Strategy in the Second Nuclear Age

STRATEGY IN THE SECOND NUCLEAR AGE

Power, Ambition,
and the Ultimate Weapon

TOSHI YOSHIHARA
and
JAMES R. HOLMES
Editors

GEORGETOWN UNIVERSITY PRESS
WASHINGTON, DC

LIBRARY OF CONGRESS CATALOGING-IN-PUBLICATION DATA

Strategy in the second nuclear age : power, ambition, and the ultimate weapon / Toshi Yoshihara and James R. Holmes, editors.
    p. cm.
  Includes bibliographical references and index.
  ISBN 978-1-58901-928-7 (pbk. : alk. paper)
  1. Nuclear warfare. 2. Nuclear weapons—Government policy. 3. Strategic forces. 4. Security, International. I. Yoshihara, Toshi. II. Holmes, James R., 1965–
U263.S773 2012
355.02'17—dc23

2012001503

♾ This book is printed on acid-free paper meeting the requirements of the American National Standard for Permanence in Paper for Printed Library Materials.

15 14 13 12   9 8 7 6 5 4 3 2   First printing

The views voiced in this volume do not necessarily represent the views of the US government or any other institution with which the authors are affiliated.

CONTENTS

CHAPTER 1

INTRODUCTION

Toshi Yoshihara and James R. Holmes

THIS IS A BOOK ABOUT STRATEGY in its broadest sense. Two centuries ago, the Prussian general and military theorist Carl von Clausewitz crafted a workmanlike yet seminal "general concept of strategy," which he defined as "the use of an engagement for the purpose of the war." This is strategy for the battlefield commander. Clausewitz scopes out from this narrowcast vision of battle as a compact, self-contained event that advances political aims. Yet strategy also involves coordinating engagements, "each of them with the others in order to further the object of the war."[1] In current US military parlance, the responsibility for relating one engagement to the next for political purposes is the province of "operational," theater-level commanders. But by consciously limiting his field of view to the "conduct of war," Clausewitz excludes a range of critical endeavors from his treatise. He terms these "preparations for war"—namely, the processes of raising, training, equipping, moving, and sustaining armed forces.[2] He acknowledges their existence, then sets them aside.

Yet prewar preparations cover much crucial ground. Peter Paret, a leading commentator on Clausewitz, takes note of his "defiantly simplistic" formulation and points out that it "can be amended or expanded without difficulty" to include functions not strictly related to the battlefield. For Paret "strategy is also based on, and may include, the development, intellectual mastery, and utilization of all of the state's resources for the purpose of implementing its policy in war."[3] In a similar vein, Michael Howard, another leading Clausewitz scholar (having cotranslated *On War* with Paret), widens the concept of strategy. Howard notes that owing to Clausewitz's far-reaching influence, "throughout the nineteenth century, 'strategy' became generally equated in the public mind with *operational* strategy" (emphasis in the original).[4] Conflating strategy with operations represents a grave oversight, in Howard's judgment.

Accentuating strategy's operational dimension to the exclusion of all others likewise slights its critical logistical, technological, and social dimensions—and thus impoverishes both scholars' and practitioners' understanding of strategy. Howard observes that these other dimensions assume new importance when operational artistry fails one or more of the belligerents. Indeed, it is commonplace for extraneous-seeming factors to decide the outcome of a trial of arms. He points out that during the American Civil War, the skill and daring of Robert E. Lee could not yield victory for the Confederacy as long as equal resolve animated both Union and Confederate leaders and citizens. It was the social and logistical dimensions that allowed President Abraham Lincoln to rally a populace that might have despaired at early battlefield reverses and to amass crushing material superiority in the field. Howard concludes that *"all other factors being equal,* numbers ultimately proved decisive" in the Civil War, and thus enabled the North to overcome the South's impressive feats of arms (emphasis in the original).[5]

Strategy, then, involves far more than battles and engagements. This is especially true of *nuclear* strategy, which is premised on fielding high-technology engines of war in peacetime to conduct wartime operations that no one wants to conduct. In this spirit, the present volume straddles Paret's and Howard's intersection between preparations for and the conduct of war. For the purposes of this study, we define "strategy" as "the political and military use or nonuse of disruptive nuclear technology." We do so because the nonuse of doomsday weaponry has been the goal of nuclear strategy since the dawn of the atomic age. We contend, nevertheless, that the states examined in the chapters that follow see value in the use of nuclear weapons for both deterrence and combat. Although the emphasis varies from chapter to chapter, all the contributors pay special heed to the logistical, technological, and social dimensions of strategy alongside the specifics of force structure and operations.

If strategy is the theme of this volume, rationality and interaction emerge as two metathemes. We define rationality broadly as the intellectual and policymaking process whereby leaders relate military means to political ends through the medium of strategy. In Clausewitzian terms, they estimate the value of the political goals at stake. Doing so lets them "discover" how many lives and how much national treasure they must expend to attain these goals, and for how long. The more pressing the goals, the greater the "magnitude" and "duration" of the effort a nation must make to achieve them.[6]

Rationality is a fragile thing, subject to countless intervening factors. In all likelihood competitors will assign different values to their national interests and political stakes. In leaders' eyes, high stakes may warrant extremely risky policies and strategies. Relatively meager stakes may leave even a preponderantly powerful state at a disadvantage in terms of political resolve. Moral factors are also at work. What reasonable people consider beyond the pale in peacetime, they may see as thinkable if not praiseworthy during crises, when options narrow, the strain on decision makers is intense, and time grows short. Or there are limits on the accuracy of human perceptions. Flawed yet deeply held assumptions deriving from history, tradition, and prevailing circumstances may be hard to modify or undo under extreme stress. Indeed, such strategic axioms may become even more entrenched in leaders' minds in times of crisis and war. They provide an intellectual reserve to tap when events rule out careful deliberation.

Interaction pits multiple rational yet imperfect actors against one another. Stability and predictability are rare when two or more "living forces" wrestle for tactical and strategic advantage.[7] Asymmetries between capabilities tend to release the brakes on restraint. Contests between the very weak and the very strong can prod one or both sides to contemplate nuclear and nonnuclear escalation. Even between powers with evenly matched nuclear capabilities, differences in conventional military power can skew the rational calculus. In short, dexterity will be at a premium.

Classic nuclear strategists have wrestled with these questions. Lawrence Freedman, for instance, observed that it became plain in the 1950s that "the sole long-term role of nuclear weapons was to deter their use by the enemy." Thus "the story of the decades of nuclear strategy . . . is of a gradual return to the simple view that, in conditions of nuclear stalemate, arsenals of these tremendously powerful weapons tend to cancel each other out."[8] Thomas Schelling postulated an international "tradition" for the nonuse of nuclear weapons, namely, "a jointly recognized expectation that they may not be used in spite of declarations of readiness to use them, even in spite of tactical advantages in their use."[9] Such factors presumably reinforce stable deterrence.

However, Colin Gray warned that there were "distinctive US and Soviet national styles in nuclear strategy" and that these ways of war "may interact in actual armed conflict with fatal consequences for the United States."[10] Strategic culture played its part in nuclear strategy and interactions. And despite Schelling's appeal to international mores discouraging the use of nuclear weapons, Bernard Brodie bewailed *the loss of the defensive function as an inherent capability of our major offensive forces* (emphasis in the original). The US Strategic Air Command, for instance, did "not become a shield if deterrence fails." The success of nuclear strategy thus depended on "our having the initiative" and "on our hitting first."[11]

Even in a stable bipolar system, then, powerful incentives work against pure rationality while amplifying the escalatory dynamics intrinsic to competitive interaction. Patrick Morgan worries about the uneven, constantly shifting character of deterrence: "While certain abstract elements of deterrence have something of a universal character, the degree and nature of its challenges and implementation are so uneven and varied, the operational conceptions of deterrence and the specifics of both challenge and response are so elaborate, that it is inevitably lodged in the varying national and political character of conflicts, shaped by the social and cultural detail of the motivations, perceptions, and analyses that drive challenges and responses."[12]

Morgan's cautionary words take on added cogency as new nuclear actors enter the arena, which compounds the dilemmas that have vexed the likes of Schelling, Freedman, Brodie, and Gray. We hope the chapters that constitute this volume will help policymakers maintain enough strategic flexibility to cope with the challenges of this new nuclear era, and thus to act judiciously yet with alacrity when strife threatens.

A More Complex Nuclear Geometry

Nuclear strategy is in flux, as it always has been. From the earliest days of the Cold War, the nuclear weapon states debated a dizzying array of concepts, doctrines, and strategies for employing an ever-evolving array of strategic and tactical weaponry. Despite all that, Cold War nuclear rivalry remained largely predictable. Two roughly comparable blocs of states, both led by nuclear-armed hegemons, faced off. The number of official nuclear weapon states remained compact, because it was capped by the Treaty on the Non-Proliferation of Nuclear Weapons, or Nuclear Non-Proliferation Treaty. The system remained manageable despite harrowing episodes like the Cuban Missile Crisis and the US/Soviet standoff during the Yom Kippur War. And yet, even while the Cold War remained in full swing, certain incidents foreshadowed an end to the stable bipolar rivalry that typified the first nuclear age. Nonproliferation experts take just pride in having restrained the spread of dooms-day weaponry. They quote President John F. Kennedy, who spoke out in 1963 on behalf of a nuclear test ban: "With all of the history of war, and the human race's history unfortunately has been a good deal more war than peace, with nuclear weapons distributed all through the world, and available, and the strong reluctance of any people to accept defeat, I see the possibility in the 1970s of the President of the United States having to face a world in which 15 or 20 or 25 nations may have these weapons. I regard that as the greatest possible danger and hazard."[13]

Despite Kennedy's grim prophecy, the official number of nuclear weapon states remained—and remains—five. Article IX of the Nuclear Non-Proliferation Treaty limited the declared nuclear weapon states to those that had "manufactured and exploded a nuclear weapon or other nuclear explosive device prior to 1 January 1967."[14] Five states—the United States, the Soviet Union, Great Britain, France, and China—had done so by the cutoff date. Certain states along the margins of the Western world nonetheless developed covert arsenals outside the treaty framework. One of those, South Africa, is covered in this volume. Another, Israel, possesses an undeclared arsenal that, now as in the first nuclear age, exerts direct influence on the configuration of power, influence, and security in the Middle East. The circle of nuclear weapon states started expanding early on, albeit not as swiftly as President Kennedy fretted that it might.

Nuclear weapons also started proliferating beyond the Western world. The People's Republic of China detonated an atomic device in 1964 and thus became the fifth nuclear weapon state. Kennedy foretold that US statesmen would find it difficult to impossible to manage diplomatic relations with a nuclear China governed by Mao Zedong, who once pronounced even a nuclear-armed United States a "paper tiger" whose overthrow was fated.[15]

Interestingly, the heated rhetoric surrounding China's prospective nuclear break-out in the early 1960s presaged recent policy debates about Iran's nuclear future. Nor were such concerns confined to the Western powers. Whether an ambitious non-Western power like China would abide by the Cold War logic of mutually assured destruction (with its unforgettable abbreviation, MAD) remained doubtful to both sides of the East/West rivalry, despite ideological kinship between Communist-ruled China and the Soviet Union. Indeed, *both* superpowers, not just the United States, contemplated preemptive strikes against the Chinese nuclear weapons complex.[16] Moscow went a step further. The Chinese historian Liu Chenshan, evidently writing with the official blessing of Beijing, has confirmed that it took direct diplomatic intervention from the Nixon administration in the 1969 Sino-Soviet border war to avert Soviet nuclear strikes on China. Washington reportedly threatened a massive counterstrike against Soviet cities if Moscow proceeded with a nuclear bombardment.[17]

In the meantime, India and Pakistan commenced clandestine nuclear research and development of their own. Then the Cold War ended. By the mid-1990s, scholars like Paul Bracken, Colin Gray, and Keith Payne had taken to prophesying that a "second nuclear age" would replace the Cold War paradigm of nuclear bipolarity.[18] For Payne the nexus between rising regional powers and the proliferation of technology related to weapons of mass destruction has fundamentally altered the strategic landscape by challenging basic Cold War assumptions about deterrence.[19] Revisionist local players armed with nuclear weapons, insists Payne, may prove impervious to the logic of deterrence that governed the superpower rivalry. Gray pithily declares that "the second nuclear age is a period defined—one can hardly say organized—by the absence of a dominant political rivalry (bipolar or otherwise)."[20] US hegemony and the strategic consequences that flow from it are the main features of this brave new world.

Bracken argues that Asia occupies the epicenter of the new nuclear era.[21] Precisely because the region has benefited enormously from industrialization and globalization, governments can now transmute wealth into military capability—including the ultimate weapon. This represents the dark side of the dynamism and innovation impelling Asian economic success. Bracken foretells that access to disruptive, increasingly abundant technology related to weapons of mass destruction will empower Asian states to nullify Western military superiority in the region. If so, they will reverse a power imbalance that dates to the days when the explorer Vasco da Gama first dropped anchor in the Indian Ocean. This is a development of world-historical significance.

The late Samuel Huntington portrayed this apparent tectonic shift in civilizational terms. He agrees with Bracken that non-Western states will shatter the Western monopoly on military power and thus complicate the familiar, relatively simple geometry of East/West deterrence. Huntington further asserts that the "proliferation of nuclear and other weapons of mass destruction is a central phenomenon of the slow but ineluctable diffusion of power in a multicivilizational world."[22] For those of pessimistic leanings, nuclear proliferation is systemic in nature. It verges on being irreversible.

It bears mentioning that the phrase "second nuclear age" was neither new nor original when it returned to vogue during the 1990s. Daniel Yergin had used it as early as 1977 to describe the patterns of proliferation that he discerned in the developing world.[23] India's "peaceful nuclear explosion" of 1974 showed how would-be nuclear powers can slip through loopholes in nonproliferation efforts that permit the civilian use of nuclear energy. Yergin illuminated the structural features of proliferation, which endure to this day. Today's Iranian nuclear challenge, for instance, harks back to the ambiguous Indian breakout of the 1970s. John F. Kennedy was prescient to worry about the nature of proliferation, despite overestimating its velocity.

As the strategic context shifts, Bracken pronounces it high time to rethink "legacy concepts" like deterrence. It would be a grave mistake to "treat the two eras the same, overlooking their basic differences."[24] The structural differences between the first and second nuclear ages include the addition of new players to deterrence; the inextricable bond between the bomb and the "power, legitimacy, and status" of postcolonial states; the prospective interactions among established nuclear weapon states and new entrants into the nuclear circle; the Asia-centric nature of nuclear proliferation; the temptation for poor countries with weak conventional forces to go nuclear; and a surfeit of technology and know-how that was unavailable to the original nuclear weapon states.[25]

In short, the international system is increasingly complex. Nuclear weapons engage nation-states' sense of themselves, arousing their leaders' and citizens' deepest passions. The barriers to nuclear entry no longer appear unbreachable. And at the same time, the technical and psychological impediments to using nuclear weapons appear smaller and smaller. Bracken urges US officials to start working on a replacement arms control effort tailored to the demands and idiosyncrasies of the second nuclear age. Only thus, he says, can this combustible mix be tamped down.[26]

Huntington agrees that the second nuclear age is different while questioning how much the West can do about it. Cold War competition involved competitive arms buildups that produced nuclear warheads in enormous numbers along with platforms to deliver them. In the post–Cold War era, he says, the West's antagonists are "attempting to acquire weapons of mass destruction, and the West is attempting to prevent them from doing so." Post–Cold War competition was a matter not of "buildup versus buildup but rather of buildup versus hold-down." Huntington declares that the outcome of such a race today is foreordained: "The hold-down efforts of the West may slow the weapons buildup of other societies, but they will not stop it."[27]

Why such conviction? Huntington observes that non-Western countries have a financial incentive to proliferate so they can profit by selling nuclear-related technology to fund their own endeavors. Moreover, aspiring local hegemons consider nuclear weapons a trump card for deterring great power intervention in their neighborhoods, and thus as an enabler for plans to reshape regional orders. Such powers also view nonproliferation efforts as the Western powers' way of perpetuating their dominance rather than as a tool for sustaining international order. India, to name one, long insisted that the grand bargain codified in the Nuclear Non-Proliferation Treaty equates to apartheid against nuclear have-nots.

One might qualify Huntington's appraisal of the second nuclear age somewhat. It certainly remains true that Western nuclear weapon states remain intent on holding down non-Western nuclear aspirants. To coin a Huntingtonian-sounding term, however, one might describe the contemporary West as having undergone a nuclear "builddown," or partial disarmament. The United States is arguably most committed to the Huntingtonian vision of a nuclear buildup, but even its successive administrations have negotiated cutbacks to the US and Russian inventories. The Barack Obama administration's outlook on nuclear strategy and forces might be termed "fewer but better," judging from plans to design replacements for the US Navy's aging fleet of *Ohio*-class nuclear-powered ballistic missile submarines (known as "SSBNs"), which form the heart of undersea deterrence. President Obama has repeatedly vowed to move toward a nuclear-free world. But out of expediency, the national security establishment is devising a smaller yet still potent deterrent force to tide the nation over until nuclear disarmament comes within reach.

Western Europe has trodden farther down the road to abolition, not only out of principle but also because of the sheer cost of procuring and maintaining SSBNs and their armament. Several years ago, British prime minister Gordon Brown publicly contemplated scaling back the Royal Navy's SSBN fleet from four boats to three, the bare minimum to keep one boat on patrol at all times. Officials in Brown's Labour government spoke of using Great Britain as a "disarmament laboratory," which would prove that disarmament can work and show how.[28] France also finds its minimal deterrent under strain. Although Franco-British talks have borne little fruit thus far, the two European middleweights have started discussing joint deterrent patrols that would keep one SSBN on station at any time. Like the United States, then, Britain and France seem to be searching for a floor: the smallest quantity of nuclear weaponry and platforms needed to buttress national security.

Russia is also in builddown mode, because it has consented to successive arms control accords with the United States. At the same time, perversely, Moscow has come to lay *greater* weight on nuclear weapons in its military strategy and doctrine. The Soviet-era military degenerated to the point of collapse during the economic upheaval of the 1990s, and Russia's conventional military might has not yet recovered. One might portray contemporary Russia, therefore, as a "regressive" nuclear weapon state—that is, a state that uses nuclear weapons as a substitute for weak or decaying conventional forces. Its nuclear doctrine has taken on offensive overtones.

This tendency is becoming more pronounced. Rising energy prices have the Russian economy on the rebound. The leadership has applied part of this newfound revenue to new SSBNs and submarine-launched ballistic missiles, including the Layner and Bulava missiles that are currently undergoing testing.[29] Even so, Russia's strategic predicament resembles Pakistan's more than it does that of fellow nuclear states from the first nuclear age. It is a state hopelessly outmatched in conventional military power yet comparable to its main antagonist in nuclear forces. In our judgment Moscow qualifies as a custodian of the first nuclear age—but only just.

Because of such complicating factors, it appears more accurate to classify post–Cold War competition as "builddown versus hold-down" rather than "buildup versus hold-down." Declining Western nuclear powers are attempting to forestall or hold down non-Western arsenals. This strategic quandary is even more vexing than the one Huntington described. On the whole, however, time has borne out Bracken's and Huntington's bleak forecasts.

Nuclear "old-timer" China, one of five nuclear weapon states acknowledged under the Non-Proliferation Treaty, has embarked on sweeping qualitative and quantitative modernization, upgrading nuclear forces that for decades remained primitive and vulnerable to disarming first strikes like the one contemplated by Soviet premier Leonid Brezhnev in 1969. Meanwhile, India and Pakistan, which tested nuclear weapons more than a decade ago, continue to refine their forces, doctrines, and strategies. North Korea appears to have settled in as the newest member of the unofficial nuclear club. In short, numerous non-Western governments are searching for doctrines and strategies that fortify nuclear deterrence.

Analytical Framework

Depending on how one counts, the second nuclear age has been in the making for nearly forty years. At the very least, more than a decade has passed since New Delhi and Islamabad convulsed South Asia with a series of nuclear tests. Whatever one wishes to call this era, the second nuclear age or some other moniker, enough time has elapsed for observers to test the principles of strategy against both longtime nuclear players and the post–Cold War entrants into the nuclear game. Three main questions guide our inquiry in this book. First, to what extent do the strategies, doctrines, operational art, and force structures among the nuclear powers examined in this study conform to classical Western definitions and understandings of strategy? Second, is there a universal logic to nuclear strategy? And third, what explains the peculiarities, if any, of the nuclear strategies among the national case studies assessed in this volume?

This book assembles a group of distinguished scholars of strategy and area studies to grapple with these questions. These contributors concentrate primarily on Asian states that have already amassed or boast the potential to acquire nuclear arsenals. Of special interest are factors that prompt states to pursue disruptive technologies and that shape how nuclear weapon states employ such weaponry once acquired. The chapter authors attempt to anticipate how new entrants into the unofficial circle of nuclear powers will interact among themselves and with nonnuclear states, and how the gatekeepers of the first nuclear age will contend with gatecrashers from the second.

But this volume is not just concerned with the dynamics between the privileged nuclear weapon states and players that inhabit the murky terrain outside various nonproliferation efforts. As noted above, the transition from the first nuclear era to the second is neither as linear nor as clear-cut as some theorists imply. China, a non-Western nuclear weapon state from the first nuclear age, is fundamentally revising its strategy, doctrine, and forces to reinforce nuclear deterrence. India's breakout occurred at the midpoint of the Cold War, whereas the origins of South Asian nuclear deterrence calculations can be traced back to the 1980s. Japan, which was a major benefactor of protection afforded by the United States and other guarantors of the first nuclear age, may be revisiting its assumptions about extended deterrence. We therefore define the parameters of the second nuclear age in broad, inclusive terms.

As a result, we should clarify certain idiosyncrasies in our case selection for the chapters that follow. Our metrics for judging whether an Asian state is a nuclear newcomer or a de facto newcomer are simple. Has the state recently developed or otherwise procured nuclear weapons? If so, the rationale for including it is straightforward. If not, has its nuclear strategy or force structure undergone a discontinuity of such scope that it is in effect embarking on a wholly new nuclear strategy, doctrine, or force structure? If a nuclear state meets either test, we believe it belongs in this volume.

First, we believe it is fitting to classify longtime nuclear states like the People's Republic of China, which detonated its first nuclear explosives in 1964, and India and Pakistan, which have been overt nuclear weapon states since 1998, as newcomers to the field of nuclear strategy. Simply put, changing circumstances sometimes warrant dramatic change to a nation-state's long-standing nuclear posture. This is the case with China. It takes time for new nuclear weapon states to settle on their preferred strategies and doctrines; witness the cases of India and Pakistan. From an intellectual standpoint, New Delhi and Islamabad find themselves roughly where Washington and Moscow were in the late 1950s, twelve years after Hiroshima and Nagasaki. Few would describe those years as a stable interval for American and Soviet nuclear strategies. The original nuclear weapon states remained newcomers, and thus their strategies are still immature.

Second, we believe that examining Japanese thinking about nuclear deterrence and strategy offers several analytical insights. Tokyo is not only reacting to the parties that are driving the second nuclear age, including North Korea and China; it is also reevaluating the efficacy of the US nuclear umbrella. The debates in Japan offer reminders that alliance politics remains a central organizing principle of nuclear stability. A Japanese nuclear breakout—a very hypothetical scenario—also illustrates the likely dynamics if states like Taiwan and South Korea opt to go nuclear in the future, presumably after the United States withdraws its security guarantees or those guarantees lose credibility in the wake of, say, a massive drawdown of the US conventional presence overseas. In a sense, then, the Japanese case offers a proxy for charting the way ahead in nuclear strategy, which can thus help policymakers think through the challenges that may ensue if American extended deterrence falters.

And finally, though many of the national cases examined in the volume are located in Asia, our analysis is premised on the notion that strategy making is a universal phenomenon that defies arbitrary geographic parameters. There is a logic of strategy that transcends place, time, and culture. The strategic calculus of states beyond East and South Asia, such as Iran and South Africa, thus merits our full attention. South Africa is often touted as a classic success story for nonproliferation. What such triumphalism overlooks is the strategic calculus that informed the advances in restraining the South African nuclear arsenal before voluntary disarmament. The proliferation period, then, offers valuable lessons for the new epoch. Iran constitutes the next major test case for nonproliferation. If the hold-down effort toward Iran fails, then the international community must come to terms with an emerging nuclear power in the Middle East, much as the United States learned to live with the Chinese bomb in the 1960s.

To recapitulate: This is not a book that focuses exclusively on Asian proliferation, deterrence, or nuclear stability. Rather, this book is fundamentally concerned with the rise of the nuclear non-Western world and the inescapable reality that both the old-timers and newcomers in this group have undertaken serious strategic thinking about the utility of the ultimate weapon they now possess. Discerning how they are doing so is part of understanding the strategic terrain in today's world.

Plan of the Book

The rest of the chapters address the themes and cases outlined above as follows. Joshua Rovner leads off in chapter 2 by putting to the test Bernard Brodie's 1946 declaration that the "chief purpose" of the US military establishment could no longer be to win wars but "to avert them." In the emerging nuclear age, insisted Brodie, the armed forces "can have almost no other useful purpose."[30] Did policy-makers uniformly subscribe to that logic during the first nuclear age, and does it still hold in the second nuclear age? Rovner points out that many questions about the rationality or irrationality of nuclear deterrence and what constituted stable deter-rence in a bipolar system were never fully settled during the Cold War.

A host of new questions arose when the first nuclear age started giving way to the second. Would nuclear aspirants like Iran, Iraq, North Korea, Libya, and Syria—nation-states that were at once authoritarian, radical, indifferent to risk, and inexpe-rienced at atomic diplomacy—abide by Brodie's logic of mutual deterrence? How could established nuclear weapon states adjust their strategies and forces to reinforce stability vis-à-vis governments that might not act by Western standards of rational-ity? Or did they need to act preemptively or preventively? Whether deterrence can work toward the "rogue states" of the second nuclear age or more forceful measures represent the best strategy is a dilemma that Rovner explores in detail, and thus lays the groundwork for the country chapters. These are questions of enormous import for the declared nuclear weapon states and indeed for the international community writ large.

In chapter 3 Helen Purkitt and Stephen Burgess examine the case of South Africa, which may seem like an outlier in a book about the second nuclear age, a largely Asia-centric phenomenon that has mostly followed the protracted struggle of the Cold War. This is a case worth revisiting, however. Purkitt and Burgess explain how the apartheid government in South Africa went about covertly building a small tacti-cal arsenal and thought about using that arsenal. To what extent did a rational cost/benefit calculus impel South African strategy and doctrine, and to what extent were the apartheid leaders driven by an irrational worldview and motives? These are questions worth pondering as the reader proceeds to consider the contemporary Asian cases in subsequent chapters.

The history of nuclear collaboration between South Africa and Israel, moreover, sheds light on the propensity of new entrants into the nuclear club to share expertise and hardware among themselves—particularly with new aspirants that are geo-graphically remote and pose no real threat to their national security. The Israeli–South African nexus foreshadowed the nexus between North Korea and Pakistan, which clandestinely abetted each other's nuclear ambitions for many years. Purkitt and Burgess's retelling of how the South African regime considered using nuclear weapons to coerce the United States into intervening in wartime offers a glimpse into the unorthodox thinking that characterizes some actors in this new era.

In chapter 4 Christopher Yeaw, Andrew Erickson, and Michael Chase conduct a comprehensive survey of China's nuclear doctrine, strategy, and force structure. Relying on a wealth of primary sources, their narrative follows China's dramatic transition from a modest posture of minimum deterrence to the "effective deter-rence" of recent years. Chinese thinking about nuclear doctrine was spellbound by Maoist dogma, and thus it remained in a state of suspended animation until the 1980s. Yet China has made significant progress across the board since the reform and opening period that began in 1978. Chinese strategists now openly debate whether the no-first-use doctrine remains prudent. Yeaw, Erickson, and Chase suggest that under certain circumstances, Beijing may be compelled to reconsider the threshold for nuclear use. As missile guidance systems improve, moreover, the Chinese may expand their conception of nuclear war from one that involves limited retaliatory attacks against civilian targets to one that includes counterforce strikes. Greater accuracy opens up new strategic vistas.

Beijing has also steadily reversed the material backwardness of its nuclear forces. It is deploying more survivable, more mobile platforms on land and at sea, and it is fielding its first assured second-strike capability. New delivery systems, such as nuclear variants of land-attack cruise missiles, may enter service in the coming years. Beyond hardware, the Second Artillery Force is reforming its training regimen to include more realistic and rigorous exercises. This will enhance the quality of China's military "software," namely, the commanders and troops who operate the forces. Yeaw, Erickson, and Chase warn, however, that a more credible Chinese deterrent posture may not necessarily translate into a stable United States–China strategic relationship. Chinese writings about signaling and escalation control suggest that Beijing's crisis behavior may actually foster miscalculations and instability.

In chapter 5 Terence Roehrig supplies an analytical framework for discerning the future trajectory of North Korea's nuclear strategy if multilateral efforts to disarm Pyongyang fail. He demonstrates how interdisciplinary approaches that marry regional studies to strategic theory can substantially advance our understanding of Asia's nuclear future. He reviews the various dimensions of deterrence theory as the starting point for foretelling how North Korea might seek to develop a credible nuclear deterrent. A key finding of this theoretical survey is that Kim Jong-un, as reflected in chapter 5, probably views nuclear weapons primarily as a guarantor of regime survival. Contradicting prevailing concerns about the potentially disruptive geopolitical consequences of North Korea's breakout, Roehrig contends that Pyongyang's nuclear arsenal will be designed primarily to deter the United States and South Korea. This interpretation would clearly recast allied priorities and planning for the defense of Seoul.

Roehrig also postulates four potential deployment options that might underwrite North Korea's nuclear strategy. The Kim Jong-un regime may seek to enhance the survivability of its nuclear deterrent posture by: (1) dispersing and hiding the arsenal in hardened facilities; (2) loading the delivery systems and warheads on road-mobile platforms; (3) deploying the weapons on board ships or submarines; or (4) basing the nuclear-tipped missiles at launch sites located near the Chinese border. The fourth option suggests that the proximity of China adds virtual strategic depth to the North Korean nuclear forces. This represents a shrewd, possibly effective political use of a geographic sanctuary to deter preemption or retaliatory strikes. Roehrig cautions against complacency, especially with respect to some of the more destabilizing postures that Kim's regime may eventually adopt. Persistent fears about the survivability of its nuclear arsenal might compel North Korea to keep its delivery systems at dangerously high levels of readiness, perhaps even hair-trigger alert. The potential for misperceptions, miscalculations, or escalation would mount. Thus a nuclear Korean Peninsula is not just a proliferation problem. It could also severely compromise the integrity of US deterrence in the Western Pacific.

In chapter 6 James Schoff furnishes the strategic context within which the debates about nuclear deterrence are taking place in Japan. Because the internal dynamics shaping these discussions are either overlooked or poorly understood, this chapter represents a valuable addition to the existing literature. The proximate stimulus for Tokyo's reassessment is North Korea's breakout following its nuclear tests in 2006 and 2009. Rapid Chinese military modernization is also feeding into Tokyo's deterrence calculus. Schoff clearly shows that perceptions of the firmness of the US commitment to the alliance architecture in Asia against the backdrop of growing regional nuclear challenges deeply influence Japanese discourses. His key finding is that threat perceptions among the two most important US allies in Northeast Asia may be drifting apart. Tokyo increasingly fears the prospect of entrapment by Washington, whereas potential for abandonment by Washington preoccupies Seoul. This divergence in allied perspectives, Schoff contends, demands immediate attention from the policymakers who are managing transpacific relations.

Schoff demonstrates that nuclear debates in Tokyo are nothing new. Since the earliest days of the Cold War, Japanese strategists and politicians have struggled to come to grips with the implications of extended deterrence. However, Schoff finds that Japanese defense planners have neither learned from nor internalized the lessons of deterrence theory, and instead have preferred to rely on the US nuclear umbrella as an intellectual crutch and a substitute for original thought. As Tokyo more seriously reconsiders the balance between nuclear and conventional deterrence, it must ascend a steep learning curve. Seoul faces a different set of concrete challenges. Pyongyang may believe that it now possesses the nuclear wherewithal to deter allied retaliation if it chooses to unleash a conventional military offensive against Seoul. This more complex deterrence calculus is taking hold at a time when Seoul has agreed (perhaps reluctantly) to assume more operational responsibilities in wartime. How Washington shores up the allied deterrent posture under trying circumstances will be a pressing priority in the coming years.

In chapter 7 James Holmes and Toshi Yoshihara engage in a provocative thought experiment about Japan's strategic options if it ever decides to break out and go nuclear. Although the authors rate Tokyo's pursuit of an independent nuclear deterrent as very unlikely, they nevertheless find analytical value in thinking about the unthinkable. Contrary to conventional wisdom, they find that going nuclear would not be easy for Japan. Tokyo would need to divert substantial funding, scarce human capital, and limited stocks of fissile materials (assuming they can be enriched to weapons grade) into a nuclear weapons program. A clandestine effort would be nearly impossible given the exposure of Japan's civilian nuclear infrastructure to very intrusive nonproliferation inspection and monitoring programs. A fait accompli strategy thus lies out of reach. It would not be an overnight affair to field affordable, effective, and reliable delivery systems. It would require time-consuming processes of training, testing (something banned by an international treaty of which Tokyo has been a devout supporter), and doctrinal development. The resource demands for such a project would be severe—especially in view of the competing costs of reconstruction following the 2011 tsunami, earthquake, and nuclear meltdown in northern Japan.

Holmes and Yoshihara add value to the literature by hypothesizing the most optimal uses of Japan's resources for developing a credible nuclear deterrent. They argue that land-based and air-launched platforms would be too vulnerable to pre-emptive strikes, especially given Japan's lack of geographic depth. They also rule out an undersea ballistic missile deterrent as a viable option owing to the prohibitive costs and the enormous technical barriers that such an exotic capability would impose on Tokyo. Finally, they conclude that nuclear-tipped cruise missiles deployed aboard conventionally powered submarines might be a superior alternative for Japan. The Maritime Self-Defense Force already possesses one of the most advanced and capable conventional submarine fleets in the world. Although an undersea deterrent might require sizable increases in force structure, such a sea-launched capability would still be financially viable for a fiscally challenged Japan. How Washington would react to such a breakout by Tokyo and whether their alliance would survive a political earthquake of this magnitude are questions worth pondering.

In chapter 8 Anupam Srivastava and Seema Gahlaut review the evolution of India's nuclear strategy and forces since the inception of a civilian nuclear program during the 1950s. The authors concentrate on the complex strategic environment confronting New Delhi, the mixed motives animating this relatively new state repre-senting an ancient civilization, and the dualism that typifies Indian nuclear strategy and doctrine as a result of this mélange of influences. Complicating matters, India found itself on the business end of international sanctions for more than two decades after its 1974 nuclear test. Rancor over being a target of nonproliferation measures shapes Indian policy to this day.

Srivastava and Gahlaut show that the Indian leadership has been fervently wed-ded to the idea of outright nuclear disarmament since the days of its founding prime minister, Jawaharlal Nehru. Yet New Delhi edged toward nuclear weapons capacity, both out of prudence and because the nuclear weapon states repeatedly rejected or ignored its entreaties on behalf of abolition. What at first glance may look like an erratic nuclear policy and strategy has in reality been a product of these competing interests and also shifts in the strategic surroundings. Srivastava and Gahlaut con-centrate on the institutional dimension of strategy, and thus they observe that fash-ioning wise bureaucratic arrangements is as important as strategic wizardry to New Delhi's nuclear strategy. India is a country on the march by any standard, and the authors close by recommending several indicators that will help outsiders track India's progress in the nuclear arena and adapt their own strategies to a newly assert-ive New Delhi.

In chapter 9 Andrew C. Winner, building on Srivastava and Gahlaut's bird's-eye view of Indian nuclear strategy, inquires into the prospects for an Indian naval undersea deterrent. Winner forecasts that stationing nuclear-tipped cruise or ballistic missiles aboard India's SSBNs would exert substantial influence on the nuclear prac-tices of its rivals, China and Pakistan. While avoiding making firm predictions, he identifies factors that will determine how the continual cycle of action and reaction among the Indian Ocean powers may play out in the coming years. Interaction, one of this volume's metathemes, forms the core of his analysis.

The material dimension of strategy plays a key part in the Indian navy's nuclear endeavors. Much of Winner's analysis remains hypothetical, because the first Indian SSBN, christened the *Arihant*, is not yet fully operational. And even when this ship has entered service, the precise nature of its armament remains unclear. It will likely carry tactical nuclear-tipped cruise missiles as an interim measure, pending the testing and deployment of a working sea-launched ballistic missile. Depending on how New Delhi appraises the strategic context, the *Arihant*'s range and payload limitations will likely compel the Indian navy to dispatch its submarine force into the China seas, which will mean holding coastal Chinese cities at risk, or to the Arabian Sea, where it can reach high-value Pakistani urban areas. Scarcely could the Clausewitzian metaphor of a collision of living forces manifest itself more vividly than in interactions between Indian, Pakistani, and Chinese forces.

In chapter 10 Timothy Hoyt paints a grim picture of Pakistani nuclear strategy and forces. The years since the 1998 nuclear tests have witnessed changes of government, armed strife and near-strife between Pakistan and India, and the rise of a transnational militant movement that now threatens Pakistan itself. Coupled with Islamabad's "truly abysmal nuclear proliferation record," writes Hoyt, these restive surroundings have given rise to "a significant risk management problem for the international community, its neighbors, and its own government."

In light of this, Hoyt dwells primarily on the threats that the Pakistani arsenal poses for regional and global harmony. As with apartheid Pretoria, a blend of realpolitik and ideational factors imparts the motive force to strategic calculations in Islamabad. India drives Pakistani strategy in both domains. New Delhi remains far superior in conventional military terms, whereas the essence of Pakistani society is being "like India, but not India."[31] Like Winner, Hoyt attempts to envision future interactions as he recounts how fellow South Asian powers and the international community have thus far responded to Pakistan's nuclear strategy and postulates how they might do so.

In chapter 11 Scott Jones and James Holmes turn their gaze westward from Pakistan to Iran, which appears intent on fielding nuclear weapons of its own. Tehran's plans to develop a nuclear energy capability, including a closed nuclear fuel cycle, have set loose an international uproar over its apparent nuclear weapons aspirations. Jones and Holmes suggest that for the Iranians, rational strategic considerations form only one part of their nuclear calculus and that the nuclear option is not a strictly partisan issue for them. Nuclear weapons have an appeal far beyond President Mahmoud Ahmadinejad's circle of hardliners. Indeed, ordinary Iranians with little love for the country's authoritarian clerical regime profess support for nuclear weapons, not only for defense and deterrence but also as a token of great power. Thus a "nuclear reversal" appears improbable, regardless of who rules Iran in the coming years.

If a wide swath of Iranian opinion indeed favors constructing a nuclear arsenal, ask Jones and Holmes, what facets of Iranian strategy, doctrine, and force structure will be common to the country's Islamic regime and to some hypothetical future regime? How would strategy differ from regime to regime, and how should the West respond to political and strategic change in Tehran? Glimpsing answers to these questions vis-à-vis this latest newcomer to the second nuclear age is clearly a matter of tremendous significance for the international community. Only by anticipating future trends can Western capitals get ahead of the problems posed by a nuclear Iran. Jones and Holmes suggest that Iran's fear of its geopolitical surroundings will drive its strategy. The nature of the regime may encourage or discourage exaggerated fears. In the final analysis, then, regime type bears directly on Iranian nuclear strategy.

In chapter 12 the editors of this volume offer their conclusion. Although this collection of essays is neither comprehensive in its coverage of existing and potential nuclear players nor exhaustive in assessing the expected roles and missions of nuclear weapons, it nonetheless represents an intellectual leap into the second nuclear age. The numerous propositions about the future nuclear postures of the newcomers contained in this book depart radically from the prevailing reluctance in academia and the policy world to contemplate acquiescence in irreversible break-outs. The contributors also venture onto unfamiliar terrain and thus reexamine the strategic axioms that have come under assault in this more complex nuclear era. Strategies and options that were once considered unthinkable are now being openly debated across the countries examined in this study. The authors also identify enduring sources of nuclear instability that could have wide-ranging strategic implications for trustees of the status quo—above all, the United States.

Notes

1. Carl von Clausewitz, *On War*, edited and translated by Michael Howard and Peter Paret (Princeton, NJ: Princeton University Press, 1976), 128, 177.

2. Ibid., 131–32.

3. Peter Paret, ed., *Makers of Modern Strategy: From Machiavelli to the Nuclear Age* (Princeton, NJ: Princeton University Press, 1986), 3.

4. Michael Howard, "The Forgotten Dimensions of Strategy," *Foreign Affairs* 57 (Summer 1979): 976.

5. Ibid., 977.

6. Clausewitz, *On War*, 92, 585–86.

7. Ibid., 77.

8. Lawrence Freedman, "The First Two Generations of Nuclear Strategists," in *Makers of Modern Strategy*, ed. Paret, 738–39.

9. Thomas C. Schelling, *The Strategy of Conflict* (New York: Oxford University Press, 1963), 260.

10. Colin S. Gray, *Nuclear Strategy and National Style* (Lanham, MD: Hamilton Press, 1986), ix.

11. Bernard Brodie, *Strategy in the Missile Age* (Princeton, NJ: Princeton University Press, 1965), 225.

12. Patrick M. Morgan, *Deterrence Now* (Cambridge: Cambridge University Press, 2003), 285–86.

13. "The President's News Conference of March 21, 1963," in *Public Papers of the Presidents of the United States: John F. Kennedy 1963*, edited by US Department of State (Washington, DC: US Government Printing Office, 1964), 280.

14. United Nations, "The Treaty on the Non-Proliferation of Nuclear Weapons (NPT)," www.un.org/en/conf/npt/2010/npttext.shtml.

15. William Burr and Jeffrey T. Richelson, "Whether to 'Strangle the Baby in the Cradle': The United States and the Chinese Nuclear Program, 1960–1964," *International Security* 25, no. 3 (Winter 2000–2001): 67.

16. Lyle Goldstein, *Preventive Attack and Weapons of Mass Destruction: A Comparative Historical Analysis* (Stanford, CA: Stanford University Press, 2006).

17. Andrew Osborn and Peter Foster, "USSR Planned Nuclear Attack on China in 1969," *Daily Telegraph* (London), May 13, 2010, www.telegraph.co.uk/news/worldnews/asia/china/7720461/USSR-planned-nuclear-attack-on-China-in-1969.html.

18. Paul Bracken, "The Second Nuclear Age," *Foreign Affairs* 79, no. 1 (January–February 2000): 146–56.

19. Keith B. Payne, *Deterrence in the Second Nuclear Age* (Lexington: University Press of Kentucky, 1996). See also Keith B. Payne, *The Great American Gamble: Deterrence Theory and Practice from the Cold War to the Twenty-First Century* (Washington, DC: National Institute Press, 2008).

20. Colin Gray, *The Second Nuclear Age* (Boulder, CO: Lynne Rienner, 1999), 25.

21. Paul Bracken, *Fire in the East: The Rise of Asian Military Power and the Second Nuclear Age* (New York: HarperPerennial, 2000).

22. Samuel P. Huntington, *The Clash of Civilizations and the Remaking of World Order* (New York: Simon & Schuster, 1996), 192.

23. See Daniel Yergin, "The Terrifying Prospect: Atomic Bombs Everywhere," *The Atlantic*, April 1977, 47; Daniel Yergin, "Order and Survival," *Daedalus* 107, no. 1 (Winter 1978): 274.

24. Paul Bracken, "The Structure of the Second Nuclear Age," E-Note, Foreign Policy Research Institute, September 25, 2003, www.fpri.org/enotes/20030925.americawar.bracken.secondnuclearage.html.

25. Ibid.

26. Ibid.

27. Huntington, *Clash of Civilizations*, 190.

28. Rebecca Johnson, "Britain's New Nuclear Abolitionists," *Bulletin of the Atomic Scientists*, July 15, 2008, www.thebulletin.org/web-edition/features/britainsnew-nuclear-abolitionists.

29. "New Russian Ballistic Missile Sub to Join Navy in 2011," *Global Security Newswire* (Nuclear Threat Initiative), December 14, 2010, www.globalsecuritynewswire.org/gsn/nw_20101214_7366.php.

30. Bernard Brodie, "The Weapon: War in the Atomic Age and Implications for Military Policy," in *The Absolute Weapon: Atomic Power and World Order*, edited by Bernard Brodie (New York: Harcourt Brace, 1946), 52, 76.

31. Stephen P. Cohen, *The Idea of Pakistan* (Washington, DC: Brookings Institution Press, 2004).

CHAPTER 2

AFTER PROLIFERATION

Deterrence Theory and Emerging Nuclear Powers

Joshua Rovner

DETERRENCE THEORY EVOLVED along with the Cold War. For some early American strategists, the relationship between nuclear proliferation and deterrence was self-evident. "Everything about the atomic bomb is overshadowed by the twin facts that it exists and that its destructive power is fantastically great," wrote Bernard Brodie in 1946. "Thus far the chief purpose of our military establishment has been to win wars. From now on it must be to avert them. It can have almost no other useful purpose."[1]

Brodie's famous declaration put deterrence in the forefront of the American strategic debate, and the rise of a bipolar international system provided the backdrop for his revolutionary ideas. Intense political competition between the United States and the Soviet Union took on ominous overtones in the shadow of growing nuclear arsenals. How could the superpowers compete with one another without risking annihilation? What did the superpowers need to do in order to reinforce deterrence and preserve the peace? Alternately, was deterrence a foregone conclusion among states with the power to destroy one another? If so, was it possible that stable deterrence would actually encourage conventional aggression among states that were sure that escalation to the nuclear level was impossible? And how could the superpowers deter conventional attacks on their allies?

These questions generated whole fields of inquiry: Economists and political scientists developed analytically sophisticated models to describe the interaction between nation-states with the means to deliver unprecedented levels of destruction. Skeptics, including historians and political psychologists, criticized these abstract models for assuming that decision makers would be able to act sensibly under conditions of high stress and for assuming that all states operated according to the same rational principles. They noted that state leaders very often appear "irrational," that is, unable to rank-order their interests and calculate the consequences of action. This is especially the case during crises, when the combination of stress and time constraints causes leaders to fall back on preconceptions and cognitive biases.[2]

Critics also argued that states' interests and preferences can change in the midst of confrontations with other powers, which complicates the task of manipulating their behavior through carefully calibrated deterrent signals.[3] Domestic politics and bureaucratic incentives may skew decisions over the use of force in ways that fall well outside the boundaries of rational deterrence theory. Finally, critics argued that different states might conceive of rationality in very different ways. What looks irrational to outsiders might make perfect sense given a state's unique history, values, and strategic culture.[4]

The debates over the requirements for stable deterrence in a bipolar system divided scholars, analysts, and policymakers for decades. They were never resolved. After the Cold War, deterrence theorists turned their attention to regional powers like North Korea, Iran, India, and Pakistan, all of which have pursued nuclear capabilities in the face of substantial international nonproliferation efforts.

The rise of nascent nuclear states created a new set of policy dilemmas. Analysts were concerned about relations with emerging nuclear powers that were inexperienced in nuclear diplomacy and unable to offer credible reassurances that they would be reliable custodians of their newly won arsenals.[5] Lacking technical experience, these states could not guarantee the quality of safeguards against accidental use or the security of sensitive technologies and fissile material.[6] Concerned about vulnerability to a preventive strike, emerging nuclear powers couched their efforts in suggestive but opaque rhetoric, which was sufficiently ambiguous to cause dangerous misperceptions.[7] Flush with nationalism and intrigued by the possibilities of nuclear coercion, they were likely to underestimate the danger of nuclear saber rattling.[8] And though they also might have been eager to use their new capabilities to push the limits of their political influence, their close proximity to nuclear rivals would limit available warning times and complicate crisis management. Observers feared that overcoming all these problems would be especially difficult for states with unstable political systems and a history of civil–military turmoil.[9]

Of particular interest were the so-called rogues: Iran, Iraq, North Korea, Libya, and Syria. Some analysts feared that the character of these states—authoritarian, radical, and risk-acceptant—made them largely impervious to deterrence. Authoritarian leaders lacked accountability for their actions and were less constrained by domestic concerns. And because these leaders were ideologically and politically radical, they were inherently difficult negotiating partners and more likely to accept enormous risks in the pursuit of grandiose aims. Some analysts concluded that these inherent dysfunctions made deterrence seem dubious at best. Conversely, the revolution in military affairs caused some US strategists to dream about lifting the fog of war and winning bloodless wars against smaller, less capable, and technologically unsophisticated enemies.[10] Extraordinary advances in precision weapons and information technology led to the belief that successful preventive strikes were possible against rogue regimes, which were probably allergic to deterrence in the first place.

Doubts about deterrence combined with enthusiasm about the revolution in military affairs led to a brief infatuation with preventive military action as the preferred solution to the proliferation problem in the late 1990s, which culminated with the war in Iraq in 2003. Kenneth Pollack expressed the fears of deterrence skeptics when he argued that a nuclear-armed Iraq would put the United States on the horns of a terrible dilemma. "Relying on pure deterrence to keep Saddam at bay once he has acquired a nuclear arsenal is terrifyingly dangerous," Pollack wrote. "It is likely to find us confronting a Hobson's choice of either allowing Saddam to make himself the hegemon of the Gulf region (and in effect or actuality controlling global oil supplies) or else fighting a war with him that could escalate to nuclear warfare."[11] The implication was that American conventional capabilities would not deter emerging nuclear powers from regional aggression, but those states *would* be able to deter the United States from intervening against them.[12] For these reasons, the George W. Bush administration's 2002 National Security Strategy was unambiguous about the dangers of relying on deterrence against emerging nuclear powers: "Given the goals of rogue states and terrorists, the United States can no longer solely rely on a reactive posture as we have in the past. The inability to deter a potential attacker, the immediacy of today's threats, and the magnitude of potential harm that could be caused by our adversaries' choice of weapons, do not permit that option." Conversely, the administration believed that military transformation would "ensure our ability to conduct rapid and precise operations to achieve decisive results."[13]

Although the zeal for preventive military strikes has abated, strategists continue to argue about whether some states are insensitive to deterrent signals. Indeed, a central question in the contemporary deterrence debate is whether emerging nuclear powers are rational enough to be deterred. Critics argue that the assumption of rationality is even less tenable today than during the Cold War. Today's emerging nuclear powers, they maintain, are likely to take extraordinary risks for reasons one may not understand. Supporters of deterrence counter that states are not interested in self-immolation; even the most bizarre and morally odious regimes will moderate their behavior if their core interests are threatened. They point out that examples of national suicide are scarce, even though certain states may take enormous risks in pursuit of their political goals.

Much is at stake in this debate. Basic questions about grand strategy, force structure, and diplomacy all rest on assumptions about the utility of deterrence in the immediate aftermath of proliferation. Supporters believe that deterrence can serve as a low-risk and low-cost interim strategy on the path toward a long-term modus vivendi between status quo powers and emerging nuclear powers. Skeptics are unwilling to take the risk that deterrence will fail, and they tend to favor alternatives like missile defense, preventive and preemptive strikes, and regime change.

Unfortunately, this debate has reached an impasse. Plenty of evidence exists to support both sides, and the lines are firmly drawn. The first section of this chapter seeks to reenergize the debate by approaching the problem from a different direction. Rather than looking at the particular characteristics of emerging nuclear powers, it explores the requirements for deterring different kinds of action. The second section offers a series of propositions about what kinds of deterrent signals are more or less likely to succeed against them. The third section considers how emerging nuclear powers conceptualize deterrence against status quo nuclear states and regional rivals. I treat this question briefly, whereas the other contributors to this volume address it in detail.

Not Whom but What to Deter

There are at least two ways of defining an "emerging nuclear power." A broad definition, used elsewhere in this volume, focuses on capabilities. According to this logic, states can "emerge" as new kinds of nuclear powers as they achieve increasingly higher technical thresholds. Nascent nuclear powers that learn how to produce fissile material are often said to enjoy a breakout capability. Although they do not possess nuclear weapons, they do possess the material and technical knowledge needed to quickly deploy a modest arsenal. Other states go further, designing and testing explosive devices and deploying a small number of deliverable weapons. As nuclear capabilities improve in terms of both quality and quantity, states may achieve a rudimentary or a reliable second-strike capability, meaning that they have confidence in their ability to retaliate to an enemy volley. Finally, states may achieve a level of nuclear development that gives them war-fighting or preemptive capabilities. Such states enjoy sophisticated and accurate weapons, varied and distributed delivery vehicles, hardened silos and related facilities, and robust command-and-control networks. There are many levels between a breakout capability and genuine first-strike arsenal, of course, and this definition allows the researcher to examine how successive breakthroughs affect the state's priorities and its strategic behavior. China conducted its first nuclear test almost a half century ago, for instance, but only recently has it gained the capability to consider using nuclear weapons for anything besides existential deterrence. Chapter 4 of this volume considers some of the implications of China's emerging capability.[14]

Although there is much to be said for the capabilities-based definition, this chapter takes a different approach. I define emerging nuclear powers as those that have tested their first nuclear explosive device within the last fifteen years. I also include states with a demonstrated capacity for indigenously producing weapons-grade fissile material. These states have overcome the major technological hurdle—designing a basic explosive device is much easier—and are therefore at the cusp of going nuclear. I focus on time rather than capabilities for two reasons. First, states that have only recently developed a nuclear capability are at the leading edge of the learning curve. They lack experience in nuclear diplomacy and may not understand the uses and limits of their newfound arsenals.[15] Conversely, states with a long nuclear pedigree also benefit from a significant learning period before they reach a new level of capabilities. Second, foreign powers are likely to be more nervous about a state's initial breakthrough than with subsequent innovations. Perhaps because they are suspicious about its motives and do not know what to expect about its behavior as a nuclear power, they may have little confidence that it will be a reliable custodian of nuclear weapons.

A closely related issue is whether status quo states can be confident about deterring emerging nuclear powers. If different states are more or less rational, so goes the current thinking, then different states should be more or less susceptible to deterrence. The goal for theorists and policymakers of late has been to identify those states that are deterrable, and then tailor deterrent signals according to their unique characteristics.[16] States unlikely to respond to any combination of threats and promises must be dealt with differently. Depending on the threat they pose, status quo powers might choose to ignore them, defend against them, physically contain them, or attack them. Summarizing this line of analysis, Colin Gray stresses the importance of "looking for deterrable foes" and taking other measures against undeterrable enemies.[17]

The debate over rationality, however, also begs the question about what kinds of action status quo powers seek to deter. If rationality varies across time and space, then it is reasonable to expect that the same deterrent threats might work against some actions but not others. Status quo powers might find it very easy to deliver clear and credible deterrent signals in order to forestall direct nuclear attacks, but they might not be able to issue credible threats against less provocative and damaging actions. As a result, the quality of modern deterrence theory, not to mention contemporary strategy against emerging nuclear powers, will rest on the ability to calibrate deterrent threats against specific actions. As Jeffrey Knopf puts it, "Rather than *whom*, the first question should be *what* to deter" (emphasis in the original).[18]

Status quo powers seek to deter at least four kinds of action: a rapid expansion of new entrants' nuclear capabilities, the transfer of fissile material and nuclear technology to other states and nonstate actors, the use of nuclear weapons as a cover for conventional aggression, and the use of nuclear weapons in war. Here I discuss these behaviors in detail. The subsequent section offers a series of propositions on what kinds of deterrence are most likely to succeed against them.[19]

Expansion of Newcomers' Arsenals

Emerging nuclear powers have important choices to make about the size, composition, and distribution of their nuclear capabilities. They might seek a "minimal" capability for the narrow purpose of deterring against attack by larger rivals.[20] Alternately, they might choose a larger force in order to ease their sense of vulnerability or as a way of expanding prestige or influence. They might choose to explore different delivery platforms, just as the United States invested in the strategic triad of submarines, manned aircraft, and land-based ballistic missiles during the Cold War. Expanding the force could also include efforts to disperse and conceal weapons, research and production centers, and associated support facilities.

Status quo powers have several possible reasons for wanting to deter an expansion of new nuclear stockpiles. A large and varied arsenal might tempt leaders of emerging nuclear powers to believe that they can extract more coercive value from nuclear weapons than is the case. This in turn would create additional pressure for neighboring countries to bolster their own defenses or seek equivalent nuclear capabilities. Regional arms races and spirals of mutual hostility and mistrust would result. Although local deterrent balances might eventually take hold, the interim period would be extraordinarily dangerous and unstable.[21] As a result, successful efforts to deter rapid expansion would alleviate the immediate consequences of pro-liferation, because such efforts would relax regional tensions and reduce local secur-ity dilemmas.

Deterring expansion would also lower the chance of a leakage of nuclear weap-ons, materials, or technologies. Large-scale nuclear efforts necessarily require more personnel and resources. Maintaining security becomes more difficult under these conditions. Similarly, deterring expansion would make international monitoring easier, especially if emerging nuclear powers were discouraged from dispersing and concealing key facilities. Cautious and deliberate expansion, as opposed to a spasm of production and deployment of nuclear weapons, would help ease the road to future arms control agreements.

If successful, efforts to deter rapid expansion would allow an emerging nuclear power's arsenal to grow fast enough to alleviate worries about vulnerability to a first strike while simultaneously holding the scale of the program in check so that it did not contribute to destabilizing second-order effects. Finding the right balance, however, is likely to prove elusive. Overly strenuous efforts to deter expansion might cause the emerging nuclear power to feel insecure, thus amplifying its incentives to "use them or lose them." Insufficient attention to deterring expansion, conversely, might exacerbate the regional security dilemma, leading to arms races, crises, and a higher chance of accidental or intentional nuclear leakage.

Transfer of Matériel or Know-How

A great deal of attention has focused on the danger that emerging nuclear powers will deliver nuclear materials, technologies, or weapons to states and nonstate prox-ies. The reasons are unsurprising, given the history of interstate cooperation on nuclear development. All five recognized nuclear weapon states under the Nuclear Non-Proliferation Treaty—the United States, Russia, France, Great Britain, and China—have assisted in other states' nuclear efforts. Like their predecessors, rising nuclear states today appear eager to share or barter their achievements. North Korea has been accused of assisting Syria's reactor program, for instance, whereas Paki-stan has been accused of looking the other way as its chief nuclear scientist, A. Q. Khan, constructed a multinational black market for enrichment technologies.

Analysts also fear that emerging nuclear powers will covertly deliver nuclear weapons to terrorist groups.[22] Although these fears have been greatly exaggerated, such an event, however unlikely, could seriously undermine American security.[23] First, nonstate actors would presumably deliver nuclear weapons using commercial transportation methods, which would be very difficult for intelligence agencies to track and intercept. Second, transnational nonstate actors are difficult to monitor because they are not attached to any specific piece of territory, meaning that intelli-gence on transnational actors will require sustained international cooperation and information sharing. Third, terrorist groups preaching martyrdom would be inher-ently difficult to deter because their operatives are already committed to suicide. Fourth, the technology needed to trace nuclear materials back to the source remains immature and somewhat unreliable. Status quo powers will have a difficult time convincing international observers that their forensic techniques can definitively locate the origin of a nuclear device, especially after the fact of a nuclear explosion. This will make it hard to credibly deter the patron state from providing weapons and know-how to terrorist proxies. As long as forensic technology remains immature, emerging nuclear powers may believe that they can remain anonymous patrons.[24]

Use as a Cover

Emerging nuclear powers may believe they can use nuclear weapons as a cover for conventional aggression and other efforts to expand their regional political influence. According to this logic, the great powers would hesitate to intervene in local conflicts if the aggressor could threaten to escalate the conflict to the nuclear level.

The established nuclear powers, having gone through the terrifying learning process of repeated Cold War crises, know enough not to brandish nuclear weapons in order to strengthen their position in local conflicts. Inexperienced nuclear states might be less inhibited and more willing to "throw their weight around."[25] Moreover, the fact that they are inexperienced might allow them to credibly deliver what Thomas Schelling called "threats that leave something to chance." This is because status quo powers might believe that they are just naive enough to risk a nuclear exchange. These conditions are not conducive to crisis stability.[26]

The use of nuclear weapons for this kind of coercion is appealing for two reasons. First, it offers a plausible edge over regional rivals, which might back down quickly rather than try to mount a defense against a nuclear-armed aggressor. In these cases emerging nuclear powers might be tempted to act on long-standing local territorial or political disputes, and if they were especially ambitious, they might seize the opportunity to fundamentally reshape the regional balance. Second, emerging nuclear powers might doubt that foreign powers will intervene if nuclear weapons are in play. The United States and other great powers may decide that the value of the regional status quo, which would not be closely bound to core national security interests, is not worth the risk. In this way regional powers could render irrelevant the massive US advantage in conventional military strength.

Use in War

The greatest danger is that an emerging nuclear power would use its weapons in war, against either local or distant enemies. Nuclear attacks could occur as part of a preplanned war-fighting strategy or through a process of inadvertent escalation. Nuclear-armed states may begin conflicts with the intent of using nuclear weapons for coercive purposes or not to use them at all. Depending on the course of the war, however, they may reconsider. A state on the verge of catastrophic defeat, for instance, might gamble for resurrection by using one or more nuclear weapons, in hopes that the damage and psychological shock of such an attack would reverse its fortunes.

Calibrating Deterrence

Deterrent strategies attempt to discourage challenges to the political status quo. Most of the theoretical literature on deterrence focuses on the use of military threats to avert military aggression, though more recent work suggests nonviolent approaches, including warnings of economic sanctions and diplomatic isolation.[27] Deterrence succeeds when possible challengers determine that the material or political costs of action outweigh the benefits. Effective deterrent signals also include explicit or implicit promises that threats will become inoperative once the challenger stands down. Without such reassurances, challengers have little reason to comply with the demands of the status quo power.[28]

Status quo states have a number of options to consider when crafting deterrent signals. Deterrence may involve military, economic, or diplomatic messages. It can be pursued unilaterally or in a coalition. Deterrent signals may be specific or ambiguous; and threats may be aimed at the target's military capabilities (counterforce) or his civilians (countervalue). In theory, the status quo state can use various combinations to deter emerging nuclear powers from the behaviors described above. What kinds of deterrent signals are most likely to succeed? Which are likely to fail, and why? The following are propositions for calibrating deterrence against rapid expansion, transfer, use as a cover, and use in war. (See table 2.1 for a summary.)

Deterring Expansion

Emerging nuclear powers have important decisions to make after they achieve a nascent capability. These include choices about the size and scope of the nuclear infrastructure, the number and type of weapons and delivery vehicles to build, and the level of transparency that they are willing to tolerate in order to satisfy international observers. More important are the *strategic* options that underlie these decisions. Emerging nuclear powers may be satisfied with a small capability to provide minimal deterrence against foreign adversaries. Small deterrent forces would also provide some independence from great powers, as well as the prestige that comes with membership in the nuclear club. If they are fearful that minimal deterrence is unreliable, however, they may seek a larger force with dispersed and concealed facilities as well as varied delivery options. Perceived vulnerability to nuclear rivals with superiority in numbers and technology is an important spur to this kind of expansion. Finally, they may increase the size and sophistication of their arsenal if they believe that they can use it to complement conventional operations and increase coercive leverage in regional conflicts.

There are at least three general ways to deter rapid expansion. First, status quo states can threaten emerging nuclear powers with diplomatic isolation. Such threats would force emerging nuclear powers to weigh the strategic benefits of a larger

Table 2.1 **Propositions on Immediate Deterrence**

Action	*Deterrent Signals*	*Complementary Reassurances*
Expansion	1. Diplomatic isolation 2. Targeted economic sanctions 3. Dissuasion	1. Diplomatic integration 2. Tacit economic rewards 3. Toleration of small arsenals
Transfer	1. Deterrence by denial and punishment via nuclear forensics 2. Indirect deterrence against facilitators	1. No punishment as long as material/technology stays within borders 2. No legal action against facilitators
Use as a cover	1. Deterrence by denial via local conventional superiority regional security arrangements 2. Ambiguous counterforce threats	1. Implicit or explicit guarantees against regime change 2. No preventive military strikes
Use in war	1. Specific countervalue threats 2. Specific warnings for political and military leaders who authorize use	1. Explicit guarantee that deterrent force will remain as long as the target complies 2. Explicit protection for political and military leaders who forbid use

arsenal against the opportunity costs of greater integration into the international system. The opportunity costs also imply a latent danger of finding themselves in the crosshairs of the status quo states. Emerging nuclear powers might believe that expansion can increase their influence over nonnuclear neighbors, but this would also invite hostility from nuclear-armed great powers.

Status quo powers can also attempt economic sanctions in order to discourage expansion. In some circumstances sanctions may be effective in influencing the strategic choices of emerging great powers. For example, regimes that rely on particular sectors of the economy to sustain their rule might be particularly sensitive to threats against those sectors.[29] Another economic signal would be a variant of what the Bush administration called *dissuasion*: the attempt to deter rival states from attempting to become peer competitors by convincing them that such an effort would be futile.[30] In terms of deterring expansion, a modified dissuasion strategy would include public reminders of the costs of seeking a large and dispersed capability, along with private suggestions that a small and relatively inexpensive deterrent force is tolerable. Such an approach, of course, would cut against nonproliferation efforts by sending mixed signals about the acceptability of nuclear weapons. It would also be difficult to send a clear signal about the limits of what is acceptable.

If dissuasion is problematic, effective military threats against expansion are even harder to conceive. Such messages strain credulity. Why would the status quo power tolerate the acquisition of nuclear weapons but risk war in order to keep the nascent arsenal from reaching some numerical or technological threshold? What level of expansion would trigger a military response? How could the leaders of status quo powers possibly rally domestic and international support for such a response? For example, North Korea is estimated to have sufficient fissile material for six to twelve nuclear weapons. It is hard to imagine that Washington could make a credible military threat to deter Pyongyang from increasing this number to fifteen, twenty, or fifty. Such precise calibration is inherently incredible and probably impossible.

Deterring Transfer

There are two basic approaches to deterring the transfer of nuclear capabilities and know-how to other states or nonstate actors. The first involves nuclear forensics, which is the capability to identify the source of fissile material even after an explosion. Nuclear facilities leave unique characteristics on uranium and plutonium, and in theory forensic experts can trace these elements back to their country of origin. Armed with this potential knowledge, status quo states might be able to deter transfer by informing nuclear producers that they will be held responsible in the event of an attack. Forensic technologies hold out the promise that nuclear suppliers cannot anonymously transfer fissile material to nonstate terrorist groups or other third parties. Nuclear forensics thus provides deterrence by denial as well as deterrence by punishment. High-quality forensic science might convince emerging proliferators that they cannot remain anonymous (denial) and may suffer retribution (punishment).[31]

There are several problems with using forensics for the purpose of deterrence, however. Beyond the technological obstacles associated with reliably determining the origin of fissile material, international agencies will have difficulty acquiring reliable samples from states of concern to test against black-market discoveries or the residue from the aftermath of an attack. Even proponents of the creation of a comprehensive database recognize the diplomatic challenges involved.[32] The amount of uncertainty involved in forensic conclusions may degrade the credibility of the deterrent signal; a nuclear supplier might plausibly claim to be the victim of a false positive. Moreover, even if forensic science progresses far enough so that analysts can be confident about their conclusions, questions remain about the appropriate deterrent threat. One scholar has recently argued for a declaratory policy that would guarantee punishment for states found to be negligent in securing their stocks of fissile material.[33]

This "negligence doctrine" would compel emerging nuclear powers to invest more in facilities security and deter them from transferring material to third parties. Unequivocal threats of retaliation may not be credible, however, especially if supplier states can plausibly claim that leakage was inadvertent. For this reason, ambiguous threats based on forensic science might be more appropriate. Automatic retaliation may also prove counterproductive in cases in which the source of nuclear material was an ally.[34]

The second approach to deterring transfer is related to recent scholarship on terrorism. Although some terrorists are absolutely committed to conducting attacks and cannot be deterred by threats of punishment, terrorists' supporters may be less willing to sacrifice all for the cause. Raising the costs of action to third parties might deter them from participating, which would make it more difficult for terrorist groups to operate. This kind of indirect deterrence may also work for deterring states from transferring nuclear material and technology.[35] Rather than sending threats and reassurances to the emerging nuclear power, the idea is to communicate with other actors that would be involved in any nuclear transfer. Because their motives may be based on profit instead of ideology or religion, threats of legal or financial punishment may suffice to deter them from cooperating with nuclear suppliers and their clients.

Deterring Use as a Cover

Extant deterrence theory is especially relevant to the problem of deterring the use of nuclear weapons to cover aggression, because the strategic problem today is much the same as the extended deterrence problem during the Cold War. Then the problem was how to credibly threaten the Soviet Union with retaliation for attacks on US allies, even if such threats created the possibility of a general war. Now the problem is how to credibly threaten nuclear-armed regional aggressors in conflicts that probably do not involve core national security interests. The credibility of US commitments is questionable in both cases, because the value of the object may be less than the risk of a nuclear exchange.

One answer given by Cold War deterrence theorists relied on a favorable balance of conventional forces. Strengthening the local balance would reinforce deterrence by denial by convincing Soviet leaders that they could not achieve their strategic goals, even in the absence of a nuclear response by the United States. The idea was to raise the conventional costs of action and the likelihood of failure without threatening Moscow's second-strike deterrent capability. This would simultaneously deter aggressiveness without threatening Soviet national security, and thus would prevent a dangerous spiral. The requirements for conventional deterrence were the subject of heated debate, but the logic was straightforward.[36]

The same logic applies today. Indeed, the argument for maintaining local conventional superiority is stronger because the United States does not need to deal with the quantitative advantages that it faced against the Soviet military during the Cold War. If deterrence by denial could support extended deterrence against a superpower enemy in its own backyard, then it should work against vastly inferior conventional foes. Regional aggressors face dubious odds of success and the very real prospect of rapid defeat, which should give them pause before they risk a confrontation. And though they might take heart in the United States' supposed aversion to casualties, advances in military technology have given US forces a much greater ability to fight conventionally without absorbing heavy losses. This eases the domestic political constraints on regional intervention and thus adds credibility to US deterrent threats.[37]

Efforts to shore up local alliances also strengthen the conventional balance. Emerging nuclear powers may believe that nuclear weapons will erode allies' mutual commitments by raising the price of solidarity. However, balancing incentives should be much stronger in these cases because of the increased threat to neighboring states. This should ease the diplomatic requirements of building and maintaining local coalitions. The Obama administration's recent efforts to extend defensive umbrellas in the Middle East and East Asia implicitly rely on this logic. Whether this will succeed over the long run is unclear, but so far there are no real signs of regional bandwagoning, and no signs that Iran or North Korea has been able to intimidate its neighbors. Although nuclear capabilities may help emerging nuclear powers deter direct military intervention, their neighbors appear to be more steadfast in opposition and more willing to balance against them.

If local conventional superiority and balancing coalitions constitute useful deterrents against use as a cover, then there is probably little utility gained by nuclear threats. It is inherently difficult to issue credible nuclear threats, especially against countervalue targets, when core national interests are not at stake. A threat to break the decades-long tradition against nuclear use, especially when the target would include civilian population centers, would probably not be taken seriously by an emerging nuclear power.[38]

Conversely, counterforce deterrence against small nuclear arsenals is more credible. Well-publicized advances in intelligence, accuracy, and warhead design may convince small nuclear powers that they are vulnerable to a debilitating conventional strike against even buried or hardened facilities. Actually achieving a successful strike is another matter, but the goal would simply be to create enough doubt to inspire caution in the targeted state. If the targeted state believes that status quo powers can hold its nuclear weapons at risk, then these weapons will lose value as a covering force for conventional operations. Moreover, counterforce strategies may be less dangerous than during the Cold War. If the United States threatened the Soviet retaliatory force, it might act incautiously during crises, lest it suffer a catastrophic first strike.[39] But today's emerging nuclear powers cannot plausibly threaten the United States. US leaders, accordingly, can issue credible counterforce threats without fears of crisis instability, while simultaneously providing reassurances that they will not act against the target's deterrent capability as long as it accepts the status quo.

It is unclear that specific threats are best. Such threats might encourage a rapid expansion of nuclear capabilities as well as more serious efforts at concealment and dispersion. Yet ambiguous threats may also create sufficient uncertainty to encourage caution without provoking unintended consequences. According to Alexander George and Richard Smoke, would-be aggressors are more likely to act if they believe they can calculate and control the risks of escalation.[40] For this reason vague threats may suffice to sow serious doubts about an emerging nuclear power's ability to manipulate events.

Deterring Wartime Nuclear Use

The surest path to deterring use as a cover is through a combination of local conventional superiority and diplomatic efforts to sustain regional balancing coalitions. Nuclear counterforce threats may also discourage emerging nuclear powers from provoking crises that would place their own deterrent capabilities at risk. Ambiguous signals may also succeed because they remove the challenger's ability to control risk in the event of war. In wartime, however, deterrence may require precisely the opposite signals. Counterforce threats are likely to be ineffective and may even prove to be counterproductive by creating perverse escalatory incentives for the weaker power. Conversely, specific countervalue threats will be much more credible after the shooting starts, and they will vividly convey the consequences for crossing the nuclear threshold.[41] Specific threats involve unambiguous guarantees of nuclear retaliation against military, government, and industrial centers if the challenger goes nuclear in the course of the war. These will almost certainly include cities.

To be clear, countervalue nuclear threats are only appropriate in very narrow circumstances. The wildly disproportionate threat to deliberately target cities is almost never credible. But in extreme circumstances such threats might be the only way to convince target states not to cross the nuclear threshold. Most worrisome is the hypothetical case, mentioned above, in which an emerging nuclear power is on the verge of conventional defeat and believes that escalation is the only way to change the outcome. Unambiguous countervalue threats might be necessary to dispel such hopes for resurrection. They would constitute a specific warning: Rather than promising a miraculous reversal of fortune, the first use of nuclear weapons will guarantee catastrophic destruction and the end of your regime.

If ambiguity makes sense during peacetime, why are specific threats appropriate during war? First, public inhibitions against nuclear use are likely to be much lower after the fighting ignites public passions. As a result, specific threats to respond in kind to nuclear escalation will be more credible than the same threats would be if delivered before the war. And if ambiguous threats always leave something to chance, they are especially dangerous against the leaders of emerging nuclear powers, who will be under immense wartime pressure and shackled with immature command-and-control systems. Leaving something to chance against such adversaries is dangerous. It raises the likelihood of a rash nuclear attack or a loss of civilian control over nuclear decisions. Either scenario could undermine diplomacy amid the stresses of combat. The loss of civilian control, furthermore, would complicate the war's termination because it would be difficult to identify a negotiating partner.

Whereas counterforce strategies are justifiable before wars begin, they become counterproductive once a war is under way. Both targeting strategies would be credible, but counterforce threats would be more dangerous because they would create a strong use-it-or-lose-it incentive for emerging nuclear powers with small and potentially vulnerable arsenals. Reassurance would also be easier when combined with countervalue signals. In other words, status quo states would hold the target state's core national interests at risk while promising to spare the deterrent force as long as the leadership does not escalate. This could provide an incentive to control escalation as well as negotiate an end to the war. The primary benefit of such signals is that they reinforce the boundary between conventional and nuclear arms. Counterforce signals in wartime would do just the opposite, blurring the line and possibly encouraging escalation.

What Do Emerging Nuclear Powers Seek to Deter?

The analytical framework presented in this chapter helps to unpack the security challenges associated with emerging nuclear powers, and it yields a number of propositions on how to calibrate deterrence against them. It also suggests some ideas about how the leaders of those states might think about deterring status quo nuclear powers as well as regional nuclear and nonnuclear rivals. Like established nuclear powers, they have a strong interest in constructing deterrent signals to preclude different kinds of actions. And like the status quo states, their concerns fall into four broad categories: conventional attack, unconventional escalation, third-party intervention, and structural asymmetry.[42]

First, emerging nuclear powers seek to deter regional rivals from conventional attack. This is especially important for states with relatively small and technologically unsophisticated conventional forces. For instance, Pakistan's small arsenal serves as a "nuclear equalizer" against India, which enjoys a better than five-to-one advantage in annual defense spending.[43] Similarly, North Korea's bluster against South Korea and the United States is typically accompanied by blunt deterrent signals. "If the US imperialists invade our dear father land even 0.001 millimeter," declared a North Korean official in one representative statement, "eight million youths and schoolchildren will smash them at one stroke . . . [and] plunge the damned US territory into a sea of flame."[44] The point of these messages, however crude, is clear enough. At the same time emerging nuclear powers also have incentives to keep their nuclear activities hidden, lest they become the targets for preventive strikes. As a result, they must balance the temptation to demonstrate their small nuclear capabilities to deter invasion against the danger of unintentionally provoking Osirak-style attacks.

Second, emerging nuclear powers may seek to deter their enemies from escalating to the nuclear level if war occurs. Controlling escalation would go some distance toward nullifying their opponents' unconventional advantages. It would also provide a set of related benefits. Emerging nuclear powers could more reliably protect their hard-won arsenals, wage protracted wars on more favorable terms, and gain an important measure of regime security by convincing enemies to limit their strategic objectives. Deterring escalation would facilitate the war's termination on acceptable terms, even if the emerging nuclear power was clearly losing on the battlefield. In these cases the stronger power would have incentives to negotiate a limited victory rather than risk catastrophe. Conversely, it would be much more dubious about any settlement after a nuclear exchange, and it would have few incentives to accept anything short of regime change.

Third, emerging powers seek to deter third parties from intervening in regional wars. As described above, status quo nuclear powers fear that emerging nuclear powers will use their arsenals as a cover for conventional aggression. But smaller states might view nuclear weapons merely as tools to prevent great power meddling in what they see as essentially local disputes.

Fourth and finally, emerging nuclear powers seek to deter status quo nuclear powers from limiting their freedom of action. Great powers try to exert "structural power" by dominating international institutions and setting the normative bound-aries for acceptable behavior. Their control of nuclear weapons puts smaller states at a disadvantage, especially if they require great power protection from regional threats. Acquiring nuclear weapons is a way of carving out some autonomy and to block great powers from domineering behavior. France's decision to build the force de frappe in the 1960s was an early example. Although French leaders relied on the US security umbrella, they did not want to become utterly beholden to US interests. Thus developing an independent nuclear capability made it possible for France to take an active and sometimes confrontational role against the United States in Euro-pean affairs.[45] The fact that US relative power today is historically unprecedented puts a premium on creative ways for smaller states to guard their autonomy. Possess-ing some nuclear capabilities may prove an important means to this end.[46]

All these propositions come with an important caveat. To say that emerging nuclear powers want to deter different kinds of behavior is not to argue that they will succeed. Tailoring specific messages to head off specific threatening actions is no easy task, and the history of first-generation nuclear states suggests that they will struggle mightily to communicate clear and effective signals to their rivals. How well and how quickly they learn to cope with this problem will affect the likelihood of misperception between traditional and emerging nuclear powers—and, more broadly, it will say much about the consequences of contemporary proliferation.

Notes

1. Bernard Brodie, "The Weapon: War in the Atomic Age and Implications for Mili-tary Policy," in *The Absolute Weapon: Atomic Power and World Order*, edited by Ber-nard Brodie (New York: Harcourt Brace, 1946), 52, 76.

2. For early criticisms of rational deterrence theory, see Stephen Maxwell, *Rational-ity in Deterrence*, Adelphi Paper 50 (London: International Institute for Strategic Studies, 1968); Alexander L. George and Richard Smoke, *Deterrence in American Foreign Policy: Theory and Practice* (New York: Columbia University Press, 1974); and Patrick M. Mor-gan, *Deterrence: A Conceptual Analysis* (Beverly Hills, CA: Sage, 1977). On signaling and the psychological barriers to communication, see Robert Jervis, *Perception and Mis-perception in International Politics* (Princeton, NJ: Princeton University Press, 1976); and Robert Jervis, Richard Ned Lebow, and Janice Gross Stein, eds., *Psychology and Deter-rence* (Baltimore: Johns Hopkins University Press, 1985).

3. Richard Ned Lebow and Janis Gross Stein, "Rational Deterrence Theory: I Think, Therefore I Deter," *World Politics* 41, no. 2 (January 1989): 208–24.

4. Colin S. Gray, *Nuclear Strategy and National Style* (Boston: Hamilton Press, 1986); Keith B. Payne, *The Fallacies of Cold War Deterrence and a New Direction* (Lex-ington: University Press of Kentucky, 2001).

5. Marc Dean Millot, Roger Molander, and Peter A. Wilson, *"The Day After . . ."* *Study: Nuclear Proliferation in the Post–Cold War World*, vol. 2 (Santa Monica, CA: RAND Corporation, 1993); Brad Roberts, *Weapons Proliferation and World Order after the Cold War* (The Hague: Kluwer Law International, 1996), 319; James J. Wirtz, "Beyond Bipolarity: Prospects for Nuclear Stability after the Cold War," in *The Absolute*

Weapon Revisited: Nuclear Arms and the Emerging International Order, edited by T. V. Paul, Richard J. Harknett, and James J. Wirtz (Ann Arbor: University of Michigan Press, 1998); Paul Bracken, *Fire in the East: The Rise of Asian Military Power and the Second Nuclear Age* (New York: HarperCollins, 1999), 114–24.

6. Scott D. Sagan, "More Will Be Worse," in *The Spread of Nuclear Weapons: A Debate Renewed*, by Scott D. Sagan and Kenneth N. Waltz (New York: W. W. Norton, 1995).

7. On the dangers of opaque proliferation, see Shai Feldman, "Managing Nuclear Proliferation," in *Limiting Nuclear Proliferation*, edited by Jed C. Snyder and Samuel F. Wells Jr. (Cambridge, MA: Ballinger, 1985); Avner Cohen and Benjamin Frankel, "Opaque Nuclear Proliferation," *Journal of Strategic Studies* 13, no. 2 (September 1990): 14–44; Susan M. Burns, "Preventing Nuclear War: Arms Management," in *Nuclear Proliferation in South Asia: The Prospects for Arms Control*, edited by Stephen Philip Cohen (Boulder, CO: Westview Press, 1991). For a more sanguine analysis of the consequences of opacity, see Devin T. Hagerty, *The Consequences of Nuclear Proliferation: Lessons from South Asia* (Cambridge, MA: MIT Press, 1998), 39–62.

8. In the aftermath of Hiroshima and Nagasaki, American officials took for granted that they would and should use nuclear weapons in the next war. In 1948, future secretary of state John Foster Dulles told then–secretary George Marshall, "Why the American people would execute you if you did not use the bomb in the event of a war." It took many years and several intense crises for the United States and the Soviet Union to settle into a stable deterrent balance. Dulles is quoted by Fred Kaplan, *Wizards of Armageddon* (New York: Simon & Schuster, 1983), 178. On the long period of instability in the first half of the Cold War, see Bracken, *Fire in the East*, 99–101; and Richard K. Betts, "Universal Deterrence or Conceptual Collapse? Liberal Pessimism and Utopian Realism," in *The Coming Crisis: Nuclear Proliferation, US Interests, and World Order*, edited by Victor A. Utgoff (Cambridge, MA: MIT Press, 2000), 71.

9. Lewis A. Dunn, "Military Politics, Nuclear Proliferation, and the 'Nuclear Coup d'Etat,'" *Journal of Strategic Studies* 1, no. 1 (1978); Betts, "Universal Deterrence," 67. Other observers worried about the destabilizing effects of proliferation absent the anchor of bipolar competition. Most important, they feared that balancing coalitions would break down quickly against nuclear-armed aggressors. See Stephen Peter Rosen, "Nuclear Proliferation and Alliance Relations," in *Coming Crisis*, ed. Utgoff; and Lyle J. Goldstein, *Preventive Attack and Weapons of Mass Destruction: A Comparative Historical Analysis* (Stanford, CA: Stanford University Press, 2006). Not all observers shared these concerns. Kenneth Waltz famously argued that the spread of nuclear weapons would lead to the spread of cautious behavior as the logic of mutually assured destruction took hold. Stephen Walt, similarly, argued that regional powers would have large incentives to balance against regional powers, which would contribute to deterrence and help contain regional aggression. See Stephen M. Walt, "More May Be Better," in *Spread of Nuclear Weapons*, ed. Sagan and Waltz; and Stephen M. Walt, "Containing Rogues and Renegades: Coalition Strategies and Counterproliferation," in *Coming Crisis*, ed. Utgoff.

10. William A. Owens, *Lifting the Fog of War* (New York: Farrar, Straus & Giroux, 2000). Owens is a former commander of the US Sixth Fleet and vice chief of naval operations.

11. Kenneth M. Pollack, *The Threatening Storm: The United States and Iraq: The Crisis, the Strategy, and the Prospects after Saddam* (New York: Random House, 2002), 335.

12. For a similar argument, see Derek D. Smith, "Deterrence and Counterproliferation in an Age of Weapons of Mass Destruction," *Security Studies* 12, no. 4 (Summer 2003): 152–97.

13. George W. Bush, *The National Security Strategy of the United States* (Washington, DC: US Government Printing Office, 2002), 15–16.

14. I thank Christopher Twomey for clarifying these distinctions. See also Michael S. Chase, Andrew S. Erickson, and Christopher Yeaw, "Chinese Theater and Strategic Missile Force Modernization and Its Implications for the United States," *Journal of Strategic Studies* 32, no. 1 (2009): 67–114.

15. Michael Horowitz, "The Spread of Nuclear Weapons and International Conflict: Does Experience Matter?" *Journal of Conflict Resolution* 53, no. 2 (April 2009): 234–57.

16. On recent US efforts at "tailored deterrence," see M. Elaine Bunn, "Can Deterrence Be Tailored?" *Strategic Forum* 225 (January 2007). For arguments about the need to understand the target in detail, see Barry R. Schneider and Jerrold M. Post, *Know Thy Enemy: Profiles of Adversary Leaders and Their Strategic Cultures*, 2nd ed. (Montgomery: US Air War College, 2003); Caroline Ziemke, "The National Myth," in *Coming Crisis*, ed. Utgoff; William Martel, "Deterrence and Alternative Images of Nuclear Possession," in *Absolute Weapon Revisited*, ed. Paul, Harknett, and Wirtz; and Colin S. Gray, *Maintaining Effective Deterrence* (Carlisle, PA: Strategic Studies Institute, US Army War College, 2003).

17. Gray, *Maintaining Effective Deterrence*, x. See also Smith, "Deterrence and Counterproliferation."

18. Jeffrey Knopf, "The Fourth Wave in Deterrence Research," *Contemporary Security Policy* 31, no. 1 (April 2010): 27.

19. Peter Lavoy lists a dozen possible dangers associated with proliferation. I divide these into two categories: structural and strategic. *Structural* problems include such issues as the lack of reliable bureaucratic and technological safeguards against nuclear attacks, as well as changes to local power balances that might encourage neighboring states to pursue preventive military action against emerging nuclear powers. *Strategic* problems describe the ways in which emerging nuclear powers might use their new capabilities. Deterring these behaviors is the focus of the first half of this paper. Helping emerging nuclear powers make the transition to responsible custodianship is the focus of the second half. Peter R. Lavoy, "The Strategic Consequences of Nuclear Proliferation: A Review Essay," *Security Studies* 4, no. 4 (Summer 1995): 695–753.

20. On minimal deterrence, see Jeffrey Lewis, *The Minimum Means of Reprisal: China's Search for Security in the Nuclear Age* (Cambridge, MA: MIT Press, 2007); and George H. Quester, "The Continuing Debate on Minimal Deterrence," in *Absolute Weapon Revisited*, ed. Paul, Harknett, and Wirtz.

21. Barry Posen suggests that this is one reason the United States would have acted forcefully against Iraq in 1990–91, even if it possessed a small nuclear arsenal. Failure to reverse Iraq's conquest of Kuwait would have reinforced the belief in the coercive power of nuclear weapons, which would have inspired rapid regional arms racing. Such a "hellishly competitive" world might stabilize eventually, but the interim period would be "very exciting." Barry R. Posen, "US Nuclear Security Policy in a Nuclear Armed World, or What If Iraq Had Had Nuclear Weapons?" in *Coming Crisis*, ed. Utgoff, 160–67.

22. Derek D. Smith, *Deterring America: Rogue States and the Proliferation of Weapons of Mass Destruction* (Cambridge: Cambridge University Press, 2006).

23. On inflated threats, see John Mueller: *Atomic Obsession: Nuclear Alarmism from Hiroshima to Al-Qaeda* (New York: Oxford University Press, 2009). On loose arguments about the danger of nuclear terrorism, see Joshua Rovner and Austin Long, "The Ties That Bind? The Dubious Link between the War in Afghanistan and the Threat of Nuclear Terrorism," unpublished paper, 2009.

24. I discuss forensics in more detail below. For a primer on forensic technology, see Klaus Mayer, Maria Wallenius, and Ian Ray, "Nuclear Forensics: A Methodology Providing Clues on the Origin of Illicitly Trafficked Nuclear Materials," *The Analyst* 130 (2005): 433–41.

25. Betts, "Universal Deterrence," 71.

26. Thomas Schelling, *The Strategy of Conflict* (New York: Oxford University Press, 1960), 193.

27. For criticism of the overly military focus of Cold War deterrence theory, see Patrick M. Morgan, *Deterrence: A Conceptual Analysis* (Beverly Hills, CA: Sage, 1977). For a commentary on recent research, see Knopf, "Fourth Wave."

28. Thomas Schelling, *Arms and Influence* (New Haven, CT: Yale University Press, 1966), 74–75. See also Thomas J. Christensen, "The Contemporary Security Dilemma: Deterring a Taiwan Conflict," *Washington Quarterly* 25, no. 4 (Autumn 2002): 7–21.

29. Jonathan Kirshner, "The Microfoundations of Economic Sanctions," *Security Studies* 6, no. 3 (Spring 1997): 32–64.

30. US Department of Defense, *Quadrennial Defense Review Report*, September 2001, 12. For some commentary, see Richard L. Kugler, "Dissuasion as a Strategic Concept," *Strategic Forum* 196 (December 2002).

31. Caitlin Talmadge, "Deterring a Nuclear 9/11," *Washington Quarterly* 30, no. 2 (Spring 2007): 21–34.

32. Michael A. Levi, "Deterring Nuclear Terrorism," *Issues in Science and Technology*, Spring 2004, www.issues.org/20.3/levi.html; Joshua Rovner, "Preparing for a Nuclear Iran: The Role of the CIA," *Strategic Insights* 4, no. 11 (November 2005); Talmadge, "Deterring," 29.

33. Anners Corr, "Deterrence of Nuclear Terrorism: A Negligence Doctrine," *Nonproliferation Review* 12, no. 1 (March 2005): 127–47.

34. On calculated ambiguity, see Robert L. Gallucci, "Averting Nuclear Catastrophe: Contemplating Extreme Responses to US Vulnerability," *Annals of the American Academy of Political and Social Science* 607 (September 2006). On the counterproductive effects of automatic retaliation, see Michael Miller, "Nuclear Attribution as Deterrence," *Nonproliferation Review* 14, no. 1 (March 2007): 33–60.

35. Robert Trager and Dessislava P. Zagorcheva, "Deterring Terrorism: It Can Be Done," *International Security* 30, no. 3 (Winter 2005–6): 87–123; Paul K. Davis and Brian Michael Jenkins, *Deterrence and Influence in Counterterrorism: A Component in the War on Al-Qaeda* (Santa Monica, CA: RAND Corporation, 2002).

36. John J. Mearsheimer, "Why the Soviets Can't Win Quickly in Central Europe," *International Security* 7, no. 1 (Summer 1982): 139–75; Barry R. Posen, *Inadvertent Escalation: Conventional War and Nuclear Risks* (Ithaca, NY: Cornell University Press, 1992), 68–128. For a skeptical view of conventional deterrence, see Eliot Cohen, "Toward Better Net Assessment," *International Security* 13, no. 1 (Summer 1988): 176–215.

37. On the implications of the revolution in military affairs on deterrence, see Patrick M. Morgan, *Deterrence Now* (Cambridge: Cambridge University Press, 2005), 203–37.

38. On the norm against nuclear use, see T. V. Paul, *The Tradition of Non-Use of Nuclear Weapons* (Stanford, CA: Stanford University Press), and Nina Tannenwald, *The Nuclear Taboo: The United States and the Non-Use of Nuclear Weapons since 1945* (Cambridge: Cambridge University Press, 2008).

39. Posen, *Inadvertent Escalation*.

40. Alexander L. George and Richard Smoke, *Deterrence in American Foreign Policy: Theory and Practice* (New York: Columbia University Press, 1974), 519–33.

41. As Barry Posen wrote regarding one emerging nuclear power, "Iran must be made to understand one simple thing: using nuclear weapons first or arranging for others to do so would be the path to certain annihilation." Barry R. Posen, "Overkill," *Foreign Affairs* 89, no. 4 (July–August 2010): 160–63, at 163.

42. For an early post–Cold War monograph that distinguishes the different coercive purposes of emerging nuclear powers, see Dean A. Wilkening and Kenneth Watman, *Nuclear Deterrence in a Regional Context* (Santa Monica, CA: RAND Corporation, 1995).

43. Ashok Kapur, "New Nuclear States and the International World Order," in *Absolute Weapon Revisited*, ed. Paul, Harknett, and Wirtz, 242. For data on comparative defense spending, see International Institute for Strategic Studies, *The Military Balance* (London: International Institute for Strategic Studies, 2009), 449.

44. Korean Central News Agency, "Koreans Vow to Cope with US War Move," December 4, 1998, available at www.kcna.co.jp.

45. Paul, "Power, Influence, and Nuclear Weapons," 33.

46. On US power, see Stephen G. Brooks and William C. Wohlforth, *World Out of Balance: International Relations and the Challenge of American Primacy* (Princeton, NJ: Princeton University Press, 2008). On ways in which smaller states might respond, see Stephen M. Walt, *Taming American Power: The Global Response to US Primacy* (New York: W. W. Norton, 2006).

CHAPTER 3

SOUTH AFRICA'S NUCLEAR STRATEGY

Deterring "Total Onslaught" and "Nuclear Blackmail" in Three Stages

Helen E. Purkitt and Stephen F. Burgess

IN THE 1970s South Africa's apartheid regime decided to develop nuclear weapons as a means of ensuring its survival in the face of rising external threats.[1] Once the regime decided to use its nuclear energy program and a mixture of imported and homegrown technology to begin building nuclear weapons, it began to devise strategies to use them and to develop missiles and aircraft to deliver them. In 1975 South African leaders discerned a sudden spike in the threat to national security owing to the USSR's intervention in Cuba and presence in Angola, along with burgeoning guerrilla activity on the part of the South West African People's Organization (SWAPO) and the African National Congress (ANC).

In response the regime considered a strategy of threatening to use or actually using tactical nuclear weapons in case the Soviets brought nuclear weapons or other weapons of mass destruction (WMD) to Angola to threaten South Africa. It also considered threatening or launching tactical nuclear attacks against SWAPO and ANC guerrilla bases and against African states like Angola that actively supported these movements—especially if these antagonists were found to possess WMD. The strategic idea of using—or even threatening to use—nuclear weapons to destroy guerrilla bases or African capital cities may seem fanciful. But it reflects the psychology of South African rulers toward threats to the survival of their regime, which in turn molded their vision of a proportionate response. Discussions about such a strategy indicate that the apartheid regime had embarked on a "search for strategies" after the arsenal already existed. In short, nuclear weapons were developed and fielded before the leadership formulated fully rational ideas about how to employ them.

At the same time, Pretoria began developing a strategy to manipulate Washington in case Moscow, its African allies, or the ANC threatened the survival of the apartheid regime. In effect this was a strategy of blackmail. South Africa was an ally of the United States and the United Kingdom during World War II and the Korean War but drew away from its erstwhile allies in the 1960s and felt abandoned by the United States by the late 1970s. In response South African leaders sought to devise a strategy that would use nuclear weapons to induce the United States to side with Pretoria in the struggle with the Soviet Bloc, especially if things started to go badly in southern Africa. The result was a three-stage strategy in which South African leaders would threaten to conduct a nuclear test, which purportedly would impel the United States to throw its support behind them. The strategic idea of using nuclear weapons to blackmail the United States into intervening on South Africa's behalf seems as whimsical as the concept of striking at militants or its neighboring states with nuclear weapons. Again, however, its strategy mirrored the outlook of its political leaders on relations with the United States, along with their perceptions of the effect that a nuclear test would create.

The senior South African politicians and military officials who authorized the development of nuclear weapons and an array of sophisticated warheads and delivery devices shared a core set of beliefs and passions about the importance of developing mass-destruction weaponry to counter a hazily defined enemy. South African leaders' shared emotions arose from a collective sense of abandonment and isolation toward their former allies that had come to treat South Africa as a pariah state. The country's mounting fear of abandonment, amplified by its resentment at Western betrayal, drove state president P. W. Botha and other leaders to direct the military-industrial sector to improve the sophistication of South African warheads and to build tactical and longer-range missiles. And the sense of urgency propelling their nuclear weapons program was only heightened by a number of factors—including the escalating, increasingly violent opposition at home; intensifying pressure from the international antiapartheid movement; the ready availability of sanctuary for ANC guerrillas in neighboring states; and a growing recognition by leaders, the Afrikaner elite, and the defense establishment that time was not on their side.[2]

The South African nuclear case bears some resemblance to the cases of France, the United Kingdom, and China. These nations developed their own nuclear arsenals in the face of overwhelming Soviet nuclear superiority, and they found it difficult to craft rational nuclear strategies in the face of assured destruction.[3] A number of states—Israel, India, Pakistan, South Africa, and North Korea—secretly developed nuclear weapons in defiance of sanctions inspired by the Nuclear Non-Proliferation Treaty (NPT). Most of them did so for the purpose of deterrence.[4] In particular, North Korea developed a strategy of nuclear blackmail against Japan, the United States, and South Korea. Pyongyang's actions may have appeared irrational but were quite logical in that Washington eventually accommodated it. Israel also developed a nuclear strategy intended to draw the United States into any future Arab-Israeli war on Tel Aviv's behalf.[5]

In this chapter we explain South Africa's nuclear strategy in comparison with the strategies of other nuclear weapon states. We show how and why the psychology of regime officials and the existence of a nuclear capability drove the making of strategy in South Africa as compared with other states. By embracing nuclear blackmail, South African leaders evidently wanted to be seen as prepared to risk everything. At the same time, they attempted to deceive both the United States and the Soviet Union.

Regime Psychology, Nuclear Weapons
Development, and Strategy Formulation

To understand why nation-states initiate secret nuclear weapons programs and strategy, it is necessary to analyze the political psychology of leaders and groups involved in decision making. Our research and that of others indicates that shared core beliefs and political resolve animating leaders and groups represent critical determinants in the decision to formulate a nuclear strategy. Once analysts understand decision makers' beliefs and the ways they frame specific problems, it becomes possible to track when and how changes in beliefs, problem framing, and collective emotional responses lead to changes in policy and strategy.[6] A short foray into South Africa's past, then, constitutes a platform for further analysis of Pretoria's nuclear weapons enterprise.

The South African leaders who came to power in 1948 exhibited what Jacques Hymans terms "oppositional nationalism," which combines a sense of national and racial superiority with paranoia.[7] Afrikaner nationalists saw themselves as "God's chosen people" in South Africa. They also believed fervently that communists and African nationalists were bent on annihilating Afrikaners, their way of life, and their regime. In the 1960s Afrikaner nationalism metamorphosed into a *laager* (i.e., "circle the wagons") complex amid mounting threats.[8] The *laager* complex manifested itself in rampant paranoia about an onslaught from Soviet-backed communists or black nationalists. It was a significant psychological impetus behind Pretoria's decision to build the bomb.[9] In the 1960s apartheid leaders cited the menace from black guerrilla movements backed by the Soviet Union and China as justification for a sixfold increase in defense expenditures. The regime became increasingly militarized. The position of secretary of defense was shifted from civilian to uniformed leaders. Parliament lost effective oversight over the military.[10] As a consequence of heightened threat perceptions, apartheid rulers and atomic scientists had few domestic political constraints with which to contend as they led South Africa into the nuclear weapons club.

Regime psychology manifested itself in a collective sense of betrayal and abandonment by longtime friends and allies. Until 1960 the regime felt that it was a part of the anticommunist Cold War alliance.[11] But from 1960 onward Afrikaner nationalist leaders, supported by the majority of whites in South Africa, increasingly felt sold out and isolated by arms embargoes and other punitive measures enacted by the United Nations and erstwhile allies such as the United States, Great Britain, and other European countries. In the 1970s these resentments were amplified by Western inaction during the Soviet-backed Cuban intervention in Angola. Now bereft of outside support, Pretoria saw little recourse other than to develop a nuclear weapons strategy.

Finding itself on death ground, then, jolted the apartheid regime into action. A surge in political protests at home coupled with the first signs of guerrilla warfare in neighboring states fueled these threat perceptions. For nearly two decades, the prospects for internal revolution and external aggression sustained support throughout the South African government for sophisticated but costly defense research and development. Pervasive fear among most Afrikaner politicians and members of the white elite of losing control of their political and economic supremacy forged a conviction that the government must build up its defenses to protect a cherished way of life and the political status quo.

However, Pretoria's anxiety was misplaced. South Africa faced less threat of invasion or WMD attack than any other state intent on building a WMD capacity. The country lay far from the Soviet Union and its WMD arsenal. Distance attenuated the chances of a Soviet missile attack or an invasion by Cuban troops almost into nonexistence. The absence of any credible threat to national existence demonstrates that the South African case is explained less by realist theory and actual threats than any other WMD case. Models drawing on political psychology and organizational and domestic politics do more to explain Pretoria's actions than cost/benefit calculations. Excessive fears of adversaries exacerbated by xenophobic nationalism induced South African leaders to magnify the severity of security threats. This became a self-perpetuating cycle. Real increases in domestic and external threats strengthened the incentive to construct a vast array of sophisticated weapon systems, including nuclear arms.

South African leaders like Prime Minister John Vorster (1966–76) and especially State President P. W. Botha (1976–89) tapped this reservoir of support for collective survival to develop nuclear weapons and launch vehicles and formulate nuclear strategy. Botha ranks as the godfather of South African nuclear weapons because he threw his unconditional support behind all nuclear-related weapons projects undertaken by the regime. He played a central role in all decisions related to the nuclear weapon and space launch programs starting in 1966, when he was appointed defense minister, until he was forced to step aside as state president after suffering a massive stroke in February 1989. WMD, including nuclear weapons and a range of launch vehicles, constituted all-important tools for implementing his "total strategy" of opposing "total onslaught" by Soviet-backed Cuban forces, communists, and black nationalists. Covert nuclear warheads and an arsenal of different types of missile systems came to be viewed as essential force multipliers for a military stretched thinner and thinner by operational demands at home and along the frontiers with South West Africa (Namibia) and Angola.[12]

Throughout the 1980s, in addition to overseeing the completion of six World War II–type atomic bombs, Botha supported research and development on state-of-the art nuclear technologies and missiles. He secured the funds needed for a multi-stage rocket system, which he envisioned as playing a dual role as both the country's premier nuclear deterrent and a civilian satellite launch vehicle. He is credited, furthermore, with being the chief architect of the South African nuclear strategy.

Botha implemented an integrated committee approach to guide the country's secret nuclear weapons program. Representatives from the Armaments Corporation of South Africa (Armscor), the Atomic Energy Commission, and the South African Defense Force took part in meetings of the planning group. The South African air force played a major and growing part in drafting secret nuclear strategy and tactics and fielding delivery systems. The air force practiced tactical nuclear attacks using Buccaneer fighter-bombers, which signified the leadership's readiness to use nuclear weapons as a war-fighting instrument. The notion of dropping tactical nuclear

weapons on guerrilla encampments or Cuban military bases seemed wildly disproportionate to the threat and thus lacked credibility. The same held true for the idea
of conducting nuclear strikes against an African capital.[13]

In the 1980s Botha and the South African military establishment exploited the
growing isolation of the country, public backing for a credible deterrent, and the
demand for long-range surveillance to develop ever-more-sophisticated warheads
and launch vehicles. And once they had embarked on this path, these apartheid
leaders found it necessary to craft a strategy for using this new hardware. Thus
timing and their long-standing commitment to maintaining sophisticated defenses
to buck ever-tighter international sanctions reinforced the apartheid leaders' determination to implement an effective nuclear deterrent strategy.

Fortunately for Pretoria, another technologically advanced state, Israel, also felt
increasingly isolated and under siege—which opened up new vistas for joint research
and development.[14] Secret meetings between Israeli and South African leaders for-
malized cooperation on air, space, and missile programs. Defense Minister Shimon
Peres and Prime Minister Vorster convened one such gathering in November 1974 in
Geneva. One product of Israeli–South African ties was the multistage space launcher
known in South Africa as the RSA 3, which entered service during the 1980s.[15]
The two states' seemingly quixotic mutual interest in building a strategic missile is
explicable because senior politicians and military officials in both Tel Aviv and Pretoria had embraced a nuclear doctrine premised on the capacity to threaten an attack
on Soviet cities. And both Israeli and South African national security strategies
emphasized deterring the Soviet Union, the real threat behind their regional enemies,
especially during an all-out attack. Common threat perceptions propelled the development of nuclear strategy in the two nations.

The two states' clandestine work on long-range missile development continued
throughout the 1980s. In all likelihood these efforts were meant to equip both mili-
taries with missiles that would make true deterrence plausible and thus transcend
their inventories of tactical weaponry.[16] How far South Africa's missile programs
had progressed is indicated by the fact that plans were well under way to build a five-
story, multistage, long-range missile capable of flying 3,000 kilometers or further.[17]
Nuclear delivery systems were reportedly so advanced that South African missiles
could reach Lagos as early as 1983.[18] South Africa, in short, was fielding a real
strategic deterrent with Israeli help by the late 1980s, just as the Cold War was
nearing its end.

The Strategy of Deterring "Total Onslaught"

In 1975 the South African government produced the "South African Jericho Weapons Missile System" memorandum, which expressed strategists' concerns about the
potential threat from Soviet and Chinese tactical nuclear weapons. Observes the
document: "Although the open use of nuclear weapons against the RSA [Republic
of South Africa] by those powers which possess such weapons and the potential to
deliver them can be discarded for the foreseeable future, we must accept that there

is a danger that an enemy assuming an African identity such as a terrorist organization, or an OAU [Organization of African Unity] 'liberation army' could acquire and launch against us a tactical nuclear weapon. China appears to be the most likely nuclear power to associate with such an adventure."[19]

This memorandum was issued a year after Prime Minister Vorster and Defense Minister Botha gave the go-ahead for a nuclear weapons program. South African politicians, strategists, and military leaders, much like their Western counterparts, were focused on the possible use of battlefield nuclear weapons and on devising strategies and tactics to counter such weaponry during the 1970s.

The memo confirms South African leaders' mounting worries that nuclear weapons could become available to subnational groups such as terrorist organizations "within the next ten years." The memo echoed the conventional wisdom, noting that "the bi-polar conformation in world conflict has broken up into a multi-polar order. Western solidarity has been shattered by recent events and divergent interests and political systems. The proliferation of nuclear weapons and the potential capability for their manufacture by smaller nations has rendered a super-power strategy irrelevant in new aspects of localised conflict."[20]

The Jericho memo illustrates how international, regional, and domestic threats had become blurred in the thinking of white South African politicians and strategic planners. This merger of threat perceptions imparted the impetus and the rationale for undertaking expensive and highly sophisticated new military research and development programs during the 1980s and for drawing up the associated nuclear strategy.

The memo and the ambitious range of missiles and other launch vehicles developed by the South Africans indicate that P. W. Botha coveted a mix of nuclear weapons with various ranges and payloads—much like his counterparts in the United States, the United Kingdom, and France. This would offer the leadership a menu of options, allowing them to use the arsenal for either defensive or offensive purposes on the strategic, theater, or tactical levels.

South Africa anticipated and planned for the possibility of the Soviets' placing nuclear weapons in Angola in the much the same way they had installed weapons in Cuba in 1962. The Soviets, however, had evidently learned their lesson from the Cuban Missile Crisis. Moscow never considered placing nuclear weapons so far outside the USSR again, and Soviet leaders never contemplated transferring control of nuclear weapons to guerrilla movements, because they wanted to maintain absolute control over the inventory. South African leaders nevertheless felt that they must plan for the worst case, in which "their backs were up against a wall."[21]

How would Pretoria harness its atomic arsenal for political use? South Africa would have threatened to launch a nuclear attack on ANC or SWAPO bases, on Luanda or on Lusaka, if Cuban troops and SWAPO fighters made significant advances in Namibia or the ANC appeared poised to seize power in South Africa. It probably would have issued threats obliquely, much as Israel threatened "dire consequences" in case an Arab offensive backed by the Soviet Union made significant gains—as in the 1973 Yom Kippur War. The West would not have reacted as long as Pretoria's atomic diplomacy remained ambiguous, but the United States and its allies would have intervened to restrain South Africa and its adversaries if apartheid leaders had overtly vowed the combat use of tactical nuclear weapons. Their strategy, then, may well have backfired. Escalation to the nuclear level, furthermore, raised the probability of Soviet retaliation using intercontinental ballistic missiles.

The 1994 public revelation that an underground nuclear-blast-proof bunker had been installed underneath a South African Defense Force building in Pretoria fueled speculation that the apartheid leaders may have accepted the prospect of an actual combat use of nuclear weapons if they found their backs against the wall. The bunker was intended to shield its occupants from a retaliatory Soviet nuclear strike. Its existence lent credibility to ANC suspicions that the apartheid regime planned to use nuclear weapons against the ANC, SWAPO, Cuban troops, or supporting states in times of extreme crisis.[22] Pretoria, however, never developed the capacity to launch a nuclear strike against Moscow or Havana. Its missiles and bombers lacked the range to strike at targets that distant.

However, South African nuclear planners did target suspected ANC military bases in neighboring countries.[23] At the time of the 1994 political transition, many ANC members believed that white Afrikaner decision makers had been desperate enough and willing to use nuclear weapons in the region, or even at home. Their conviction constituted a source of distrust among parties at the start of the negotiations that ended apartheid rule. Also driving the regime was the siege mentality that gripped most top decision makers during the Vorster and Botha eras, along with beliefs that white rule in South Africa represented one of the last outposts of "civilized Western culture" in Africa. Although these beliefs seldom appeared explicitly in political statements, they were inseparable from the ideology common to whites who supported the Botha government.[24]

The Three-Stage Strategy of "Nuclear Blackmail"

In the late 1970s and early 1980s Botha, his strategists, and top Armscor officials developed a three-stage nuclear "blackmail" strategy of deterrence. This new strategy was more calibrated than threatening to assault African capitals, Cuban troops, or guerrilla bases. Nuclear use was more thinkable under the new approach, which gave Botha and other leaders greater credibility and flexibility in approaching the United States and other erstwhile allies.

During stage one Pretoria would assume a posture of uncertainty and thereby refuse to confirm or deny the existence of South African nuclear weapons to the outside world. Instead, the country would practice a policy of "progressive disclosures," which entailed gradually communicating its nuclear capabilities through a succession of leaks and outside revelations in response to requests for explanations of unexplained occurrences. Stage one was designed to counter a rising security threat and to embroil the United States, the United Kingdom, and France in southern African affairs.

Stage two was designed for situations in which South Africa confronted an overwhelming security threat, such as a Cuban-led invasion. At this point South Africa planned to make its nuclear capability known to the United States and other Western powers on a confidential basis in a bid for diplomatic intervention and even military aid.

Stage three would involve disclosing to the United States and other powers that the South African military planned to conduct an underground nuclear test.[25] The leadership saw stage three as a "last step," to be taken only if South Africa faced a full-scale invasion by Soviet-backed Cuban forces and ANC and SWAPO fighters.[26] Pretoria believed the prospect of losing South Africa to the Soviet Bloc would elicit some sort of United States–backed intervention, especially if coupled with a nuclear test that could escalate into a thermonuclear exchange. If Washington demurred, Pretoria could proceed with the test and let the chips fall where they would.

Israel's remarkable success at using nuclear weapons as leverage with the United States inspired the South African concept of nuclear blackmail. The Nixon administration reportedly resupplied the Israeli military during the 1973 Arab-Israeli War after the Israelis threatened to unsheathe their nuclear sword.[27] The success of the Israelis' blackmail was obvious to the South African leaders. According to official sources, government policymakers hoped that a demonstration test would bring aid to South Africa or convince the threatening nation to "back off." In interviews officials maintained that nuclear weapons were "quick fix" tools of political influence and nuclear blackmail.[28]

A strategy of nuclear blackmail seemed unworkable during the Carter administration (1977–81). South African leaders saw the administration persisting with the policy that began in January 1976 with the Clark Amendment and the US "abandonment" of South Africa in Angola, where the military suffered defeat at Cuban hands.[29] The Carter administration also brought pressure on Pretoria to help restore black majority rule in Zimbabwe and to end apartheid after the Soweto uprisings of 1976. Administration officials also criticized and leveled sanctions against South African moves to develop and test nuclear weapons. The administration worked with Congress to pass the Nonproliferation Act of 1978, a measure South Africa leaders believed was aimed at them. Congress subsequently terminated an agreement to sell highly enriched uranium to South Africa—a move apartheid leaders regarded as an unforgivable act of betrayal.

The November 1980 election of Ronald Reagan, who saw South Africa as a long-standing ally in two world wars and the Cold War, ushered in a new policy of "constructive engagement" with South Africa. State President P. W. Botha and other apartheid leaders sensed that the Reagan administration would be more sympathetic to South Africa's struggle against a "total onslaught" by the Soviet Union, its allies, and its partners. Regime strategists conceived of the three-stage strategy as a way to signal to the Reagan administration for help rather than blackmail it. The international community clearly would have seen the strategy as a kind of blackmail if it had been put into effect.

To execute the three-stage nuclear strategy, Pretoria needed missiles capable of delivering nuclear weapons. Armscor officials pointed out, reasonably enough, that the credibility of such a strategy hinged on deliverability—the actual capacity to strike against the targets under threat.[30] If the government opted to reveal the existence of its nuclear devices to the United States and other Western powers, these devices must be real war-fighting implements. If they were only test devices, the Western powers might see little need to intervene on Pretoria's behalf.

The leadership reaffirmed the three-stage strategy and the nuclear weapons program in the mid-1980s in an extensive review of South African defense policy. The changing defense system, competing demands for increasingly scarce public resources, and the high cost of the nuclear weapons program compelled Botha to order the review. The strategic review prompted the government to realign its nuclear- and missile-related priorities. Botha decided to produce just seven nuclear weapons, enough to achieve the deterrence and blackmail goals of a demonstration force. He did allow work on advanced nuclear concepts to continue.[31]

In the second half of the 1980s the regime faced a clangor of unrest and protests at home along with increasingly well-armed opponents in Angola. South African leaders nonetheless took solace in their demonstrable nuclear capability, a form of insurance against a serious military threat or the worst-case scenario of a "total onslaught."

It appears that South African officials may have used their possession of nuclear weapons as political leverage over the West during the negotiations that ended the Angolan conflict. By 1987 advanced weaponry, such as Soviet-built MiG warplanes and antiaircraft missiles, was pouring into Angola. The high-technology MiGs might challenge South African control of the air. Pretoria fretted that a loss of air superiority would compel it to call up thousands of reservists to continue the war on the ground.[32] In 1987, accordingly, Armscor received an order from the country's top leadership to reopen its nuclear test site in the Kalahari Desert.[33] A water tower was placed over one of the shafts to provide a plausible cover story as Armscor employees pumped water out of the two shafts. The manner in which the test site was constructed, however, allowed sophisticated surveillance satellites to easily observe the actions being taken. It is possible that the government was implementing stage two or even preparing for stage three—even though government insiders insisted that the nuclear program never got past stage one of the blackmail strategy.[34]

In June 1988 Cuban forces fought off South African troops in a battle outside Calueque, Angola. Cuban air superiority played a major role in this battle. South African commanders made adjustments on the ground to counter their loss of unchallenged control of the skies. Even so, the shifting balance of forces must have fueled fears in Washington and the international community that Pretoria would soon conduct a nuclear test.[35]

In 1988 an international diplomatic initiative sponsored by the United States, the Soviet Union, Portugal, and other Western countries succeeded in brokering a cease-fire among South Africa, Cuba, and Angola. Under the Tripartite Agreement of 1988, Cuban and South African forces withdrew from Angola, Namibia was granted independence, and almost fourteen years of war within Angola came to a temporary end.[36] The end of this protracted bush war eliminated the immediate regional threat to the South African government. Former apartheid officials pointed to the improved threat environment, combined with the collapse of the Soviet Bloc in 1989, as the principal reasons why "the South African Defence Establishment could stop short of bringing the nuclear option into play."[37]

Conclusion

Several aspects of the South African experience with nuclear strategy are relevant for understanding the factors and themes that impel states to pursue nuclear weapons and state-of-the-art missiles, along with strategies for using them. Ideology was central to Pretoria's thinking. Senior political leaders possessed of an "oppositional nationalist" psychology determined the shape and scope of covert nuclear and missile programs and strategy. Isolated states like South Africa and Israel exhibited a strong tendency to band together and engage in clandestine cooperative arrangements to develop nuclear weapons, launch systems, and strategies capable of deterring aggression and defending the homeland.

Threat perceptions propel political leaders' quest for sophisticated nuclear weapons, launch vehicles, and effective strategy. Perceptions of high threat convince taxpayers and their leaders to pay the financial and diplomatic costs associated with developing WMD and the means and strategies to use them. Abatement of the threat, conversely, can prompt a decision to disarm.

The South African experience underscores the critical part played by political leaders shaping secret nuclear weapons programs. Botha—who served successively as defense minister, prime minister, and state president—was truly the godfather of the nuclear program and strategy. He embodied the *laager* complex. For proof of his dominant influence, consider how quickly these programs were dismantled. Pretoria abandoned them less than a year after F. W. de Klerk came to power in 1989.

Only a handful of people knew the full scope of the South African nuclear program and strategy. Nevertheless, it took a major interagency effort on the part of well-trained, determined white South Africans who felt under siege by external and internal enemies. Without this sense of fatalism, it would be difficult to replicate a similarly broad, sophisticated program elsewhere. On a sobering note, the South African case shows that any country with a national airline and a modest defense industry can build crude delivery platforms for nuclear weapons and develop a strategy to use them.[38]

The South African case also suggests that rogue states can secure technology and expertise by working covertly with fellow isolated states, deploying sanctions-busting arms procurement agents in countries around the world, and entering into covert partnerships with other states and individuals. Though few nation-states will amass the resources and expertise to challenge major powers' superiority in nuclear delivery systems, the South African case suggests that more and more countries will build dual-use satellite launch rockets that can easily be converted into long-range missiles.[39] Thus the South Africa case stands as a stark reminder that it is easy to exchange a satellite for a nuclear payload once a country possesses a multistage rocket. This subterfuge made it hard for outside intelligence services to prove with sufficient fidelity that South Africa had embarked on a nuclear weapons program.

The evolution of the South African nuclear weapons program underlines how broader domestic and international political trends can converge to give rise to clandestine programs like this one. Only informed political analysis can furnish insight into motives or sophisticated covert behavior. Technical means alone cannot unearth covert programs. Few South Africa analysts were surprised in 1993 when Pretoria acknowledged the existence of its nuclear endeavors. Ever since the 1960s, the apartheid regime had been widely suspected of launching secret military projects. This was a logical consequence of the militarization of South African society and of political leaders' decision to develop an indigenous arms industry. Even so, many Western politicians professed shock at the breadth, degree, and sophistication of South African nuclear and missile programs. Similarly, few political observers were surprised to learn about nuclear and missile cooperation between South Africa and Israel, but many of them were surprised at how closely the two states worked. And few foresaw that the apartheid regime would contemplate using nuclear weapons as tools of political influence in the 1980s.

South Africa's nuclear strategy demonstrated the extent to which global, regional, and even domestic threats can become blurred in the minds of politicians and strategic planners, especially those prone to extreme nationalism and paranoia. The South African case fits into a pattern in which elites develop nuclear weapons, doctrine, and strategy as the international environment shifts and the regime's thinking struggles to adjust.

The South African case demonstrates the hazards of inverting strategy, policy, and procurement, especially amid a changing nuclear geometry. The oppositional nationalist psychology of regime leaders and scientists led Pretoria to obtain nuclear hardware, which in turn drove the nation's quest for doctrine, strategy, and even policy. This raises disturbing questions about how to sustain deterrence given today's complex strategic configuration. This is especially true in Southwest Asia, where Iran and other states may develop nuclear weapons without a clear deterrent strategy and where they may be tempted to resort to first-strike strategy.

The South African case is far from irrelevant to the contemporary world, despite the quixotic nature of the apartheid regime and its worldview. If a rational strategic calculus had prevailed, Pretoria would have forgone its nuclear option. Threats to the apartheid regime were asymmetrical, and nuclear weapons could do little to deter them. As an insurance policy, South Africa could have maintained "threshold state" status, allowing the military to speedily build nuclear weapons or perhaps develop a "recessed nuclear deterrent" like India's.

The South African case holds lasting value in the second nuclear age because it spotlights the importance of relating regime psychology to decisions pertaining to nuclear weapons and strategy. When the threat subsides and regime paranoia eases, the utility of nuclear weapons ceases, the costs appear too steep to bear, and nations can step back. In 1989, finally, South Africa's apartheid regime leaders were contemplating a transfer of power to the black majority. A confluence of events—the end of the Cold War and the impending halt to Afrikaner rule—relegated the South African nuclear deterrent to the dustbin of history.

Notes

1. Helen E. Purkitt and Stephen F. Burgess, *South Africa's Weapons of Mass Destruction* (Bloomington: Indiana University Press, 2005); Helen E. Purkitt, "The Politics of Denuclearization," paper presented at Defense Nuclear Agency's Fourth Annual International Conference on Controlling Arms, Philadelphia, June 21, 1995; David Albright, "South Africa and the Affordable Bomb," *Bulletin of Atomic Scientists*, July–August 1994, 37–47; David Albright, *South Africa's Secret Nuclear Weapons* (Washington, DC: Institute for Science and International Security, 1994), 1–12; Renfrew Christie, "South Africa's Nuclear History," paper presented at Nuclear History Program Fourth International Conference, Nice, June 23–27, 1992; Peter Liberman, "The Rise and Fall of the South African Bomb," *International Security* 26, no. 2 (Fall 2001): 45–86; William J. Long and Suzette R. Grillot, "Ideas, Beliefs, and Nuclear Policies: The Cases of South Africa and Ukraine," *Nonproliferation Review* 7, no. 1 (Spring 2000): 24–40; Leonard S. Spector and Jacqueline R. Smith, *Nuclear Ambitions: The Spread of Nuclear Weapons 1989–1990* (Boulder, CO: Westview Press, 1990); Waldo Stumpf, "South Africa's Nuclear Weapons Program: From Deterrence to Dismantlement," *Arms Control Today* 25, no. 10 (December 1995–January 1996): 4–7; Hannes Steyn, Richard van der Walt, and Jan van Loggerenberg, *Armament and Disarmament: South Africa's Nuclear Weapons Experience* (Pretoria: Networks Publishers, 2003).

2. F. W. de Klerk, *The Last Trek: A New Beginning* (London: Macmillan, 1998); David Ottaway, *Chained Together: Mandela, de Klerk, and the Struggle to Remake South Africa* (New York: Random House, 1993); Allister Sparks, *The Mind of South Africa: The Story of the Rise and Fall of Apartheid* (London: Mandarin, 1990).

3. Jacques E. C. Hymans, *The Psychology of Nuclear Proliferation: Identity, Emotions, and Foreign Policy* (Cambridge: Cambridge University Press, 2006); Bruce D. Larkin, *Nuclear Designs: Great Britain, France, and China in the Global Governance of Nuclear Arms* (New Brunswick, NJ: Transaction, 1996); John C. Hopkins and Weixing Hu, *Strategic Views from the Second Tier: The Nuclear Weapons Policies of France, Britain, and China* (New Brunswick, NJ: Transaction, 1995). From the late 1940s through the mid-1950s, the United Kingdom and France followed the precedent of the two global superpowers and began to develop nuclear weapons. Ostensibly, the two Western European nations wished to protect themselves against the Soviet Union, as US security guarantees were losing credibility, especially after the United States opposed the United Kingdom and France in the Suez crisis of 1956. However, by the late 1950s, as nuclear devices were assembled and tested, it appeared that they were being developed for the maintenance of prestige, especially as the status of the two former imperial powers waned.

4. Deon Geldenhuys, *Isolated States: A Comparative Analysis* (Johannesburg: Jonathan Ball Publishers, 1990); Brad Roberts, "Strategies of Denial," in *Countering the Proliferation and Use of Weapons of Mass Destruction*, edited by Peter L. Hays, Vincent J. Jodoin, and Alan R. van Tassel (New York: McGraw-Hill, 1998), 63–88.

5. Seymour M. Hersh, *The Samson Option* (New York: Random House, 1991), 217–26.

6. D. Sylvan and J. Voss, eds. *Problem Representation and Political Decision Making* (Cambridge: Cambridge University Press, 1998); Yacov Y. I. Vertzberger, *The World in Their Minds: Information Processing, Cognition and Perceptions in Foreign Policy Decision Making* (Stanford, CA: Stanford University Press, 1990). These works build on earlier research on the importance of understanding a group's shared scripts and stories

about past events and history, as well as the importance of understanding how groups of foreign policy decisionmakers frame the problems at hand. See R. P. Abelson, "The Psychological Status of the Script Concept," *American Psychologist* 33 (1981): 273–309. Richard C. Snyder, H. W. Bruck, Burton Sapin, and Valerie Hudson, *Foreign Policy Decision Making (Revisited)* (New York: Palgrave Macmillan, 2002); Helen Purkitt and James W. Dyson, "US Foreign Policy towards Southern Africa during the Carter and Reagan Administrations: An Information Processing Perspective," *Political Psychology* 7, no. 3 (September 1986): 507–32.

7. Hymans, *Psychology of Nuclear Proliferation*, 25.

8. William H. Vatcher, *White Laager: The Rise of Afrikaner Nationalism* (New York: Praeger, 1965).

9. Purkitt, "Politics of Denuclearization," 8.

10. Kenneth Grundy, *The Militarization of South African Politics* (London: I. B. Tauris, 1986); Robert S. Jaster, *The Defence of White Power: South African Foreign Policy under Pressure* (London: Macmillan, 1989).

11. Purkitt and Burgess, *South Africa's Weapons*, 34–37. The close working relations among South African political and military leaders with the United Kingdom and the United States in the 1950s created numerous opportunities to increase the country's capacity for WMD development and strategies for using WMD. In terms of the initial commitment to build a nuclear bomb, South Africa's military, scientific, and industrial interests in developing the country's natural uranium resources and exploiting this resource to help develop the capabilities needed to produce nuclear energy was an important factor.

12. Steyn, van der Walt, and van Loggerenberg, *Armament and Disarmament*, vii–x.

13. Jacob W. Kipp, "Russia's Nonstrategic Nuclear Weapons," Foreign Military Studies Office, May 2001, www.ciaonet.org/cbr/cbr00/video/cbr_ctd/cbr_ctd_06.html. It must be emphasized that the South Africans in the 1970s were looking to develop tactical nuclear weapons as well as long-range missiles, as they saw a variety of threats on the horizon. This point helps underscore how important tactical nuclear weapons have been, although they have not received as much attention as the "museum pieces" in the literature—probably because their existence was classified until November 1996, when the minister of defense, General Igor Rodionov, mentioned them as a deterrent threat against NATO expansion. Rodionov had spent a year fighting with civilian leaders over the proper course of military reform. Pressured to confine reform to the armed forces and focus on personnel reductions, Rodionov warned that NATO expansion could cause Russia to perceive a nonstrategic nuclear threat on its western frontiers. He was quoted as saying, "we might objectively face the task of increasing tactical nuclear weapons at our border."

14. Chris McGreal, "Brothers in Arms: Israel's Secret Pact with Pretoria," *The Guardian,* February 7, 2006, www.guardian.co.uk/world/2006/feb/07/southafrica.israel. The former Israeli ambassador to South Africa, Alon Liel, was quoted as saying, "We created the South African arms industry. . . . They assisted us to develop all kinds of technology because they had a lot of money. When we were developing things together we usually gave the know-how and they gave the money. After 1976, there was a love affair between the security establishments of the two countries and their armies."

15. Lieutenant General Pierre Steyn, interviewed by Helen Purkitt, Midrand, South Africa, June 1994. South Africans played a major role in the founding and development

of the Israeli Air Force. This and other linkages help to explain why the air forces of the two countries continued to cooperate in the 1970s and 1980. There was a secret component to this collaboration. For instance, the Israeli Air Force used South African Air Force installations for research and development and testing.

16. The most widely cited source that details secret South African–Israeli agreements remains Seymour M. Hersh, *The Samson Option* (New York: Random House, 1991), 220–21. Hersh provides a detailed description of Israel's nuclear deterrent strategy. South African military officials made similar statements about the importance of maintaining a balance of nuclear capabilities at both the global and regional levels during the 1970s. For a discussion of South Africa's nuclear strategy, see Steyn, van der Walt, and van Loggerenberg, *Armament and Disarmament*. For a discussion of its efforts to develop the capabilities needed to implement this strategy, see William E. Burrows and Robert Windrem, *Critical Mass: The Dangerous Race for Super Weapons in a Fragmenting World* (New York: Simon & Schuster, 1994).

17. See Frank V. Pabian, "South Africa's Nuclear Weapon Program: Lessons for Non-proliferation Policy," *Nonproliferation Review* 3, no. 1 (Fall 1995): 11; Nick Badenhorst, "South Africa's Nuclear Program," unpublished paper, 2000; and Peter Hounam and Steve McQuillen, *The Mini-Nuke Conspiracy; Mandela's Nuclear Nightmare* (London: Faber & Faber, 1995). Helen Purkitt received confirmation of the existence of a project to build a five-story missile during a July 2002 interview with one of the chief weapons researchers who was involved in rocket research from the beginning of South Africa's programs.

18. Hersh reported that South Africa and Israel negotiated the secret nuclear agreements in 1972; Hersh, *Samson Option*. Badenhorst cites the content of a declassified report by the US Central Intelligence Agency that claimed that South Africa supplied the Israelis with depleted uranium for antitank rounds and with natural uranium rods throughout the early 1970s; Badenhorst, "South Africa's Nuclear Program," 39. Liberman also discusses the content of these secret agreements, including the possibility of joint construction of an intercontinental missile; Liberman, "Rise," 63.

19. Quoted by Michael Schmidt, "Proof of SA Nuclear Plan," *Sunday Times* (Johannesburg), October 12, 2003, 5; quotation from 1975 top-secret South African memo titled "The Jericho Weapons Missile System," which was declassified in 2003; "Treasons of Conscience," *Weekly Mail & Guardian*, August 11, 2000, available at www.sn.apc.org/wmail. The memo referred to the Jericho II missile that Israel was developing and that Israeli minister of defense Shimon Peres had promised to South African prime minister Vorster in a secret meeting in Geneva in 1974. Military analysts in South Africa had paid attention to the decisive role played by air power and a modern air defense system in Israel's ability to defeat a numerically superior coalition of neighboring countries during the Yom Kippur War of 1973. In Geneva, the two signed an agreement providing for strategic cooperation between the two countries. The agreement was a mutual defense pact according to which "the two countries would assist each other in wartime by supplying spare parts and ammunition from emergency stocks. Each country agreed that its territory would be used to store all types of weapons for the other country." According to Dieter Gerhardt, a senior commander in the South African Navy who for many years spied for the Soviet Union, under a later clause in the agreement called "Chalet," Israel agreed to arm eight Jericho II missiles with "special warheads" for South Africa.

20. Schmidt, "Proof of SA Nuclear Plan," 5.

21. This was a favorite phrase that was used repeatedly by senior military, Armscor, and political officials to explain the nuclear strategy during interviews conducted by Helen Purkitt in South Africa in 1994.

22. Peter de Ionno, "SA Military's Amazing Underground Bomb-Proof Laager," *Sunday Times* (Johannesburg), May 22, 1994; Albright, *South Africa's Secret Nuclear Weapons*, 2.

23. The maps attached to the secret memo indicate the maximum reach of a missile with a range of 500 kilometers. If deployed along the northern border of South Africa or other territories controlled by South Africa (i.e., South West Africa), Lusaka and the capital cities of several other African countries that hosted ANC rebel camps were within range of the weapon system.

24. For another analysis that emphasizes the importance of understanding the political leadership's shared beliefs, see Long and Grillot, "Ideas, Beliefs," 24–40.

25. J. W. De Villiers, Roger Jardine, and Mitchell Reiss, "Why South Africa Gave Up the Bomb," *Foreign Affairs* 72, no. 5 (November–December 1993): 101. Stumpf, "South Africa's Nuclear Weapons Program," 4–7.

26. Helen Purkitt and Stephen Burgess heard remarkably similar descriptions of South Africa's three-stage nuclear deterrent strategy in separate interviews with senior members of the South African military, Armscor staff members, Atomic Energy Commission staff members, and political officials in 1994, 2000, and 2001.

27. Hersh, *Samson Option*.

28. Interviews conducted by Helen Purkitt in South Africa during 1994.

29. Willem Steenkamp, interviewed by Helen Purkitt, Cape Town, 1994. See also Willem Steenkamp, *South Africa's Border War, 1966–1989* (Gibraltar: Asanti, 1989), 69.

30. Albright, *South Africa's Secret Nuclear Weapons*, 8.

31. Stumpf, "South Africa's Nuclear Weapons Program," 5; interviews conducted by Helen Purkitt with senior Armscor managers, 1994.

32. Interviews conducted with senior military officials and with Helmoed-Romer Heitman (*Jane's Defense Weekly*), Willem Steenkamp, and other experts on South African defense matters in Cape Town, conducted by Helen Purkitt, July 1994 and July 1997. See also Steenkamp, *South Africa's Border War.*

33. Stumpf, "South Africa's Nuclear Weapons Program," 4–7; interviews with Armscor officials conducted by Helen Purkitt, July 1994.

34. Stumpf, "South Africa's Nuclear Weapons Program," 4–7; interviews with Armscor officials conducted by Helen Purkitt, July 1994.

35. Chester A. Crocker, *High Noon in Southern Africa: Making Peace in a Rough Neighborhood* (New York: W. W. Norton, 1992); Steenkamp, *South Africa's Border War*; interviews conducted by Helen Purkitt, June and July 1994.

36. It is not known whether the reopening of the Vastrap test site, other subtle threats to use WMD on the ground, or battlefield actions played a role in subsequent international diplomacy.

37. Steyn, van der Walt, and van Loggerenberg, *Armament and Disarmament*, 94.

38. This point is one that several senior officials involved in South Africa's former covert nuclear program repeatedly stressed in interviews with Helen Purkitt in 1994.

39. Helen Purkitt, "The Proliferation Significance of South Africa's Former Space-Launch Vehicle Program," unpublished paper, 2008.

CHAPTER 4

THE FUTURE OF CHINESE NUCLEAR POLICY AND STRATEGY

Christopher T. Yeaw, Andrew S. Erickson, and Michael S. Chase

THE DEVELOPMENT OF China's missile force has been among the most impressive and most closely watched aspects of Chinese military modernization over the past two decades. Beyond its growing and increasingly sophisticated arsenal of conventional missiles, China's nuclear modernization is focused on improving the ability of its forces to survive an adversary's first strike and making its nuclear deterrence posture more credible in a missile defense environment. At the theater level, China maintains nuclear-armed, solid-propellant, road-mobile DF-21 (CSS-5) medium-range ballistic missiles (MRBMs) as the cornerstone of its regional nuclear deterrence capability. As for its strategic nuclear capabilities, China still deploys a relatively small number of silo-based DF-5A (CSS-4 Mod 2) intercontinental ballistic missiles (ICBMs), and Beijing is moving toward a more survivable posture based on solid-fueled, road-mobile ICBMs. Indeed, both the DF-31 (CSS-10 Mod 1) and DF-31A (CSS-10 Mod 2) road-mobile ICBMs have been deployed to units within the Second Artillery Force during the past few years.[1] The DF-31 (CSS-10 Mod 1) is capable of reaching targets throughout Europe and Asia and also parts of the northwestern United States, whereas the longer-range DF-31A (CSS 10 Mod 2) is capable of targeting almost all of the continental United States.[2] In addition, China may be developing a new road-mobile ICBM that could be equipped with multiple, independently targetable reentry vehicles. China is also attempting to further diversify its nuclear forces by deploying a new submarine-launched ballistic missile and nuclear-powered ballistic missile submarine.

Along with these force modernization developments, China's nuclear deterrence strategy has evolved from what was essentially a version of "minimum deterrence," which relied on a handful of nuclear weapons to notify potential adversaries that any nuclear attack on China would elicit "assured retaliation," toward a new approach that China's 2006 Defense White Paper characterizes as requiring a "lean and effective nuclear force capable of meeting national security needs."[3] Some Chinese scholars have described this evolving approach as "dynamic minimum deterrence," conveying that it retains key features of China's traditional strategy while adjusting it to keep pace with changes in the security environment and emerging threats.[4] Li Bin describes

China's nuclear strategy as "counter nuclear coercion," highlighting what many Chinese scholars characterize as its long-standing emphasis on countering superpower nuclear threats.[5] China's pursuit of "effective deterrence" is thus less a departure from its traditional "assured retaliation" approach than an effort to ensure that its "assured retaliation" strategy will be seen as credible despite challenges posed by an evolving security environment and advances in capabilities for adversary intelligence, surveillance, and reconnaissance; conventional precision strikes; and missile defense.[6] But even this evolutionary departure from past practices is so significant that Beijing qualifies as a nuclear newcomer for the purposes of this volume.

Drawing on a variety of sources—including Chinese-language military publications, academic and technical journal articles, and military media reports, as well as unclassified US government publications on Chinese military power—we examine recent developments in Chinese nuclear strategy and force structure. Our key findings are twofold.

First, China is moving from a "minimum deterrence" posture, premised on ambiguity about its modest and vulnerable nuclear capabilities, toward a more secure second-strike deterrence posture whereby nuclear deterrence operations are integrated with conventional missile force strike operations. Nuclear forces help deter nuclear attack while contributing to escalation control in a conventional conflict. For example, in the event of a conventional conflict with another major power, it seems likely that the Second Artillery would conduct nuclear deterrence operations, such as dispersing mobile nuclear forces and attempting to send a message in order to deter the adversary not only from using nuclear weapons or coercing China with nuclear threats but also to deter the adversary from carrying out conventional strikes against targets such as China's nuclear forces, nuclear power stations, large-scale hydroelectric power facilities, and important strategic targets in and around Beijing and other major cities.

Second, China's nuclear missile force developments and the Second Artillery's evolving approach to nuclear and conventional missile force campaigns will have major implications for the United States–China strategic relationship and could lead to crisis instability under certain circumstances. In particular, although a secure second-strike capability will likely result in greater strategic stability in the long term, it may not do so immediately or automatically. Some recent developments could result in considerable instability in the event of a crisis or conflict between China and another major military power, such as the United States. China retains its long-standing no-first-use (NFU) policy, but Chinese sources raise questions about what exactly Beijing would construe as equivalent to "first use" on the part of an adversary. Some deterrent actions discussed in Chinese publications could easily be misunderstood, possibly leading to inadvertent escalation. The principal recommendation that emerges from our findings is that dialogue on issues of mutual concern is required to mitigate these risks.

Historical Background

Throughout the Cold War, as M. Taylor Fravel and Evan Medeiros argue cogently, China was willing to accept a "striking" degree of vulnerability by developing only a "small and vulnerable nuclear force structure."[7] They suggest two major reasons: (1) Mao Zedong and his successor Deng Xiaoping viewed nuclear weapons as tools for deterrence in the form of "assured retaliation," not war fighting; and (2) the People's Liberation Army (PLA) lacked "experience and expertise" to "develop nuclear strategy and an associated operational doctrine."[8] Subsequently, however, "this situation evolved as expertise and attention to nuclear issues grew and as external events required China's response. This change led China to examine, systematically, the requirements of a credible second-strike capability, which it appears to have achieved."[9] To these factors, we add a third. As Dennis Blasko emphasizes, "technology determines doctrine" in China's case.[10] Initially, China lacked the technological capabilities to achieve assured retaliation; it now possesses such capabilities and is constantly improving its arsenal to ensure that it continues to meet this core objective.

Following the establishment of the People's Republic of China in 1949, the ruling Chinese Communist Party was determined to end a century of humiliation at the hands of foreigners and the consequent compromise of China's autonomy. During the next several years, important events underscored the value of nuclear weapons in this regard. The USSR, which had conducted its first nuclear test in 1949, demonstrated that it was an increasingly unreliable security partner, and it would later renege on its alleged promises to provide China with a nuclear weapon. The Korean War of 1950–53 subjected China for the first time to US nuclear threats, a challenge that would intensify in the Taiwan Strait crises of 1954–58. By the mid-1950s Mao concluded that China needed nuclear weapons to prevent bullying or coercion by the nuclear powers: "In today's world, to ensure that we will not be bullied by others, we cannot but possess this thing."[11] Similarly, Chinese authors often emphasize that China was compelled to develop nuclear weapons in response to "nuclear blackmail and nuclear threats," or to counter nuclear coercion.[12]

The PLA's first ground-to-ground missile force unit was established in July 1959. According to a Chinese source, "at that time, there were only three battalions; the force could not conduct campaign training." In June 1964, the first missile base was constructed. Then, on October 16, 1964, China detonated its first nuclear weapon. A detailed statement issued later that day revealed central tenets of Beijing's nuclear philosophy that persist to this day in official statements: "China cannot remain idle in the face of ever-increasing nuclear threats from the United States. . . . The Chinese government solemnly declares that China will never at any time or under any circumstances be the first to use nuclear weapons. . . . The Chinese government will . . . exert every effort to promote, through international consultations, the . . . complete prohibition and thorough destruction of nuclear weapons."[13]

During the next two years, notes the authoritative volume *The Science of Second Artillery Campaigns* (hereafter, *SSAC*), the PLA established six missile bases and twelve missile regiments, but "each missile regiment was managed separately by relevant schools and academies and the artillery forces in the military area command while implementing separate missile technology and tactical training." Consequently, China's nascent missile force "did not have the capability to conduct training at the campaign level."[14]

In July 1966 the Second Artillery Force was created, "signifying that the establishment and development of the missile forces had entered an important phase." Each missile regiment was formally incorporated into one of the corresponding missile bases and implemented relevant technical and tactical training, thus establishing the necessary foundation for campaign training.[15] On June 17, 1967, China tested its first hydrogen bomb.[16]

Although the establishment of the Second Artillery Force represented an important development from an organizational perspective, China still lacked an effective retaliatory nuclear strike capability. According to an article written by a professor at the Second Artillery Command College, because China "did not possess effective means of secondary nuclear strikes," its deterrent posture during this period was basically one of "existential nuclear deterrence."[17] The development and deployment of nuclear-capable ballistic missiles of gradually increasing ranges proved to be a tortuous process. The first major achievement came in September 1966, when China deployed its first nuclear-armed ballistic missile, the roughly 1,000-kilometer-range DF-2 (CSS-1) MRBM. The DF-3 (CSS-2) intermediate-range ballistic missile (IRBM) followed in May 1971. These missiles gave China at least some ability to strike regional targets, but even after the deployment of the DF-4 (CSS-3) long-range ballistic missile in 1980 brought targets as far away as Moscow and Guam within range of China's nuclear forces, China still lacked a nuclear delivery system capable of reaching the continental United States.[18]

China also lacked an explicitly articulated nuclear strategy. Intellectual development lagged hardware, as is often the case with nuclear newcomers. The relative immaturity of China's nuclear strategy and doctrine was a consequence of the constraints imposed by adherence to Mao's military theories, the domestic tumult of the Cultural Revolution, and the limitations of Chinese nuclear warhead and ballistic missile technology.[19]

Thus it was not until the early 1980s that changes in the political situation and advances in the Second Artillery's nuclear force capabilities finally enabled China to begin thinking seriously about articulating a nuclear strategy. Chinese strategists soon began deliberating about moving beyond "existential nuclear deterrence."[20] In terms of nuclear capability, one event that made this transition possible was the August 1981 deployment of China's first ICBM, the DF-5, albeit only in two silos. As China's nuclear capability gradually increased, its nuclear strategy and doctrine also began to evolve in a more sophisticated direction. Even as China maintained its nuclear policy, including its commitment to NFU, and its focus on "assured retaliation" remained relatively unchanged, its nuclear deterrence strategy underwent considerable development after the beginning of the reform and opening period.

During the past thirty years, according to an article by Zhao Zekuan, a professor at the Second Artillery Command Academy, China's force structure developments to support its nuclear deterrence strategy have progressed through three distinct stages.[21] The first, which took place under Deng's leadership, was "minimum nuclear deterrence." In November 1983 Deng declared: "We have some nuclear weapons, . . . so if you want to destroy us, you will face some retaliation." The key characteristics of this approach were "limited development," "being streamlined and effective," and "you will face some retaliation if you try to destroy us."[22] During this period China's nuclear retaliatory capability was extremely limited and relied heavily on uncertainty about numbers and locations to deter an enemy first strike. China's ability to strike more distant targets remained highly limited. Although work on an extended-range variant of the DF-5, the DF-5A, began in the mid-1980s, only four of the 13,000-kilometer-range DF-5As were deployed in silos by the early 1990s.[23]

The second stage in the evolution of China's post-Mao nuclear strategy was one in which nuclear forces were seen as contributing to a broader strategic deterrence posture, an approach articulated during Jiang Zemin's tenure as the core of China's third-generation senior leadership group. Strengthening nuclear deterrence was one key objective, but it was part of a much wider concept of strategic deterrence, which also encompassed many other types of capabilities.[24] Jiang Zemin encapsulated China's approach by saying, "Our possession of such power is a great deterrence for countries possessing nuclear weapons, so that they will not dare to act recklessly." The main characteristics of China's approach to nuclear deterrence during this period were "taking nuclear weapons as the core power of strategic deterrence," "combining multiple means of deterrence," and ensuring that hostile countries would "not dare to act recklessly."[25]

Although enhancing nuclear deterrence was clearly an important part of this approach, the phrase "combination of multiple means" underscored the importance of other types of forces and capabilities, including conventional missiles. Indeed, one of the key developments during this period was the establishment of the Second Artillery Force's conventional missile force. It began forming its first conventional missile unit in August 1991 and formally established its first conventional missile brigade in April 1993.[26] That year,[27] the Central Military Commission assigned the Second Artillery the task of "dual deterrence and dual operations" (双重威慑, 双重作战, *shuangzhong weishe, shuangzhong zuozhan*),[28] which emphasizes the importance of deterrence and combat roles for both the conventional and nuclear missile forces.[29]

China's first conventional ballistic missile force unit was established in 1993. Within a few years China's nascent conventional missile capability reached the forefront of its coercive diplomacy toward Taiwan. During the 1995–96 Taiwan Strait crisis, the conventional missile force conducted two "large-scale conventional deterrence firing exercises," known as "Magic Arrow-95" and "Joint 96–1."[30] Some Chinese observers evaluate the missile launches as a successful display of force that deterred Taiwan from moving further toward formal independence.

The third, current stage of China's post-1978 nuclear deterrence posture has materialized under Hu Jintao's leadership. The main feature of this era, which builds upon thinking that dated back to the 1980s, is its emphasis on nuclear deterrence that "meets the needs of national security" and is "development oriented," "reliable," and "strong."[31] One of the most important developments during this period has been the deployment of the road-mobile DF-31 and DF-31A ICBMs in 2006 and 2007, respectively. Another key development, since the Second Artillery Force assumed responsibility for it in 1993, has been the rapid growth of the conventional missile force. Although the development of this force is beyond the scope of this chapter, it must be noted that this force has given China a potent new capability to conduct regional strikes, either independently or as part of a joint campaign. Indeed, according to *SSAC*, "During future joint combat operations the Second Artillery will not merely act as the main force in providing nuclear deterrence and nuclear counterstrike power, but will also act as the backbone force in conventional fire-power assaults."[32]

China's Current Nuclear Strategy

China's 2006 Defense White Paper, the most authoritative public statement of how Beijing views the security environment and proper strategic responses to it, provided the first official explanation of China's nuclear strategy. It summarizes the key elements of China's approach to nuclear weapons as follows:

> China's nuclear strategy is subject to the state's nuclear policy and military strategy. Its fundamental goal is to deter other countries from using or threatening to use nuclear weapons against China. China remains firmly committed to the policy of no first use of nuclear weapons at any time and under any circumstances. It unconditionally undertakes not to use or threaten to use nuclear weapons against non–nuclear weapon states or nuclear-weapon-free zones, and stands for the comprehensive prohibition and complete elimination of nuclear weapons. China upholds the principles of counterattack in self-defense and limited development of nuclear weapons, and aims at building a lean and effective nuclear force capable of meeting national security needs. It endeavors to ensure the security and reliability of its nuclear weapons and maintains a credible nuclear deterrent force. China's nuclear force is under the direct command of the Central Military Commission (CMC). China exercises great restraint in developing its nuclear force. It has never entered into and will never enter into a nuclear arms race with any other country.[33]

The doctrinal underpinnings of this approach were outlined in the 1987 edition of *The Science of Strategy* (*Zhanlüexue*), which outlines the mission of the nuclear missile force as follows: "In peacetime, the mission of the Second Artillery is to bring nuclear deterrence into play, so as to deter enemies from launching a nuclear war against China, and to support China's peaceful foreign policy. . . . In wartime, the strategic mission is to prevent conventional war from escalating into nuclear war, and to contain the escalation of nuclear war; and—if China suffers the enemy's nuclear attack—to conduct a nuclear counterattack, striking the enemy's strategic targets and weakening its war potential and strategic attack forces."[34]

A variety of authoritative publications on missile force campaigns and nuclear deterrence that have been published during the past decade shed further light on China's nuclear strategy.[35] For example, the editors of the 2001 edition of *The Science of Strategy*, published by the PLA's Academy of Military Science, divide nuclear deterrence strategies and postures into three categories: "maximum deterrence," "minimum deterrence," and "medium strength deterrence." China's concept of "effective deterrence," which is based on an assured retaliation capability that must evolve in response to changes in the offensive and defensive capabilities of potential adversaries, appears most similar to the concept of "medium strength nuclear deterrence." The volume's editors, Peng Guangqian and Yao Youzhi, indicate that "medium-strength" deterrence requires " 'sufficient and effective' nuclear strike force to threaten an opponent by imposing on him unbearable destruction to a certain extent so as to attain one's deterrent objective."[36] Indeed, Fravel and Medeiros note that "this definition—especially the explicit reference to the concepts of sufficiency and effectiveness—strongly resembles PLA descriptions of China's own nuclear strategy and is consistent with the concept of deterrence through assured retaliation."[37]

One question that some of these newly available sources address is what types of enemy actions China believes its nuclear capability can help deter. These sources suggest that Chinese strategists expect nuclear deterrence not only to prevent an enemy from using nuclear weapons against China but also to deter certain types of strategic conventional attacks. According to SSAC:

> Deterring the escalation of warfare refers primarily to the application of nuclear weapons to carry out active and passive deterrence, in order to prevent a conventional war from escalating into a nuclear war; to prevent the enemy from carrying out a conventional strike against our nuclear facilities and creating nuclear leakage; and to prevent the enemy from causing unbearably tremendous losses to our major, strategic facilities through medium and high-powered air raids against us. The demonstration of power causes the enemy to dread that the possible consequence of its actions will be that its losses will exceed its gains, thereby causing the enemy to change its plans for risky activities and achieving the goal of restricting the war to a certain scope.[38]

This illustrates one of the ways in which the editors of the volume view nuclear weapons as a "backstop to support conventional operations."[39] Specifically, according to the authors of SSAC, "From the perspective of international strategic patterns, nuclear weapons are a strong nuclear backstop for ensuring the status of large countries and they are a potentially huge deterring resource. In local conventional wars under informatized conditions, just by moderately revealing one's nuclear strength, one is able to apply many types of deterrent methods flexibly. An enemy that is using informatized, conventional air raids against us cannot but consider prudently how high the price might be, thereby achieving the goal of supporting conventional operations."[40]

Nuclear deterrence thus plays an important role during conventional conflicts in deterring both nuclear attack and certain types of conventional escalation. According to SSAC, "Second Artillery nuclear missile units are the main forces involved in nuclear counterstrikes, and are mainly responsible for important nuclear deterrent and counter–nuclear deterrent duties during joint campaigns."[41]

Chinese doctrinal publications like *SSAC* continue to reflect the official NFU policy, as outlined in other books, articles, and official documents like China's National Defense White Papers, in that they assume the Second Artillery nuclear forces would launch their weapons only after an enemy first strike. For example, *SSAC* indicates that Chinese missile forces would have to conduct nuclear counterstrikes after suffering heavy damage from an enemy nuclear attack:

> Based on the principle that our country will not be the first to use nuclear weapons under any circumstances, the strategic nuclear forces of the Second Artillery will implement nuclear counterattacks only after the enemy has carried out nuclear attacks against China, and only in accordance with the orders of the supreme command. Therefore, as a whole, nuclear counterattack campaigns will be implemented under nuclear conditions. If the enemy launches nuclear attacks against our country, it will definitely treat the operational positions and nuclear missile weapon systems of the Second Artillery as its key targets. After Second Artillery operational areas suffer such attacks, the battlefield situation becomes very complex and the environment extremely harsh. Our personnel, weapons and equipment, battle positions, roads and bridges, and reconnaissance, communications, and command and control systems will suffer serious damage and destruction. The nuclear counterattack campaign of the Second Artillery will have to be implemented under very difficult conditions.[42]

This is also consistent with the writings of Chinese scholars who assert that China will continue to adhere to a NFU policy. Major General Yao Yunzhu, a senior researcher at the PLA Academy of Military Science who serves on the Defense White Paper drafting team, emphasizes that "no first use . . . has been most frequently and consistently repeated in numerous Chinese government statements ever since China became a nuclear weapon state in 1964."[43] She adds: "The most important element of China's nuclear policy is renunciation of the first-use option."[44] Rong Yu and Peng Guangqian elaborate that "although some people believe China's NFU policy is not credible, China has never wavered from its promise during the past 40 years."[45] Rong and Peng see the NFU policy as a stabilizing factor in crisis situations and as "conducive to escalation control."[46]

Nonetheless, interviews and a variety of publications suggest that Chinese strategists continue to debate matters of nuclear policy. Among the issues that reportedly have been under discussion at various points during the past decade are the merits of continuing to adhere to this NFU policy. Indeed, some Chinese strategists have argued that the NFU policy is an unnecessary, self-imposed strategic constraint. Chinese analysts have considered at least three scenarios under which Beijing might consider discarding the traditional NFU policy. The first is under the wartime condition of retaliation for conventional strikes on strategic or nuclear targets and facilities. Here it is useful to examine *Intimidation Warfare* (hereafter, *IW*)—edited by Lieutenant General Zhao Xijun, the Second Artillery Force's deputy commander from 1996 to 2003—which echoes many of the statements outlined in *SSAC* and sheds additional light on China's possible calculus and tactics in various scenarios.

According to the now-retired Zhao, "In a conventional war, when the enemy threatens to carry out conventional strikes against one's nuclear facilities or other major strategic targets, in order to protect the nuclear facilities, prevent nuclear leakage, and to arrest the escalation of conventional war to nuclear war, one should employ nuclear weapons to actively carry out nuclear deterrence against the enemy."[47]

The second possibility occurs under the much more likely condition of external intervention in a high-intensity crisis or conflict. Specifically, Chinese authors have suggested that Beijing could "lower the nuclear threshold" to deter US military intervention in a Taiwan scenario. This lowering of the nuclear threshold seems to indicate a shift in the declaratory policy to something less restrictive than no first use, and it is separate from elevation of the alert level. According to an article in *Military Art*, one of the PLA's most important journals, "When we are under the pressure of circumstances to use military force to reunify the motherland's territory, we may even lower the threshold of using nuclear weapons to deter intervention by external enemies."[48]

The third scenario is when Chinese leaders believe that territorial integrity is at stake. Some Chinese strategists seem to indicate the possibility of first use under particularly dire circumstances, such as a scenario in which the PLA is on the verge of suffering a politically catastrophic defeat in a conventional military conflict over Taiwan. And as Zhao summarizes: "Of course, there are quite a number of scholars in the military academic theoretical community of China, who—based on the characteristics of modern high-tech warfare—are studying the issue of the conditional threat of use of nuclear weapons."[49]

Other portions of *SSAC* envision similar conditions under which it may sometimes be necessary to adjust nuclear policy or lower the nuclear threshold to deter an enemy from launching conventional attacks against strategic targets such as Chinese nuclear facilities, dams, or electrical infrastructure, or the capital or other major cities, or to avert catastrophic conventional defeat. The relevant passage is worth quoting at length:

> Reducing the nuclear deterrence threshold refers to the following situation: when a militarily powerful country armed with nuclear missiles and depending on its absolute superiority in high tech conventional weapons carries out medium or high strength continuous air raids against our major strategic targets, and when our side lacks a good plan for resisting the enemy, the nuclear missile forces should follow the orders of the supreme command, adjust their nuclear deterrence policies in a timely fashion, and actively carry out powerful nuclear deterrence against the enemy in order to deter the strong enemy from continuously carrying out conventional air raids against our major strategic targets. The following are opportune moments for nuclear missile units to reduce the nuclear deterrence threshold. First, when an enemy threatens to carry out conventional strikes against our nuclear facilities (or nuclear power stations), in order to prevent the creation of large-scale, disastrous nuclear leakage, one's own nuclear missile units must sharply oppose the enemy and use nuclear missiles to carry out effective deterrence, thus restraining the enemy from carrying out its scheme of using conventional air raids against

our nuclear facilities. Second, when an enemy threatens to carry out conventional strikes against our major strategic targets related to the safety of the people, like large-scale hydroelectric power stations, one should adhere to the deterrence orders of the supreme command and threaten to use nuclear missiles against the enemy in order to ensure the absolute security of our major strategic targets. Third, when an enemy threatens to carry out medium or high strength conventional strikes against our capital, important major cities, and other political and economic centers, the nuclear missile units should follow the orders of the supreme command and resolutely issue threats of the use of nuclear weapons to the enemy. This should be done in order to achieve the goal of reducing the strength of the enemy's air raids or deterring the enemy from carrying out air strikes. Fourth, when conventional warfare continues to escalate and the overall strategic situation is extremely unfavorable for us, and when national security and survival are seriously threatened, in order to force the enemy to stop its war of invasion and save the country from danger, the nuclear missile units should follow the orders of the supreme command and carry out effective nuclear deterrence against the enemy.[50]

The specific methods and means for "reducing the nuclear threshold" under any of the above-noted circumstances may include launch exercises and warnings disseminated though the media. The purpose is to shake the enemy psychologically and "conquer the enemy without fighting."[51] Accordingly, depending upon the level of threat presented by the enemy, it may even be necessary to "disseminate the aim points at which [China's] nuclear missiles are aiming."[52] A reduction in the nuclear deterrence threshold may also include changing the declaratory nuclear policy.[53]

Chinese strategists also suggest that there is some ambiguity when it comes to determining what constitutes first use by an adversary. As two such commentators state, "establishing definitely whether the adversary has broken the nuclear threshold is not necessarily a straightforward issue," because conventional attacks may have equally devastating effects in certain cases. Specifically, they raise the question of whether a conventional attack on a country's nuclear forces could be considered tantamount to the first use of nuclear weapons. "On the surface, this is merely a conventional attack," they write, "but in effect, its impact is little different from suffering a nuclear strike and incurring similarly heavy losses." The result could be that the conventional attack would "be seen as breaking the nuclear threshold," with the result that the party suffering the attack "will find it difficult to refrain from a nuclear counterattack."[54] Chinese strategists have made similar comments with reference to conventional strikes against China's strategic command-and-control structure.[55] As Fravel and Medeiros point out, "Whether intended or not, the existence of such a debate generates increased ambiguity about the conditions under which China might use nuclear weapons, thereby strengthening China's deterrent."[56]

These statements highlight conditions under which China's NFU policy might face considerable pressure, or perhaps might not apply if China judges an adversary's actions as in some way equivalent to a nuclear first strike. Nonetheless, it seems that this debate has ended, at least for now, with a decision to maintain the NFU policy. This is reflected by China's 2010 Defense White Paper, which states: "China consistently upholds the policy of no first use of nuclear weapons, adheres to a self-defensive nuclear strategy, and will never enter into a nuclear arms race with any other country."[57] *SSAC* and *IW* were clearly part of this debate; but they may not represent the last word on the subject, because they are now more than seven years old. Indeed, Chinese scholars suggest that Beijing would approach any actual decision to authorize the use of nuclear weapons with great caution, and that such a decision would only be made under the most extreme circumstances. For example, Rong and Peng state that given the immense damage that would be caused, the decision to use nuclear weapons would be "only imaginable if core national interests are in peril, such as the survival of the state or nation."[58] Furthermore, Chinese sources underscore that only the "supreme command" (*tongshuaibu*), the highest-level political and military leadership and likely a highly deliberative body, is authorized to make a decision about the employment of nuclear weapons.[59]

Nuclear Counterstrike Campaigns

Consistent with the NFU pledge, the nuclear counterstrike campaign is the only nuclear missile force campaign outlined in Chinese military publications.[60] Doctrinally, the PLA defines a nuclear counterstrike campaign as "the operational action composed of nuclear strikes that is implemented by the nuclear missile large formation of the Second Artillery based on the uniform planning and highly centralized command in order to achieve specific strategic goals or strategic campaign goals."[61] Other services are envisioned as participating in strikes as follows: "Joint nuclear counterattack campaigns usually take the nuclear forces of the Second Artillery as their main component, with the nuclear forces of the navy's nuclear submarines and the nuclear forces of the air force's bomber units unifying three dimensions of nuclear counterattack operational activities."[62] This passage is somewhat perplexing, in that China's nuclear-powered ballistic missile submarines (known as "SSBNs"), are not yet operationally deployed, and it is unclear whether China's bombers maintain a nuclear strike role, but it appears to indicate that Chinese strategists envision a requirement for the nuclear missile forces of the Second Artillery to coordinate with the other services.

Publications like *SSAC* indicate that nuclear counterattack campaigns could consist of both initial nuclear strikes and follow-on nuclear attacks. Indeed, Chinese strategists indicate that the Second Artillery should be capable of "carrying out a number of waves of nuclear missile strikes after initial nuclear strikes."[63] Follow-on strikes could consist of repeat strikes against targets that were not destroyed by the initial nuclear strike, or they could be carried out "in order to maintain the huge amount of pressure and psychological fear against the enemy."[64]

Such a complex concept of nuclear warfare appears to be at odds with the conventional wisdom regarding Chinese concepts of nuclear counterattack as consisting mainly of countervalue retaliatory strikes designed solely to inflict punishment, and thus to deter the outbreak of nuclear war in the first place.

Chinese military publications also offer some insight into how Chinese strategists think about questions of nuclear targeting. The targeting strategy for the nuclear counterattack campaign has as its core the mission of "carrying out missile strikes on the enemy's important strategic and campaign targets, in accordance with the intentions of higher levels, in order to frustrate the enemy's strategic plans, shake the enemy's will, cripple the enemy's command systems, retard the enemy's warfare activities, weaken the enemy's warfare potential, and prevent an escalation of nuclear warfare."[65] Under the guiding ideology of "integrated deterrence and warfare and focused strikes," targeting aims at "vital targets" in order to [make an impact on] everything by striking one point, and paying a small price to achieve a large victory." Again the concept of escalation control comes into view, and this guides much of the targeting, for "correctly selecting the targets for striking the focal point is a precondition for carrying out the ideology of focused strikes." Striking at the focal point is aimed at "stopping the enemy at the first opportunity."[66] Targeting is designed to bring swift victory at minimal cost.

Categories of targets parallel in many respects the traditional targeting categories in the United States and Russia. Target categories include strategic weapon bases, strategic rear-area bases, military command headquarters, political and economic centers, heavy industry facilities, transportation and communication nexuses, and heavy military industry groups.[67] The selection of targets in the execution phase must be very deliberate so as to achieve just the right psychological effect upon the adversary: "The target must be reasonable and the deterrence not to be too high that the enemy cannot accept it and cause the deterrence to fail, or even to drive it to the extreme and not to be deterred. It should not be too low, either, as it will make the enemy have no feel of the deterrence and the objective of deterrence unable to be achieved." Additionally, there seems to be a very rational process within the Second Artillery Force whereby weapons are allocated to targets according to various factors such as range, reaction time, penetration capability, yield ("destruction capabilities of various models of warheads"), missile inventory, and reserve force requirements.[68]

China's Nuclear Missile Force Capabilities

Backstopping the PLA's growing arsenal of short-range and theater conventional missiles are its theater and strategic nuclear missile forces, which provide the ultimate escalatory or counterescalatory threat. In addition to its theater nuclear capabilities and silo-based ICBMs, the deployment of the road-mobile DF-31 and DF-31A ICBMs and the development of the JL-2 submarine-launched ballistic missile (SLBM) are enhancing the survivability of China's once highly vulnerable strategic missile force. In addition, China may be able to create a nuclear triad by deploying nuclear-armed air-launched cruise missiles aboard PLA Air Force

(PLAAF) bombers, though it appears that the Second Artillery's land-based nuclear force will remain the core of China's deterrent capability for the foreseeable future.[69]

Nuclear MRBMs and IRBMs

China currently deploys the DF-3 (CSS-2) IRBM and DF-21 and DF-21A (CSS-5 Mod 1 and CSS-5 Mod 2) MRBMs for regional nuclear deterrence missions.[70] The DF-3 (CSS-2), first deployed in 1971, is a single-stage, liquid-propellant IRBM with a maximum range of about 3,000 kilometers (1,900 miles). The US Air Force National Air and Space Intelligence Center (NASIC) estimates that the DF-3 (CSS-2) is "transportable" but has "limited mobility." China has about fourteen to eighteen liquid-fueled DF-3 (CSS-2) IRBMs and about five to ten CSS-2 launchers.[71] Many observers expect the DF-3 (CSS-2) IRBMs to be retired from service soon.[72]

China has been making the transition to a more survivable, road-mobile theater nuclear force featuring the CSS-5 Mod 1 and CSS-5 Mod 2 MRBMs. According to the 2009 NASIC report on foreign ballistic missile and cruise missile systems, the PLA has fewer than fifty launchers each for its nuclear-armed CSS-5 Mod 1 and CSS-5 Mod 2 MRBMs.[73] The CSS-5 Mod 1 and CSS-5 Mod 2 are both two-stage, solid-propellant, road-mobile missiles with maximum ranges of more than 1,750 kilometers (more than 1,100 miles).[74]

Intercontinental Ballistic Missiles

The silo-based DF-5 (NATO designator CSS-4) ICBM—a liquid-propellant, two-stage missile—has been the mainstay of China's intercontinental nuclear deterrence force since its initial deployment in 1981. China currently deploys about twenty silo-based DF-5A (CSS-4 Mod 2) ICBMs, which have a range of at least 13,000 kilometers (more than 8,000 miles), enough to strike targets throughout the continental United States.[75] The US intelligence community has judged for a number of years that China is capable of deploying a version of the DF-5 ICBM equipped with multiple, independently targetable reentry vehicles (MIRVs).[76] China has made no official statements regarding whether it intends to deploy a MIRVed version of the DF-5, but researchers affiliated with China's Second Artillery Force and missile and aerospace industry have published several studies on MIRV-related research in recent years.[77]

Converting the DF-5s to a MIRV configuration, if China were to decide to do so, would dramatically increase the number of warheads that China could deliver against "soft targets," such as major cities and large military installations, in the continental United States. According to one analyst, "Chinese military experts also talk increasingly frequently about a deployment of five to seven warheads atop the existing silo-based missiles as a counter to US missile defense. Steps such as these could result in an increase from 20 to 100 or more nuclear weapons deployed by China capable of reaching the United States."[78] Chinese researchers have also discussed employing decoys to penetrate an enemy missile defense system. Whatever the exact numbers of warheads and decoys carried by each missile, MIRVing the DF-5 ICBMs would clearly represent a major increase in China's strategic nuclear capability.

China is also deploying two road-mobile ICBMs, the DF-31 and DF-31A. The DF-31 (CSS-10 Mod 1) is a three-stage, solid-propellant, road-mobile ICBM with a maximum range of more than 7,200 kilometers (more than 4,500 miles). The DF-31 is probably intended to replace China's aging limited-range DF-4 missiles. The DF-31 is deployed on a mobile erector launcher, and thus it is likely intended mainly to cover targets in Russia and Asia, but its range is sufficient to reach US missile defense sites in Alaska, US forces in the Pacific, and targets in parts of the western United States.[79] After a protracted development history that began in the 1980s, China conducted the first developmental flight test of the DF-31 in August 1999. Following this initial flight test, the system remained under development for several more years, despite numerous predictions that its deployment was imminent. It was finally deployed in 2006.[80] By 2010, according to the US Department of Defense (DoD), China had deployed fewer than 10 DF-31 launchers.[81]

The DF-31A (CSS-10 Mod 2) is a three-stage, road-mobile ICBM with a maximum range of more than 11,200 kilometers (more than 7,000 miles). The DF-31A's longer range allows it to reach targets throughout most of the continental United States. A 2009 DoD report on Chinese military power states that China began deploying the DF-31A (CSS-10 Mod 2) in 2007. As of 2010 China had fielded 10–15 DF-31A launchers.[82]

China also still has sixteen to twenty-four of its older, shorter-range, liquid-fueled DF-4 (CSS-3) ICBMs.[83] The DF-4 is a two-stage, liquid-propellant missile with a range of about 5,400 kilometers (more than 3,400 miles). The DF-4 can be deployed in silos, but it is also transportable. China has about ten to fifteen launchers, according to NASIC.[84] Many observers anticipate that China will decommission its limited-range DF-4s now that it has deployed the DF-31 ICBM.

In addition, China may also be developing one or more additional ICBMs. A 2010 DoD report indicated that China could be developing a new road-mobile ICBM that could be equipped with MIRVs.[85] This statement should be seen in the context of numerous media reports that have appeared over a number of years suggesting that other ICBMs might be under development. Indeed, rumors about a possible DF-41 ICBM program have been in circulation for more than a decade, but some suggest that the program may have been canceled.[86] More recently, a Hong Kong magazine reported that China is "speeding up" the development of a new DF-51 ICBM, but the article provided no information on its mission or characteristics.[87]

Submarine-Launched Ballistic Missiles

China's undersea deterrent is undergoing a generational change with the emergence of the Type-094, or Jin-class, nuclear-powered ballistic missile submarine. The Jin represents a substantial improvement over China's first-generation Type-092, or

Xia-class, SSBN. The Xia-class boat (hereafter, Xia) was launched in the early 1980s but never conducted a deterrent patrol. China currently has one Xia intended to carry 12 CSS-NX-3 (JL-1) SLBMs with a relatively short maximum range of about 1,600 kilometers (more than 1,000 miles), but it is not considered operational.[88] After its disappointing experience with the Xia, China appears determined to build enough Type-094 SSBNs to enable the PLA Navy (PLAN) to conduct near-continuous deterrent patrols. The US Office of Naval Intelligence forecasts that China will build a "fleet of probably five Type-094 SSBNs . . . to provide more redundancy and capacity for a near-continuous at-sea presence."[89] Each of these second-generation SSBNs will be outfitted with twelve developmental JL-2 SLBMs that have an estimated range of at least 7,200 kilometers and are equipped with penetration aids.[90] At least two Jin-class SSBNs have been launched, but the JL-2 (CSS-NX-14) SLBM, a three-stage SLBM with a maximum range of about 7,200 kilometers (more than 4,500 miles), reportedly remains under development,[91] having failed "several of what should have been the final round of flight tests."[92] Chinese sources claim that a successful JL-2 test, possibly limited to missile surfacing control, finally occurred in the summer of 2011.[93]

Possible Nuclear Land-Attack Cruise Missiles

Nuclear-armed land-attack cruise missiles (LACMs) could also be deployed as a complement to China's nuclear ballistic missiles. Indeed, DoD assesses that the new air- and ground-launched cruise missiles China is developing may be capable of carrying nuclear warheads.[94] If armed with nuclear warheads, the PLA's emerging LACM capabilities could supplement China's theater and strategic ballistic missile forces. According to the 2009 DoD report, "New air- and ground-launched cruise missiles that could potentially perform nuclear missions would similarly improve the survivability, flexibility, and effectiveness of China's nuclear forces."[95] Likewise, the 2009 NASIC report on worldwide cruise missile and ballistic missile capabilities states that the DH-10 missile in particular could be capable of carrying a conventional or nuclear warhead.[96] Whether China will ultimately choose to deploy nuclear-armed ground- or air-launched cruise missiles, however, remains unclear. Indeed, as Jeffrey Lewis has noted, the DoD report does not state that China has deployed nuclear-armed LACMs; it simply indicates that some Chinese cruise missiles may be capable of carrying nuclear warheads. There is no conclusive evidence that a nuclear warhead has been so assigned.[97]

Possible Tactical Nuclear Weapons

Relatively little research has addressed Chinese views on nonstrategic, or tactical, nuclear weapons. The available literature suggests that China has been interested in tactical nuclear weapons for some time, especially during the period when Beijing was concerned about a potential Soviet invasion. Scholars have been unable to determine conclusively whether China currently possesses any tactical nuclear weapons.[98]

Discussions of coordination between the Second Artillery Force and the nuclear forces operated by the PLAN and the PLAAF in some Chinese sources seem to suggest that the PLAAF may retain the capability to deliver nuclear bombs, presumably against close-in targets. Conversely, China's 2006, 2008, and 2010 Defense White Papers discuss the nuclear capabilities of the Second Artillery and PLAN but mention only conventional missions for the PLAAF, which implies that the air force may play no part in nuclear deterrence.

Additionally, Chinese sources hint at potential Chinese interest in other types of tactical nuclear forces, including short-range ballistic missiles with nuclear warheads and neutron-bomb-type (enhanced radiation) warheads. According to Zhao Xijun, "The missiles of the tactical missile force usually carry conventional warheads. They can also carry a nuclear warhead or a special warhead according to the needs of the task and strike targets."[99] It is unclear from the context of this passage, however, whether Zhao is referring specifically to Chinese missile forces or to tactical missile forces in general. Even more ambiguously, *SSAC* mentions neutron bombs as follows: "Neutron bombs in particular are small-scale hydrogen bombs that increase the strength of nuclear radiation in the early period after being detonated. On the battlefield, they can be used in large numbers and they are extremely lethal to humans."[100] Again, however, it is far from clear whether this passage is intended to imply that China has such weapons in its arsenal or simply to serve as a brief overview of the characteristics and capabilities of neutron bombs. Because available materials are far from definitive, it is unclear what types of nonstrategic nuclear weapons China currently maintains, if any; and how, if at all, such forces figure into Chinese nuclear war plans.

Training

In January 2011 Second Artillery Force commander Jing Zhiyuan and political commissar Zhang Haiyang issued an order emphasizing the central role of training in further enhancing the combat capabilities of the missile force. Jing and Zhang urged the missile force to "uphold military training as a key focus in expanding and deepening preparation for military struggle, the basic way to generate, consolidate, and enhance combat power, and regular, core work in the development of [missile force] units." Reflecting this high-level emphasis on the importance of training, Chinese military media reports suggest that Second Artillery training is growing in realism and complexity. In particular, as part of the PLA's broader program of training reforms, the Second Artillery is making progress in areas such as training under more realistic combat conditions, which incorporate opposition "blue forces"; electronic warfare; nighttime and adverse weather training; air defense and tactics to counter intelligence, surveillance, and reconnaissance (ISR); and more rigorous training evaluations. These developments represent significant progress in the rigorousness of Second Artillery training.

The Second Artillery emphasizes that "troops should train as they will fight," which means that exercises should take place under realistic conditions so as to temper the skills their units will need in actual combat. Jing and Zhang demand "flexible application of principles and tactics" in keeping with making training as realistic as "actual war."[101] For one model brigade, this entails "updating concepts, innovating boldly, and putting [them] to real-war tests."[102] Chinese military media reports indicate that some recent exercises have simulated a loss of communications links, which has forced units to switch to backup communications. Others have tested emergency repair capabilities such as erecting replacement bridges, clearing blocked roads, and repairing damaged facilities. Another important way in which many PLA exercises now attempt to enhance the level of realism is by incorporating simulated opposing forces. Second Artillery units frequently conduct opposing force exercises as part of this drive to train under more realistic and challenging conditions.[103] One recent exercise reportedly featured sophisticated blue force efforts from young, well-educated personnel familiar with foreign military capabilities.[104] Such a use of simulated adversaries in exercises is particularly noteworthy because it makes training more realistic and challenging, encourages officers to take the initiative in response to changing situations, and gives troops exposure to possible adversary tactics. It bespeaks a clear understanding that warfare is an exceedingly interactive enterprise.

Other reports indicate that training is sometimes designed to force participating units to deviate from their prepared plans. This is done to prepare officers and soldiers to cope with actual combat situations in which they may lose the ability to communicate with higher headquarters or find that the enemy has reacted to their actions in unexpected ways. Along these lines, Second Artillery Force units have practiced moving to alternate launch sites and erecting temporary launchpads when primary launch positions are "destroyed" during exercises.[105] Since the late 1990s Second Artillery training has also emphasized inter-theater deployments, which entail considerable operational and logistical challenges. Chinese military media reports indicate that Second Artillery units are also conducting nighttime maneuver training.[106]

The Second Artillery Force has also practiced a variety of techniques to counter enemy ISR, precision strike, jamming, and electronic warfare (EW) attacks.[107] In keeping with the emphasis on training in a "complex electromagnetic environment" contained in recent General Staff Department training guidelines, this is intended to improve the PLA's ability to operate in an EW environment and to allow military units to practice various types of counterreconnaissance, offensive EW, and counter-EW techniques. The Second Artillery has followed these guidelines by conducting exercises that emphasize EW training, according to Chinese military media reports.[108] Many exercises have focused on employing countermeasures against enemy ISR systems, and some have incorporated simulated enemy precision air strikes and electronic jamming. In addition, Chinese media reports indicate that the Second Artillery is conducting exercises that test its ability to employ increasingly sophisticated decoys and camouflage methods to defeat adversary airborne and space-based ISR capabilities, including optical, infrared, and radar imagery systems.[109]

The PLA has also conducted numerous multiservice exercises in recent years, which have provided considerable opportunities for the Second Artillery Force to improve its experience conducting joint operations and joint command and control.[110] For example, in the summer of 2006 the PLA conducted the North Sword–07 exercise, in which Second Artillery units operated alongside two ground-force divisions, PLAAF units, and People's Armed Police troops. The exercise scenario involved long-distance maneuvers, intelligence collection, and mobile counterattack operations.[111]

Still another important area of emphasis in training is command automation and missile force command and control. Current senior leadership training guidance highlights the importance of the "informatization" of the missile force and the development of "information system-based 'system of systems' operations capabilities."[112] Chinese military media reports also highlight the Second Artillery's employment of an "integrated command platform" that enables commanders to coordinate and direct the operations of multiple brigades and launch units with different types of equipment,[113] and to conduct structured attack training.[114] Related exercises have involved deploying a new field command post.[115]

The Second Artillery Force is also making greater use of simulations, computer war games, and command post exercises to improve the planning and decision-making skills of commanders and their staffs. These are relatively low-cost techniques that allow officers and soldiers to accumulate valuable experience at lower expense and risk than live-fire exercises. The Second Artillery has been employing simulators to prepare its forces to operate developmental missile systems before they are deployed.[116]

Finally, a sometimes overlooked but very important element of the PLA's training reform program is the emphasis on standardization of training and the development and application of more stringent criteria for the examination and evaluation of military training. This emphasis on rigorous screening and evaluation is reflected by the recent promotion of "two commanders, one operator" testing and evaluation, which focuses on assessing the capabilities of missile launcher and launch battalion commanders and specialist operators in the Second Artillery.[117] This marks a particularly important change in that more rigorous evaluation of training helps identify problems and shortcomings, thereby improving readiness and combat capabilities. In addition, the Second Artillery Force has issued a series of regulations intended to standardize training practices and promote more robust testing and evaluation of nuclear and conventional missile force units.[118] Chinese military media reports indicate that training assessment is becoming increasingly realistic and that units are being compelled to address shortcomings identified as part of the evaluation process. Commanding officers reportedly are held accountable when units fail to measure up to training standards, and are obligated to identify problems and draw up plans for improvement to raise the level of training.

Key Drivers

The principal driver behind these developments in doctrine, force structure, and training is China's growing concern about the viability of its traditional deterrent posture. Chinese analysts recognize that a more survivable posture is required to make deterrence credible and effective in the face of growing challenges posed by improvements in ISR, missile defense, and conventional precision strike capabilities. Concerns about the threat posed by enemy conventional strike capabilities are reflected in Chinese military publications. For example, according to *Science of Campaigns* (2000), in addition to guarding against nuclear or possibly other attacks by weapons of mass destruction, the Second Artillery Force's strategic missile forces must also be prepared to defend against conventional attacks using long-range precision guided munitions.[119] The concept of "close protection," which features prominently in discussions of the importance of improving the survivability of the missile force, is geared toward dealing with these threats. China is also responding actively to the development and deployment of the US missile defense system.

Chinese analysts view US pursuit of a missile defense system as a particularly serious threat to the viability of China's nuclear deterrent. According to Wang Zhongchun, "Once the system is completed, the United States will obtain a strategic deterrent force with both offensive and defensive capabilities, which could pose serious challenges to the limited nuclear deterrent capabilities of medium-sized nuclear countries." Chinese analysts state that ballistic missile defense (BMD) will make it easier for the United States to consider the first use of nuclear weapons. According to Rong Yu and Peng Guangqian:

> Today, with the gradual shaping of the American shield, offensive action is far easier. . . . If the United States does not have foolproof confidence to erase the adversary's nuclear arsenal in a first strike, it will have to deliberate on the possibility of a counterattack. However, should the United States possess the strategic defense capabilities, its first strike would leave only a few nuclear weapons available for the adversary to launch a retaliatory counterattack, which would be within the capacity of its missile defense system to intercept; a second strike would then eliminate the remainder of the adversary's nuclear force. It is apparent that, with the BMD system, US decision makers would be greatly emboldened when facing the choice of launching a preemptive or even preventative nuclear attack.[120]

China clearly places a high priority on ensuring that its forces are capable of fulfilling deterrent and countercoercion missions. Chinese strategists have concluded that an effective deterrent posture requires not only the ability to survive a conventional or nuclear first strike but also the capacity to penetrate, overwhelm, or otherwise neutralize US missile defense systems.

The United States–China Strategic Security Relationship, Declaratory Policy, and the Risks of Crisis Instability

China is concerned about "destabilizing" US conventional weapons developments that it believes threaten its nuclear deterrent. Although China's declaratory policy suggests that it will not compete in an arms race, movement toward a more robust force structure is occurring as a consequence of US development of BMD and conventional "prompt global strike" (PGS). Expectations about US BMD developments in particular are clearly a major factor shaping China's calculations about how many weapons it needs to support a nuclear strategy of effective deterrence.

From Beijing's perspective, Chinese strategists have argued that US missile defense systems and proposed conventional global strike programs would degrade strategic stability by compromising China's assured second-strike capability. Specifically, Chinese scholars have suggested that such capabilities would make it easier for the United States to contemplate a first strike against China. Indeed, Chinese analysts view US pursuit of a missile defense system as a serious threat to the viability of China's nuclear deterrent.[121] Some state that BMD will make it easier for the United States to consider the first use of nuclear weapons.[122]

US proposals to deploy PGS capabilities, which have been mentioned in several recent policy documents, including the 2010 Quadrennial Defense Review and the Nuclear Posture Review, have also raised concerns among China's analysts that such capabilities could undermine its strategic stability. Recently, some Chinese scholars have expressed concerns that even if US missile defense and PGS systems have little or no real impact on China's assured second-strike capability, they may still give US planners and decision makers a false sense of superiority, which potentially could lead to US attempts to coerce China with nuclear threats in a crisis.[123] They raise the possibility that even the illusion of "nuclear primacy" could lead to more aggressive behavior on the part of the United States.[124]

Moreover, some military publications and the comments of some Chinese strategists are not fully in line with declaratory policies like NFU. This raises potential doubts about Beijing's commitment to such policies in certain circumstances. This is of potential concern, particularly given the fact that United States–China nuclear relations remain less formal than those that prevailed between the United States and the USSR, which could have sinister implications for a possible crisis or instability. China's official policy is NFU, and Beijing asserts that it requires lean and effective nuclear deterrence that meets the needs of national security.

To be sure, there is a disconnect between China's official posture and certain sections of books like *IW* and *SSAC*, particularly the ones that contemplate conditions under which NFU would not really apply, or that indicate the nuclear force is useful for deterring conventional attacks and for escalation control. But other sections of the same publications are very much consistent with Beijing's official policy, such as those in which the authors state that the Second Artillery Force would need to conduct nuclear counterstrike operations in a harsh environment because they would already have been hit by an enemy first strike. In sum, then, there is some inconsistency between official policy and *some* parts of the books, but other parts are more closely aligned with the declaratory policy. One plausible explanation is that these differences reflect debate over these issues at the time the books were published. Another is that they were intended at least in part to induce caution among potential adversaries by indicating that under certain circumstances, conventional attacks against strategic targets in China could lead to nuclear escalation, notwithstanding China's NFU policy.

Perhaps of greatest concern, authoritative doctrinal publications reveal disturbing overconfidence in China's ability to maintain escalation dominance and strategic clarity. For example, instability may result if the alerting or de-alerting of strategic forces creates a temporary state of increased vulnerability. Miscalculation is another particularly troubling possibility, one that could be heightened by uncertainty over the message that one side is trying to convey to the other or by overconfidence in the ability to control escalation. Some of the signaling activities described in Chinese publications could easily be misinterpreted as preparations to conduct nuclear missile strikes, undercutting crisis stability even if Beijing actually intends to strengthen deterrence. Discussions such as these in Chinese publications on missile force operations suggest a complex and evolving attitude toward deterrence and escalation control and reflect discussions and debates among strategists about refining deterrence strategy in response to emerging challenges.

Some Chinese sources contain references that raise troubling questions about miscalculations that could result from attempts to bolster the robustness of deterrence during a crisis or amid a conventional conflict. Escalation could ensue. The first is that during mid-intensity nuclear deterrence operations, in order to "create credible situations," "liquid fueled missiles are engaged in simulated replenishments."[125] Although this signal is intended to put the enemy under the severe psychological strain of realizing that China's missile forces have entered the "pre-mobilization state" in hopes of causing the adversary to "abandon certain activities,"[126] the authors apparently fail to consider the potential for grave miscalculation on the part of the adversary. This is an especially alarming possibility, in that such activities could greatly accelerate escalation rather than cause the adversary to back down. Another potentially escalatory move envisioned by Zhao is the launch of long-range (intercontinental) missiles with nonnuclear warheads, "so as to create psychological shock in the opponent."[127] Although he offers no caution about the risks of unintended escalation, this could be a very destabilizing action, especially during a conflict with another nuclear power—much as Chinese commentators warn about PGS.

Nevertheless, some Chinese authors do acknowledge that actions intended to deter an adversary could instead provoke escalation. Zhao himself cautions that deterrent operations could accidentally trigger escalation if staged improperly: "Whether the timing for conducting the military deterrence of the missile forces is correctly chosen will directly affect the progress of deterrence and its outcome. If the appropriate timing is chosen, then deterrence will deter the enemy, contain the eruption of war, and obtain the objective of peace with the small price of deterrence. If inappropriate timing is chosen, then deterrence may cause the situation to deteriorate, even leading to the eruption and escalation of war."[128] Unfortunately, however, such discussions in Zhao's volume and other relevant publications are underdeveloped.

Conclusion

Beijing is no longer content to rely on a minimal deterrence force posture from which the threat of nuclear retaliation with a handful of surviving weapons would be considered sufficient to constrain an adversary. Therefore, it is modernizing its theater and strategic nuclear forces by enhancing survivability, increasing striking power, and countering missile defense developments. The deployment of road-mobile ICBMs is improving the survivability of Chinese nuclear forces by making them more challenging to locate and target. The deployment of the Jin-class SSBNs will diversify China's strategic deterrent by adding a sea-based nuclear retaliatory capability. Moreover, with the deployment of the DF-31 and DF-31A ICBMs and the anticipated introduction of the JL-2 missiles on board the Jins, China is finally attaining a credible nuclear deterrent based on a survivable second-strike capability. Our assessment is thus consistent with those of many Chinese analysts, who conclude that the deployment of land-based mobile missiles and SSBNs will "fundamentally ensure the reliability and credibility of China's nuclear force."[129]

As mentioned in the previous section, there are a number of reasons to be concerned that the transition to a more secure second-strike capability will not necessarily translate immediately or automatically into greater strategic stability. Indeed, it is entirely possible that these developments could in fact contribute to interactions that might decrease crisis stability under certain circumstances, particularly if planners and decision makers in either country fail to consider the potential implications of certain actions. Washington will thus need to proceed carefully to avoid precipitating counterresponses that are contrary to US interests, such as a larger-than-planned Chinese nuclear force buildup, further development of counterspace capabilities, or potentially destabilizing higher alert levels.

At the same time, however, the introduction of road-mobile strategic missiles and SSBNs will increasingly enable China to achieve its desired posture of effective deterrence. The modernization of Chinese nuclear forces and the transition from silo-based to road-mobile nuclear missiles and SSBNs might thus enhance the stability of strategic deterrence. Indeed, deterrence theory suggests that a more secure second-strike capability should enhance stability by encouraging both the United States and China to behave much more cautiously.[130]

Consequently, as China continues to modernize its nuclear and missile forces, preserving strategic stability promises to become a far more important aspect of the United States–China security relationship in the coming years. Indeed, successfully managing what could become a dangerous balancing act will require much of both parties. The United States will need to exercise considerable self-restraint, given the asymmetries that will continue to characterize the United States–China nuclear balance, despite China's recent enhancement of its nuclear and conventional missile capabilities. Planners and decision makers in the United States will also need to acquire an in-depth understanding of Chinese views on strategic signaling, crisis management, and escalation control, particularly in the context of a conflict over Taiwan. Meanwhile, Chinese planners and decision makers will need to have a similarly realistic understanding of US views and motivations.

This emerging dynamic within the United States–China strategic relationship thus underscores the need for greater United States–China dialogue and engagement on strategic issues. Although China historically has been reluctant to increase transparency, especially in the realm of its nuclear missile forces, its growing capabilities may create a new level of confidence on Beijing's part, and perhaps even a nascent recognition that modest increases in transparency could help safeguard shared interests in regional security and strategic stability.

Notes

1. National Air and Space Intelligence Center (hereafter, NASIC), *Ballistic and Cruise Missile Threat*, April 2009, Federation of American Scientists website, www .fas.org/programs/ssp/nukes/NASIC2009.pdf, 3.

2. Ibid., 19.

3. Information Office of the State Council of the People's Republic of China, *China's National Defense in 2006*, December 2006, http://news.xinhuanet.com/english/2006–12/ 29/content_5547029.htm. See also Evan S. Medeiros, "'Minding the Gap': Assessing the Trajectory of the PLA's Second Artillery," in *Right-Sizing the People's Liberation Army: Exploring the Contours of China's Military*, edited by Roy Kamphausen and Andrew Scobell (Carlisle, PA: Strategic Studies Institute, US Army War College, 2007), 143–90.

4. Chu Shulong and Rong Yu, "China: Dynamic Minimum Deterrence," in *The Long Shadow: Nuclear Weapons and Security in 21st Century Asia*, edited by Muthiah Alagappa (Stanford, CA: Stanford University Press, 2008), 161–87.

5. Li Bin, "中国核战略辨析" [Understanding China's Nuclear Strategy], 世界经济与政治 [World Economics & Politics] 9 (2006): 16–22.

6. Analyzing Chinese nuclear nomenclature is challenging, particularly because official sources are incomplete and take a "lowest common denominator" approach. The only official bilingual document to date that has been endorsed by the Second Artillery and China's nuclear weapons establishment, as well as US experts, offers the following definitions. Minimum deterrence: "Threatening the lowest level of damage necessary to prevent attack, with the fewest number of nuclear weapons possible." Limited deterrence: "There is no consensus on the definition." Maximum deterrence: "A term used in the past by some Chinese military scholars to describe a form of deterrence whereby with a strong nuclear superiority as support, the threat of a massive nuclear strike is used to deter the adversary." Tailored deterrence: "Flexible deterrence capabilities and operational doctrines specifically designed according to the specific psychological, political, ideological, and economic characteristics of the targeted actor." Committee on the US–Chinese Glossary of Nuclear Security Terms, *English–Chinese, Chinese–English Nuclear Security Glossary* (Washington and Beijing: National Academies Press and Atomic Energy Press, 2008), 36, 33, 35, 74, www.nap.edu/catalog/12186.html.

7. M. Taylor Fravel and Evan S. Medeiros, "China's Search for Assured Retaliation: The Evolution of Chinese Nuclear Strategy and Force Structure," *International Security* 35, no. 2 (Fall 2010): 48.

8. Ibid., 51–52.

9. Ibid., 86.

10. Dennis J. Blasko, "'Technology Determines Tactics': The Relationship between Technology and Doctrine in Chinese Military Thinking," *Journal of Strategic Studies* 34, no. 3 (June 2011): 355–81.

11. Zhao Zekuan, "New Development of Nuclear Deterrence Theory and Practice in the New Period," *China Military Science* 1 (2009): 16–20.

12. Wang Wenrong, ed., *Zhanlüexue* [The science of strategy] (Beijing: National Defense University Press, 1999), 348.

13. *Break the Nuclear Monopoly, Eliminate Nuclear Weapons* (Beijing: Foreign Languages Press, 1965), 1–5. See also John Wilson Lewis and Xue Litai, *China Builds the Bomb* (Stanford, CA: Stanford University Press, 1988), 241–43.

14. Yu Jixun, *The Science of Second Artillery Campaigns* (hereafter, *SSAC*) (Beijing: People's Liberation Army Press, 2004), 53. Yu Jixun was a high-ranking missile force officer.

15. Ibid., 53.

16. Lewis and Xue, *China Builds the Bomb*, 205–6.

17. Zhao, "New Development of Nuclear Deterrence."

18. John Wilson Lewis and Hua Di, "China's Ballistic Missile Programs: Technologies, Strategies, Goals," *International Security* 17, no. 2 (fall 1992): 15.

19. Lewis and Xue, *China Builds the Bomb*, 190–218.

20. Zhao, "New Development of Nuclear Deterrence," 17.

21. Ibid., 17.

22. Ibid., 17.

23. Lewis and Hua, "China's Ballistic Missile Programs," 19.

24. Dennis J. Blasko, "Military Parades Demonstrate Chinese Concept of Deterrence," *China Brief* 9, no. 8 (April 16, 2009), www.jamestown.org/single/?no_cache = 1&tx_ttnews%5Btt_news%5D = 34869.

25. Zhao, "New Development of Nuclear Deterrence," 17.

26. Lan Rongcheng and Li Wei, "Review of Second Artillery Building in the Past 60 Years," *China Military Science* 4 (2009).

27. Tien Ping, "核政策有调整空间" [Space for readjustment in nuclear policy], 香港商報訊 [Hong Kong Commercial Daily], June 23, 2003.

28. This is the official Chinese translation. "Deterrence" might be better translated as "coercion" here.

29. *SSAC*, 54.

30. Ibid.

31. Zhao, "New Development of Nuclear Deterrence," 18.

32. *SSAC*, 138. We believe that *SSAC* represents the Second Artillery's best effort at producing a high-level professional military handbook for missile-force personnel, but it should be noted that the Second Artillery is not the final arbiter of decisions about nuclear policy and strategy issues, which are presumably considered by China's highest-level civilian and military leaders.

33. Information Office of the State Council of the People's Republic of China, *China's National Defense in 2006* (Beijing: People's Republic of China, 2006), http://news.xin huanet.com/english/2006–12/29/content_5547029.htm.

34. *Zhanlüexue* [The science of strategy] (1987), 115.

35. These include Wang Hongqing and Zhang Xingye, eds., *Zhanyixue* [The science of campaigns] (hereafter, *SOC*) (Beijing: National Defense University Press, 2000); Xue Xinglin, ed., *Zhanyi Lilun Xuexi Zhinan* [Campaign theory study guide] (Beijing: National Defense University Press, 2001); and Zhang Yuliang, ed., *SOC* (Beijing: National Defense University Press, 2006).

36. Peng Guangqian and Yao Youzhi, eds. *Zhanlüexue* [The science of strategy] (Beijing: Military Science Press, 2001), 235.

37. Fravel and Medeiros, "China's Search for Assured Retaliation," 78.

38. *SSAC*, 273–74.

39. Ibid., 273.

40. Ibid., 274.

41. Ibid., 144.

42. Ibid., 59.

43. Yao Yunzhu, "Chinese Nuclear Policy and the Future of Minimum Deterrence," *Strategic Insights* 4, no. 9 (September 2005), www.nps.edu/Academics/centers/ccc/publications/OnlineJournal/2005/Sep/yaoSep05.html.

44. Yao Yunzhu, "China's Perspective on Nuclear Deterrence," *Air & Space Power Journal*, Spring 2010, www.airpower.au.af.mil/airchronicles/apj/apj10/spr10/yao.html.

45. Rong Yu and Peng Guangqian, "Nuclear No-First-Use Revisited," *China Security* 5, no. 1 (Winter 2009): 89, www.chinasecurity.us/images/stories/Rong_and_Peng(1).pdf.

46. Rong and Peng, "Nuclear No-First-Use Revisited," 88.

47. Zhao Xijun, ed., *Intimidation Warfare: A Comprehensive Discussion on Missile Coercion* (hereafter, *IW*) (Beijing: National Defense University Press, 2005), 173.

48. Zhang Peimin, "How to Develop the Means of Strategic Deterrence," *Military Art* 2 (February 2004): 34.

49. *IW*, 92.

50. *SSAC*, 294.

51. *IW*, 33.

52. *SSAC*, 295.

53. *IW*, 33.

54. Rong and Peng, "Nuclear No-First-Use Revisited," 85.

55. Author interviews with Chinese strategists, China, 2006.

56. Fravel and Medeiros, "China's Search for Assured Retaliation," 80.

57. State Council Information Office, *China's National Defense in 2010*, March 31, 2011, http://merln.ndu.edu/whitepapers/China_English2010.pdf.

58. Rong and Peng, "Nuclear No-First-Use Revisited," 88.

59. See, e.g., *SOC 2000*, 371.

60. See, e.g., Xue Xinglin, *Zhanyi Lilun Xuexi Zhinan*, 384–93.

61. *SSAC*, 46.

62. Ibid., 297.

63. Ibid., 307.

64. Ibid.

65. Ibid., 298.

66. Ibid., 126.

67. *IW*, 17.

68. Ibid., 152–53.

69. "Joint counterstrike" presumably means Second Artillery and SSBNs. Some references mention the possibility of PLAAF participation, even though it is unclear whether the PLAAF actually retains any such capability.

70. *IW*, 14.

71. Ibid., 17.

72. US Department of Defense, *Military and Security Developments Involving the People's Republic of China, 2009* (Washington, DC: Office of the Secretary of Defense,

2009) (hereafter, DoD 2009), www.defense.gov/pubs/pdfs/China_Military_Power_Report_2009.pdf, 24.

73. NASIC, *Ballistic and Cruise Missile Threat*, 17.

74. Ibid., 17.

75. Ibid., 21.

76. Robert Walpole, "Foreign Missile Developments and the Ballistic Missile Threat," Statement for the Record to the Senate Foreign Relations Committee, September 16, 1999, www.cia.gov/news-information/speeches-testimony/1999/walpole.htm.

77. See, e.g., Tan Shoulin, Zhang Daqiao, and Yu Zhijun, "The Optimization and Evaluation of the Warhead Separation Sequence of Multiple Independent Reentry Vehicle Missiles," *Journal of Ballistics* 3 (2006).

78. Brad Roberts, "Book Review: Nuclear Minimalism," *Arms Control Today*, May 2007, www.armscontrol.org/act/2007_05/BookReview.asp4.

79. Robert Walpole, "Statement for the Record to the Senate Subcommittee on International Security, Proliferation, and Federal Services on the Ballistic Missile Threat to the United States," February 9, 2000, www.cia.gov/news-information/speechestestimony/2000/nio_speech_020900.html4.

80. DoD 2009, 24.

81. US Department of Defense, *Military and Security Developments Involving the People's Republic of China, 2010* (Washington, DC: Office of the Secretary of Defense, 2010) (hereafter, DoD 2010), 66.

82. Ibid., 66.

83. This estimate comes from NASIC, *Ballistic and Cruise Missile Threat*. The 2009 Department of Defense report states that China maintains about twenty DF-4s.

84. Ibid., 21.

85. US Department of Defense, *Military and Security Developments Involving the People's Republic of China, 2011* (Washington, DC: Office of the Secretary of Defense, 2011), 3.

86. Pamela Pun, "Experts: DF-41 Could Force US to Adjust Its Strategy," *Hong Kong Standard*, October 15, 1999.

87. Chin Chien-li, "A Critical Biography of General Peng Xiaofeng, Political Commissar of the Second Artillery Corps," *Frontline* 90 (December 2006), 64–67.

88. NASIC, *Ballistic and Cruise Missile Threat*, 25.

89. US Office of Naval Intelligence, "Seapower Questions on the Chinese Submarine Force," December 20, 2006, Federation of American Scientists website, www.fas.org/nuke/guide/china/ONI2006.pdf.

90. Ibid.

91. NASIC, *Ballistic and Cruise Missile Threat*, 3.

92. DoD 2010, 34.

93. "我们终将蛟龙托水而出, 腾空飞翔, 威震四海" [We will eventually let the flood dragon emerge from the water, fly forth, and shock the four seas with its might], 我的中國網 [My China Net], August 17, 2011, http://mychinanet.com/bbs/subject.aspx?board＝1&topic＝61542&mtopic＝61542.

94. DoD 2009, 24.

95. Ibid.

96. NASIC, *Ballistic and Cruise Missile Threat*, 29.

97. See Jeffrey Lewis, "DH-10," July 14, 2008, *Arms Control Wonk*, www.arms controlwonk.com/1945/dh-10. As Lewis points out, "the language is could and would, not do and will" (emphasis in the original).

98. See Robert S. Norris and Hans M. Kristensen, "Chinese Nuclear Forces, 2008," *Bulletin of the Atomic Scientists* 64, no. 3 (July–August 2008): 42–45, www.thebulletin .org/files/064003009.pdf; Charles Ferguson, Evan S. Medeiros, and Phillip C. Saunders, "Chinese Tactical Nuclear Weapons," in *Tactical Nuclear Weapons: Emergent Threats in an Evolving Security Environment*, edited by Alistair Millar and Brian Miller (London: Brassey's, 2003); and Kenneth W. Allen, "China's Perspectives on Non-Strategic Nuclear Weapons and Arms Control," in *Controlling Non-Strategic Nuclear Weapons: Obstacles and Opportunities*, edited by Jeffrey A. Larsen and Kurt J. Klingenberger (Maxwell, AL: Air University Press, 2001).

99. *IW*, 16.

100. *SSAC*, 274.

101. Jing Zhiyuan and Zhang Haiyang, "第二炮兵二0一一年军事训练动员令, Dier paobing erlingyiyi nian junshi xunlian dongyuanling" [Mobilization order for the Second Artillery's Military Training in 2011], 火箭兵报, *Huojianbing bao* [Rocket forces news], January 1, 2011.

102. Xu Changlei and Li Yongfei, "导弹劲旅插上信息化'翅膀'" [Mighty missile force adds informatized wings], 火箭兵报, *Huojianbing bao*, May 1, 2010.

103. See, e.g., Xu Changlei, Chen Leixiang, and Li Yongfei, "某旅瞄准训练转变, 设置对抗演练新课目, *Moulu miaozhun xunlian zhuanbian, shezhi duikang yanlian xin kemu*" [A certain brigade takes aim at transformation of training, sets up new opposing-force training exercise subjects], 火箭兵报, *Huojianbing bao*, February 19, 2011.

104. Li Yan, Zhang Xianqiu, and Ge Song, "某训练基地狡黠'蓝军'逼'红军'增长'狼性'" [At a certain training base, the sly "blue force" pushes the "red force" to increase their "aggressiveness"], 火箭兵报, *Huojianbing bao*, June 21, 2010.

105. Yu Juncheng, "临时发射场即刻建成, *Linshi fashechang jike jiancheng*" [Temporary launchpad established immediately], 火箭兵报, *Huojianbing bao*, May 20, 2006, 1.

106. Ma Zhongbo, "全员全装全要素, 多路多向多课题, Quanyuan quanzhuang quan yaosu, duolu duoxiang duo keti" [All-personnel, all-equipment, and all-element exercise involving multiple approaches, directions, and subjects], 火箭兵报, *Huojianbing bao*, August 1, 2006.

107. Yan Xifei, Tang Licheng, and Zhang Jiangang, "'蓝军'在行动" [Blue force in action], 火箭兵报, *Huojianbing bao*, June 11, 2010.

108. "Second Artillery Red-Blue Force Confrontational Exercise Emphasizes Training in a Complex Electromagnetic Environment," *Liberation Army Daily*, August 26, 2006.

109. Wang Tie and Wu Yanbing, "All-Army Camouflage Specialty Group Deputy Head Wang Xiangwei: My Profession Is 'Fraud and Deception,'" *China Youth*, October 1, 2003, 24–26.

110. US Department of Defense, *Annual Report to Congress: Military Power of the People's Republic of China* (Washington, DC: Office of the Secretary of Defense, 2006), 16, www.dod.gov/pubs/pdfs/China%20Report%202006.pdf.

111. US Department of Defense, *Annual Report to Congress: Military Power of the People's Republic of China* (Washington, DC: Office of the Secretary of Defense, 2007), 24, www.defense.gov/pubs/pdfs/070523-China-Military-Power-final.pdf.

112. Jing and Zhang, "Dier paobing erlingyiyi nian junshi xunlian dongyuanling."

113. Chang Sheng and He Tianjin, "某基地加强逐级集成训练提升核心军事能力纪实" [On-the-spot report: base steps up level-by-level integrated training, boosts core military capabilities], 火箭兵报, *Huojianbing bao*, June 21, 2010.

114. Ding Haiming and Liang Pengfei, "中国战略导弹部队演兵场目击之三第二炮兵 4 支导弹旅联合训练实弹发射精准命中目标" [Four Second Artillery missile brigades in joint training conduct live launches, hit targets exactly], 解放军报, *Jiefangjun bao* [Liberation Army daily], July 17, 2009. According to this report, which describes a strategic missile force exercise, "the battlefield situation is presented in real time on a large electronic screen in the forward command post. In the joint training, an integrated command platform simultaneously directs the combat operations of several missile brigades and hundreds of launch units, on the one hand communicating with frontline missile brigades and launch battalions, exercising precise command and control over the missile group's launches."

115. Xu Changlei, "某部新型野战指挥所演兵场上显神威" [A certain unit demonstrates prowess on the training ground with its new field combat operations command post], 火箭兵报, *Huojianbing bao*, May 11, 2010.

116. "PLA's New Missile Tested Successfully and Begins to Equip Strategic Rocket Forces," *Liberation Army Daily*, October 16, 2006.

117. See, e.g., Yue Xiaolin, Li Fumin, and Yu Xihong, "某基地致力强化核心战位人员的核心作用, '两长一手'演兵场上竞风流, *Mou jidi zhili qianghua hexin zhanwei renyuan de hexin zuoyong*" [A certain base exerts works toward strengthening the core function of core battle position personnel: Admirable competition on "two commanders, one operator" exercise ground], 火箭兵报, *Huojianbing bao*, July 31, 2010.

118. Zhang Ligang, He Tianjin, and Kang Fashun, "第二军事训练会议在某基地召开, *Dier paobing junshi xunlian huiyi zai mou jidi zhaokai*" [Second Artillery military training conference held at a certain base]," 火箭兵报, *Huojianbing bao*, August 15, 2006.

119. *SOC 2000*, 371.

120. Rong and Peng, "Nuclear No-First-Use Revisited," 81.

121. Wang Zhongchun, "Nuclear Challenges and China's Choices," *China Security*, Winter 2007, 62, www.wsichina.org/cs5_4.pdf.

122. Rong and Peng, "Nuclear No-First-Use Revisited," 89.

123. Li Bin and Nie Hongyi, "An Investigation of China–US Strategic Stability," *World Economics & Politics* 2 (2008): 60–61.

124. Ibid., 61.

125. *IW*, 185.

126. Ibid.

127. Ibid., 186.

128. Ibid., 172.

129. Wang Zhongchun, "Nuclear Challenges," 62.

130. This is strongly and seminally argued by Thomas C. Schelling, *The Strategy of Conflict* (New York: Oxford University Press, 1960), 251; and Thomas C. Schelling, *Arms and Influence* (New Haven, CT: Yale University Press, 1966), 235.

CHAPTER 5

NORTH KOREA'S NUCLEAR WEAPONS PROGRAM

Motivations, Strategy, and Doctrine

Terence Roehrig

On OCTOBER 9, 2006, North Korea (the Democratic People's Republic of Korea) exploded a nuclear device and joined the ranks of the world's nuclear powers. The yield of this test was well below those of other entrants, probably less than 1 kiloton and smaller than that for which North Korean leaders and technicians had hoped. The explosion succeeded in demonstrating a rudimentary nuclear weapons capability and stirring up the security environment in East Asia. On May 25, 2009, North Korea conducted a second nuclear test despite numerous warnings from Washington, Beijing, Seoul, Tokyo, and others. Evidence indicated that this test was more successful, and that it thus generated a yield estimated at 2 to 4 kilotons. This further cemented North Korea's position as a de facto nuclear weapon state.

Efforts continue to resume the Six-Party Talks on North Korean nuclear disarmament and convince North Korea to relinquish its nuclear capability. It appears increasingly unlikely, however, that North Korea will ever fully give up its nuclear weapons. Pyongyang might be willing to curtail or freeze certain dimensions of the program, or it might claim that it has given up its nuclear weapons while refusing to allow the International Atomic Energy Agency to fully verify the assertion. In any case, the likelihood of the comprehensive, verifiable denuclearization of North Korea is quickly fading. Indeed, on September 30, 2009, North Korea cited the US nuclear threat when it declared that its "dismantlement of nuclear weapons is unthinkable even in a dream as long as there exist[s] the sources that compelled it to have access to nukes."[1] There is little chance that the advent of new leadership in Pyongyang will change matters. The new paramount leader, Kim Jong-un, probably views a nuclear arsenal as a backstop for his regime's survival.

With the likelihood that North Korea will retain some level of nuclear weapons capability, analysis then turns to Pyongyang's nuclear strategy and doctrine. What role do nuclear weapons play in the country's security calculations (doctrine), and what are its specific strategies for using these assets? Using deterrence theory as an analytical framework, I examine possible avenues for North Korea's nuclear weapons strategy and doctrine. Although the direction of its nuclear weapons program is unclear, if it chooses to go beyond its current, small-scale program and develop an operational force of some kind, the United States, South Korea (the Republic of Korea), and others must give careful consideration to understanding North Korean strategy and doctrine. Even with the possibility that it develops only a small operational nuclear force, North Korea will enhance its ability to deter South Korea and the United States, something that it can do already to a degree with its conventional capability. Nuclear weapons also raise serious concerns about Pyongyang's strategy, which might include placing its forces on hair-trigger alert or assuming a posture involving launching with little strategic warning because of these forces' vulnerability. Its status as a nuclear state, furthermore, might embolden it to be more provocative and willing to resort to brinkmanship, because it believes that it holds the ultimate deterrent of nuclear weapons. All these dimensions pose greater danger for the region, particularly for stability in a crisis.

The remainder of this chapter addresses deterrence theory and its relevance for North Korea, examines possible directions for the country's strategy and doctrine, and assesses the probable impact of these developments on regional peace and security.

Nuclear Weapons, Deterrence Theory, and North Korea

Deterrence theory is a common starting point for assessing the strategy and doctrine of most nuclear-armed states. It should be noted at the outset that North Korea has said little about its nuclear strategy and doctrine, and it remains unclear whether it will follow a typically Western conception of nuclear deterrence.[2] Most likely, it will construct some indigenous version that borrows from multiple sources and repackages the doctrine as homegrown. Concepts of deterrence theory nonetheless remain the best guide available to assess North Korean strategy and doctrine.

Deterrence is the use of threats to convince an adversary not to take some action. An important dimension of the threat is that it must impose unacceptable costs on the challenger, persuading it to refrain from taking the action. If the adversary concludes that the costs are sufficiently high, theory maintains that deterrence is likely to be successful. There are two types of deterrence threats: deterrence by denial and deterrence by punishment.[3] Deterrence by denial occurs when states seek to deter adversaries by possessing sufficient military power to prevent the challenger from achieving its objectives. In the context of a military invasion, the defender could either defeat the invasion or, short of victory, make any attack so costly that the challenger would decide the assault was not worth the effort.[4] With the advent of air power and the development of nuclear weapons, threats began to change, allowing for deterrence by punishment. States could now bypass the defenses and ground forces of their adversaries and strike directly at population centers and industrial sites. States might also possess the ability to punish with conventional weapons like long-range artillery, rockets, and conventionally armed ballistic missiles. These systems are very different from nuclear weapons but could still pose the prospect of unacceptable cost, especially if able to hit strategic nodes, government facilities, or cities.

Nuclear weapons had a particularly significant impact on deterrence by punishment. With these weapons, states are able to threaten devastating attacks on an enemy homeland that raise the costs to far higher levels than conventional forces can impose. Moreover, a state does not need to have conventional superiority to issue threats of nuclear punishment, and there is no need for precise calculations of the military balance for deterrence to be successful. Kenneth Waltz notes that "with nuclear weapons, stability and peace rest on easy calculations of what one country can do to another."[5] The threat to punish is also not necessarily tied to any possibility of winning. Patrick Morgan argues that with conventional forces, states can threaten to fight if attacked or seek revenge after winning a conflict. If it possesses nuclear weapons, a state can threaten punishment whether it can win or not.[6]

First- and Second-Strike Capability

An important dimension of a nuclear force is whether it has first- or second-strike capability. First-strike capability refers to a state's ability to launch a surprise attack that successfully takes out an adversary's nuclear weapons and other necessary assets and thus eliminates the possibility of retaliation. Because achieving a successful first strike is a very difficult and dangerous task, states interested in possessing this capability develop large nuclear forces with accurate delivery systems. Whether a first strike will succeed is exceedingly uncertain, even with the most robust force. If it fails, the attacking state will find itself exposed to devastating retaliation. States that fear they are vulnerable to a first strike are more likely to adopt a launch-on-warning posture, in an effort to ensure that their forces are not caught on the ground before they can retaliate.

If the target of a first strike also possesses a significant conventional capability, a nuclear first strike might also need to hit conventional force targets to remove the danger of conventional retaliation. During the Cold War this was not a serious concern for the United States and the Soviet Union because they did not share a border and neither superpower could readily invade the other. US allies, however, were keenly aware of this dynamic. North Korea and South Korea do share a border, whereas Seoul lies well within range of hundreds of North Korean artillery pieces and multiple rocket launcher systems. North Korean conventional capability is a central factor in strategic deterrence calculations on the Korean Peninsula.

For a second-strike capability, a state must be able to absorb an enemy's attack while retaining sufficient survivable nuclear forces to retaliate afterward. There is no way, however, to calculate precisely what "sufficient" forces means. Sufficiency is whatever it takes to deter the attack in the first place. Given the horrendous destructive potential of nuclear weapons, the chance of even a few deliverable warheads' surviving could be sufficient to deter. Traditional ways to ensure a second-strike capability include maintaining a large nuclear weapons force. Sheer size makes it difficult for an adversary to hit all the necessary targets. States can also deploy

[handwritten margin notes: True. But convent weapons are still effective uses as deterrents & gen weapons]

their warheads in hardened sites such as underground silos or mountain bunkers, which bolsters survivability. Or they can employ stealth and mobility, deploying ballistic missile submarines, or perhaps mobile missiles that move between different destinations on land, which makes targeting difficult and uncertain. States that possess a second-strike capability are less likely to rely on launch-on-warning strategies, because they have more confidence in their ability to ride out an attack while retaining enough nuclear capability to respond. As a result these states are more likely to adopt a launch-under-attack posture. Their forces generally are not on a hair-trigger alert status, which improves stability in a crisis.

States that seek a first-strike capability are likely to employ what are known as "counterforce" targeting criteria. Such an approach mainly targets the adversary's retaliatory capabilities and other military assets. The success of a first strike is contingent on the ability to knock out the other side's ability to respond. Counterforce targeting requires large numbers of warheads and accurate delivery systems. In contrast, a second-strike capability usually adopts a "countervalue" posture, which focuses less on the other side's military capabilities and more on punitive strikes, usually against cities. A state with a limited number of warheads generally adopts a countervalue posture, because it possesses too few warheads for a first strike that will successfully disarm an adversary. Punishment and countervalue targeting do not require especially accurate delivery systems to achieve their goals.

Deterrence Situations

Deterrence can also be used in a variety of circumstances. This points to some important distinctions between deterrence situations. First, deterrence can refer to either "primary" or "extended" deterrence. Primary deterrence refers to a state's actions to protect its homeland, whereas extended deterrence refers to a state's intent to deter actions against an ally or some other state. This is a crucial distinction. Few would doubt a defender's commitment to respond if its homeland were attacked, but many questions arise in an extended deterrence situation. Most important, will the defender back its ally in a crisis? Is protecting the ally considered a sufficiently important interest to risk a nuclear exchange that might follow if deterrence fails? There is no guarantee that a state will honor its commitment when this obligation might bring severe destruction on its homeland. During the Cold War many questioned the United States' commitment to protect Europe, and thus asked whether the United States would really sacrifice Washington for London or Paris. Doubts about this prompted France and the United Kingdom to develop modest nuclear arsenals of their own. The North Korean case is one of primary deterrence. Pyongyang is intent on guaranteeing the survival of the regime, and it has no ally to protect. Thus there can be little doubt that it will respond if attacked.

Second, deterrence can be part of either a symmetrical or an asymmetrical situation; and in each of these differing situations, the power relationships of the adversaries can create different dynamics. For instance, during the Cold War the

US–Soviet relationship was a symmetrical confrontation because both sides possessed relatively similar military capabilities. But when the Cold War ended, attention shifted to situations of asymmetrical deterrence where power differentials were significant. In particular, many wondered if so-called rogue states such as Iran, Iraq, and North Korea could be deterred through traditional conceptions of deterrence. In addition, asymmetrical deterrence can work in the other direction with relatively weaker states that are seeking to deter more powerful challengers.[7]

Rationality

Deterrence theorists often assume that leaders of states act rationally. Ideally, rational decision makers assemble a list of potential options, assess the associated costs and benefits for each option, and then choose the course of action that produces the most benefit for the least cost. Nuclear weapons make these calculations easier because the costs of a nuclear exchange are so high and so obvious. Scholars have often criticized the rationality assumption, and there are certain difficulties with accepting this premise.[8] Yet perfect rationality is not required for deterrence to work, particularly with nuclear weapons. Nuclear deterrence need not rest on precise calculations of costs and benefits that produce a rational outcome. Even with an imperfect assessment of these factors, the high costs of nuclear weapons will dominate most calculations and impose a sufficient degree of rationality on most decision makers.

With regard to North Korea, many questioned the rationality of Kim Jong-il. In 1999, during testimony before the Senate Armed Services Committee, US Forces Korea commander General John Tilelli Jr. spoke of North Korea as an "unpredictable regime."[9] The regime's provocative language and regular use of brinkmanship lent credence to public perceptions that Kim Jong-il was irrational—and the popular media only cemented the image of his craziness. The movie *Team America* and a cover photo of Kim in *The Economist* magazine (with the title "Greetings Earthlings") solidified the prevailing impression.[10] However, it is also possible to argue that North Korean leaders are very rational in their ability to use minimal resources to successfully pursue their interests. Rationality does not mean freedom from making mistakes, but it does imply a certain level of predictability. For Kim Jong-il, regime survival was the paramount objective that informed his regime's rationality. The same doubtless holds true for his successor, Kim Jong-un.

The rationality assumption in deterrence often focuses on the challenger. Will that state make rational calculations of costs and benefits, and thus be deterred? In the context of Korean security, North Korea is usually viewed as the adversary to be deterred, and an analysis typically queries whether North Korean leaders will make the calculations necessary for successful deterrence. In the case of the country's nuclear weapons capability, however, Pyongyang is the one that is attempting to implement a deterrent strategy to prevent an attack by the United States, and perhaps South Korea. In this case, the perceptions of North Korea's irrationality help strengthen its deterrence strategy, because its adversaries believe that it "just may be crazy enough" to use nuclear weapons.[11] Thus, perceptions of irrationality and unpredictability can be a means for achieving rational ends.

Credibility

For deterrence to be successful, it must be credible. In his book *The Requirements of Deterrence*, William Kaufmann identifies three criteria for a credible deterrence strategy: capability, cost, and resolve.[12]

Capability. Capability entails convincing an antagonist that one possesses the military means to carry out any threat one makes. It is not absolutely necessary that the capability be explicit. Israel has never conducted a nuclear test, yet no one doubts that it possesses nuclear weapons. The level of North Korea's nuclear capability is unclear, although it has conducted two nuclear tests. Evidence from its first explosion indicated that the yield was less than 1 kiloton, well below the yield of most nuclear tests. Its second nuclear test was more successful, but the precise dimensions of its capability remain a matter of speculation.

Regarding the number of weapons in the North Korean arsenal, estimates range from a minimum of four nuclear weapons to a maximum of seventeen. Such estimates usually rely on approximations of the amount of plutonium that the country has been able to reprocess. In January 2009 the country provided its first indication of the number of warheads it may possess. Selig Harrison, director of the Asia program at the Center for International Policy and a frequent visitor to North Korea, returned from a visit there, where officials had told him that they had "weaponized" close to 31 kilograms of plutonium, enough for four or five nuclear warheads. Harrison noted that it remained unclear what "weaponization" meant, but the implication was that Pyongyang has constructed nuclear weapons.[13]

Weaponization is an important issue. It is one thing to conduct a nuclear weapons test. It is quite another to miniaturize the technology sufficiently to build a warhead that can fit atop a ballistic missile or within the bomb bay of an aircraft. Converting rudimentary technology into a working payload is at once a difficult task and crucial for a viable nuclear capability. There is no way to verify the weaponization claim, and it is also possible that Pyongyang was fabricating information to obtain leverage with the incoming Obama administration. At this juncture, it appears that North Korea has not mastered this critical step, but it will likely continue working at this task.

The question of weaponization also raises the issue of North Korean delivery systems and the types of targets they are capable of reaching. One of the country's military strengths is its ballistic missile force. It first showed interest in acquiring ballistic missiles and technology in the 1980s, when it obtained a Scud B ballistic missile from Egypt. Its technicians reverse-engineered and improved on that missile, and thus constructed more advanced models. Sometime in 1988, the country began work on the Nodong 1, an improved version of the Scud. The Nodong is a single-stage, medium-range ballistic missile with a range of 1,350 to 1,500 kilometers, depending on the size of the warhead.[14] It is a likely candidate for deploying any future North Korean nuclear warheads. Its extended range would let Pyongyang hold all of Japan and all US personnel stationed there—including on Okinawa—at risk. Estimates indicate that North Korea has approximately 800 short- to intermediate-range ballistic missiles, including 600 Scuds capable of reaching Seoul and other parts of South Korea, along with 200 Nodongs.[15]

Anxieties over North Korea's ballistic missile capability escalated further in August 1998, when Pyongyang launched the three-stage Taepodong missile, allegedly to put a satellite into orbit. The missile's development had begun in 1987, when Kim Jong-il grasped the importance of having a missile that could reach the United States. He reportedly remarked, "if we can develop this we have nothing to fear. Even the American bastards won't be able to bother us."[16] On July 4, 2006, a few months before its nuclear test, North Korea conducted another round of ballistic missile tests, launching six short-range missiles and one Taepodong 2. Depending on the payload, a successful Taepodong 2 flight could reach Hawaii or Alaska, but the test failed. On April 5, 2009, North Korea launched another three-stage Taepodong 2, allegedly to put a satellite into orbit. The launch failed, but it demonstrated that Pyongyang had made progress in its ballistic missile program. In June 2009 General James Cartwright, vice chairman of the Joint Chiefs of Staff and former head of US Strategic Command, testified before the Senate Armed Services Committee that it would be three to five years before North Korea might have a missile that could reach the West Coast. Cartwright predicted, however, that Pyongyang would not manage to manufacture a nuclear warhead small enough to fit on the missile by then.[17] But in January 2011 Secretary of Defense Robert Gates warned that North Korea might have a ballistic missile capable of reaching the United States in five years and that North Korea's nuclear weapons program "is becoming a direct threat to the United States."[18] In other words, if North Korea increases the range of its missiles sufficiently to strike the United States, it can threaten the US homeland. As a result, it could impose a greater cost on the United States and would be a direct threat to US security. But it remains unclear whether and when North Korea will achieve the necessary engineering breakthroughs.

Although most attention centers on North Korea's plutonium program, concern also remains for its potential to build nuclear weapons using highly enriched uranium (HEU). Revelations of an HEU-based program surfaced during United States–North Korea meetings in October 2002, which eventually led to the unraveling of the 1994 Agreed Framework. The program had been relatively quiet until September 4, 2009, when Pyongyang sent a letter to the president of the UN Security Council announcing that North Korea was about to enter the final phase of enriching uranium.[19] In November 2010 North Korean officials revealed a new facility to a visiting Stanford University physicist, Siegfried Hecker, that contained close to 2,000 centrifuges for uranium enrichment, and the facility's advanced nature surprised many knowledgeable observers. The full extent of North Korea's HEU efforts remains uncertain for the time being.

Finally, there is also a political dimension connected to North Korea's capability. Since the early 1990s, the United States, South Korea, China, Japan, and Russia, either bilaterally or in the Six-Party Talks, have been trying to convince North Korea to give up its nuclear weapons program. It has stated on several occasions that it is committed to denuclearize but that it will not do so until certain conditions have been met, particularly by the United States—which must establish normal relations with North Korea, abolish its "hostile policy" toward the North, conclude a formal peace treaty to end the Korean War, and remove its nuclear threat and nuclear umbrella from the Korean Peninsula, among other conditions.

Despite North Korea's two nuclear tests, however, the participants in the Six-Party Talks (with the obvious exception of North Korea) have refused to recognize North Korea as a nuclear weapon state. And this is true in a legal sense. The Nuclear Non-Proliferation Treaty acknowledges only those nuclear weapon states that had exploded nuclear bombs by 1968. In an operational sense, however, the story is much different. In November 2008 the US Defense Department published a report titled *Joint Operating Environment 2008: Challenges and Implications for the Future Joint Force*, whose authors noted that "the rim of the great Asian continent is already home to five nuclear powers: China, India, Pakistan, North Korea, and Russia."[20] Subsequently, in the journal *Foreign Affairs*, Secretary of Defense Robert Gates stated that "North Korea has built several nuclear bombs."[21]

North Korea was quick to jump on these items, proclaiming, "it is the first time that a US government report has acknowledged and announced that North Korea is a nuclear weapon state."[22] Pyongyang deliberately conflated the reality that it has attained a weapons capability with the politics of joining the closed nuclear club. The United States' acknowledgment of operational reality does not constitute admission of the latter. Criticism nonetheless followed these acknowledgments of North Korea as a nuclear power. In a daily briefing session State Department spokesman Sean McCormack refuted the assertion, and he noted the recognition "is not our national policy, and that the document [*Joint Operating Environment 2008*] . . . they referenced does not represent the official views of the United States."[23] Finally, the Obama administration has made clear that it will not recognize North Korea as a nuclear weapon state. The administration thus recognizes that North Korea's nuclear capability is not only a military and security issue but also a political one.

Cost. As noted above, successful deterrence necessitates not only a capability but also the possession of military force capable of imposing unacceptable costs on an adversary. Cost is closely tied to capability. Without sufficient capability, it may be very difficult to impose steep enough costs to alter an opponent's decision-making calculus. However, it is worth pointing out that imposing costs is not solely a matter of threatening military penalties. To fully employ this dimension of deterrence, the defender must have a detailed understanding of what the challenger values. Without this assessment, the defender risks threatening "costs" that hold at risk things of relatively little value to the challenger—which increases the likelihood that deterrence will fail.

Relying on conventional weapons to impose unacceptable costs may limit the defender's options, particularly in an asymmetrical deterrence situation where the defender is the weaker of the two states. However, the stronger state in the asymmetrical relationship may not need nuclear weapons to deter the weaker state, because the strategic effect will be the same. Moreover, the interests involved between the two states also play a role here. If the challenger is a more powerful global actor, its interests in the region may be far less important than those of the weaker state. This is particularly so if the weaker defender is in a primary deterrence situation. Consequently, the defender may need to threaten only a modest penalty to raise the costs high enough to deter the challenger.[24] Although conventional weapons raise questions about the ability to increase costs, nuclear weapons are far clearer on this dimension. With even a small nuclear arsenal set to launch-on-warning, a state can inflict serious damage on a challenger. The destructive capacity of nuclear weapons simplifies a challenger's cost/benefit calculus by posing the stark prospect of cataclysmic devastation. As Kenneth Waltz argues, "in a conventional world, one is uncertain about winning or losing. In a nuclear world, one is uncertain about surviving or being annihilated. If force is used, and not kept within limits, catastrophe will result. That prediction is easy to make because it does not require close estimates of opposing forces."[25] If even a lesser nuclear state can place a handful of nuclear weapons on target, the costs may be devastating and unacceptable.

Resolve. The final criterion necessary for successful deterrence is resolve: The defender must demonstrate to the challenger that it is determined to carry out its threat if deterrence fails. Because North Korea's deterrent policy is an example of primary deterrence, there is little doubt that it would respond if attacked. But the link between resolve and successful deterrence is not always so clear. Even if a defender's threat to respond is ironclad, a challenger may still attack, believing that it can eliminate the defender's ability to retaliate before the defender can respond. Or the challenger may assign such value to its objectives that it is prepared to absorb the inevitable costs of retaliation. The two circumstances may coincide if the challenger is more powerful militarily, believes its strengths can overcome the defender's capabilities and resolve, and sees the perceived costs as manageable.

Conversely, even an uncertain threat to respond may deter an enemy if the costs are exceedingly high, as is the case with nuclear weapons. As long as a state appears willing to launch-on-warning or has an arsenal big enough that a few nuclear weapons will survive an attack, the specter of destruction may be more than enough to deter. The classic conception of this is Thomas Schelling's "threat that leaves something to chance." Schelling argued that "a response that carries some risk of war can be plausible, even reasonable, at a time when a final, ultimate decision to have a general war would be implausible or unreasonable. A country can threaten to stumble into war even if it cannot credibly threaten to invite one."[26] Thus, resolve does not always rest on exact calculations but instead is a shifting relationship between certainty and the costs of retaliation.

North Korea's Nuclear Motivations and Doctrine

North Korean strategic nuclear doctrine flows in part from Pyongyang's motives for obtaining nuclear weapons. Many studies have addressed this issue. They point to several explanations, including concern for North Korea's security, the desire for a bargaining chip to extract economic and political concessions from South Korea and the United States, the pursuit of a payload that can be married with the nation's ballistic missile capability and sold for valuable hard currency, and finally, as a way for Kim Jong-un to ingratiate himself with his military and solidify his hold on power.[27]

Determining North Korean intentions is difficult. Pyongyang's motives probably combine the interests mentioned above. North Korea's public pronouncements, however, focus predominantly on security concerns and the need to deter the United States. These sentiments need not be taken completely at face value, because it is often unclear what is part of North Korean posturing and what is its actual position. However, repetition appears to point to the importance of deterrence in the nation's strategic doctrine. On February 10, 2005, when North Korea formally declared that it was a nuclear power, it noted that "the US disclosed its attempt to topple the political system in [North Korea] at any cost, threatening it with a nuclear stick. This compels us to take a measure to bolster its nuclear weapons arsenal in order to protect the ideology, system, freedom and democracy chosen by its people." Consequently, North Korean nuclear weapons "will remain [a] nuclear deterrent for self-defense under any circumstances."[28] On October 3, 2006, in an effort to justify its upcoming nuclear test, North Korea maintained that

> a people without [a] reliable war deterrent are bound to meet a tragic death and the sovereignty of their country is bound to be wantonly infringed upon. This is a bitter lesson taught by the bloodshed resulting from the law of the jungle in different parts of the world. [North Korea's] nuclear weapons will serve as [a] reliable war deterrent for protecting the supreme interests of the state and the security of the Korean nation from the US threat of aggression and averting a new war and firmly safeguarding peace and stability on the Korean Peninsula under any circumstances.[29]

Later, on January 17, 2008, the North Korean Ministry of Foreign Affairs issued a rejoinder to the US position that bilateral relations can be normalized only after North Korea relinquishes its nuclear weapons capability. The ministry declared that North Korea

> made nuclear weapons to defend itself from the US nuclear threat, not in the anticipation of such things as the normalization of the relations with the US or economic assistance. It is the reality on the Korean Peninsula that we can live without normalizing the relations with the US but not without [a] nuclear deterrent. . . . If there is something to be desired by us, it is not to normalize the relations between [North Korea] and the US but to boost the nuclear deterrent in every way to more firmly defend the security of our nation. . . . Though the bilateral relations are normalized in a diplomatic manner, [North Korea's] status as a nuclear weapon state will remain unchanged as long as it is exposed even to the slightest US nuclear threat.[30]

Finally, following the passage of UN Security Council Resolution 1874 in June 2009—the latest in a series of measures designed to prevent proliferation from North Korea—the North Korean Ministry of Foreign Affairs argued: "Had any other country found itself in the situation of [North Korea], it would have clearly realized that

[it] has never chosen but was compelled to go nuclear in the face of the US hostile policy and its nuclear threats. It has become an absolutely impossible option for [North Korea] to even think about giving up its nuclear weapons. It makes no difference to [North Korea] whether its nuclear status is recognized or not."[31]

Han S. Park notes that most North Koreans believe it is their nuclear capability that protects them from a US invasion. According to Park, "when one asks any North Korean about the reason for the US invasion of Afghanistan and Iraq, one will get one answer only: Those countries were invaded because they did not have the military capability to defend themselves. Every North Korean is also likely to offer the view that the United States would not have attempted either invasion if the target country had had nuclear weapons."[32]

Although North Korea has tested a nuclear device, insists that it is a nuclear power, and has claimed that it has "weaponized" four or five warheads, it is unlikely to have even a small operational nuclear force for some time. As discussed before, achieving full operational status will demand breakthroughs in several difficult technologies, including miniaturizing a warhead to the proper size to fit on a missile, constructing a warhead that can survive reentry, solving fueling challenges with ballistic missiles, and building the necessary deployment and maintenance infrastructure. The estimates of fissile material provide some indication of North Korea's nuclear capability, but judging the future direction of Pyongyang's nuclear force remains dicey.[33] North Korean leaders, moreover, continue to imply that if certain conditions are met, they might yet be willing to abandon their nuclear endeavors. In January 2009, during a visit with a senior Chinese official, the news agency Xinhua quoted Kim Jong-il as saying, "The North Korean side will commit itself to the denuclearization of the North Korean Peninsula [sic], and hopes to coexist peacefully with other involved parties. North Korea is not willing to see tensions emerge in the peninsula, and is willing to strengthen consultation and cooperation with China to push forward the Six-Party Talks."[34] Efforts to restart negotiations continue yet have borne little fruit early in Kim Jong-un's rule. Indeed, an abortive April 2012 "satellite launch"—an endeavor scarcely distinguishable from a ballistic missile test—likely represented a new gesture of defiance. Yet North Korea may never be sufficiently satisfied with the security environment and thus may continue, slowly, to develop a more operational nuclear capability embodied in a small nuclear force.

Nuclear Strategy and Capability

If North Korea indeed chooses to keep pursuing an operational nuclear weapons force, this force will likely remain small, perhaps in the range of thirty to seventy warheads—the approximate number in the Pakistani and Indian arsenals. Most likely, if North Korea goes in this direction, it will remain at the lower end of this range. North Korean leaders are likely to determine that a small nuclear force is sufficient for their deterrence needs. Moreover, considering the country's economic problems, it may be unable to sustain a large and costly nuclear weapons infrastructure. If this is the case, at least four main issues will arise that pertain to North Korea's possible nuclear strategy.

First, the North Korean force will be too small to consider a first strike. Given the numbers and relative inaccuracy of North Korean missiles, Pyongyang would have a difficult time opting for a counterforce strategy that targeted an opponent's military facilities. Instead, it would likely opt for a countervalue strategy, and thus threaten retaliation through punitive strikes on an adversary's cities. Though target lists are typically classified, North Korea's would likely include Seoul, other South Korean cities, Japanese population centers, and US military bases in South Korea and Japan. Targeting US bases would not be part of a counterforce strategy, but rather a way to hold at risk assets, such as forward bases and personnel critical to the United States' presence in the region that are valued by the United States—which would ensure that Washington remained deterred.

Given North Korea's conventional military doctrine, it is possible that Pyongyang might conceive of nuclear weapons, in particular those deployed on short-range missiles, as part of its offensive strike plans. It has already incorporated numerous artillery assets, multiple rocket launchers, and conventionally armed Scud and Nodong missiles into its war plans. Including nuclear weapons in the mix would certainly complicate South Korean and US efforts to target the missiles, because some would be conventionally armed, whereas others would boast nuclear warheads. Both before and after its October 2006 nuclear test, however, North Korea unambiguously pledged that it would "never use nuclear weapons first."[35] Its past and present leaders probably are well aware that initiating a conflict, either conventional or involving nuclear weapons, would spell the end of their regime.

Instead, North Korea will probably seek a second-strike capability in which at least a portion of its nuclear forces survives an initial attack, whether conventional or nuclear, with the capacity to retaliate and inflict unacceptable punishment. If it can credibly threaten a nuclear counterstrike with even a few warheads, this may be enough to restrain any South Korean or US efforts to invade or bring down the regime.

The key question is how North Korea would ensure some degree of survivability for its nuclear forces. If, during a crisis, Pyongyang chose to deploy missiles on launchpads that were in the open and susceptible to detection by satellite, these would be vulnerable to a preemptive attack. Such an exposed posture would encourage North Korea to launch-on-warning, a very unstable proposition during a crisis. Several alternatives are possible. First, North Korea could store road-mobile, nuclear-tipped missiles in hardened sites, particularly locations in the mountains of the Korean Peninsula. Pyongyang has already demonstrated exemplary tunneling capability. Such a capability would let it construct launch facilities that would be extraordinarily resistant to enemy strikes. These locations would provide protection and concealment during peacetime, and the missiles could be rolled out when necessary for firing.

A second possibility is the deployment of nuclear-capable missiles on a road-mobile system under which the missiles are loaded on mobile launchers and moved about randomly along North Korea's network of roads. These missiles could be moved into hardened shelters for protection and concealment if there was a crisis. However, a road-mobile force would create other difficulties, including maintaining command and control over these weapons and developing missiles and warheads sufficiently rugged to withstand the jarring of road travel while remaining capable of an accurate launch. These are not easy technologies to master and could be very difficult to implement during a crisis or combat situation. Because most of North Korea's missile force is liquid-fueled instead of solid-fueled, furthermore, Pyongyang would face additional challenges with maintenance and safety while the force was on strategic alert.

A road mobile system that might be postured for launch-on-warning raises some important challenges for command and control. Authority in North Korea is centralized and emanates almost exclusively from its leader, Kim Jong-un. He simultaneously holds the positions of chairman of the National Defense Commissions, general secretary of the Korean Workers' Party, and supreme commander of the Korean People's Army.[36] There is little doubt that command and control in the North Korean military begins with Kim Jong-un. Most likely, the decision to launch nuclear weapons would require a direct order from him. However, a road-mobile system would be susceptible to communication disruptions. Communication failures would also jeopardize the ability of these road-mobile systems to launch-on-warning because they might not be aware of an incoming attack until it was too late. To ensure that these systems could operate as intended might require some degree of delegation of command authority to local officers. However, a highly centralized government such as that of North Korea is unlikely to grant such authority to lower levels for fear of losing control of these highly valued military assets.

A third possibility is the eventual development of submarine- or ship-launched ballistic missiles. In September 1993 North Korea bought twelve decommissioned Russian submarines, including Golf II–class boats, from a Japanese company for scrap. When operational, these submarines could each carry up to three Soviet SS-N-5 submarine-launched ballistic missiles. North Korea is also working on a new missile based on the Soviet SS-N-6 (R-27, or Taepodong-X). This missile is intended as a land-based mobile weapon, but reports indicate that North Korean engineers are striving to adapt it for deployment on board a submarine or surface combatant. The missile has an estimated range of 2,500 kilometers. The purchase of the Golf II–class submarines did not include the missiles or electronic firing systems, but it did include significant subsystems that, if suitably adapted, could accommodate the R-27/Taepodong-X.[37] If North Korea managed to deploy even a limited submarine missile force, it would significantly improve the survivability of its nuclear weapons, allowing it to threaten the US homeland. In short, a North Korean submarine capability would transform military and strategic calculations for all players in East Asia.

Fourth, a final method of "hardening" North Korean missiles against enemy action, and increasing their survivability in a crisis, is to construct launch sites close to the Sino-Korean border. In September 2008, during a closed-door session with the South Korean National Assembly, South Korean defense minister Lee Sang-hee identified a new North Korean launch facility located approximately 40 to 50 kilometers from the Chinese border. The base is designed for missiles larger than those launched from the site on North Korea's east coast. It may be intended for military purposes, or it may be designed to support the North Korean space program. Lee noted that the site was approximately 80 percent complete. Other analysts have observed that the Tongch'ang-dong site is larger and more advanced than its forebears. The North

Korean missile program is clearly continuing to grow, which demonstrates Pyong-yang's desire to develop both ballistic missile and space launch programs.[38] Although not physically "hardened," the site's proximity to China would make it difficult to hit without sending nuclear debris across the border and risking collateral damage—side effects that could embroil Beijing in a conflict. Thus, locating nuclear weapons at this site would bolster their survivability, and in turn Pyongyang's deterrent.

If Pyongyang entertains serious doubts about the ability of the force to ride out an initial attack, North Korean forces might adopt a launch-on-warning posture. As noted above, this means that they would not wait to absorb an attack before retaliat-ing. Instead, North Korea would launch its retaliatory attack upon receipt of a strate-gic warning, so that enemy missiles or air strikes would hit empty North Korean launch facilities. North Korea would also face the dilemma of deciding whether the assault was limited or intended to end the regime. If the attack were limited, perhaps to punish Pyongyang for some transgression, a North Korean nuclear response would escalate the conflict and pose a risk that the regime would come to an end. From Pyongyang's perspective, it might not matter if the attack on the North were conven-tional or nuclear; an effort to take out North Korea's nuclear weapons through either nuclear or conventional preemption would probably have the same strategic effect. Clearly, launch-on-warning is a dangerous force posture that would put North Korean forces on high alert, in danger of launching with little warning or by mistake.

Implications for Security on the Korean Peninsula

The implications of an operational North Korean nuclear capability are troubling. North Korea is unlikely to use nuclear weapons in any offensive military action, and Pyongyang has given a no-first-use pledge. The regime would be condemned internationally not only for an invasion of the South but also for its use of nuclear weapons. Under these circumstances, South Korea and the United States would likely move to eliminate the regime, which would put an end to this security problem once and for all. If the regime were in its last days, it is possible that it might lash out with a nuclear strike. Needless to say, regime collapse represents an uncertain and dangerous scenario.

Most likely, North Korea will rely on nuclear weapons to deter a United States–South Korea invasion and to use for political leverage. In February 2009 Dennis Blair, the US director of national intelligence, noted in congressional testimony that "Pyongyang probably views its nuclear weapons as being more for deterrence, inter-national prestige, and coercive diplomacy than for war fighting and would consider using nuclear weapons only under certain narrow circumstances. . . . Pyongyang would not attempt to use nuclear weapons against US forces or territory unless it perceived the regime to be on the verge of military defeat or risked an irretrievable loss of control."[39]

Pyongyang will do its best to maintain a force that has some level of survivability, and thus sow doubt that a preemptive strike could eliminate all its nuclear weapons.

If it is able to continue increasing the range of its ballistic missiles, this will eventually allow it to threaten the US homeland, which would drastically change Washington's strategic calculus. Once North Korea has improved its nuclear weapon and ballistic missile capabilities to the extent that it can hit the United States, it will become a more direct and serious threat to US security. For South Korea and Japan, this will become a reality as soon as North Korea weaponizes a warhead for placement on a Scud or Nodong ballistic missile.

However, the credibility of even this posture raises some difficult questions. Patrick Morgan notes that in asymmetrical deterrence situations like the one on the Korean Peninsula, threats to retaliate are more complicated. For deterrence to be credible, the challenger must believe that the defender will actually carry out its threats. Yet if North Korea were to execute a threat involving nuclear weapons, it would escalate the conflict and thus provoke a stronger military challenger to respond with even greater force—perhaps its own nuclear weapons. The defender's use of nuclear weapons, then, would escalate the conflict to its disadvantage and perhaps bring about its own downfall. Consequently, a challenger might not find a threat from Pyongyang to use nuclear weapons credible. The challenger might call North Korea's bluff in the belief that Pyongyang does not wish to see its regime come to an end.[40]

Thus, demonstrating credibility in a relationship of asymmetrical deterrence involves an inherent contradiction. Can North Korea credibly threaten the use of nuclear weapons, given the likelihood that doing so would bring about its demise? Yet the perception of an irrational North Korean regime that might lash out may be sufficient to deter South Korean and US actions, which would provide the necessary deterrent effect for North Korea.[41] Given even the possibility of North Korean retaliation, based on Schelling's concept that "the threat that leaves something to chance," Pyongyang's threats might be sufficient to deter an attack. It is important, moreover, to recall that Pyongyang may not necessarily need nuclear weapons to successfully deter Seoul and Washington. As noted above, Pyongyang has hundreds of artillery pieces and multiple rocket launchers trained on Seoul, which could destroy the South's capital before they could be hit. A preemptive strike would need to take out these conventional assets along with any North Korean nuclear weapons—a daunting task that bolsters North Korea's ability to deter.

The size and relative vulnerability of the North Korean force raises further questions. Because North Korea's force is small and vulnerable to a preemptive strike, it may be on hair-trigger alert and driven by a "use or lose" rationale. Even a limited conventional strike by US or South Korean forces, or possibly an exercise, could be misread by Pyongyang as the prelude to a full-scale invasion. Moreover, if facing the possibility of regime change, North Korea might believe that it has little to lose in responding with nuclear weapons. These dimensions raise serious concerns for the stability of the North Korean force and the dangers of escalation in a crisis.

In all probability, North Korea's leaders may believe that its nuclear capability has increased their political influence and expanded their room to maneuver through brinkmanship. Provocative rhetoric and actions are already a staple of North Korea's diplomacy. Nuclear weapons allow its leaders to push the envelope further because they believe these ultimately destructive arms can deter action against them if the situation escalates. Thus, nuclear weapons will give North Korea a trump card if its provocative behavior inflames an issue beyond its control.

Conclusion

The future of North Korea's nuclear program is very uncertain. North Korea may return to the Six-Party Talks, where it will surely be pressured to relinquish its nuclear capability. Some hold out hope that with the right deal, North Korea may yet be convinced that denuclearization is the best course of action for the future of the regime. But considerable evidence and logic indicate that North Korea will never fully and verifiably give up its nuclear program. After all, North Korea lives in a dangerous neighborhood, and nuclear weapons address some important security concerns. North Korea may choose to remain a nuclear weapon state based on the military and political power an unconventional arsenal confers, both at home and abroad.

This chapter has assumed North Korea will retain its nuclear weapons, eventually developing them into a small but operational force intended to deter South Korea and the United States. It is not a foregone conclusion that events will bear out this assumption. But if it does—if Pyongyang remains a nuclear power, honing its rudimentary capability into an operational force—its efforts will complicate East Asian security immensely. If the Six-Party Talks ultimately fail to achieve denuclearization, all countries in the region will need to work at maintaining a stable security environment, encouraging North Korea to adopt a nuclear strategy that retains a "no first use" policy, strong command-and-control, and a stable nuclear weapons posture. Deterrence on the Korean Peninsula will take on a new dimension—North Korean nuclear weapons—and all parties will need to figure out how to live with it to maintain peace and security in the region.

Notes

1. "DPRK's Will to Strive for Building Nuclear-Free World Reiterated," Korean Central News Agency, September 30, 2009.

2. Peter Hayes, "The Stalker State: North Korean Proliferation and the End of American Nuclear Hegemony," *Policy Forum Online* 06–82A, Nautilus Institute, October 4, 2006, www.nautilus.org/fora/security/0682Hayes.html.

3. Glenn Snyder, *Deterrence and Defense* (Princeton, NJ: Princeton University Press, 1961), 9–16. See also John J. Mearsheimer, *Conventional Deterrence* (Ithaca, NY: Cornell University Press, 1983), 28–30.

4. Ibid.

5. Kenneth N. Waltz, "Nuclear Myths and Political Realities," *American Political Science Review* 84, no. 3 (September 1990): 734.

6. Patrick M. Morgan, *Deterrence Now* (Cambridge: Cambridge University Press, 2003), 13–14.

7. Terence Roehrig, "Restraining the Hegemon: North Korea, the United States and Asymmetrical Deterrence," *Pacific Focus* 20, no. 2 (Fall 2005): 7–51.

8. See Alexander L. George and Richard Smoke, *Deterrence in American Foreign Policy: Theory and Practice* (New York: Columbia University Press, 1974), 75; Robert Jervis, Richard Ned Lebow, and Janice Gross Stein, *Psychology and Deterrence* (Baltimore: Johns Hopkins University Press, 1985); and Patrick M. Morgan, *Deterrence: A Conceptual Analysis* (Beverly Hills, CA: Sage, 1983), 42–79.

9. General John H. Tilelli Jr., Statement before the Senate Armed Services Committee, 106th Congress, 1st Session, March 4, 1999.

10. *The Economist*, June 17–23, 2000.

11. See Denny Roy, "North Korea and the 'Madman Theory,'" *Security Dialogue* 25, no. 3 (September 1994): 307–16.

12. William W. Kaufmann, *The Requirements of Deterrence* (Princeton, NJ: Center for International Studies, 1954), 19.

13. Choe Sang-Hun, "North Korea Says It Has 'Weaponized' Plutonium," *New York Times*, January 18, 2009, www.nytimes.com/2009/01/18/1orld/asia/18korea.htm.

14. For the details on North Korean ballistic missiles, see Joseph S. Bermudez Jr., *The Armed Forces of North Korea* (New York: I. B. Tauris, 2001), and Daniel A. Pinkston, *The North Korean Ballistic Missile Program* (Carlisle, PA: Strategic Studies Institute, US Army War College, 2008), www.strategicstudiesinstitute.army/mil/pdffiles/PUB842.pdf.

15. Pinkston, *North Korean Ballistic Missile Program.*

16. Federation of American Scientists, "Taep'o-dong 2 (TD-2)," www.fas.org/nuke/guide/dprk/missle/td-2.htm.

17. James Cartwright, "Hearing to Receive Testimony on Ballistic Missile Defense Programs in Review of the Defense Authorization Request from Fiscal Year 2010 and the Future Years Defense Program," US Senate Armed Services Committee, June 16, 2009, http://armed-services.senate.gov/Transcripts/2009/06%20June/09–44%20-%206 –16–09.pdf.

18. Elisabeth Bumiller and David E. Sanger, "Gates Warns of North Korea Missile Threat to US," *New York Times*, January 11, 2011, www.nytimes.com/2011/01/12/world/asia/12military.html.

19. "DPRK Permanent Representative Sends Letter to President of UNSC," Korean Central News Agency, September 4, 2009, available at www.kcna.co.jp.

20. US Department of Defense, *Joint Operating Environment 2008: Challenges and Implications for the Future Joint Force* (Washington, DC: US Government Printing Office, 2008), 32, www.jfcom.mil/newslink/storyarchive/2008/JOE2008.pdf.

21. Robert Gates, "A Balanced Strategy: Reprogramming the Pentagon for a New Age," *Foreign Affairs* 88, no. 1 (January–February 2009): 32.

22. "US Recognizes DPRK as Nuclear Weapons State," Korean Central News Agency, December 11, 2008, available at www.kcna.co.jp.

23. Sean McCormack, "Daily Press Briefing," US Department of State, December 10, 2008, http://2001–2009.state.gov/r/pa/prs/dpb/2008/113078.htm.

24. Bruce W. Bennett, Christopher P. Twomey, and Gregory F. Treverton, *What Are Asymmetric Strategies?* (Santa Monica, CA: RAND Corporation, 1999), 3.

25. Scott D. Sagan and Kenneth N. Waltz, *The Spread of Nuclear Weapons: A Debate Renewed*, 2nd ed. (New York: W. W. Norton, 2002), 9.

26. Thomas C. Schelling, *Arms and Influence* (New Haven, CT: Yale University Press, 1966), 97–98.

27. Michael J. Mazarr, *North Korea and the Bomb: A Case Study in Nonproliferation* (New York: St. Martin's Press, 1995); Victor D. Cha and David C. Kang, *Nuclear North Korea: A Debate on Engagement Strategies* (New York: Columbia University Press, 2003); Michael O'Hanlon and Mike Mochizuki, *Crisis on the Korean Peninsula* (New York: McGraw-Hill, 2003); Mike Chinoy, *Meltdown: The Inside Story of the North Korean Nuclear Crisis* (New York: St. Martin's Press, 2008); and Joel S. Wit, Daniel B. Poneman, and Robert L. Gallucci, *Going Critical: The First North Korean Nuclear Crisis* (Washington, DC: Brookings Institution Press, 2004).

28. "DPRK FM on Its Stand to Suspend Its Participation in Six-Party Talks for Indefinite Period," Korean Central News Agency, February 10, 2005, available at www.kcna.co.jp.

29. "DPRK Foreign Ministry Clarifies Stand on New Measure to Bolster War Deterrent," Korean Central News Agency, October 3, 2006, available at www.kcna.co.jp.

30. "DPRK Foreign Ministry's Spokesman Dismisses US Wrong Assertion," Korean Central News Agency, January 17, 2009, available at www.kcna.co.jp.

31. "DPRK Foreign Ministry Declares Strong Counter-Measures against UNSC's 'Resolution 1874,'" Korean Central News Agency, June 13, 2009, available at www.kcna.co.jp.

32. Han S. Park, "Military-First Politics (Songun): Understanding Kim Jong-il's North Korea," in *Academic Paper Series: On Korea*, vol. 1 (Seoul: Korea Economic Institute, 2007), 126.

33. For an assessment of North Korea's nuclear future, see Jonathan D. Pollack, "North Korea's Nuclear Weapons Program to 2015: Three Scenarios," *Asia Policy* 3 (January 2007): 105–23.

34. Lucy Hornby and Jack Kim, "Kim Jong-il Says Wants Denuclearization of Peninsula," *Washington Post*, January 23, 2009, www.washingtonpost.com/wp-dyn/content/article/2009/01/23/AR2009012300470.html.

35. "DPRK Foreign Ministry Clarifies Stand"; "DPRK Foreign Ministry Spokesman Totally Refutes UNSC 'Resolution,'" Korean Central News Agency, October 17, 2005, available at www.kcna.co.jp.

36. See Bermudez, *Armed Forces*, 20–55.

37. See Steven A. Hildreth, *North Korean Ballistic Missile Threat to the United States*, CRS Report for Congress RS21473 (Washington, DC: Congressional Research Service, 2009); "CNS Special Report on North Korean Ballistic Missile Capabilities," Center for Nonproliferation Studies, March 22, 2006, 2, http://cns.miis.edu/stories/pdfs/060321.pdf.

38. "N Korea 'Builds New Missile Site,'" BBC News, September 11, 2008, http://news.bbc.co.uk/2/hi/asia-pacific/7609718.stm; Haroon Siddique, "North Korea 'Building New Missile Base,'" *The Guardian*, November 4, 2008, www.guardian.co.uk/world/2008/nov/04/northkorea-missiles.

39. Dennis C. Blair, "Annual Threat Assessment of the Intelligence Community for the Senate Select Committee on Intelligence," report for US Senate, February 12, 2009, 24–25, http://intelligence.senate.gov/090212/blair.pdf.

40. Morgan, *Deterrence Now*, 270–72.

41. Roehrig, "Restraining the Hegemon," 7–51.

CHAPTER 6

CHANGING PERCEPTIONS OF EXTENDED DETERRENCE IN JAPAN

James L. Schoff

Nᴏʀᴛʜ ᴋᴏʀᴇᴀ'ѕ 2006 ᴀɴᴅ 2009 nuclear weapon tests and the subsequent "debates" in Japan about whether the nation should ponder its own nuclear deterrent renewed attention to the subject of Japan and nuclear weapons. Pundits and policymakers in both the United States and Japan contemplated the implications of Pyongyang's nuclear breakout, and many wondered if this marked the beginning of fundamental change in Japanese thinking on these issues. Just as North Korea's long-range missile test over Japanese airspace in 1998 contributed significantly to Japan's decision a few years later to embrace America's missile defense development program, might the nuclear tests eventually prove to be a similar watershed moment in Japanese defense policy? Would there be a rising tide of Japanese sentiment in favor of reexamining the Three Non-Nuclear Principles of nonpossession, nonmanufacture, and nonintroduction?

The short answer to the nuclear question in Japan is "no." There is little evidence to suggest that Japan has notably more interest in developing an indigenous nuclear deterrent as a result of North Korea's tests, and Japan has not taken steps to shorten its theoretical lead time for launching a domestic nuclear weapons program.[1] The perceived threats are not sufficient to warrant such a dramatic policy shift, and Japan's alliance with the United States is still considered up to the challenges at hand. Moreover, Japanese nuclear weapons development has been even less likely in the near term since the more liberal, pacifist-influenced Democratic Party of Japan (DPJ) came to power after winning a historic election in September 2009. The 2011 Fukushima nuclear disaster of course did nothing to cure the Japanese people's nuclear allergy.

North Korea's nuclear tests and continuing missile programs are, however, examples of Japan's eroding security position in the region, and they contribute to a growing sense of vulnerability among the defense policy elite in Japan. These anxieties are compounded by China's military modernization, its space exploration, and its rising economic and diplomatic influence in the region. Japan has always been dependent on energy imports, which constitute about 94 percent of its primary energy supply, but its reliance on food imports is also high (more than 60 percent of its calorie intake), and instability in the Middle East and the rising share of food imports from China have exacerbated Tokyo's unease.[2]

For more than half a century, Japan's alliance with the United States has helped to mitigate these uncertainties, and the so-called US nuclear umbrella has been a primary symbol of America's commitment to regional security and Japan's defense. Japanese perceptions of extended deterrence are changing subtly, however, as both the regional security landscape and Japanese domestic politics undergo transformation. The monopoly on policymaking long held by high-level bureaucrats and conservative politicians in Japan broke apart dramatically when the DPJ assumed the reins of government in late 2009, giving greater voice to left-leaning and populist leaders. Where policy insiders once worried most about a possible US abandonment of Japan and its core interests, prevailing public concerns about Japan's becoming entangled in US foreign policy adventurism and conflict abroad now carry more weight. Meanwhile, Japan's wariness about China's rising power lies just below the surface, which contributes to fluid and unpredictable attitudes toward deterrence and the role of the United States–Japan alliance.

Unsurprisingly, the North Korean nuclear tests and domestic political change in South Korea have also affected perceptions of extended deterrence in America's other major Northeast Asian ally. For decades, South Korea's top security concern was an overwhelming lightning strike by North Korea's massive army. Forward-deployed US conventional and tactical nuclear forces were a vital component of the allies' deterrent strategy. This was less of a nuclear "umbrella" than it was a nuclear "spear" to deter and, if necessary, defeat a North Korean ground assault. US tactical nuclear weapons represented an integral part of the allies' plan to defend Seoul in the 1960s and 1970s, when North Korea maintained a sizable conventional military advantage.

As the United States and South Korea strengthened their conventional capabilities vis-à-vis North Korea's military infrastructure in the 1980s and early 1990s, it became possible for the United States to withdraw all its nuclear weapons from South Korean territory. Seoul's liberal governments in the late 1990s and early 2000s voiced fewer and fewer concerns about US abandonment compared with earlier years, and Seoul sought to reduce the country's dependence on Washington for deterrence support. More recently, however, the pendulum has swung back again. North Korean nuclear gains have prompted calls in the South for the United States to reaffirm its nuclear umbrella. By the late 2000s the newly elected conservative administration of Lee Myung-bak was emphasizing the importance not only of the US nuclear umbrella but also of possibly enhancing the nation's "nuclear sovereignty" by expanding its control over the nuclear fuel cycle. This ostensibly constituted a move to earn the right to reprocess spent nuclear fuel and reduce waste, but some considered it an initial hedge in case Seoul one day determined that the country needed an indigenous nuclear deterrent.[3]

It is common within alliances for countries to struggle with the tension between fears of abandonment and fears of entanglement. This has been abundantly true in East Asia. Where a country resides on that spectrum often informs its decision making at critical junctures, whether it means allowing the introduction of US nuclear weapons to its ports or its soil or insisting on greater political and operational distance between the partners. For many years since the late 1990s, Japan worried more about abandonment than entanglement when it came to tough deterrence questions. South Korea tilted in the other direction. More recently, the allies' perceptions have seemingly moved in opposite directions. It is important to understand why this is the case, how significant and lasting a change this could be, and what it implies for deterrence in the region. To get some perspective on the answers to these questions, it is helpful to review the history of deterrence debates in both countries.

For a variety of reasons, this chapter focuses on Japan as the critical path for nuclear deterrence in the region. The US nuclear umbrella over South Korea remains important—increasingly so, in fact—but the political sensitivity associated with extended deterrence is higher in Japan. It takes more effort to reassure Tokyo, whereas South Korea enjoys options for defense spending and offensive strike that Japan has denied itself based on how it interprets its Constitution. Theoretical contingencies involving nuclear weapons are more numerous in the Japanese case (involving China, North Korea, and even Russia), whereas South Korean scenarios typically involve only North Korea. Seoul is inherently reluctant to use nuclear weapons on Korean soil, moreover, especially now that the allies enjoy qualitative conventional superiority.

A major reason why South Korean scenarios mainly involve North Korea is because US forces on the peninsula do not enjoy the same strategic flexibility they do in Japan, and this will remain true for the foreseeable future. This exposes the United States–Japan alliance to wedge strategies. An adversary could threaten the use of nuclear weapons as a means of intimidating Tokyo. One plausible scenario would see China resort to nuclear saber rattling to discourage Japanese leaders from consenting to the use of American air assets from Kadena Air Force Base in a Taiwan contingency. A US nuclear posture sufficient for deterrence and for defending Japan, then, should also satisfy Washington's other allies in the region; but the reverse is not necessarily true. This dynamic will likely persist, but changing perceptions of deterrence in Northeast Asia could challenge long-held assumptions.

Extended Deterrence and Japan: Past and Present

For decades extended deterrence was thought of in relatively simple terms in Japan, as characterized by robust US security commitments to its allies overseas and underwritten predominately by a nuclear umbrella to deter war with the Soviet Bloc. The US commitment to counter the Soviet threat was largely unquestioned in Tokyo, and the details about how deterrence worked mattered little. This helped shape an environment that allowed Japan to be fervently nonnuclear in its public statements and government policies.

Although one-third of the known nuclear weapon states in the world (China, North Korea, and Russia) are immediate neighbors of Japan, Japan remains a non–nuclear weapon state. Tokyo has long worked fervently in international forums to promote nuclear nonproliferation and disarmament.[4] Japan's Atomic Energy Basic Law, which was enacted in 1955, clearly states that research on, the development of, and the use of atomic energy will be limited to peaceful purposes. Japan joined the International Atomic Energy Agency in 1957. In 1967 Prime Minister Sato Eisaku announced that his government had adopted the Three Non-Nuclear Principles: no possession, no production, and no introduction. Japan affixed its signature to the Nuclear Non-Proliferation Treaty (NPT) in 1970 and ratified the accord in 1976. Japan supported the indefinite extension of the NPT in 1995 and signed the International Atomic Energy Agency's Additional Protocol to the NPT in 1998. Sato's role in solidifying Japan's commitment to abstain from developing nuclear weapons was largely responsible for making him Japan's only recipient of the Nobel Peace Prize in 1974—even though it later came to light that he considered his nuclear disavowal a "mistake" and that Washington and Tokyo had in fact negotiated a secret agreement allowing for the introduction of certain kinds of nuclear activities.[5]

That Japan remains the only nation ever to suffer a nuclear attack, combined with its pacifist Constitution prohibiting the maintenance of "war potential," has long made the mere mention of a possible nuclear option for Japan a third rail in Japanese politics. Japanese public opinion has never favored nuclear weapons, and more than a few Japanese policymakers have damaged their careers by calling for fuller and more open debate on the topic. The North Korean nuclear tests, however, seemed to weaken this taboo. After all, a nuclear North Korea has long been considered a catalyst that could push Japan over the nuclear threshold. For example, Japanese foreign minister Muto Kabun stated in 1993 that "if North Korea develops nuclear weapons and that becomes a threat to Japan, first there is the nuclear umbrella of the United States upon which we can rely. But if it comes down to a crunch, possessing the will that 'we can do it ourselves' is important."[6] Japanese officials and opinion leaders have uttered similar sentiments over the years, while the government has consistently argued that possessing nuclear weapons is not unconstitutional, theoretically speaking.

The truth is that raising the nuclear issue in Japan, although certainly sensitive, has never been forbidden as absolutely as many Japan watchers contend. Nor is Japan's so-called nuclear allergy necessarily a genetic condition. There have always been a small number of influential nuclear advocates in postwar Japan, and a major reason why they remain in the minority is because Japan has enjoyed the luxury of nuclear deterrence supplied by the United States. The credibility of the United States–Japan alliance and the extended deterrent has been a mainstay for Japan's sense of security, along with another important factor: the absence of a serious, consistent existential threat to Japan. Whenever events have called one or both of these factors into question, Tokyo has taken to rethinking its nonnuclear posture—at least on the hypothetical plane.

China's first nuclear test, which came in 1964, represented one example of such a reconsideration. Senior leaders of the Liberal Democratic Party (LDP) called on the government to reexamine Japan's nuclear policies. US officials were surprised at Prime Minister Sato's suggestion that Japan should possess nuclear weapons if the Chinese Communists did, and that although the Japanese public at large appeared unready for such a break with past policy, the younger generation could evidently be "educated" to be more flexible on this point.[7] In the end Japan decided to forgo nuclear weapons, but the government was careful to hedge against changing circumstances in two ways.

Tokyo's first hedge was to confirm that the United States remained committed to using nuclear weapons in defense of Japan if necessary, and to address certain logistical details to assure that this commitment remained feasible. In January 1965, for example, Sato asked US defense secretary Robert McNamara to deploy nuclear weapons against China if "war" broke out with Japan. McNamara gave this assurance.[8] The second hedge involved developing the basis for an indigenous nuclear weapon program in case one were to ever become necessary. According to an important policy-planning study prepared by the Ministry of Foreign Affairs (MOFA) in 1969, for example, "regardless of joining the NPT or not, we will keep the economic and technical potential for the production of nuclear weapons, while seeing to it that Japan will not be interfered with in this regard."[9]

Unfurling the Nuclear Umbrella

The United States–Japan alliance established by the 1960 Treaty of Mutual Cooperation and Security (a.k.a. the United States–Japan Security Treaty) did not explicitly countenance extended deterrence or a nuclear umbrella protecting Japan.[10] Public aversion to any mention of nuclear weapons was intense at the time, and Japan's somewhat rosy appraisal of the security situation in East Asia did not compel policymakers to seriously question the necessity and credibility of the US nuclear umbrella. China's first nuclear test in 1964 modified Tokyo's views to some degree, but the public response to the nuclear test by the Japanese government was muted, and in any event China was not a target of Japanese defense planning.[11]

Though as early as 1965 Prime Minister Sato and others occasionally talked openly about the idea of sheltering under an American "nuclear umbrella," this remained a controversial subject in the mid-1960s. Left-wing politicians in the Diet argued that extended deterrence was nothing more than a policy pushed by Washington to amplify US influence over non–nuclear weapon states.[12] More than a few Japanese feared being embroiled in a nuclear exchange on the Korean Peninsula or between the United States and the Soviet Union. Sato's 1965 request to McNamara for nuclear protection, consequently, was shrouded in secrecy.

Even inside the bureaucracy, some arguments deviated from the government's quiet acceptance of American nuclear protection. In early 1966, for example, Shimoda Takezo, then MOFA's administrative vice minister, stated in a press conference that he thought Japan was not under the US nuclear umbrella.[13] This comment gave way to a MOFA "unified viewpoint" a few days later. This statement was phrased in a handy double negative, in essence conveying that it was not accurate to say that Japan was not covered by the nuclear umbrella. As noted above, in fact, Sato had already taken the initiative in January 1965 to clarify the US commitment to Japan. His action formed the modern basis for US extended deterrence vis-à-vis Japan.[14]

Sato, initially a supporter of Japanese nuclear armament, changed his mind when confronted with Washington's strong nonproliferation policy and his own government's internal studies suggesting that reliance on US nuclear arms was the best policy for Japan. None of the conceivable alternatives—domestic nuclear weapons production, nuclear sharing with the United States, or Japan overtly denying itself American nuclear protection—appeared viable at that time to most Japanese policymakers. Hence Sato subsequently pushed Washington to clarify its commitment to Tokyo's defense on several occasions, especially in 1965 and 1967 meetings with President Lyndon Johnson.[15] Still, the joint statement promulgated by the two leaders after their January 1965 meeting referred only obliquely to nuclear matters; President Johnson "reaffirmed the United States' determination to abide by its commitment under the treaty to defend Japan against any armed attack from the outside."[16]

Little by little, discussion within Japan and between the allies about extended deterrence and the nuclear umbrella became more open and more common. The main drivers behind this phenomenon in the middle to late 1960s included China's nuclear breakout, the pending 1970 deadline for extending the United States–Japan Security Treaty after its initial ten-year term, and international debate about the NPT, including issues such as the deployment of nuclear weapons to non–nuclear weapon states and how to provide for the security of those states. Combined with other factors, this led Sato to enunciate his Three Non-Nuclear Principles in 1967, to articulate his Four Pillars policy in 1968, and eventually to sign the NPT in 1970 (though Japan waited six years before ratifying the treaty).

The Four Pillars policy was important because it left no doubt about Japan's reliance on the US nuclear umbrella. The policy identifies the Three Non-Nuclear Principles as one pillar. The other three pillars include (1) promoting nuclear power for peaceful purposes, (2) promoting global nuclear disarmament, and (3) relying on the US nuclear deterrent for protection from "the international nuclear threat."[17] With the Four Pillars policy, the nuclear umbrella was officially and fully unfurled—or at least formally acknowledged as such—and it has remained unfurled ever since.

From Japan's perspective, the umbrella was ostensibly intended only to deter a nuclear attack. It was not meant to deter a conventional attack. This was clearly stated whenever the government mentioned the nuclear umbrella in public.[18] From the historical record it remains unclear whether both allies held that position in common or whether one (or both) believed that nuclear weapons could play a broader role in deterrence.

Japanese scholars themselves note that throughout the Cold War Japan rarely discussed extended deterrence in the United States–Japan alliance. Only recently have academics and policymakers begun to examine these concepts more closely, taking a theoretical and strategic perspective that appears uniquely Japanese.[19] This is not to say that Japanese defense planners paid no attention to deterrence-related issues during the Cold War, but they generally approached deterrence in a passive way that reflected their country's dependence on the US nuclear umbrella and forward-deployed US forces. To the extent that scholars did study deterrence, their endeavors were usually confined to describing the theories developed in Europe and the United States and what was going on in NATO vis-à-vis the Soviet Union.

During the Cold War it mattered little exactly how deterrence functioned in East Asia, as long as United States–Japan political and security commitments seemed strong and credible. The United States' nuclear and conventional military capabilities were so overwhelming from the Japanese perspective that Tokyo seldom concerned itself with details. Japan's national security needs were relatively simple and modest, and US power was more than enough to satisfy them as long as the bilateral relationship was solid. With deterrence requirements seemingly well under control, and owing to political sensitivities surrounding military issues, Japan's policies toward deterrence and national defense during the Cold War were more an exercise in political correctness than a product of real strategic calculations.[20]

Arguably, Japan is now only just beginning to incorporate deterrence theory into its defense planning, as evidenced by its articulation of a "dynamic deterrent" concept in its "National Defense Program Guidelines from Fiscal Year 2011." United States–Japan bilateral discussions about deterrent strategy only became regularized in 2011 and do not connect directly to joint decisions about procurement, deployments, or training. The political correctness mentioned here remains an important factor. One sign of this is MOFA's view that the US debate about modernizing or replacing old nuclear warheads is primarily an arms control issue—even though this debate has direct implications for whether the nuclear umbrella shielding Japan will remain viable over the long haul.

The Debate over Defense and Deterrence in Japan

In the early days after the Japan Defense Agency (JDA) was founded in 1954, Japanese defense officials drew up plans to construct and equip Self-Defense Forces (SDF) to protect the country. The first defense plan was ambitious; it envisioned a future military capable of defending itself, with about two thousand aircraft and a large naval fleet consisting of up to seven aircraft carriers. The fleet was meant primarily to counter the threat emanating from the Soviet Union.[21] The second defense plan, which was completed in 1961, better reflected the political and economic realities of the time. The revised United States–Japan Security Treaty had been signed by then. Under this pact the allies decided that Japan need only defend itself within Japanese territory. Tokyo had no need to think about power projection or to create special medical, transportation, or other support units. Such units could reasonably be supplied by the domestic civilian infrastructure. Still, the main driver behind Japanese defense planning was the objective of "threat repulsion," or responding to potential threats, even if this simply meant possessing the ability to hold off an invader long enough for US forces to mobilize and "take over the situation."[22]

Soviet capabilities were on the increase throughout the 1960s. In 1969, accordingly, President Richard Nixon articulated the Guam Doctrine, which emphasized that US allies held primary responsibility for their own defense. Debate emerged in Tokyo regarding how to respond to the growth of Soviet power and to Nixon's sobering words.[23] Threat-based planning demanded that Japan build up its own forces in response to Soviet moves; the Guam Doctrine offered a political opportunity to move from "necessary defense capability" (*shoyo boeiryoku*) toward "independent defense" (*jishu boei*). This was precisely the direction advocated in 1970 by new JDA director, Nakasone Yasuhiro, and in the proposed fourth defense plan, which espoused large budget increases and an emphasis on independent capabilities. But this plan came under fierce attack in the Diet, attracted widespread public opposition, and was quickly withdrawn. The government found itself forced to take a different approach to defense planning, which entailed solidifying minimal or basic defense while turning away from threat-based forces and military strategy.

Kubo Takuya, then the director of the Defense Bureau, penned a bellwether document reflecting Tokyo's decisive turn back to basic defense. Despite opposition from the JDA and the SDF, the reasoning expressed in his memo eventually became a kind of touchstone for postwar defense planning. His so-called KB thesis rationalized a small defense establishment and a close alliance with the United States.[24] "There is no probable threat [to Japan]," he wrote, "though there is a possible threat. . . . Thus, Japan will not aim to build up its defense capability enough to address currently forecast future threats. Instead, Japan will consider a basic standing defense to be the goal of the defense program."

Because there was no "probable threat," Kubo argued, defense spending should be limited to about 1 percent of gross domestic product. He explained that insufficient human resources, land area, and budgets made it unrealistic for Japan to maintain a maximal defense. He insisted that such a posture would be too expensive to achieve in the first place and to sustain over time.[25] In his estimate ground forces need not be the main factor for calculating the power balance between the Soviet Union and Japan, an island nation far different from the continental European NATO member nations adjoining the Warsaw Pact. Japan enjoyed the luxury of focusing on naval forces and air power. The SDF was not significantly inferior to Soviet forces in these domains—especially when US forces were factored in.

Critics derided Kubo for having proposed a "beyond-the-threat theory" or an "escape-from-the-threat theory." In the words of one former JDA official, "The idea of threat opposition was like the ABCs of defense preparation. There was a lot of criticism saying that if Japan lost its footing with regard to this fundamental component, the future of its defense capability would be in jeopardy."[26] But JDA officials proffered few real answers of their own for the kinds of potential threats the country faced, particularly with regard to nuclear weapons. Another former JDA official recalled, "Not long after Nakasone arrived, he asked us to work out the defense capability estimates for both a nuclear-weapon-equipped force and a conventional force." In other words, what kind of conventional military deterrent would be necessary to counter the Soviet Union on its own, if Japan opted for such a force? "I was told that we were doing this 'to determine how much merit should be placed on nuclear weapons.' . . . We tried to figure it out, but eventually we had to come back with the answer that we just didn't know."[27]

Kubo assumed that Japan had no need to develop nuclear weapons to bolster its national prestige, and he believed that nuclear weapons had no military utility for Japan. Japan was too dense and too small, he reasoned; Japan would always lose more than it gained in a nuclear exchange. No one would believe that Japan would actually use its nuclear weapons, and that reality vitiated their potential deterrent effect. "There is no choice but to rely on the US extended deterrence," he concluded, and so Japan should focus on maintaining its trustworthy and friendly bilateral relationship with the United States, making itself important to both West and East, and strengthening bilateral military cooperation.[28] Interestingly, Kubo also suggested that Japan "establish a structure to develop considerable nuclear armament capability at any time, . . . [so] the United States will get worried about unstable international relations due to nuclear proliferation and will desire to maintain the United States–Japan security effort including extended deterrence"[29]

The mainstream idea among Japanese military analysts at that time was so-called rational deterrence theory. Rational deterrence assumes that if even the possibility of retaliation is as low as 1 percent, a challenger will be deterred from military action by the unimaginably high destructive power of nuclear forces. As Kubo and others argued, for Japan the credibility of the US nuclear umbrella was primarily a psychological matter. The only thing Japan could and should do was trust the United States, as long as Washington publicly promised to defend Tokyo. One MOFA official explained it this way: "When it comes to the nuclear umbrella, it is like a talisman from the United States. Japan is not sure how it works, but they put their faith in it and believe it will protect them."[30]

But extended deterrence is more than just a psychological matter for Japan—as defense analysts and academics argued in a secret government-sponsored report on nuclear weapons compiled in 1968–70. What was most important, the report explained, was the thinking of both sets of policymakers involved in a potential conflict—say, with the United States as the "deterrer" and China as the "deterree." In such a scenario it made little difference what Japan thought. The report concluded that Japan could do little but rely on the US nuclear umbrella, regardless of whether it was credible in Japanese eyes.[31] This outlook helps explain Japan's sensitivity to warming United States–China relations or to increased US vulnerability to Chinese strategic nuclear forces. Either development would tend to boost Chinese confidence that the United States would not retaliate on Japan's behalf with full force.

As the Cold War wound down, theoretical and strategic analyses of extended deterrence began appearing more frequently in Japan's academic community. Some began to question assumptions about deterrence and the alliance, though scholars could not agree on why they doubted the US security guarantee. Ogawa, for example, maintained that the credibility of extended deterrence depends on the ethnic, cultural, and historical ties between the provider and recipient of deterrence, and that the strategic importance of the country being protected has little effect on deterrence credibility. As a result, he reasoned, America's strong historical and cultural ties with Europe meant that the nuclear umbrella over NATO was sturdier than the one covering Japan.[32]

Others, like Noguchi, argued that a country will risk its own security to protect others only when its national interest is in jeopardy, and so the idea of shared interests and codependence is crucial. Self-interest and material factors are more important than psychological bonds rooted in common culture or history. Noguchi worried that after the Cold War, in a unipolar world, Washington might not value its alliances as strongly as it had before. In turn, the credibility of extended deterrence could suffer.[33] For several years after the Cold War, however, this academic debate remained just that—academic. The preponderance of American power meant that few in Japan believed there was anything that could seriously threaten the alliance. Or, more accurately, few believed that any country could threaten the United

States. As before, the workings of deterrence within the alliance were simply not a matter of pressing interest for Japanese defense planners.

A notable exception to Japan's near-indifference to deterrence arises from China's and North Korea's development and modernization of medium- and long-range ballistic missiles. Fears of a Chinese or North Korean missile attack explain why Tokyo has gone to the time and expense of deploying missile defenses. During the Cold War Japan considered the US nuclear umbrella to be "existential deterrence" because the prime focus of deterrence was preventing large-scale Soviet aggression. Some Japanese scholars now argue, however, that regional contingencies, coercive diplomacy, or asymmetrical threats represent the main challenges. As a result, Japan should assess the pros and cons of other types of deterrence, including deterrence by denial through missile defenses, an indigenous preemptive strike capability, or indigenous nuclear armament.[34]

Bolstering the missile defense component of deterrence represents an attractive step for Japan. After North Korea launched a Taepo Dong missile through Japanese airspace in 1998, it became easier politically to support such a program. Public support increased further in 2003, after Pyongyang expelled international nuclear inspectors and resumed reprocessing plutonium for use in nuclear weapons. Missile defense fits with Japan's defensive-minded military stance and its preference to deter through denial. It has also helped strengthen the alliance with the United States, because joint development of missile defenses ranks high among Washington's priorities.

Codevelopment and codeployment has by no means been cost free for Tokyo, however, and not just in financial terms. Since Japan agreed in December 2003 to collaborate on putting a new missile defense system in place, the government has spent an annual average of 1.3 trillion on the program—which has commensurately reduced the funds available for other defense budget categories. Japan has also incurred diplomatic criticism from China and Russia, which have insisted that missile defense could be a destabilizing force in the region and would compel them to develop more and better missiles. If Beijing and Moscow follow through on such warnings, Japanese designs could well backfire, which would force China in particular to depart from minimum deterrence and build up overbearing missile forces.

Many Japanese scholars are quick to note that missile defense plays only a supplemental role in the alliance's overall deterrent posture. They emphasize that in the case of China, allied conventional superiority is more important than missile defense.[35] This comes in part from the dilemma of extended deterrence. As one Japanese scholar explains, deterrence providers seek to limit conflicts to the region they are protecting, in order to avoid an all-out war endangering their own homelands.[36] The United States, it follows, will do everything it can to prevent the escalation or expansion of an East Asian regional conflict. If it cannot do this through overwhelming conventional superiority, then it could default to a policy akin to appeasement, seeing such a posture as the only way to avoid resorting to nuclear weapons. As a former MOFA diplomat explained, "the conventional superiority advantage is critical, because it obviates the whole debate about whether or not Washington would 'sacrifice Los Angeles to save Tokyo' in a nuclear exchange."[37] So even though nuclear weapons constitute a major psychological component of extended deterrence—and the component that is most talked about—Japan has increasingly shifted its gaze to the conventional aspects.

In essence this is a Japanese version of the old European fear of "decoupling." During the Cold War some Europeans fretted that the United States might detach itself from its strategic commitment to Western Europe in the face of an overbearing Soviet Union. Decoupling fears waxed and waned throughout the Cold War, depending on the intensity of the security situation. Now some in Japan are concerned about the implications of current trends in East Asia, and they thus suggest that "if the United States–China military balance in East Asia reaches parity, then the credibility of the US nuclear umbrella will be gravely shaken."[38] Following this line of thinking, China's nuclear force modernization program combined with continued US cuts should exacerbate the decoupling problem for Japan, unless allied conventional superiority is maintained.

Looking Ahead in Japan

There are four basic schools of thought about how Japan ought to stiffen deterrence: (1) those who advocate self-help, implying greater security independence from the United States; (2) those who support the alliance but advocate hedging assertively against the potential for US abandonment ("hedging for substance"); (3) those who support hedging, but primarily as a means of deterring abandonment ("hedging for show"); and (4) those who seek greater military cooperation with the United States as a way to deter abandonment (urging Tokyo to make itself an "indispensable ally").[39] Under Prime Minister Junichiro Koizumi and many of his LDP successors in the 2000s, the fourth group held sway, but a few security policy choices drifted into the second and third categories, such as missile defense, the development of Hyuga-class helicopter-carrying destroyers, and the launching of intelligence satellites. Since World War II true security independence has never been a serious option for Japan, but political change and realignment in Japan has the potential to shake up the traditional status quo in this area.

The DPJ generally supports the alliance with America, albeit with a slightly more independent streak compared with the LDP due to conflicting political ideologies. One could even argue that former DPJ secretary-general Ozawa Ichiro's emphasis on obtaining UN authorization before undertaking military involvement abroad is closest to the first group of independence advocates, but the truth is that the DPJ is fractured when it comes to attitudes toward the alliance. Some accentuate the fear of entanglement and thus point to the potential danger of aligning too closely with the United States. Others take Kubo's "possible threat" premise one step further. Such advocates tend to view security threats as downright unlikely, which calls into question the necessity of keeping the current US force structure in Japan. Some even see the US military presence as the problem rather than the solution when it comes to reducing external threats. This partly explains why some within the DPJ are comfortable with asking Washington to remove the forward-deployed US Marines from Japan completely (as they did in 2010), rather than simply relocate from their current base near Naha on Okinawa to a less densely populated part of Japan.

Because many see nuclear threats to Japan as particularly unlikely, the DPJ government has taken steps to deemphasize the breadth and prominence of the US nuclear umbrella, for example by requesting the US government to restrict "the role of nuclear weapons . . . to deterrence of the use of nuclear weapons and that the use of nuclear weapons against [non–nuclear weapon state] members of the NPT be banned."[40] The Yukio Hatoyama administration also contravened earlier government lobbying efforts in Washington by explicitly telling US officials that it has no problem with the United States' retiring aging nuclear TLAM/Ns, and it went out of its way to bring to light—and repudiate—past secret agreements with the United States allowing for the introduction of US nuclear weapons to Japan under certain circumstances.[41] Although the DPJ government continues to emphasize the utility of US nuclear weapons for maintaining deterrence for as long as such weapons exist in the world, it has been much more supportive of US proposals for reducing the number of US nuclear weapons and their role in American defense strategy.

All this suggests that advocates of security independence are gaining some strength, though this probably has more to do with diminished threat perceptions than with a fear of US abandonment that would require Japan to make major defense-related investments to bolster its own deterrent capability. In other words, there is no broad call for strengthening Japanese defense capability to take over missions left by the United States. It is quite possible, however, that these reduced threat perceptions could just be a temporary illusion caused in part by the DPJ government's inexperience—some would say naïveté—and the recent dearth of provocative acts akin to North Korea's 1998 missile launch over Japan, the confrontation with a North Korean spy boat in late 2001, or a serious geostrategic conflict with China. On this last point, a simple skirmish between a Chinese fishing boat and Japanese Coast Guard vessels near the disputed Senkaku Islands in 2010 raised the public profile of this underlying tension between the two regional powers.

In the near term, Japan's sensitivity to extended-deterrence questions might ebb and flow depending on events and political realignment, but over time it is likely to gravitate back toward an approach of hedging (for substance or show) or of a "closer alliance with the United States," given its underlying dependence on global stability and economic openness. In this sense, the KB thesis still holds true, even as the nuclear component of extended deterrence recedes. This should ultimately yield a more practical and operationally sound concept of deterrence, as the allies reinforce their commitment and devise a strategy aimed at employing conventional forces and creating a more mature regional security architecture to maintain escalation control in critical situations. The process of getting to that point should create opportunities to reshape extended deterrence for the twenty-first century in ways that strengthen and diversify the allies' security and political relationships, possibly in closer partnership with other nations. Revamping extended deterrence would help underwrite stability in the region and reassure Japan as the United States seeks a lower nuclear profile. This should be the goal; but achieving it will require political commitment and leadership. Much depends on the nature and trajectory of China's rise, as well as on North Korea's nuclear weapon and missile development.

Although Tokyo appears to be deemphasizing extended-deterrence issues at this moment, US officials should not overestimate this trend, because the underlying dynamics have not changed appreciably. Political change in Japan could have a long-term effect on these dynamics, especially when considered alongside factors such as America's fiscal health and regional threat perceptions. It is too early to tell at this point. For now, the nuclear umbrella remains vital to Japan, even as the conventional aspects of extended deterrence become increasingly important to helping Tokyo resist coercive diplomacy and shore up deterrence at the margins. The United States–Japan relationship also supports United States–South Korea extended deterrence. In this sense, even though Japanese and South Korean perceptions of extended deterrence are moving in opposite directions, the challenge of alliance management is now more interconnected, complex, and dynamic than ever before.

Notes

1. One exception to this statement could be Japan's loosening of legal restrictions regarding the use of space for defense purposes (discussed in this report), but the motivation for this move can also be explained in the context of missile defenses and intelligence gathering.

2. See Agency for Natural Resources and Energy of the Japanese Ministry of Economy, Trade, and Industry, "Energy for Japan 2008" (in Japanese), www.enecho.meti .go.jp/topics/hakusho/2008/index.htm; and Japanese Ministry of Agriculture, Forestry, and Fisheries, "The Great East Japan Earthquake: MAFF's Information" (in Japanese), www.maff.go.jp/j/zyukyu/zikyu_ritu/011.html.

3. "South Korea May Need Its Own Deterrent," *Chosun Ilbo* (Digital Chosun), May 26, 2009.

4. North Korea is not recognized as a nuclear weapon state from a diplomatic standpoint, but it can be put in this category for defense planning purposes.

5. See "Memo: Sato Said Ban on Nukes Was 'Mistake,'" *Yomiuri Shimbun* (*Daily Yomiuri Online*), March 11, 2010; and "Japan-US Secret Pacts Confirmed, Government Policy Shift Expected," Kyodo News Agency, March 9, 2010.

6. Sam Jameson, "Foreign Minister Says Japan Will Need Nuclear Arms If North Korea Threatens," *Los Angeles Times*, July 29, 1993.

7. Kurt M. Campbell and Tsuyoshi Sunohara, "Japan: Thinking the Unthinkable," in *The Nuclear Tipping Point: Why States Reconsider Their Nuclear Choices*, edited by Kurt M. Campbell, Robert J. Einhorn, and Mitchell B. Reiss (Washington, DC: Brookings Institution Press, 2004), 222.

8. "Sato Sought US Nuclear Strike in Japan–China War," *Asahi Shimbun*, December 22, 2008.

9. "Foreign Ministry Advocated Maintaining Nuclear Potential," *Mainichi Daily News*, August 2, 1994.

10. In fact, the "alliance" was not explicitly named as such in Japanese official statements and documents until May 8, 1981, in a joint statement by Prime Minister Suzuki Zenko and President Ronald Reagan. This created a small controversy back in Japan, where the media questioned if this was now a "military alliance" or an "anti-Soviet alliance," and eventually Foreign Minister Ito Masayoshi had to explain in the Diet that

the "alliance" term was nothing more than an affirmation of the close political, economic, and cultural affairs between the two countries. See "Japanese Aide Denies Formation of Anti-Soviet Alliance with US," Associated Press, May 12, 1981.

11. See Nishihiro Seiki oral history interview conducted by Tanaka Akihiko and Murata Koji, National Security Archive US-Japan Project Oral History Program, November 16, 1995, www.gwu.edu/~nsarchiv/japan/ohpage.htm.

12. House of Councilors, Proceedings of the Special Committee Considering the Proposed Japan-Korea Treaty, Session 9 (in Japanese), House of Councilors, Tokyo, December 3, 1965, http://kokkai.ndl.go.jp/.

13. Kurosaki Akira, *Nuclear Weapons and the US–Japan Relationship: American Nuclear Nonproliferation Diplomacy and Japan's Choices 1960–1976* (in Japanese) (Tokyo: Yushisha, 2006), 196–97.

14. "Sato Sought US Nuclear Strike."

15. Kurosaki, *Nuclear Weapons.*

16. "Joint Statement of Japanese Prime Minister and US President Johnson," January 13, 1965, in *Documentary History of US–Japanese Relations, 1945–1997*, 625–27; US Department of State, *Public Papers of the Presidents: Lyndon B. Johnson, 1965* (Washington, DC: US Government Printing Office, 1966), 40–42; *The World and Japan Database*, Tokyo Institute of Oriental Culture, University of Tokyo, www.ioc.u-tokyo.ac.jp/~worldjpn/documents/texts/JPUS/19650113.D1E.html.

17. Minutes of the Proceedings for Questions with Regard to the Foreign Minister's Speech (in Japanese), 58th Japanese National Diet General Session 3, January 30, 1968.

18. Most Japanese government reports (e.g., *Japan's National Defense Program Guideline FY2005–*) reiterate the policy that US nuclear weapons are a deterrent against a nuclear attack on Japan. See, e.g., Japan Defense Agency, *Defense of Japan 2006* (Yamagata Prefecture: Fujisho, 2006), 428. Some, however, have suggested a broader role in deterring other unconventional attacks. See Council on Security and Defense Capabilities, *Japan's Visions for Future Security and Defense Capabilities* (a.k.a. Araki Report) (Tokyo: Council on Security and Defense Capabilities, 2004).

19. See Ogawa Shinichi, "The Theoretical Assessment of the Nuclear Umbrella" (in Japanese), *Kokusaiseiji* [International Politics] 90 (March 1989); and Noguchi Kazuhiko, *The Reconstruction of Extended Deterrence Theory: From the Perspective of Credibility and Interest* (in Japanese) (Tokyo: Tokai University Press, 2005).

20. See Jimbo Ken, "Rethinking Japanese Security: New Concepts in Deterrence and Defense," in *Japan's Nuclear Option: Security, Politics, and Policy in the 21st Century*, edited by Benjamin Self and Jeffrey Thompson (Washington, DC: Henry L. Stimson Center, 2003), and Tanaka Akihiko, *Security: A Search for Fifty Years of Post-War History* (in Japanese) (Tokyo: Yomiuri Shimbun-sha, 1997).

21. Nishihiro interview, 1995.

22. Maruyama Takashi oral history interview conducted by Tanaka Akihiko and Murata Koji, National Security Archive US-Japan Project Oral History Program, April 12, 1996, www.gwu.edu/~nsarchiv/japan/ohpage.htm.

23. The Guam Doctrine also promised to "provide a shield if a nuclear power threatens the freedom of a nation allied with us."

24. Kubo wrote the memo "A Framework to Consider the Arrangement of Japan's Defense Capabilities" in 1971. Kubo often marked his memos with "KB" at the top.

25. Kubo Takuya, "A Framework to Consider the Arrangement of Japan's Defense Capabilities" (in Japanese), in *The World and Japan Database*, Tokyo Institute of Oriental Culture, University of Tokyo, 1971, www.ioc.u-tokyo.ac.jp/~worldjpn/documents/texts/JPSC/19710220.O1J.html.

26. Maruyama interview, 1996.

27. Hoshuyama Noboru oral history interview conducted by Tanaka Akihiko, Murata Koji, and Iokibe Makoto, National Security Archive US-Japan Project Oral History Program, April 19, 1996, www.gwu.edu/~nsarchiv/japan/ohpage.htm.

28. Kubo, "Framework," 1971.

29. Ibid.

30. Author's interview with an MOFA official, July 30, 2007.

31. Kase Yuri, "The Costs and Benefits of Japan's Nuclearization: An Insight into the *1968/70 Internal Report*," *Nonproliferation Review* 8, no. 2 (Summer 2001): 55–68.

32. Ogawa, "Theoretical Assessment."

33. Noguchi, *Reconstruction*.

34. Jimbo, "Rethinking Japanese Security."

35. See, e.g., Umemoto Tetsuya, "Missile Defense and Extended Deterrence in the Japan-US Alliance," *Korean Journal of Defense Analysis* 12, no. 2 (Winter 2000); and Kawakami Takashi, "Strategy of Japan: The Road Map of Alliance Transformation" (in Japanese), Tokyo Foundation Report, June 2007, www.tkfd.or.jp/admin/file/pdf/labres/24.pdf.

36. Nakanishi Terumasa, "Extended Deterrence: The Historical Path and Its Nature" (in Japanese), in *Strategic Theoretical Analysis on East–West Relations* (in Japanese), edited by Sato Seizaburo (Tokyo: Japan Institute for International Affairs, 1990), 75–108.

37. Author's interview with a former MOFA official, August 1, 2007.

38. Nakanishi Terumasa, "The Start of Japan's Nuclear Debates," in *Debates on "Japan's Nuclear Armament": How to Survive this Critical Moment of National Existence* (in Japanese), edited by Nakanishi Terumasa (Tokyo: PHP, 2006).

39. For examples of advocates of these various approaches see, respectively, Group Ichigaya, "Tomorrow Will Never Come for a Japan without Nuclear Weapons" (in Japanese), *Shokun!* February 2007; Maehara Seiji, "Can the Establishment of 'the Ministry of Defense' Make Japan 'a Normal State'?" (in Japanese), *Shokun!* March 2007; Kitaoka Shinichi, "Five Options to Deter North Korea's Nukes" (in Japanese), *Chuokoron*, December 2006; and Ishiba Shigeru, "Can the Establishment of 'the Ministry of Defense' Make Japan 'a Normal State'?" (in Japanese), *Shokun!* March 2007. Interestingly, there is no single Japanese-language equivalent for the word "hedge." Japanese defense analysts and scholars often use the English word when conveying this strategy in a security context. More generically, *hoken o kakeru* is one neutral option (be insured, get insurance), and another phrase with a slightly negative (or sly) connotation is *futamata o kakeru* (have it both ways, sit on the fence, or a foot on each side, which can also refer to dating two girls at the same time, for example).

40. "Text of Letter from Foreign Minister Okada Katsuya to US Secretary of State Hilary Rodham Clinton" (in Japanese), December 24, 2009, released January 22, 2010 by the Japanese Foreign Ministry, http://icnndngojapan.files.wordpress.com/2010/01/20091224_okada_letter.pdf.

41. Ibid.; "US to Retire Nuclear Tomahawk Missiles, Japan Told," *Kyodo News Agency*, February 22, 2010.

CHAPTER 7

THINKING ABOUT THE UNTHINKABLE

Tokyo's Nuclear Option

James R. Holmes and Toshi Yoshihara

WILL JAPAN GO NUCLEAR? Doubtful—but what if it did? It is possible to envision circumstances that would impel Tokyo and the Japanese populace to cast aside their long-standing dread of nuclear weapons and to construct an arsenal of their own for the sake of national survival. The Japanese dread about nuclear endeavors was reinforced by the 2011 Fukushima nuclear disaster, but even Fukushima might not be an insurmountable obstacle if survival were at stake. Menacing strategic surroundings or a collapse of the United States–Japan Security Treaty are two of these. If some nightmare scenario did come to pass, the common wisdom is that Japan could build a working bomb in short order. In 1991 Richard Halloran averred that "Japan is *N* minus six months," although he saw no evidence that Japan entertained any ambition to tap its latent weapons capability.[1] In 2007 Gary Sick, a well-known commentator on Middle East affairs, reported having been privately told that Japan "could do it, sort of, over a long weekend."[2] Japan, that is, may now qualify as a "threshold state," a term "commonly understood to mean possession of the indigenous ability to acquire nuclear weapons within a relatively short time frame, ranging from a few hours to several months."[3]

Japan inhabits a tough neighborhood, and the US military position in Asia looks increasingly wobbly. Nearby North Korea conducted a nuclear test in 2006 and paid no penalty for defying the Six-Party framework. Japanese thinkers have studied the rise of China closely and what it portends for Japan, which of course is positioned just off the Asian seaboard. Beijing has mounted an aggressive naval buildup during the past decade, and thus it has gained confidence in its capacity to subdue Taiwan militarily if need be while holding US navy aircraft carrier task forces at bay. Taiwan adjoins Japan's southern strategic frontier, meaning that Tokyo could not look with equanimity on a cross-strait war or a return of the island to mainland rule. Indeed, Japanese imperialist expansion more than a century ago was designed precisely to secure its southern strategic flank, the backdoor to its Ryukyu Islands chain, which stretches to the coast of Taiwan.[4] Since the Sino-Japanese War of 1895, Taiwan has been in "friendly hands" for more than a century. As such, Japanese policymakers do not take the possibility of a forcible Chinese acquisition of Taiwan lightly.

To complicate matters, as Chinese strategists look to the "day after Taiwan," they are considering how to exert influence on the sea lines of communication that connect Chinese ports with commercial shipping routes that bear vital resources from the Middle East and Africa. China's turn toward the South China Sea and the Indian Ocean may give Beijing not only more control over its own maritime security but also more control over the maritime communications on which the resource-dependent Japanese economy depends.

Seen in realist terms, then, China's maritime rise threatens to degrade Japan's strategic position in the region. Tokyo may ultimately conclude that self-help represents the only way to shore up its position. The skyrocketing costs of developing and procuring weaponry are driving the force structure of the US military inexorably downward in numbers. Just one example: The Pentagon's estimates of future US navy fleet numbers now run as low as 150 ships, a fraction the size of the nearly 600-ship navy of the 1980s.[5] Even the 313-ship fleet espoused by the navy leadership now appears fanciful, with 283 ships currently in active service and little prospect of accelerating shipbuilding rates enough to increase the fleet's inventory by thirty vessels.[6] US allies like Japan monitor such trends closely. A precipitous decline in conventional US military capacity in the region could have major diplomatic ramifications—it would undercut America's staying power in the western Pacific, give rise to Japanese fears of abandonment, and unsettle the entire Asian security architecture. More to the point, Tokyo would likely interpret such a decline as foreshadowing an end to the US nuclear guarantee.

Accordingly, an effort to see through a glass darkly, and thus discern Tokyo's nuclear options and their likely consequences, is not only worthwhile but also imperative for both analysts and practitioners of Asian affairs. First, therefore, we briefly consider the motives that would induce Japan's leadership to make such a radical break with the antinuclear sentiments of the postwar era. Second, we consider the prospect of Japanese "nuclear hedging," an approach whereby Tokyo builds up the capacity to develop nuclear weapons and keeps its strategic options open while it continues to abide by its commitments under the Nuclear Non-Proliferation Treaty. Third, we consider the technical feasibility of a swift Japanese nuclear breakout, and we pay particular attention to assumptions that Tokyo could stage a breakout within a year of deciding to do so.[7] Fourth, we identify possible force structures and strategies that could be available to Japan if its leadership were to indeed decide that it was in the national interest to cross the nuclear weapons threshold. Fifth and finally, we identify areas for future research, with the aim of generating a literature that would be of immediate use for policymakers in Washington and Tokyo.

Why Go Nuclear?

Debate has swirled around prospective Japanese nuclear aspirations at least since 1958, when Prime Minister Nobusuke Kishi told the Diet that the nation's postwar "peace Constitution" did not forbid a strictly defensive nuclear arsenal. Successive governments, however, disclaimed the words of the hawkish Kishi. By 1967 Prime

Minister Eisaku Sato was spelling out "Three Non-Nuclear Principles," informing lawmakers that his government would not manufacture, possess, or "allow the introduction of" nuclear arms into Japan. Sato's principles earned him the 1974 Nobel Peace Prize and have remained the gold standard for Japanese nonproliferation policy ever since. However, it is noteworthy that even Sato was acutely aware of Japan's vulnerability in the dangerous Cold War security environment. Following China's nuclear breakout in October 1964, Sato quickly sought reassurances from the United States that Washington would extend its nuclear umbrella to Japan.[8] In a conversation with Secretary of Defense Robert McNamara during a state visit to the United States, Sato declared, "Should a war break out [between Japan and China], we expect the United States to immediately launch a retaliatory nuclear strike [against China]."[9] Presumably, America's extended deterrence was a critical precondition to Sato's willingness to forgo the nuclear option.

In any event, Japan's "nuclear allergy" persists to the present day. Matake Kamiya explains Tokyo's self-imposed injunction against bomb making in terms of the general pacifism codified in Japan's peace Constitution, lingering memories of the atomic bombings of Hiroshima and Nagasaki, and antimilitary sentiments dating from the interwar years.[10] As a result, concludes Kamiya, opposition to nuclear weapons "is deeply embedded in postwar Japanese culture and society. . . . it is still far stronger, even today, than those who warn of impending Japanese nuclear armament realize."[11] The vast majority of observers in both Japan and the West are inclined to agree with Kamiya, though for different reasons. Indeed, very few scholars have lent credence to rationales for a nuclear buildup.[12]

Tetsuya Endo, a former vice chairman of the Atomic Energy Commission of Japan, argues that whereas Japan possesses the technical capabilities to stage a nuclear breakout, the material costs combined with the prospects of international isolation would deter Tokyo from pursuing such an option.[13] Brad Glosserman cautions that Japan likely would not survive intact as a nation-state following a nuclear exchange—even a limited one—owing to its lack of strategic depth and the extremely high population density throughout the Japanese archipelago.[14] Llewelyn Hughes identifies a series of domestic institutional factors, ranging from constitutional to informal constraints, that have anchored Tokyo securely to the US nuclear guarantee.[15] Others believe that Japan is actively pursuing other strategic options, including strengthening its own conventional military capabilities and deepening its alliance ties to the United States, as substitutes for an independent nuclear deterrent.[16] In sum, normative, material, geographic, institutional, and strategic considerations militate against Japan's going nuclear.

There is no denying these constraints. And yet the logic of national security—of threat and response—is not so readily dismissed, even under the special circumstances prevailing in postwar Japan. The prevailing skepticism, moreover, has precluded serious discourse on practical and critical steps—including the development of nuclear doctrine, command and control, and force structure—that Tokyo would need to implement if it embarked on a breakout. Therefore, it is useful to postulate strategic rationales and chart a road map for Japanese nuclearization. Scott Sagan outlines three hypotheses to explain why nation-states seek nuclear weapons:

1. According to Sagan's "security" model, governments "build nuclear weapons to increase national security against foreign threats, especially nuclear threats." George Shultz memorably summed up the security approach: "Proliferation begets proliferation."[17] Two policies are possible when threats arise, says Sagan. Sounding a Thucydidean note, he maintains that "strong states do what they can, . . . adopting the costly, but self-sufficient, policy of developing their own nuclear weapons." Weak states, by contrast, "do what they must: They can join a balancing alliance with a nuclear power, utilizing a promise of nuclear retaliation by that ally as a means of extended deterrence."[18] Doubts about the credibility of a nuclear ally's security guarantee presumably bring pressure on even weak states, or on states like Japan that rely on an alliances for other reasons, to seek nuclear capability. This is the logic of self-help.

2. Sagan's "domestic politics" model "envisions nuclear weapons as political tools used to advance parochial domestic and bureaucratic interests." The three protagonists in nuclear policymaking typically include the nuclear energy establishment, the armed forces, and politicians. The former two actors may have bureaucratic interests in going nuclear, because this would give them leverage in budgetary processes and thus allow them to attract resources. "When such actors form coalitions that are strong enough to control the government's decision-making process, . . . nuclear weapons programs are likely to thrive." Or, conversely, when a coalition opposes nuclear weapons or the various actors find themselves at loggerheads on this question, more ambiguous results are likely.[19] A clash among domestic interests seldom yields neat, entirely rational policies.

3. Under Sagan's "norms" model, "nuclear weapons decisions are made because weapons acquisition, or restraint in weapons development, provides an important normative symbol of a state's modernity and identity." Government decisions are driven "not by leaders' cold calculations about the national security interests or parochial bureaucratic interests but rather by deeper norms and shared beliefs about what actions are legitimate and appropriate in international relations." A nuclear arsenal is a token of modernity, legitimacy, and great power. As Sagan points out, an interactive relationship exists between norms and the bureaucratic actors from his second model. As norms mature over time, they tend to be codified into bureaucratic procedures and practices, and thus they influence calculations vis-à-vis important matters like whether to seek nuclear capability.[20] Beliefs and convictions color rational cost/benefit analyses.

In the Japanese case, it appears, one of Sagan's models is in tension with the other two. Rational security calculations point to a growing threat, an ally in relative decline, and thus a weaker position for Japan in Asia. Those who incline to this way of thinking tend to see a nuclear breakout as potentially unavoidable. But foreign policy, observe Graham Allison and Philip Zelikow, represents "the extension of politics to other realms."[21] They liken foreign policy to a collage, and thus they depict it as an amalgam of bargains struck, compromises reached, and coalitions formed on a variety of issues—often under pressure.[22] Proponents of Japanese nucle-arization will inevitably encounter deep-seated resistance, both from the electorate and from bureaucratic institutions in which antinuclear attitudes are entrenched.

Discord is the product of this societal indecision. Applying Allison and Zelikow's metaphor in the context of Sagan's three models, Japanese policymakers will incline strongly to pursue some middle way between pronuclear and antinuclear factions. If successful, they will maximize their liberty of action, appease important parties with a stake in the outcome, reinforce US support for the security alliance, and avoid setting off a public outcry.

Option 1: Nuclear Hedging

If we have interpreted events correctly, Tokyo will hedge its bets on whether to go nuclear—if indeed it has not already embarked on such an approach.[23] Japan's leadership, that is, will postpone a decision for as long as possible, monitoring its security surroundings while quietly building up the planning and strategy-making processes, expertise, infrastructure, and matériel to make it possible to field a modest arsenal within a reasonable amount of time. This is not an uncommon approach for governments. Notes Ariel Levite, "Would-be proliferants rarely make formal decisions to acquire the bomb or for that matter to give it up before they absolutely have to (e.g., before they are on the verge of attaining or eliminating a nuclear capability), if then." Having a "nuclear 'option'" often makes sense in pure realpoli-tik terms.[24]

Evelyn Goh defines hedging in general terms as "taking action to ensure against undesirable outcomes, usually by betting on multiple alternative positions." This makes sense, says Goh, when the leadership cannot decide on "more straightforward alternatives" because it rates the costs of such alternatives as too high or the payoffs as too low.[25] More to the point, Levite defines "'nuclear hedging' as a national strategy lying between nuclear pursuit and nuclear rollback."[26] John F. Kennedy famously predicted that fifteen to twenty nuclear weapon states would emerge by the end of the 1960s.[27] That clearly has not happened. It nevertheless appears that hedging offers the middle way for which embattled Japanese policymakers and strat-egists will be looking as they try to satisfy the partisans of Sagan's models of nuclear decision making.

In this scenario, much of the hedging will take place within the domestic arena. Moving beyond mere calls for debate on the nuclear question, the Japanese policy community would begin a more serious discourse on breaking out. For example, the prime minster could openly and formally revisit and reaffirm the constitutionality of nuclear armament, perhaps by appointing some type of blue-ribbon commission. Such a move would be as much about shaping public opinion and expectations as about developing concrete plans to be implemented.

A gradual, transparent, and deliberate analytical process thus would aim to move the nuclear issue within the bounds of routine political discourse for the Japanese state and society. Llewelyn Hughes astutely observes that recent institutional reforms have centralized power in the prime minister's office, which has bolstered that body's ability to set and impose Japan's national security agenda. This and other reforms, Hughes concludes, have "ensured that the formal barriers to nuclearization are surmountable."[28] It is therefore conceivable that future efforts to further strengthen executive authority would signal the will and expected capability to overturn constraints on pursuing an independent nuclear option.

Persuasive rhetoric toward important audiences will be critical to any hedging strategy. Japanese leaders will need to navigate among the domestic interests examined by Sagan; reassure the watchdog International Atomic Energy Agency (IAEA) and the international community that Japan has no desire to break its commitments under the Nuclear Non-Proliferation Treaty; and concurrently apply pressure on the United States not to draw down its conventional military commitment to Japan or, worse still, furl the nuclear umbrella under which Japan shelters. Indeed, added pressure on Washington to make its nuclear strategy and decision-making processes more transparent to Tokyo would implicitly signal that Japan's nonnuclear posture is not absolute.

In other words, if the United States fails to more meaningfully integrate Japan into its nuclear plans, then Tokyo might have no choice but to pursue an independent option. Alternatively, Tokyo might modify its Three Non-Nuclear Principles and thus lift its self-imposed ban on the introduction of nuclear weapons onto Japanese territory. This would represent a precursor to limited deployments of US nuclear weapons to strengthen deterrence.[29] The deployment of Pershing intermediate-range missiles in Europe during the 1980s offers a useful precedent. Such a move might eventually open the way for joint management of the nuclear weapons positioned in the home islands, similar to existing United States–NATO arrangements.[30] A strategy of calculated ambiguity that at once played up Japanese capacity to go nuclear and remained noncommittal on Japanese intentions of doing so would offer Tokyo its best diplomatic option if security conditions continued to decay in East Asia.

Option 2: Black Swans and Nuclear Breakout

What would it take to empower the adherents of Sagan's security model and thus allow their views to win out over domestic interests opposed to nuclear weapons, and over norms of decades' standing? A central feature of Japan's security strategy is the nation's utter dependence on the US nuclear umbrella. As Yukio Satoh succinctly explains, "The US extended nuclear deterrence will continue to be Japan's only strategic option to neutralize potential or conceivable nuclear and other strategic threats."[31] As such, barely perceptible signs of weakness in the US nuclear posture (either perceived or real) could trigger alarm and overreactions in Japan.

Japanese concerns about the Obama administration's recent moves to advance nonproliferation and disarmament objectives attest to such sensitivities. Specifically, Japanese policymakers fret that "extended deterrence could weaken if Washington appears too eager to placate China and Russia on these [global disarmament] issues in pursuit of the nonproliferation objective or if it permits a latent North Korean nuclear capability in exchange for safeguards against proliferation."[32] In 2006 North Korea's nuclear test compelled the Japanese government to seek public reassurances from the United States that extended deterrence remained intact.[33] Not surprisingly, even skeptics on the matter of Japanese nuclearization concede that an erosion of US credibility could fundamentally reshape the Japanese strategic calculus. The Congressional Research Service forcefully contends that "perhaps the single most important factor to date in dissuading Tokyo from developing a nuclear arsenal is the US guarantee to protect Japan's security."[34] The causes and the process by which Washington's extended deterrence could be undermined in Tokyo's eyes are beyond the scope of this chapter. Nevertheless, we contend that a gradual or sudden collapse of the nuclear umbrella would be among the most decisive stimuli for a Japanese nuclear breakout.

Indeed, historical precedents in Cold War Asia provide ample evidence of the proliferation-related consequences of real or perceived American indifference to the region. Perceptions of declining US credibility and of weaknesses in the nuclear umbrella spurred concerted efforts on the part of past American allies to break out. Under the Nixon Doctrine, which called on allies to bear heavier burdens, Washington withdrew a combat division from the Korean Peninsula in 1971. As a consequence, according to Seung-Young Kim, "Korean leaders were not sure about US willingness to use nuclear weapons," despite the presence of tactical nuclear weapons on Korean soil.[35] Such fears compelled President Park Chung-hee to initiate a crash nuclear weapons program. To compound matters, President Jimmy Carter's abortive attempt to withdraw all US forces and nuclear weapons from the Korean Peninsula accelerated Park's pursuit of an independent deterrent.

Similarly, China's nuclear test in 1964 kindled "fear that Taiwan might be wiped out in a single attack, with US retaliation coming too late to prevent destruction."[36] This lack of confidence in US security guarantees impelled Chiang Kai-shek to launch a nuclear weapons program. The Sino-US rapprochement of the early 1970s further stimulated anxieties among Nationalist leaders about the potential abandonment of Taiwan. In fulfilling its pledges under the Shanghai Communiqué, which began the normalization process, the United States substantially reduced its troop presence on the island. As Nancy Bernkopf Tucker argues, "The withdrawal of American forces from Taiwan compelled the Nationalists to think more seriously about alternative ways of protecting themselves," including nuclear weapons.[37] Recently declassified materials document growing American alarm at the prospect of a nuclear breakout on the island throughout the decade.[38]

In both cases, sustained American pressure combined with reassurances persuaded the two East Asian powers to forgo the nuclear option. The Taiwanese and South Korean experiences nonetheless show that states succumb to proliferation temptations as a result of a deteriorating security environment, heightened threat perceptions, and declining confidence in the United States. Although Japan certainly faces far different and less worrisome circumstances, these two case studies serve as a reminder to analysts to not casually wave away the possibility of a Japanese nuclear option.

As noted above, analysts and Japanese politicians evince conviction that Japan could develop a nuclear deterrent in a relatively short period. We are unpersuaded by this apparent optimism and conventional wisdom. It is true that Japan possesses all the trappings of a nuclear power. Yet the path to a credible nuclear status is likely to be long and winding. Above all, Japan needs the material capacity to develop a bomb.[39] With fifty-five nuclear power plants in operation around the country and the nuclear sector's large reserves of reactor-grade plutonium, Japan enjoys access to a readily available supply of fissile material. According to *Sankei Shimbun*, Japan possesses enough plutonium on its own soil and in reprocessing plants overseas to produce 740 bombs.[40] How readily usable this reactor-grade material would be for weapons purposes, however, remains a matter of dispute among technical specialists. An internal government report unearthed by *Sankei Shimbun* reportedly concluded that Japan would need several hundred engineers, ¥200 to ¥300 billion (or $2 to $3 billion), and three to five years to fabricate a usable nuclear warhead.[41]

The real question would be timing. It is doubtful in the extreme that Japan could circumvent its safeguards agreement with the IAEA undetected for long.[42] Although the cases of Iran and North Korea demonstrate that it is possible to bypass the IAEA, Japan holds itself to much higher, more stringent standards, having assented to one of the most intrusive, regular inspection programs in the world.[43] Furthermore, think of the diplomatic blowback. One can only imagine the uproar if such an effort on the part of Japan—heretofore a consistent, sincere opponent of nuclear weapons— were to be exposed to public and international scrutiny.

Thus, Japanese policymakers must consider the extent to which Tokyo can withstand mounting external pressure to cease and desist while its nuclear complex amasses enough bomb-making material for a viable arsenal. Tokyo cannot expect to deceive the international community, presenting the world with a fait accompli. It would probably need to make its intentions clear at the outset—and endure international opprobrium—well before reaching the breakout threshold.

Even assuming that Japan can procure enough fissile materials to build an arsenal, its engineers would still need to leap over several technical barriers. First, Japan would need to devise an effective, efficient delivery system. The most direct route would be to arm Japan's existing fleet of fighter aircraft with nuclear bombs or missiles. The fighters in the Air Self-Defense Force (SDF) inventory, however, are constrained by (1) vulnerability to preemptive strikes while still on the ground at their bases; (2) limited range, for Japan possesses no strategic bombers; (3) susceptibility to interception by enemy fighters while en route to their targets; and (4) vulnerability to increasingly sophisticated integrated air defense systems. Compounding these shortcomings, Japan is surrounded by water, which substantially increases flight times to targets on the Asian mainland.

In light of these factors, ballistic or cruise missiles would likely rank as Japan's weapon of choice.[44] There would be two main challenges. First, if Tokyo chose to rely on a missile delivery system, then it would need to produce a workable, miniaturized nuclear warhead that could be mounted atop an accurate cruise or ballistic missile. Such a feat is not beyond Japanese engineering prowess, but it would involve significant lead time. Second, it would need to develop the delivery system for nuclear payloads. Even the US defense-industrial sector, with its half century of experience in this field, takes years to design and build new missiles. Japan could conceivably convert some of its civilian space-launch vehicles into ballistic missiles, but it would need to perfect key components, such as inertial guidance systems. And unless Japan could purchase Tomahawk cruise missiles off the shelf from the United States—a doubtful prospect given Tomahawks' highly offensive nature, and thus the political sensitivity of such a sale—Tokyo would in effect find itself compelled to start from scratch if it opted for long-range cruise missiles. Procuring and integrating satellite guidance, terrain contour matching, and other specialized techniques and hardware would demand long, hard labor from Japanese weapon scientists.

There is also the question of testing. Japan would need to ensure the safety and reliability of its nuclear arsenal. There is no substitute for an actual nuclear test that would prove this new (for Japan) technology while bolstering the credibility of Japanese deterrence. But the Japanese archipelago is simply too small and too densely populated for a test to be conducted there safely—even leaving aside the potential for a political backlash, given the memories of Hiroshima and Nagasaki it would conjure up. Tokyo could detonate a device near some Japanese-held island in the Pacific, such as Okinotori-shima. But again, the diplomatic furor from flouting the Comprehensive Test Ban Treaty (CTBT) would be intense, and the Japanese populace would think back to the *Lucky Dragon* incident following the Bikini tests of the 1950s. One only need recall the uproar over French and Chinese tests on the eve of the CTBT's entry into force. Thus, for Japan, computer simulations may be less optimal but would certainly be more palatable from a political standpoint. The Israeli experience may be instructive for any Japanese bomb-making efforts.

The technical dilemmas reviewed here demonstrate that there is no shortcut to a nuclear breakout, even for a technological powerhouse of Japan's standing. The Congressional Research Service notes that, "if one assumes that Japan would want weapons with high reliability and accuracy, then more time would need to be devoted to their development unless a weapon or information was supplied by an outside source."[45] Kan Ito, a commentator on Japanese strategic affairs for nearly two decades, concurs; he admonishes observers who predict a rapid breakout for being "utterly presumptuous. . . . It is dangerous to believe such a misconception. It will take fifteen years for Japan to build up its own autonomous nuclear deterrence capability that is truly functional."[46] Although one may quibble with Ito's fifteen-year timeline, which seems unduly pessimistic, the time required to develop and field a credible deterrent would probably be measured in years rather than the weeks or months cavalierly bandied about.

Strategy, Doctrine, and Force Structure

Beyond the technical and tactical decisions associated with breaking out, Japan would need to develop comprehensive policies and processes to harness its nuclear arsenal. As noted above, strategic ambiguity about Japanese intentions and capabilities is probably impossible. As a nation that has long cherished its democratic institutions and its unquestioned civilian control of the military, Tokyo would need to issue formal public statements and official documents regarding Japanese nuclear doctrine. Such declarations, which would be intended for public and international consumption, would presumably predate the SDF's deployment of a deterrent force, which in turn would help reassure Japan's neighbors, friends, and allies, especially the United States.

Japanese officials would probably frame their doctrine strictly in terms of Japan's unique strategic position and local circumstances. Geostrategic realities would dictate that Japan renounce the war-fighting utility of nuclear weapons, hold fast to an unconditional no-first-use policy, and adopt an exclusively retaliatory nuclear posture. Japan is simply too small and vulnerable to contemplate any but the most minimal deterrent options. The goal of Japanese nuclear strategy would be to credibly threaten limited nuclear strikes against one or several countervalue targets, deterring first use by an adversary. Such a punitive approach has long underwritten the doctrines of smaller nuclear powers such as France and China.

None other than former prime minister Yasuhiro Nakasone has expressed confidence that a defensive, minimalist nuclear posture would suffice for Japan. With candor rare among Japanese politicians, he states: "I believe it is constitutional for Japan to possess small-size nuclear weapons as long as we use them only for the purposes of defending our country. A small-size nuclear weapon has a strength that is less than one-third of the power of the atomic bomb dropped on Hiroshima. Even the US Congress allows research on such small-size nuclear weapons. In order to raise Japan's defense capability in case of emergency, our Constitution should allow Japan to possess small-size nuclear weapons."[47]

Although Nakasone does not stipulate the size he prefers for Japan's nuclear arsenal, he clearly believes that the destructive power of low-yield weapons would generate sufficient deterrent effects vis-à-vis would-be enemies. Keishi Saeki of Kyoto University articulates a similar logic for an independent Japanese deterrent: "Possession of retaliatory nuclear arms consists of a means to retaliate against nuclear attacks by other nations. In other words, we must resign ourselves to accepting the initial nuclear attack. And such conditions should alleviate to a certain degree threats against other Asian nations. Moreover, the option of retaliatory nuclear arms requires preventive preemptory strikes against imminent potential (very highly probable) nuclear attacks from other nations. Accordingly, aside from possession of nuclear arms, probably necessary will be the procurement of precision guided weapons and a missile defense system, and intelligence-gathering activities."[48]

Saeki provides a useful framework for matching means to his proposed retaliatory option. Other Japanese analysts have also offered surprisingly concrete proposals for deploying a credible, defensively oriented deterrent. A former member of the Ground Self-Defense Force argued as early as 1996 for an undersea deterrent. Nisohachi Hyodo persuasively and methodically discounts the utility of land- and air-launched delivery systems, as well as systems deployed in the surface fleet.[49] Fixed silos would be most vulnerable to preemptive strikes, while Japan is too small to make maximum use of rail- or road-mobile launchers. Aircraft could be destroyed on the airfields in a first strike, and surface combatants could be tracked and sunk with little warning by nuclear attack submarines. As such, Japan's only option is to deploy conventionally powered submarines armed with submarine-launched ballistic missiles. For Hyodo, two submarines, each carrying only one missile and "roaming in separate sea zones," would be adequate to deter one target country.

In contrast a former deputy minister under the Koizumi administration, Kenzo Yoneda, is not so quick to dismiss the possibility of fitting surface warships with nuclear-tipped cruise missiles. Yoneda postulates that land-attack cruise missiles with a range of 1,000 kilometers—akin to the US Tomahawk, but with a shorter range—deployed onboard the Maritime Self-Defense Force's Aegis destroyers would constitute an important component of Japan's nuclear posture.[50] Although Yoneda furnishes no specific estimates of how many missiles it would take to comprise a credible seaborne deterrent, his emphasis on cruise missiles, which carry far smaller payloads than intercontinental ballistic missiles, dovetails with Nakasone's call for "small-size nuclear weapons." The relatively short ranges Yoneda envisions, moreover, imply a modest regional deterrent force for Japan.

Kan Ito argues that Japan must possess 200 to 300 nuclear-armed cruise missiles deployed on "small destroyers and submarines" to establish minimum deterrence.[51] Ito presumably supports using existing platforms like Aegis destroyers and the latest diesel submarines as launch platforms. He also makes a compelling case against ballistic missiles, contending that ballistic missiles are far more destabilizing than cruise missiles because of sharp differences in speed and destructive potential. Relatively slow, single-warhead, low-yield cruise missiles would signal Japan's determination to blunt opponents' preemptive strategies while remaining in an unmistakably retaliatory posture. This approach, Ito concludes, would be more conducive than a ballistic missile force to a stable Asian military balance.[52] Clearly, then, even hardliners and proponents of nuclearization embrace a defensive-minded nuclear doctrine.

The aforementioned options are not mutually exclusive. Japan could very well adopt a mix of delivery systems, or the SDF could phase in more sophisticated weaponry and platforms as they become available. It is therefore worth exploring the risks, rewards, and technical feasibility of some of the proposals reviewed above. First, Japan would be hard pressed to choose submarine-launched ballistic missiles as the backbone of its deterrent. The Maritime SDF's existing conventional submarines are too small to carry such missiles. Although a fleet of ballistic missile submarines (known as "SSBNs," which stands for nuclear-powered ballistic missile submarines), would represent the ideal platform for a guaranteed second-strike capability, the technological hurdles would severely challenge even Japan's top-notch scientific and engineering community. To name just one such hurdle, the SDF possesses no naval reactors. Developing and building the propulsion plant for an SSBN would be an enormous undertaking in itself. The cost of building, maintaining, and deploying multiple SSBNs—the Maritime SDF would need two to three boats to keep one on patrol at any given time—would tax a defense budget already under strain. Tetsuo Sawada of the Tokyo Institute of Technology estimates that a single SSBN armed with ballistic missiles would cost Japan a breathtaking $5 billion, whereas a credible deterrent force involving several submarines would reach an astronomical ¥10 trillion, or in excess of $100 billion.[53]

We therefore judge an undersea ballistic missile deterrent improbable for Japan unless the security outlook were to become truly dire and thus justify an effort of such magnitude and duration. Cruise missiles, by contrast, are cheaper and easier to develop. Indeed, much of the technology is readily available off the shelf in the marketplace. Because Japan would aim retaliatory strikes at large cities, its cruise missiles would not need to be particularly accurate. Major Asian metropolises like Pyongyang, Beijing, and Shanghai are near the coast, which would make penetrating enemy airspace relatively easy. The target set would fall well within the range of missiles like those espoused by Kenzo Yoneda. In theory, only one bird would need to get through for Japan's minimum deterrent to be credible. Ito's call for 200 to 300 missiles thus may be somewhat excessive. Even assuming high attrition rates due to malfunctions or enemy interception, a few dozen nuclear-armed cruise missiles would likely suffice.

In all probability, Japanese cruise missiles, which would be far smaller than medium-range ballistic missiles, would be fired from conventional submarines—presumably from torpedo tubes, given how difficult it would be to retrofit these boats with vertical launchers—to maximize the survivability of the deterrent force. We forecast that Tokyo would need time to perfect the techniques and procedures for launching cruise missiles from submerged conventional submarines. Thus, once the missiles became available in sufficient quantities, they could be quickly deployed in vertical launch canisters onboard Aegis destroyers as a stopgap measure. Two to three destroyers could cruise simultaneously in disparate locations in the Pacific, which would enhance redundancy and survivability. Cruise missiles could also be fired from fighter aircraft at long distances. For instance, missiles launched from an F-2 fighter plane based in Okinawa would be able to reach most of China's major coastal economic centers. Such redundancy at sea and in the air might temporarily meet Japan's strategic requirements until the undersea option was fully functional.

We acknowledge the drawbacks to deploying cruise missiles aboard conventional submarines. They are slow in comparison with their nuclear-powered brethren, their range is short because of fuel consumption, and they can remain on patrol for only a short period. SDF conventional submarines thus would likely find themselves confined to patrol grounds near Japanese coasts, rendering them vulnerable to detection. Even so, air-independent propulsion will offset the detection problem once installed in Japanese boats, allowing them to remain underwater for longer stretches. The availability, number, and modest cost of these proven assets far outweigh their technical shortfalls.

Keeping two boats on station at all times would likely meet Japan's deterrent needs. SDF boats would presumably operate from the existing submarine bases at Kure and Yokosuka. This would allow easy access to patrol grounds in the Sea of Japan and along the Asian seaboard south of the Japanese home islands. Kure in particular makes for an ideal base, with a central location in the Inland Sea, ready egress into both the Pacific Ocean and the Sea of Japan, and easily defensible approaches. Once they reached their patrol grounds, Japanese boats could reach coastal metropolises, especially once technical improvements increase SDF cruise missiles' range to rival that of TLAM-Ns. The Maritime SDF could diversify its portfolio, as it were, operating in different expanses to threaten different targets and complicate an adversary's antisubmarine warfare efforts. Tokyo could choose to surge additional submarines at any given time, moreover, straining the antisubmarine warfare capabilities of prospective adversaries. Up to eight boats could conceivably be sent to sea, according to the back-of-the-envelope calculations provided below. In light of the Chinese navy's inattention to antisubmarine warfare, this limited nuclear capability represents a potent one indeed.

Finally, there is the matter of force sizing and budgeting. With more than forty destroyers and nearly twenty submarines, Japan doubtless boasts one of the largest and most advanced navies in the world. Nevertheless, undersea deterrent patrols would likely demand substantial, though not prohibitive, increases in the size of the submarine fleet. We assume that the Maritime SDF would deploy a separate submarine group dedicated exclusively to nuclear strikes, while maintaining adequate numbers for traditional operations such as sea-lane security and sea denial. Such a decision would remove the nuclear-armed boats from potentially risky frontline duties along the Asian littoral environment, which would enable crew members to accumulate hard-earned experience and sharpen the specialized skills needed for deterrent patrols in the Pacific.

How would Tokyo finance a new arm of its submarine force? To maintain its qualitative edge in undersea warfare, the Maritime SDF has traditionally decommissioned submarines at an unusually rapid rate and has introduced more advanced boats to replace older ones. To support the nuclear mission, accordingly, the maritime service could easily extend the service life of its fleet by at least ten years, which would allow for the conversion of existing boats and the introduction of new submarines without undermining Japan's overall undersea prowess. The US navy's conversion of four *Ohio*-class SSBNs to serve as cruise missile platforms, or SSGNs, offers a precedent for this sort of effort.

What about numbers? We believe a deterrent force of twelve cruise missile submarines would let the SDF keep two boats on patrol at all times. How do we arrive at this figure? Although Japanese mariners understandably divulge few details about the technical specifications of SDF submarines, we estimate—very conservatively—that their fuel capacity would permit Japanese diesel boats to remain on patrol for one month. (As a crude measuring stick, the endurance for the ubiquitous, German-built Type 209 is advertised at fifty days at the outside.[54]) If so, approximately six boats would be necessary for the SDF to keep one on station:

▶ One boat would be deployed at any given time, with three others undergoing routine upkeep, crew training, and local operations between deterrent cruises. This would permit a four-boat rotation, with each vessel making three patrols annually. This is a leisurely operating tempo by US navy standards, and thus sustainable indefinitely for the SDF.

▶ Using the US navy thumb rule that it takes three units to keep one in full readiness for deployment, we further assume that an additional two boats would be in extended overhaul at any time, subtracting them from the rotation. This leaves us with our six-to-one ratio between boats in the Maritime SDF inventory and those actually at sea. Again, this may overstate matters, as the American thumb rule assumes six-month deployments, with all the wear and tear extended cruises impose. Japanese units face fewer demands, and so the SDF could well get by with less.

Multiplying by two—again, with one squadron presumably based at Kure and another at Yokusuka—yields a total of twelve boats. Should Japan's strategic position continue to deteriorate, Japanese strategists may conclude that a bigger margin of deterrence—and thus a bigger undersea fleet—is necessary for national defense.[55] If so, additional six-boat increments could lie in store. But the more modest fleet sketched here, we believe, would provide more than ample retaliatory capacity for "minimal deterrence with Japanese characteristics."

Such a fleet would be affordable despite the real, nettlesome budgetary constraints that Tokyo confronts. Modest increases in the defense budget (measured as a percentage of gross domestic product) would generate sufficient resources (in absolute terms) to pay for such a buildup. If the Japanese government came to see the security environment as menacing enough to warrant a nuclear breakout, it would likely reprogram funds to support a naval buildup to support nuclear deterrence. Tokyo has long fixed its defense expenditures at about 1 percent of gross domestic product, amounting to more than $40 billion a year. The Japanese government would certainly need to shatter this self-imposed, somewhat arbitrary ceiling. If Tokyo were to increase the defense budget by 20 percent, to 1.2 percent of gross domestic product, then the additional $8 billion a year could furnish the financial foundation for a major modernization and expansion of the submarine fleet. The average cost of a single conventional submarine on the world market (anywhere between $200 and $400 million per boat) suggests that Japan possesses the financial clout to meet these new force structure requirements.

Concluding Thoughts

In closing, it is worth reemphasizing that this study eschews assessing the likelihood of Japan's going nuclear. Ample work already exists on the pros and cons of nuclearization. As was noted at the start of this chapter, we concur in general that it is highly unlikely that Tokyo will pursue an independent nuclear arsenal for the foreseeable future. The United States–Japan alliance is arguably in the best shape ever, while mainstream Japanese policymakers remain confident of the credibility of American extended deterrence. However, we believe that this largely valid consensus on the improbability of a nuclear breakout has precluded constructive discourse on practical US policy alternatives if Tokyo were to undertake a radical change of course. Although it may be distasteful to contemplate such a scenario, we are convinced that there is genuine analytical utility in thinking about the unthinkable. Chief among our findings through this mental exercise is that Japan will not break out in the literal sense of the term. Rather, it will proliferate in slow motion.

This study by no means constitutes an exhaustive exploration of Japan's nuclear options and their possible consequences. Four main areas of research would be worth pursuing further:

► First, a comparative analysis of historical models—in particular the British and French experiences during the Cold War—might offer fruitful insights and potential models for Japan to emulate. Findings regarding the extent to which these smaller nuclear arsenals complemented or fit within the broader US nuclear strategy would be particularly useful for Japanese policymakers.

► Second, and closely related, this study has focused exclusively on a potential Japanese nuclearization process. It would be useful to make an effort to foresee the plausible range of impacts such a momentous decision could have on the United States–Japan alliance on the "day after" a breakout. We incline to doubt the security partnership would collapse overnight, especially if Tokyo initiated open, constructive consultations ahead of time. Even so, the transpacific alliance would never be the same. Would Washington furl its nuclear umbrella in a fit of pique? Or would Tokyo and Washington transcend the initial discord, integrate their nuclear strategies, and develop a transpacific deterrent, much as the United States–United Kingdom alliance formulated a transatlantic deterrent to Soviet aggression?

► Third, a Japanese nuclear breakout would certainly release shockwaves across the Asian capitals. How would Japan's retaliatory posture and forces interact with the Chinese nuclear doctrine and North Korea's nuclear program? Would Tokyo's entry into the nuclear club spur both horizontal and vertical proliferation?

► Fourth, but certainly not least, there are technical questions to resolve. As noted above, the timing of any Japanese effort to breach the nuclear threshold would depend in large part on the availability of weapons-usable fissile material. How easily could Japanese nuclear engineers put the nation's stockpile of reactor-grade plutonium to use manufacturing nuclear warheads? It seems reasonable to suppose that Tokyo could convert this material for use in nuclear payloads over time—the main question is when.

These questions are eminently worth pondering. We make no pretense of offering the last word on the subject of Japanese nuclear options. But we hope this is a useful first word in a sorely needed discussion of naval strategy and deterrence in Asia.

Notes

1. Richard Halloran, *Chrysanthemum and Sword Revisited: Is Japanese Militarism Resurgent?* (Honolulu: East-West Center, 1991).

2. Global Security Newswire, December 7, 2007, www.nti.org/d_newswire/issues/print.asp?story_id = 1D790077-D5CC-45E9-B8A9-C1D999CAF38D.

3. Ariel E. Levite, "Never Say Never Again: Nuclear Reversal Revisited," *International Security* 27, no. 3 (Winter 2002–3): 66n17.

4. It is noteworthy that the Japanese launched major air strikes against the Philippines from Kaohsiung in its initial moves to conquer Southeast Asia.

5. US Joint Forces Command, Presentation on "A Framework for Discussing US Joint Force Structures during the Next Administration," November 12, 2008, slide 4. The 150-ship figure assumes that Congress and the administration adopt the budget figures put forward by Representative Barney Frank (D-MA). Frank's proposal translates into a 45 percent real cut in defense spending from the fiscal year 2008 total of $703 billion, which included supplemental allocations.

6. Director of Warfare Integration, US Office of the Chief of Naval Operations, *Report to Congress on Annual Long-range Plan for Construction of Naval Vessels for FY 2009* (Washington, DC: US Government Printing Office, 2008), 3–12; "US Navy Active Ship Force Levels, 2007 to 2008," Naval Vessel Register, Naval Historical Center, www.history.navy.mil/branches/org9-4.htm.

7. See, e.g., William Choong, "Will Japan Go Nuclear?" *Straits Times*, October 23, 2006, http://rspas.anu.edu.au/papers/sdsc/analysis/Will_Japan_Go_Nuclear.pdf; and Mark Erikson, "Japan Could 'Go Nuclear' in Months," *Asia Times*, January 14, 2003, www.atimes.com/atimes/japan/EA14Dh01.html.

8. For a sense of Tokyo's surprise and alarm at Beijing's nuclear breakout, see "China's Rapid Rise as Nuke Power Surprised Japan, US," Kyodo World Service, February 25, 2005.

9. "Sato's Nuclear Request," *Asahi Shimbun*, December 24, 2008.

10. Matake Kamiya, "Nuclear Japan: Oxymoron or Coming Soon?" *Washington Quarterly* 26, no. 1 (Winter 2002–3): 65–67.

11. Ibid., 65–67.

12. For a sampling of this sparse literature, see Clifton W. Sherrill, "The Need for a Japanese Nuclear Deterrent," *Comparative Strategy* 20 (2001): 259–70.

13. Tetsuya Endo, "How Realistic Is a Nuclear-Armed Japan?" Association of Japanese Institute of Strategic Studies, July 20, 2007.

14. Brad Glosserman, "Straight Talk about Japan's Nuclear Option," *PacNet* 50A, October 11, 2006; Brad Glosserman, "Japan Peers into the Abyss," *PacNet* 20, March 20, 2008.

15. Llewelyn Hughes, "Why Japan Will Not Go Nuclear (Yet): International and Domestic Constraints on the Nuclearization of Japan," *International Security* 31, no. 4 (Spring 2007): 67–96.

16. Hajime Izumi and Katsuhisa Furukawa, "Not Going Nuclear: Japan's Response to North Korea's Nuclear Test," *Arms Control Today* 37, no. 6 (July–August 2007): 51–56; Mike M. Mochizuki, "Japan Tests the Nuclear Taboo," *Nonproliferation Review* 14, no. 2 (July 2007): 303–28.

17. George Shultz, "Preventing the Proliferation of Nuclear Weapons," *Department of State Bulletin* 84, no. 2093 (December 1984): 17–21.

18. Scott D. Sagan, "Why Do States Build Nuclear Weapons? Three Models in Search of a Bomb," *International Security* 21, no. 3 (Winter 1996–97): 55, 57.

19. Ibid., 55, 63–64.

20. Ibid., 55, 73–76.

21. Graham Allison and Philip Zelikow, *Essence of Decision: Explaining the Cuban Missile Crisis*, 2nd ed. (New York: Longman, 1999), 256.

22. Ibid., 257.

23. Levite, "Never Say Never," 71–73. See also Yuri Kase, "The Costs and Benefits of Japan's Nuclearization: An Insight into the *1968/70 Internal Report*," *Nonproliferation Review* 8, no. 2 (Summer 2001): 55–68.

24. Levite, "Never Say Never," 67.

25. Evelyn Goh, *Meeting the China Challenge: The US in Southeast Asian Regional Security Strategies* (Washington, DC: East-West Center, 2005), 2–4. See also Evelyn Goh, "A Strategic Insurance Policy," *Asia Times*, September 6, 2006, www.atimes.com/atimes/China/HI06Ad02.html, and Evan S. Medeiros, "Strategic Hedging and the Future of Asia-Pacific Stability," *Washington Quarterly* 29, no. 1 (Winter 2005–6): 145–67.

26. Levite, "Never Say Never," 59.

27. Joseph Cirincione, Jon B. Wolfsthal, and Miriam Rajkumar, *Deadly Arsenals: Tracking Weapons of Mass Destruction*, 2nd rev. ed. (Washington, DC: Carnegie Endowment for International Peace, 2005), 18.

28. Hughes, "Why Japan Will Not Go Nuclear," 91.

29. Hisahiko Okazaki, "Time to Consider a Nuclear Strategy for Japan," *Daily Yomiuri*, April 7, 2007.

30. Terumasa Nakanishi, a professor at Kyoto University, argues explicitly that "US nuclear weapons will be deployed in Japan as arms exclusively for the defense of Japan, and Tokyo and Washington will share the buttons to fire them. Japan and the United States should have a joint system to operate nuclear weapons." See "North Korea's Nuclear Threat: Should Revision of the 3 Nonnuclear Principles Be Discussed?" *Daily Yomiuri*, March 22, 2007.

31. Yukio Satoh, "Reinforcing American Extended Deterrence for Japan: An Essential Step for Nuclear Disarmament," *AJISS-Commentary*, no. 57, February 2009.

32. James L. Schoff, "Does the Nonproliferation Tail Wag the Deterrence Dog?" *PacNet* 9, February 5, 2009.

33. See Joint Statement of the US-Japan Security Consultative Committee, *Alliance Transformation: Advancing United States-Japan Security and Defense Cooperation*, May 1, 2007. The report declared that "the full range of US military capabilities—both nuclear and non-nuclear strike forces and defensive capabilities—form[s] the core of extended deterrence and support[s] US commitments to the defense of Japan."

34. Emma Chanlett-Avery and Mary Beth Nikitin, *Japan's Nuclear Future: Policy Debate Prospects, and US Interests*, CRS Report to Congress (Washington, DC: Congressional Research Service, 2008), 10.

35. Seung-Young Kim, "Security, Nationalism and the Pursuit of Nuclear Weapons and Missiles: The South Korean Case, 1970–82," *Diplomacy and Statecraft* 12, no. 4 (December 2001): 56.

36. David Albright and Corey Gay, "Taiwan: Nuclear Nightmare Averted," *Bulletin of Atomic Scientists* 54, no. 1 (January/February 1998): 55.

37. Nancy Bernkopf Tucker, *Taiwan, Hong Kong, and the United States, 1945–1992: Uncertain Friendships* (New York: Twayne, 1994), 146.

38. William Burr, ed., "New Archival Evidence on Taiwanese 'Nuclear Intentions,' 1966–1976," *National Security Archive Electronic Briefing Book No. 19*, October 13, 1999.

39. For a sampling of Japan's options for developing a nuclear warhead, see Noritsugu Takebe, "A Domestic Warhead Development Plan," *Gunji Kenkyu*, August 1, 2005, 28–43.

40. "Japan's Nuclear Capability: Model of Peaceful Use; Owns Plutonium Enough for 740 Atomic Bombs," *Sankei Shimbun*, November 8, 2006.

41. "Japan Needs 3–5 Years to Build Nuclear Warheads," Kyodo World Service, December 25, 2006; "Unaware of Reported Government Documents on Nuke Warhead: Shiozaki," *Jiji Press*, December 25, 2006.

42. "Japan Profile," Nuclear Threat Initiative Website, October 2008, www.nti .org/e_research/profiles/Japan/index.html.

43. Shinichi Ogawa and Michael Schiffer, "Japan's Plutonium Reprocessing Dilemma," *Arms Control Today* 35, no. 8 (October 2005): 20–24.

44. If the threat environment deteriorates so precipitously as to warrant an immediate breakout, it is possible to imagine the SDF relying on air delivery as an interim measure.

45. Chanlett-Avery and Nikitin, *Japan's Nuclear Future*, 6.

46. Kan Ito, "China's Nuclear Power Will Control the World by 2020," *Shokun*, January 1, 2006, 34–45.

47. Yasuhiro Nakasone, "Japan's National Defense Strategy for the 21st Century," *Voice*, April 1, 2004, 50–57.

48. Keishi Saeki, "Qualifications and Limitations of Nuclear Arms in Japan," *Chuo Koron*, September 1, 2003, 36–39.

49. Nisohachi Hyodo, "A Plan to Deploy Nuclear Warheads in Japan," *Shokun*, October 2, 1996.

50. The TLAM-N, the nuclear variant of the Tomahawk, boasted a range of 2,500 kilometers until withdrawn from the US Navy fleet in 1991.

51. Kan Ito, "Are We Prepared to Deal with Kim-Chong-Il's Evil Bombs?" *Shokun*, April 1, 2003, 86–94.

52. Ito, "China's Nuclear Power Will Control the World."

53. "North Korea's Nuclear Threat/Japan Could Build N-Weapons, But . . .," *Yomiuri Daily*, March 21, 2007.

54. "Type 209," GlobalSecurity.org, www.globalsecurity.org/military/world/europe/ type-209-specs.htm.

55. William Murray, a retired submariner, estimates that Japan would need some twenty-four missile-armed boats to provide an adequate margin of deterrence. Using our six-to-one ratio, that would allow the SDF to keep four submarines on deterrent patrol at any time. Phone discussion between James Holmes and William Murray, Newport, February 23, 2009.

CHAPTER 8

THE INFLUENCE OF BUREAUCRATIC POLITICS ON INDIA'S NUCLEAR STRATEGY

Anupam Srivastava and Seema Gahlaut

INDIA HAS PREMISED its nuclear strategy on developing an effective deterrent while at the same time pushing aggressively for a worldwide rollback of nuclear arsenals. Indian strategy, then, derives both from practical military concerns—the stark reality of nuclear neighbors to the subcontinent's east and west—and from a fervent, long-standing, apparently sincere devotion to the ideals of nonproliferation and disarmament. Scientific, technical, and doctrinal advances are critical to the military element of strategy, whereas forceful diplomacy carries forward the nonproliferation element. The dualism inherent in Indian thinking about nuclear weapons, which blends idealism uneasily with realism, helps explain the sometimes-quixotic character of Indian strategy.

Like China and most other Asian continental powers, India confronts a complex, multidirectional, multifaceted strategic environment. Its traditional rival, Pakistan, lies to the northwest, and China is to the northeast. Rivals could station ballistic missile submarines in nearby waters or use the Indian Ocean's sea lanes to transport weapons-related matériel, menacing Indian security directly or abetting the proliferation of nuclear weapons to "rogue regimes" or nonstate groups. New Delhi's strategy, consequently, must come to terms with myriad factors. This chapter reviews four clusters of questions pertaining to Indian nuclear strategy in this strategic environment, with the aim of peering ahead to discern how New Delhi may manage strategy in the second nuclear age.

One strand in India's atomic past that stands out in our account is bureaucratic politics and culture. Institutions promise to shape the making and execution of strategy, much as they have since the inception of the Indian nuclear program. Agencies bring distinctive worldviews to their endeavors. These views often clash during interagency initiatives, shaping—and at times misshaping—the products of these organizations' joint labors. The German sociologist Max Weber shed light on the benefits and drawbacks of bureaucracy. He depicted the bureaucratic method of organization as a marvel of efficiency, one of the cornerstones of the modern administrative state. He viewed bureaucracy as a kind of mechanical extension of the will of the sovereign, implying that these institutions could be relied on to carry out rulers' directives both swiftly and efficiently.

The "monocratic," or highly centralized, bureaucracy earned special plaudits from Weber, who maintained that, because it concentrated power in the hands of a few, accountable officials, was "finally superior both in intensive efficiency and in the scope of its operations."[1] It was rational in a way that more traditional modes of organization were not. Weber likened bureaucratic organizations to engineering systems; thus he insisted that the "fully developed bureaucratic apparatus compares with other organizations exactly as does the machine with the non-mechanical modes of production." Such an apparatus boasted such virtues as precision, speed, "strict subordination," and a "reduction of friction and of material and personal costs."[2] "The choice," he insisted, was "only that between bureaucracy and dilettantism in the field of administration."[3]

To be sure, enthusiasts of modern public administration did acknowledge, usually in a roundabout fashion, that bureaucratic institutions had some intrinsic shortcomings. Although they were well suited to performing routine functions, large organizations found it exceedingly difficult to alter their methods, even when the need for such change seemed compelling. Weber testified indirectly to the inflexibility of administrative institutions; he thus admitted that, once "fully established, bureaucracy is among those social structures which are the hardest to destroy."[4] The individual official was "only a small cog in a ceaselessly moving mechanism which prescribes to him an essentially fixed route of march. The official is entrusted with specialized tasks, and normally the mechanism cannot be put into motion or arrested by him, but only from the very top."[5]

Only top leaders, then, could realistically hope to steer administrative organizations in a different direction. Because of their training and career incentives, lesser officials were invariably jealous of the interests of the overall organization. As Weber explained, "the individual bureaucrat is, above all, forged to the common interest of all the functionaries in the perpetuation of the apparatus," sometimes at the expense of the larger national interest.[6] These elements made administrative institutions, built as they were on the "settled orientation of *man* for observing the accustomed rules and regulations," extraordinarily resistant to change.[7] Indeed, concluded Weber, modern administrative organization made real political revolution, "in the sense of the forceful creation of entirely new formations of authority," practically impossible.[8]

Weber did pay tribute, albeit in an offhand and cursory way, to the notion that elected officials could impose their will on bureaucratic institutions through judicious personnel appointments. He posited that appointing carefully selected individuals to preside over the bureaucracy was better than electing them.[9] The wisely chosen official acted as a "Caesar," or "a free trustee of the masses."[10] By installing like-minded officials in the bureaucracy, elected officials stood at least some chance of inducing a course change in organizations that were highly resistant to outside pressure—even pressure from their formal superiors.

At times, Indian political leaders have found it difficult to bend government agencies to their will in order to rationalize nuclear strategy. How they will fare at installing strong leadership—yoking these institutions to top-level policy and strategy—promises to be a key metric of Indian progress in fielding an effective deterrent. And whether they can design efficient institutional arrangements and install the right personnel to lead and manage them will be one arbiter of India's nuclear future. India's strong tradition of civil supremacy over military matters should help, but success is far from foreordained.

The Gradual Acceptance of the Utility of Nuclear Weapons

India has been a proponent of global nuclear disarmament since the 1950s. Indeed, India was the first country to propose a comprehensive nuclear test ban, putting forth a resolution in 1952. The major powers rejected this initiative, and its substance was diluted in the 1963 Partial Test Ban Treaty, a compact to which India acceded. New Delhi nevertheless persisted with its calls for universal disarmament and for wider test bans. It also took an active hand in the discussions that yielded the Nuclear Non-Proliferation Treaty (NPT). It objected heatedly, however, to the creation of two categories of signatories—nuclear weapon states and non–nuclear weapon states—in the final version of the accord. The leadership ultimately refused to sign the NPT. New Delhi issued its last major call for "universal disarmament" in 1988. Seeing its entreaty rebuffed prompted the Indian leadership to fundamentally rethink a nuclear strategy predicated on nuclear abolition.

In the interim, Indian foreign policy exhibited a mix of the idealism characteristic of newly independent states tempered with the experiences of an ancient civilization. The nation's founding prime minister, Jawaharlal Nehru, vigorously promoted the Non-Aligned Movement as a "third way" for the developing world in the Cold War, rather than siding with the North Atlantic Treaty Organization or the Warsaw Pact. The prime minister considered China as India's great ally in this idealistic pursuit, along with Egypt, Yugoslavia, and Indonesia. As such, Nehru felt stunned and betrayed when Mao Zedong's China deployed overwhelming force to beat India decisively in a brief but bloody border war in 1962. After the war, he was disheartened and politically weakened, and he never fully recovered from this blow and died a disillusioned man in May 1964.

Independent of these developments, India's civilian nuclear program had developed significantly during the 1950s, benefiting in part from a US team's visit under the Atoms for Peace program launched by President Dwight D. Eisenhower in 1953. An Indian research reactor, Apsara, commenced operations by 1956. Defeat at Chinese hands strengthened the voice of proponents of a nuclear weapon option. These voices clamored even more loudly following Nehru's death and China's first atomic test, which took place in October 1964. Chinese bombmaking owed much to material and technological assistance furnished by the Soviet Union, whose apparent success with state-guided economic development had prompted Nehru to initiate an Indian Five-Year Plan based on the Soviet Gos Plan.

Nehru's successor, Lal Bahadur Shastri, continued pushing for global disarmament. At the same time, however, he gave the go-ahead for scientists to expedite research that would equip India with the technical capacity and know-how to build a nuclear weapon if a political consensus were to demand one in the future. Shastri died suddenly in 1966 while finalizing a Soviet-brokered cease-fire at Tashkent to conclude the 1965 Indo-Pakistani War. His demise brought Indira Gandhi to office. Prime Minister Gandhi largely maintained Shastri's policies while the domestic weapons-oriented research-and-development effort made steady progress. In 1974 Gandhi authorized one test of a "peaceful nuclear explosive," largely to shore up her domestic political support, before reverting to the earlier policy. The prime minister reversed course despite strong pressure from advisers who implored her to allow a series of tests and thus consummate the natural progression typical of all other nuclear weapon states.[11]

Official ambivalence about nuclear strategy persisted into the late 1980s, when two developments weakened the Indian government's resistance to pursuing a working bomb. First, Indian intelligence received reports in late 1986 that China had transferred a proven nuclear weapon design to Pakistan. A. Q. Khan, the head of Pakistan's nuclear efforts, indirectly confirmed the transfer in an interview with a prominent Indian journalist; he told his interlocutor that Indian military calculations henceforth ought to accept the reality of a credible Pakistani nuclear weapons capability. Khan made this startling statement a few weeks before India conducted a major annual war exercise, Operation Brasstacks. New Delhi confirmed much later that Beijing had supplied Islamabad with the design for the bomb that Chinese engineers detonated at Lop Nor in 1966.[12] And even worse from the Indian standpoint, the evidence suggested that the United States had turned a blind eye to the Sino-Pakistani collusion on this issue.[13]

The second watershed event for reevaluating India's nuclear strategy came in 1988, when the young Indian prime minister, Rajiv Gandhi, unveiled a comprehensive plan espousing phased disarmament on the part of the nuclear weapon states. Silence greeted the proposal. The Soviet invasion of Afghanistan in December 1979 and the Ronald Reagan administration's subsequent effort to repulse the occupiers had resurrected Pakistan's status as the United States' frontline ally in South Asia. On the one hand, US policy set loose a massive flow of resources to arm and train the mujahedeen. On the other, Washington and its allies overlooked A. Q. Khan's concerted efforts to acquire Western materials and technology for Islamabad's weapons program.[14] New Delhi found the latter development especially worrisome.

In Indian eyes, these adverse developments flanking the subcontinent affirmed the value of a proven Indian nuclear weapons capability. New Delhi pressed ahead on both tracks, preparing to test a bomb while making a last-ditch push for universal disarmament. US intelligence services detected two attempts on Indians' part to conceal preparations for testing, even as New Delhi lobbied forcefully for the Comprehensive Test Ban Treaty (CTBT) at the Conference on Disarmament in Geneva.

As noted above, New Delhi had lobbied for decades in favor of an outright ban, and it took an active hand in the CTBT negotiations. Late in the talks, however, negotiators inserted an entry-into-force clause into the final draft at the behest of

China and Australia. This clause was unprecedented among international treaties, identifying India as one of forty-four nuclear-capable countries that must become parties to the CTBT for it to take effect.[15] India saw the clause as an attempt to abridge its sovereign right to remain clear of a treaty it deemed incompatible with its national interest. It also feared that governments backing the treaty would impose sanctions to compel nonsignatories to consent to the pact.

Before the window of opportunity closed or sanctions could be levied, the Indian government authorized a series of five nuclear tests. Indian weapons engineers executed the tests on May 11 and May 13, 1998.

The Development of India's Nuclear Doctrine and Strategy

The May 1998 tests, dubbed "Shakti-2" ("Power"), set loose an international furor, which was accompanied by a debate about the size and scope of the arsenal that the country would eventually build, the impact of that arsenal on the balance of power in South Asia—including neighboring China—and whether it signaled a permanent departure from long-standing Indian support for universal disarmament. New Delhi responded by assuring both regional and distant powers that it would take a measured approach. Indian officials announced a moratorium on further testing and instituted the National Security Advisory Board (NSAB) to draft a nuclear doctrine.

Implicit in the NSAB's mandate was that its input would be advisory, whereas the national security establishment would formulate and implement a detailed doctrine over time. The other principal mission entrusted to the NSAB was to develop a doctrine setting forth an accurate, reasonably detailed framework in the public domain about the eventual scale, scope, and mode of deployment of Indian nuclear weapons, delivery systems, and associated infrastructure and facilities. In late 1999, operating within these parameters, the NSAB released a doctrine outlining plans to build a "credible minimum deterrent."[16] Major provisions of the document envisioned:

▶ a sufficient, survivable, and operationally ready nuclear "triad";
▶ robust systems for command, control, communication, and intelligence;
▶ effective early-warning capabilities;
▶ comprehensive planning and training for nuclear operations consistent with Indian strategy; and
▶ the "political will" to employ such forces, if and when required.

The framers of this doctrine envisaged building a triad of sea, air, and mobile land-based systems, because they believed that such an arrangement would offer mobility, redundancy, and the capacity to disperse quickly. This would maximize survivability, and thus the credibility of deterrence. The primary focus of command, control, communication, and intelligence development would be survivability. The force itself must be capable of shifting to alert status even if degraded through repeated enemy strikes. The doctrine explicitly rejected the first use of nuclear weapons. Nuclear arms would exist exclusively to deter a nuclear attack. They would be employed solely to retaliate in kind against a nuclear assault.

The much-anticipated NSAB doctrine instantly came under intense, occasionally pungent scrutiny and criticism, both within India and among foreign commentators. One well-informed Indian analyst pronounced it full of "shibboleths and platitudes," jeering at it as "a totally harmless document that is of little or no use to anyone involved in translating a doctrine into a workable operational plan. Its only virtue is that nothing in it went very strongly against the sentiment of any member of the NSAB and conversely all members could identify themselves with some portions of it."[17]

This observation was unduly harsh, in large part because no government publicly divulges sensitive details about military strategy. The document nevertheless left several key questions unanswered. For instance, it provided no details about how the weapons would be stored. Would the warheads be mated with their delivery systems or kept separate? Would the warheads be stored fully assembled, or disassembled with nuclear and nonnuclear components held separately? Such information would reveal much about New Delhi's view of the threat environment—namely, how long Indian leaders believed they would have to decide whether to use nuclear munitions in combat.

Although the NSAB draft doctrine did clearly spell out a no-first-use policy, while disavowing the use of nuclear weapons against non–nuclear weapon states, it did not clarify whether New Delhi reserved the right to retaliate against nonstate actors. It also did not amplify why early-warning capabilities are necessary if India is content to field a retaliation-only deterrent—that is, an invulnerable second-strike force. Some analysts speculated that the initial document described features that remained "aspirational" in 1999. Whether the government intends to follow through will become apparent over time from reviewing official statements, technology acquisitions, and force deployments.

The Institutional Structure Amplified and Refined

In 2002 the Cabinet Committee on Security—the top national body vested with decision-making powers—provided further details about Indian nuclear doctrine. It maintained that rapid Chinese nuclear modernization and Pakistan's reserving the option of a first strike compelled India to pursue a more survivable, more credible nuclear posture. Salient provisions of the committee's statement included:

▶ India will build and maintain a credible minimum deterrent.
▶ Nuclear weapons will be used only in reply to a nuclear attack on Indian territory or on Indian forces anywhere.
▶ Nuclear retaliation against a first strike will be massive and designed to inflict unacceptable damage.

▶ Only the civil leadership can order nuclear retaliatory attacks, acting through the Nuclear Command Authority (NCA).

▶ Nuclear weapons will not be used against non–nuclear weapon states.

▶ India reserves the right to use nuclear weapons to retaliate against a major biological or chemical attack against it, or against Indian forces deployed anywhere.

▶ India will continue enforcing strict controls on exports of nuclear- and missile-related materials and technologies, participating in Fissile Material Cutoff Treaty negotiations, and observing its moratorium on nuclear testing.

▶ India remains committed to the goal of a nuclear-weapons-free world enforced through global, verifiable, nondiscriminatory measures.[18]

The 2002 document went into some detail on the makeup and functions of the NCA, the body that governs the use of Indian nuclear weapons. A Political Council chaired by the prime minister and an Executive Council chaired by the national security adviser constitute the NCA. The Executive Council offers expert input for NCA decision making and executes directives from the Political Council, which is the sole body empowered to order the use of nuclear weapons.

The Cabinet Committee on Security document also indicated that command-and-control arrangements, targeting strategy for retaliatory attacks, and operating procedures for various stages of alert and launch were already in existence, and that a commander in chief had been appointed to oversee the Strategic Forces Command, and thus to manage and administer all Indian strategic forces. It noted, furthermore, that India had put in place alternate chains of command to guarantee the armed forces' ability to conduct retaliatory nuclear strikes under all eventualities.

By 2003 the government had disclosed additional information about the NCA.[19] The members of the Cabinet Committee on Security make up the Political Council, along with the national security adviser. The Executive Council brings together the chairman of the Chiefs of Staff Committee (COSC) of the three armed services, the three service chiefs, the heads of the intelligence agencies, and officials representing organs from the scientific establishment that have a hand in the nuclear program.

The triservice Strategic Forces Command (SFC) was instituted in 2003 to administer all Indian strategic nuclear assets. The SFC is India's third triservice command. As expected, primary authority over the SFC went to the Indian air force "because the first two—the Integrated Defence Staff and the Andaman and Nicobar Command—had gone to the army and the navy, respectively."[20] The SFC commander in chief exercises control of the full triad of strategic nuclear assets, including land-based missiles, air- or space-delivered weapons, and sea-based platforms. There are some exceptions to this. The 333 Prithvi Missile Group and the 334 Prithvi Missile Group remain under air force control, for instance, as do the dual-capable Mirage 2000, Jaguar, and Su-30 MKI combat aircraft—warplanes capable of delivering conventional or nuclear payloads. Short-range Agni I missiles stay with the Army Artillery Corps. The SFC exercises operational control of all these systems when required. The SFC was temporarily based in Delhi in 2003, but it was subsequently relocated elsewhere.

Despite these institutional innovations, however, India has not yet created the post of chief of the Defense Staff to supply the government with single-point military advice and manage the country's nuclear arsenal.[21] This shortfall persists despite repeated recommendations from many sources, including the Kargil Review Committee (2001), a subsequent Group of Ministers' Report (2001) on reforming the national security system, and statements from successive service chiefs and the chair of the COSC.[22] According to a December 2009 report, the government is soliciting input from various political parties before acting on this advice.[23]

Appointing a chief of the Defense Staff who ranks above the three service chiefs should bolster cohesion between the armed forces on interservice doctrinal, planning, procurement, and operational issues.[24] To put the prospects for tighter coordination into perspective, however, outgoing chairs of the COSC—another post designed to generate single-point military advice—have commented wryly that the post is inherently dysfunctional and thus of suboptimal value to the NCA.[25] In all likelihood Max Weber would disapprove of this fragmentation and diffusion of bureaucratic authority and accountability, and he would castigate the Indian government for unwittingly encouraging interservice feuding at the expense of rational strategy, operations, and force planning (see figure 8.1).

Figure 8.1   India's Nuclear Command-and-Control Structure

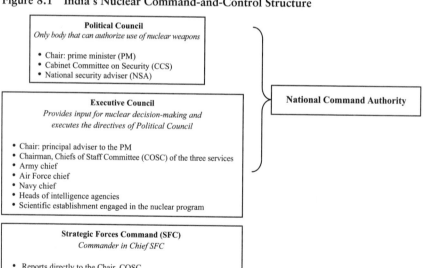

The Search for Synergy between Doctrine and Capabilities

In light of these shortcomings, it is perhaps predictable that India has compiled a decidedly mixed record in establishing doctrinal guidelines suitable for a credible second-strike capability, setting up the relevant institutional infrastructure, designing and constructing the offensive and defensive hardware necessary to accomplish the specified objectives, and adjusting strategy and force structure to stay abreast of an evolving threat environment. Although reassessment and adaptation are discussed in a subsequent section, we first examine how India's burgeoning military capabilities and technologies are influencing the further refinement of doctrine and in turn are being affected by doctrinal change.

The Defense Research and Development Organization (DRDO) is the government's chief arm for developing defense systems and technology. DRDO has worked closely with the Indian army during the past decade to field Prithvi ("Earth") surface-to-surface missiles, which boast a range between 150 and 250 kilometers, with a low circular error probable. The Prithvi underwent extensive user trials and subsequent design modifications before serial production commenced. Two variants are now operational and fully deployed.[26]

India's longer-range missile—Agni ("Fire")—boasts several variants differing in range and payload. The modified Agni I, with a solid-fueled engine and a range of 700 to 800 kilometers, has now completed all user trials, has entered serial production, and is fully operational. The Agni II is propelled by a two-stage solid-fueled engine to a range of 2,000 to 2,500 kilometers. It has been repeatedly tested from silos and mobile firing platforms. The missile has entered limited production and is nearing "induction," or operational status. Powered by a two-stage solid-fueled engine, the modified Agni III has been tested twice with mixed results. It did not come close to its maximum design range of 3,500 to 4,000 kilometers. It is still undergoing design modifications and will likely undergo additional user trials for another three to four years before serial production begins. India's longest-range missile, the Agni IV or Surya ("Sun"), will have a projected range of 6,000 to 8,000 kilometers. It remains on the drawing board, far from taking flight. New Delhi did stage a successful test of an Agni V ballistic missile in April 2012. The Agni V can strike at Bejing or Shanghai.

As noted above, the Agni I force will remain under the operational control of the Army Artillery Corps, whereas the command of the Agni IIs, Agni IIIs, and future variants will stay with the air force. In addition, the air force fields squadrons of Jaguar, Mirage-2000, and Sukhoi-30 MKI strike fighter aircraft, an undisclosed number of which have been modified to carry nuclear payloads. It remains to be seen how this apportionment of different weaponry among the military services will work out. For instance, assigning control of the Agni Is to the Indian army suggests that the military views these as tactical weapons, implying that the longer-range variants and perhaps aircraft-delivered munitions are strategic weapons. Whether Pakistan would consider Agni Is stationed along the Indo-Pakistani frontier as tactical in nature is doubtful, because even short-range birds could strike within massive swaths of Pakistani territory. The asymmetries that are likely to complicate confrontations between big and small nuclear newcomers could feature prominently in Indo-Pakistani encounters, owing in part to such perceptual disparities.

After receiving the smallest share of the defense budget for more than four decades, the Indian navy has risen sharply in prominence during the past decade. The navy has distinguished itself for making effective use of scarce resources to continue its steady modernization. The service has also gained visibility because of New Delhi's plan to make the undersea leg of its nuclear triad a working reality by developing nuclear-powered ballistic missile submarines and sea-launched ballistic missiles. The navy's endeavors are covered in depth in chapter 9.

The Indian defense budget has consistently remained under 3 percent of gross domestic product. The budget stood at $32 billion for 2010, registering year-on-year growth of only 3.8 percent above 2009—the lowest increase since 2001.[27] The armed forces' procurement budget has averaged $5 billion to $7 billion annually since 2005 and is expected to continue to grow. The Indian navy's share of the procurement budget is now $1.54 billion and is expected to continue growing, furnishing capital and technology for major upgrades into the foreseeable future.[28]

The Indian navy's most notable recent success came with the development of the advanced technology vessel (ATV). This is India's first indigenously built nuclear-powered submarine, though constructed with significant Russian assistance. After years of struggling to reduce the size and weight of the onboard nuclear reactor, the navy and the Department of Atomic Energy finally managed to miniaturize the plant enough to fit it within the ATV's hull. After the success of initial trials, the ATV began extensive sea trials in mid-2009 and is expected to become fully operational around 2014.[29]

The Indian navy's other major success came through developing DRDO's most successful antiship cruise missile, the PJ-10 BrahMos. This Mach 2.8 missile, which can strike at targets up to 290 kilometers distant, can be launched from surface or undersea combatants. Both the Russian and Indian navies are taking delivery of BrahMos missiles. This highly mobile missile will provide India with a range of attack options, for example, by amplifying the striking power of forward-deployed submarines against Pakistani (and ultimately Chinese) warships.[30]

New Delhi has also worked diligently during the past decade to develop and deploy robust missile defenses. Although this system will not itself employ nuclear-tipped missiles, it will be designed to intercept and destroy incoming missiles carrying conventional or nuclear payloads. The open-architecture, multilayered system currently under development will provide point and area defense. It will eventually be scaled up to provide nationwide defense. The system integrates long-range Russian surface-to-air missiles (S-300 PMU 1 for the Indian army, and S-300 V for the Indian air force), several shorter-range missiles, early-warning aircraft (including IL-76 and AN-50 planes, some of which can provide midair refueling), and the indigenously built Rajendra radar. In addition, India is inducting Israeli systems like the more powerful Green Pine radar and longer-range Arrow interceptors into its missile defense architecture. New Delhi is negotiating with Washington to purchase a customized version of the Patriot Advanced Capability theater missile defense system (PAC-2 or PAC-3). India was an early and strong supporter of President George W. Bush's missile defense initiative of 2004. Indian scientists and military officers have observed live missile defense tests on US soil on at least three occasions since 2003.[31]

Alongside these developments, a wider array of allied capabilities is also becoming available, which provide Indian security planners with additional options as they refine the nation's second-strike nuclear doctrine and posture and enhance its conventional defensive shield against future conventional attacks and nuclear first strikes. For instance, the Indian navy has added a new dimension to its fleet by launching an indigenous warship, code-named Project 15 Alpha. This *Kolkata*-class destroyer represents a generational advance over its predecessor, the *Delhi*-class destroyer. *Kolkatas* boast enhanced stealth features, significant land-attack capabilities, and more advanced weapons and sensors.[32]

Furthermore, India has collaborated with France since 2002 to build six *Scorpene*-class diesel-electric submarines at its Mazgaon naval docks. French shipbuilder DCNS—which has also joined with the Spanish firm Novantia to supply *Scorpenes* to Chile, Malaysia, and Brazil—is now taking its Indian collaboration much further. DCNS is entering into a joint venture with Walchandnagar Industries Ltd. to make components for submarines as well as for other naval applications.[33] In the aviation sector, Boeing and India's HCL Technologies Ltd. recently inaugurated a joint Center of Excellence that will provide engineering design, development, and support for applications critical to flight testing. The Boeing Test and Evaluation Unit will use the Center of Excellence across its entire line of products and services.[34]

For its part, DRDO has been subjected to considerable government scrutiny following long delays and cost overruns in the delivery of major combat systems. DRDO is undergoing significant restructuring to bolster its effectiveness and efficiency.[35] Outside pressures have helped bring about marked improvements in DRDO's delivery of a range of missiles, combat vehicles, and other systems since 2008. Its partnership with Israel, moreover, has helped DRDO improve the design of its main battle tank and selected military satellites. Clearly, institutional culture influences not just the handling of existing weaponry but also the capabilities and hardware at the Indian military's disposal. Liberating the armed forces and defense-related agencies from excessive dependence on foreign suppliers would bolster bureaucratic efficiency, help "indigenize" the defense industrial base, and improve interoperability among various types of military hardware. India suffers from the practice of purchasing equipment both from domestic firms and from multiple foreign suppliers.

On an even wider canvas, New Delhi has focused on upgrading its technical capacity to respond to insurgencies, terrorism, and other asymmetrical threats. Consequently, the government has expanded the scope and extent of private-sector participation in defense—a move welcomed by energetic corporate participants. With regard to "offsets," India has leveraged its massive procurement budget, requiring foreign suppliers to incorporate Indian-built components and services into major defense contracts. Depending on the value of the contract, the foreign supplier must ensure that between 35 and 50 percent of the products and services that go into a system are developed by Indian companies. This indirectly improves the domestic private sector's capacity and technology base. Offsets complement the steady growth in Indian capabilities across a diverse range of engineering, precision manufacturing, and cutting-edge technologies. In turn, India is honing its capacity to field conventional defenses while making allied improvements in nuclear weapon platforms and delivery systems.

All these advances have given India's leadership greater confidence in the armed forces' ability to carry out an ambitious nuclear strategy. For example, the government has acknowledged the value of "total battlefield awareness and readiness," namely the capacity to detect, identify, track, and target units throughout the battlespace. The Integrated Defense Staff Headquarters recently released three joint operational doctrines, a Joint Doctrine for Subconventional Operations, a Joint Doctrine for Electronic Warfare, and a Joint Doctrine for Maritime Air Operations. These documents emphasize enhancing the armed forces' joint war-fighting capabilities, noting that "wars would be fought not only in air, on land and sea but also in cyberspace, on electronic fronts, along information highways and media fronts"—demanding maximum unity of effort.[36]

On a related front, an influential former army officer claimed that because Pakistan issued a nuclear warning during Operation Brasstacks (in 1987), "the Indian NCA and its alternative structures—both on the ground and in the air—were war-gamed and funds committed for the minimum essential protection to withstand an NBC [nuclear, biological, or chemical weapon] and electro-magnetic pulse threat from Pakistan."[37]

Despite such salutary developments, disunity of effort persists in many areas. Observes one India-watcher, "In the absence of strong political guidance as to the nation's strategic goals and the conditions under which the armed forces would be employed, the armed services are being forced to improvise."[38] Indeed, the three services have formulated three separate war-fighting doctrines premised on their distinct service perspectives. The Indian army has articulated "a doctrine that puts the air force in a subordinate role of providing close air support to ground troops, while the air force's own doctrine and acquisition pattern emphasizes strategic bombing and air-to-air combat. Meanwhile, both services have largely ignored the navy, which is pushing to develop a broader reach requiring numerous large-ticket items such as aircraft carriers and nuclear submarines that will compete with the army and air force for a share of the procurement budget."[39]

The debate over doctrine will help mold the system that India eventually deploys. Another foreign analyst contends that creating a credible minimum deterrent "represents a technically demanding and economically costly enterprise" demanding "high force survivability; robust C3I [command, control, communication, and intelligence]; reliable weapon systems; and a range of systems explicitly devoted to security and safety of the arsenal and all that sustains it."[40] Still another argues that for the near to medium terms, the Indian deterrent will remain a scaled-down version of the envisaged force, combining manned bombers with short- and medium-range missiles. And "while India already possesses second-strike capacity vis-à-vis Pakistan, its ability to hit 'high-value' targets in China is far more circumscribed."[41]

Some Indian analysts counter that when properly structured, credible minimum deterrence offers the safest and most stable nuclear doctrine possible. Given secure, survivable second-strike forces and a no-first-use doctrine, they say, the force can remain relatively small—and thus will eliminate the need for forward deployments, tactical nuclear systems, and war-fighting doctrine, and reduce the incentives to adopt a hair-trigger alert posture.[42]

One potential challenge for Indian political leaders is to overcome their traditional reluctance to involve the military in the uppermost decision-making bodies. Military officers will be vital in nuclear planning, devising strategic and tactical warning procedures, developing interservice coordination for joint operations, and guaranteeing the safety of deployed weapons. An ongoing challenge for Indian defense planners is to refine capabilities and doctrine in light of rapid military modernization in China and Pakistan, close bilateral cooperation between the two prospective adversaries, and changes in their relations with India along disputed Sino-Indian and Indo-Pakistani borders. The institutional challenges detailed here could throw sand in the gears of Indian nuclear strategy and operations.

India's Strategic Environment

India faces a two-front nuclear challenge. China is bolstering its nuclear portfolio while maintaining close ties with Pakistan. A rising India doubtless helps drive China's doctrine and forces while providing the main impetus for Pakistan's nuclear efforts.

Chinese Doctrine, Capabilities, and Deployments

Although Indian officials see cause for concern in their strategic surroundings, they have not launched into a crash program aimed at fielding a large arsenal. Despite occasional expressions of alarm about the strategic environment, this bespeaks a degree of comfort with the situation in South Asia. Chinese nuclear forces are nothing new for India, whereas the strategic balance vis-à-vis Pakistan favors India. India and China have fought no major wars since their 1962 clash. And that war was a legacy of the British, whose so-called MacMahon Line was far more clearly demarcated on the map than on the ground. Neither Beijing nor New Delhi ever accepted the line in its entirety. The Sino-Indian war left an approximately 90,000-square-kilometer border region in dispute. The cease-fire line was later converted into the Line of Actual Control and has remained the de facto boundary ever since.[43] The border region remained fairly quiet until 2008 owing to the harsh climate, inhospitable terrain, and considerable troop deployments on both sides. That year, however, China took several actions that New Delhi blames for reigniting tensions.

It bears mentioning that China has settled border disputes with eight of its nine neighbors, India being the lone exception. Why China has declined to settle its differences with a nuclear India remains a matter of conjecture. On its face, China's nuclear doctrine is nonthreatening. Beijing has left its no-first-use pledge in place even as it has modernized its modest force. At the same time, China reserves the right to use nuclear weapons "in defense of its territory." Given that China claims the Indian state of Arunachal Pradesh, large parts of other Indian states in the northeast, and parts of Kashmir in the northwest as Chinese soil, Indian officials and analysts take cold comfort in Beijing's no-first-use stance.

During the past two decades, moreover, China has upgraded its military, in part by deploying batteries of short- and medium-range nuclear-tipped missiles in its southwestern provinces bordering India. Some Western analysts have pointed out that China has retired its DF-3A missiles, "the most appropriate missile for use against Indian targets," while rejecting a likely replacement, the DF-25.[44] However, an analysis of recent commercial satellite photographs tells a different story: an extensive deployment area with nearly sixty launchpads for medium-range missiles in Central China, near Delingha and Da Qaidam in the northern part of Qinghai Province. This represents a far larger deployment area than was previously known, which is suitable for different types of launchpads, for command-and-control facilities, and for a storage site for missile deployment equipment at a facility in downtown Delingha.[45]

There was another sign of improvement in the Chinese nuclear-capable missile arsenal: In 2005 only 33 of the Chinese Second Artillery's 91 ballistic missiles were solid-fueled, or 36 percent. By 2008 the share of solid-fueled ballistic missiles had grown to 55 percent, or 67 of 121 weapons. This percentage will rise further as modern DF-31 and DF-31A intercontinental ballistic missiles are deployed to replace the retiring DF-3As and DF-4s, and—more tellingly—as Beijing deploys JL-2 sea-launched ballistic missiles on its *Jin*-class nuclear-powered ballistic missile submarines. MIRVed DF-31s and JL-2s will be targeted against the United States, and Beijing is deploying short-range ballistic missiles in its four provinces opposite Taiwan. Even so, the Second Artillery increasingly possesses "excess inventory" of missiles that could easily be repositioned to hold Indian targets at risk.

It is true that Beijing has fielded nuclear missiles against India for decades, whereas New Delhi is only now beginning to deploy missiles with enough range to reach much of Chinese territory. But recent Chinese behavior has excited growing anxiety among Indian security planners, and deepening military cooperation between Beijing and Islamabad prompts fears of a two-front war. How India perceives Chinese policy and what conclusions it is reaching with regard to China's long-term intentions and conduct will help mold Indian nuclear strategy and forces. Tracking Indian commentary on these matters constitutes a matter of some importance for Western officials and scholars who hope to craft a wise strategy toward South Asia. A sense of crisis clears the mind. If serious forebodings were to take hold in New Delhi, the national security establishment might muster the resolve to impose discipline on the process of devising wise bureaucratic arrangements to govern the deployment and use of nuclear weapons.

Pakistani Doctrine, Capabilities, and Deployments

As discussed above, India's nuclear weapons program was put on the fast track after the failure of the 1988 Rajiv Gandhi universal disarmament proposal and reports that Pakistan had acquired a nuclear weapons capability without conducting overt tests. By 1998 India and Pakistan had fought three major wars, in addition to continued skirmishes over Kashmir and near-crises over military maneuvers close to the border. Some analysts had hoped that "the sheer destructiveness of nuclear weapons and a clearly enunciated doctrine governing their employment (might) serve to impose a certain degree of caution and restraint on the military actions of both sides."[46] India's no-first-use pledge was also expected to reassure Pakistan.

The February 1999 peace process appeared to validate these hopes. In May 1999, however, India sent troops to Kargil to expel Pakistani occupying forces. The result was a bloody war that ended with a Pakistani withdrawal brokered by Washington. Indian officials believed that General Pervez Musharraf had supported the infiltration of insurgents and Pakistani troops to occupy the Indian mountains before and even during the February 1999 peace summit. Wherever the responsibility lay, Kargil made it obvious that nuclear weapons had not put an end to armed conflict between India and Pakistan.

Pakistan has always identified India as a mortal security threat. Islamabad sees the acquisition of nuclear weapons as a measure to offset New Delhi's pronounced conventional superiority. Logically, therefore, it adopted a doctrine premised on first use of nuclear weapons while sketching a number of nonnuclear "redlines" that would trigger massive retaliation and countervalue targeting if India crossed them. In a 2002 interview, the head of Pakistan's Strategic Plans Division confirmed that Islamabad would use atomic weapons if

► India attacks Pakistan and conquers a large part of its territory (space threshold),
► India destroys a large part of either its land or air forces (military threshold),
► India attempts to strangle Pakistan economically (economic coercion), or
► India pushes Pakistan into political destabilization or creates large-scale internal subversion in Pakistan (domestic destabilization).[47]

Pakistani officers have suggested unofficially that there exist two other redlines:

► Indian forces' crossing the Line of Control to an extent that threatens Pakistani control over Azad Kashmir (i.e., Pakistan-controlled Kashmir) or
► an Indian attack on any Pakistani power generation facility or nuclear installation.[48]

Pakistan's nuclear stockpile is estimated at 65 to 80 weapons, with enough fissile material to construct an additional 50 weapons. Delivery options for these munitions include fighter aircraft with an operational range of 300 to 525 miles and missiles with ranges from 50 to 800 miles. Because technological constraints keep Islamabad from targeting all of India, it is building longer-range missiles, such as the Shaheen II (1,550 miles) and Ghauri II (2,200 miles). Warheads are reportedly kept separate from delivery systems, whereas missiles are deployed in mobile launchers to ensure speedy and credible use in the event of a crisis.[49]

Pakistan has opted for a "credible first-use nuclear posture that sacrifices a substantial degree of assertive and centralized control over its nuclear assets, especially in crisis situations."[50] Accordingly, "the essential parts of each weapon may be assembled without the presence of weapons safeguards, and individual commanders may have the capability of acting with or without input from Pakistan's National Command Authority."[51] Because delegated authority for launch-on-warning is an essential component of Islamabad's first-use doctrine, this introduces a degree of instability into Indo-Pakistani military calculations, although both nations have initiated a series of confidence-building measures to ameliorate the situation.[52]

Armed Conflict Remains Possible in the Second Nuclear Age

Indian officialdom believes Pakistan has consciously pursued cross-border insurrection as an asymmetrical strategy against India at least since the 1980s, when it armed and trained Sikh separatists seeking an independent homeland in Punjab. During the 1990s Islamabad shifted its target to Kashmir. The 1999 Kargil war showed that even both contenders' open demonstration of nuclear weapon capability, accompanied by the possibility of nuclear escalation, might not deter armed conflict.

During the past decade, moreover, Pakistan has further consolidated its military and nuclear cooperation with China. This includes upgrading conventional weapons platforms, developing a joint strike fighter, and using Pakistani-controlled territory in Kashmir to build a road link with mainland China through the Karakoram Pass. For its part, China has helped modernize the container seaport at Gwadar, in Baluchistan Province. At the same time, al-Qaeda's attacks on US targets on September 11, 2001, and the US response in Afghanistan returned Pakistan to the status of a major non-NATO ally of the United States.

This places Islamabad in the enviable position of being close to both Beijing and Washington and of using its strategic location as leverage with both capitals. Having such powerful patrons amplifies Pakistan's latitude for dealing with India. And lately, with the Pakistani army supporting US and NATO forces in Afghanistan while engaging radical outfits within its own territory, there is mounting evidence that Islamabad is targeting Islamic militancy on its western front. It evidently remains unprepared to go after militants on its eastern front—its border with India. It has used Washington's growing dependence adroitly to secure substantial military assistance. This includes not only a range of equipment suitable for counterterrorism but also F-16s, radar installations, long-range maritime reconnaissance aircraft, and land-attack missiles that will most likely be deployed against India.

The asymmetrical Pakistani strategy discerned by Indian officials has created a security dilemma for New Delhi. The nexus between terrorism and nuclear brinkmanship has given rise to vehement debates over nuclear strategy. India's political leadership long held the view that even a measured response to terrorist attacks might provoke major retaliation from Pakistan. But in the interim, the consequences of terrorist attacks on India have steadily mounted. This includes spectacular attacks, such as the one on the Kashmiri Parliament, the December 2001 assault on the Parliament in New Delhi, and the November 2008 attacks on multiple targets in Mumbai. An estimated 22,000 Indians have been slain and another 150,000 have been injured in terrorist violence since the 1980s.[53]

In response, India has invested heavily in upgrading its technical and human capacity to respond to terrorists' strikes. United States–India counterterrorism cooperation has also deepened since 9/11. During the trial in Mumbai of Ajmal Kasab, the lone surviving assassin from the 2008 terror attacks, he confessed to his crimes and to undergoing training in Pakistan. The US Federal Bureau of Investigation provided evidence of interceptions of satellite telephone contacts demonstrating that Kasab's handlers in Pakistani intelligence gave real-time instructions to the attackers as Indian commandos mounted a counterattack.[54] The US trial of David Headley, who confessed to masterminding the Mumbai attacks, further implicated the Pakistani establishment in Indian eyes.[55]

United States–India counterterrorism cooperation—including exchanges of human, technical, and signals intelligence—suggests that elements within Pakistan's security establishment have exploited the porous boundaries separating India from Nepal and Bangladesh. Militants have purportedly infiltrated across the borders into India, and large quantities of fake currency have been introduced to destabilize the economy. Small arms provide militants the wherewithal to strike targets across the country, including transportation hubs, scientific meetings, and other economic nodes. Although India anticipates receiving additional US help to upgrade its coastal defenses and counterterrorism capability, it also recognizes the limits on the pressure Washington can apply on Islamabad to uproot what India terms the "infrastructure of terrorism."

To cope with what they see as a hydra-headed menace, Indian defense officials and analysts have debated embracing what is called the Cold Start Doctrine. Cold Start would involve launching a limited surprise strike against Pakistan short of a nuclear war. According to one analyst, quick mobilization and action will serve two purposes aside from surprising the enemy. First, it will "compel the (Indian) political leadership to give political approval ab initio and thereby free the armed forces to generate their full combat potential from the outset." Slow mobilization "gives the political leadership in India time to waver under pressure, and in the process deny the Indian army its due military victories." Second, lengthy preparations allow time for "Pakistan's external patrons . . . to start exerting coercive pressures and mobilizing world opinion."[56] Backers of such an approach, in short, hope to circumvent domestic and international politics for the sake of the armed services' institutional interest in battlefield success.

Offensives under the Cold Start Doctrine would be designed not to cross Pakistan's nuclear redlines. Advocates believe that even if Islamabad planned to deliberately escalate a limited war, "Pakistan's external strategic patrons can coerce or dissuade both sides to avoid a nuclear conflict. But once Pakistan uses a nuclear first strike, no power can restrain India from going in for its nuclear retaliation; and the consequences in that case stand well discussed in strategic circles. Pakistan would [be] wiped out."[57] For their part, Pakistani analysts warn that "if operationalized, the 'Cold Start' Doctrine will force Pakistan to reevaluate its policy of keeping its nuclear arsenal in 'separated' form and move towards placing its strategic capability in a higher state of readiness, including mating warheads to delivery systems."[58]

Ratcheting up nuclear threats to deter a limited cross-border offensive constitutes a predictable Pakistani reaction. This persistent security conundrum induced India to abandon the "composite dialogue," which consists of government-to-government negotiations on seven areas of bilateral dispute. Islamabad had rejected New Delhi's preference for separating the seven issues in hopes of making progress through parallel negotiations on the six less contentious issues. Instead, Islamabad insists on a grand bargain that would resolve even the thorniest imbroglio, Kashmir. Pakistani officials have repeatedly tried to generate external support for this position; for example, by requesting direct mediation from Washington. New Delhi opposes any such outside intervention, although it has accepted US facilitation of the matter.

Following the Mumbai attacks, India stated that no Indo-Pakistani dialogue would be possible until the perpetrators were brought to justice. Working with the US Federal Bureau of Investigation, Indian officials handed more than fifteen dossiers to Pakistan that contained evidence to support prosecutors conducting the trial in Pakistan. Nonetheless, New Delhi has come to doubt that direct talks will resolve any of the outstanding disputes. Unless there is a discernible shift in Pakistan's strategy, India will continue upgrading its counterterrorist capabilities while preparing for hostilities. An emerging consensus holds that a Mumbai-style terrorist attack abetted by Pakistan would force India to take decisive military action—even at the risk of nuclear escalation.

New Delhi, it appears, attaches such value to the political object of quashing cross-border terrorism that it is prepared to incur the costs and hazards that would accompany a nuclear confrontation. The logic of deterrence may not hold between nuclear newcomers under all circumstances.

India's Growing Engagement with the Global Nuclear Nonproliferation Effort

Despite its efforts to craft a viable strategy for employing its nuclear arsenal, New Delhi still considers nuclear abolition a core principle of its nuclear strategy. If other nations will forgo the nuclear option, India insists that it is also prepared to do so. (How easily it could do so, now that it possesses a working arsenal backed by influential interests, is another question entirely.) As noted above, India was an ardent proponent of a global ban on nuclear testing starting in the 1950s, and Indian statesmen took to espousing universal disarmament well before the NPT came into force in 1970. The 1998 nuclear tests and subsequent weaponization have added nuance to Indian advocacy, but the fundamental tenets of support for verifiable universal disarmament persist. Indian prime minister Manmohan Singh reaffirmed New Delhi's stance at the 2010 Nuclear Security Summit, where he called for "universalization of the policy of no first use" and posited that "to be successful, nonproliferation should be universal, comprehensive and non-discriminatory and linked to the goal of complete nuclear disarmament."[59]

India has consistently objected to the fact that the NPT creates two categories of states with different rights and obligations and that it does too little to promote universal disarmament. Even so, India has consistently abided by the most crucial aspect of the NPT—horizontal nonproliferation—by refusing to provide weapons-related items, technologies, or know-how to other states. New Delhi's strong record of substantive compliance was a major factor in Washington's decision to negotiate a civil nuclear cooperation agreement. In turn the nuclear deal reinforced Indian ties with the global nonproliferation effort.[60]

India was one of the first nations to become a member of the International Atomic Energy Agency (IAEA), which it joined in 1957. New Delhi serves on the IAEA's Board of Governors, makes one of the developing world's largest contributions of funds and technical expertise, and has placed its reactors under IAEA safeguards for more than three decades. Annual IAEA reports regularly commend its reactor design and safety record.[61] It has signed most IAEA conventions related to physical security and materials control and accounting, including the Convention on Physical Protection of Nuclear Materials (CPPNM) and the 2005 amendment to the convention. In recent years it has conducted nine regional training courses on nuclear security in cooperation with the IAEA.

As part of the United States–India civil nuclear cooperation agreement, India submitted a "separation plan" approved by the IAEA's Board of Governors in 2008 that lists all twenty-two reactors currently in operation, along with associated mining, fuel fabrication, and research facilities. The plan identifies fourteen reactors and specifies when each will come under IAEA safeguards. The last one will fall under international oversight starting in 2014. The remaining eight reactors are designated as belonging to the Indian "weapons complex" and thus will remain off limits. The separation plan creates a firewall aimed at ensuring that all international participation remains confined to the civilian nuclear complex. In 2009, furthermore, India signed and ratified an Additional Protocol to the NPT, stating that all future civilian plants will be placed under IAEA safeguards. Because India plans to enhance its nuclear energy production, from the current 4,230 megawatts to 20,000 megawatts by 2030, more than 90 percent of Indian reactors and unsafeguarded fissile material will eventually come under IAEA safeguards. This represents a considerable boost for global nonproliferation efforts to secure nuclear materials.

India proposed a Comprehensive Test Ban Treaty in the 1950s but declined to sign it in 1996. Since conducting the 1998 tests, it has observed a self-imposed moratorium on further testing. New Delhi may ultimately sign and ratify the CTBT. For now, its official policy is that it will convert its moratorium into a legally binding undertaking if other states ratify the CTBT.[62] Its maneuvering room in this matter has narrowed considerably since it negotiated the civil nuclear cooperation agreement, which effectively states that if it conducts another test, each of the forty-five member states of the Nuclear Suppliers Group (NSG) can use its national laws or discretion to determine whether to suspend or cease all nuclear cooperation with India. Put simply, the costs to India of conducting another round of weapons testing have multiplied.

With regard to the Fissile Material Cutoff Treaty (FMCT), India has consistently supported an early start to negotiations at the Conference on Disarmament in

Geneva. Technical issues relating to verifiability dogged the FMCT in the past decade, along with questions about full access to the facilities operated by the five official nuclear weapon states. But since 2001, negotiations at the Conference on Disarmament have been blocked twice. In the period 2001–3, China insisted on parallel "prevention of arms racing in outer space" negotiations. Since 2009 Pakistan has lobbied to expand the scope of the FMCT to eliminate existing stockpiles rather than merely prevent future fissile material production. Many specialists see this demand as a delaying tactic that gives Islamabad time to expand its inventory of weapons-grade fissile material.[63]

Having been the target of violent extremism, India has energetically backed nonproliferation efforts targeted against nonstate actors and terrorist groups. It upgraded the legal basis for its export controls in May 2005, enacting a comprehensive "WMD [weapons of mass destruction] and Prevention of Unlawful Activities Act" that complied with UN Security Council Resolution 1540 of August 2004. Resolution 1540 directed all UN member states to institute effective export controls as a measure to combat weapons proliferation. The WMD Act also harmonized India's control list for WMD and dual-use items and technologies with the control lists published by the NSG and the Missile Technology Control Regime. Furthermore, the WMD Act's guidelines include an undertaking not yet fully accepted by some members of the NSG; it forbids transfers of enrichment and reprocessing technology and equipment to countries that do not already possess them.[64]

India is a member of the Global Initiative to Combat Nuclear Terrorism, and it is a party to the Suppression of Unlawful Activities at Sea Convention and an associated protocol. In part this accord is designed to interrupt weapons proliferation at sea. As noted above, New Delhi has also signed the CPPNM and its amplifying amendment. As Prime Minister Singh pointed out at the Nuclear Security Summit, moreover, "since 2002, we have piloted a resolution at the UN General Assembly on measures to deny terrorists' access to weapons of mass destruction. We fully support the implementation of Security Council Resolution 1540 and the UN Global Counter Terrorism Strategy." Singh also announced that India would establish a "Global Center for Nuclear Energy Partnership, visualized as a state-of-the-art facility conducting research and development of design systems that are intrinsically safe, secure, proliferation resistant and sustainable."[65]

On the nuclear energy side of the equation, New Delhi's long-standing, extensive global engagement has deepened further in the past few years. India has a limited indigenous supply of uranium but is home to one of the world's largest thorium deposits. As such, its Department of Atomic Energy has worked for decades on a three-stage approach, in which the final stage employs neutrons and plutonium-239 as breeders that generate vast quantities of energy using thorium as a feedstock. Drawing upon this research, India has "recently developed an Advanced heavy-water reactor based on low-enriched uranium and thorium with new safety and proliferation-resistant features." In 2005, India became a member of the International Thermonuclear Experimental Station in Cadarache, France.[66] And if the Global Fuel Bank becomes a reality, India has the capability and intent to join it as a technology contributor and as a fuel-receiving member.

The Impact of Indian Nuclear Strategy and Growing Power on Regional and Global Order

Indians extol collaborative enterprise and the application of science for the benefit of humankind. This mindset animated India's early approach to harnessing nuclear technology for energy, nuclear medicine, and agriculture while stiffening its early opposition to nuclear explosive testing and buildups of offensive nuclear weapons. The rigors of contemporary realpolitik have clearly undermined this purely idealistic stance, however, and a more pragmatic strand of thinking has become progressively dominant in the Indian strategic discourse since the 1970s.

A watershed moment came when India elected to stay away from signing the CTBT in 1996 and crossed the nuclear Rubicon in 1998. New Delhi then proceeded to articulate a nuclear doctrine and develop or acquire capabilities to endow its military with a credible second-strike force, ready to respond if deterrence breaks down or a conventional conflict escalates to a nuclear exchange. Assessments of Indian nuclear doctrine and strategy during the past few years have provided increasingly granular insights into how New Delhi is refining its approach to keep pace with the capabilities of its principal security threats.

The Regional Order: Asia

India's nuclear history reveals that it has been a "reluctant weaponizer." Although it is creating a sizable nuclear force, its leadership remains rooted in a doctrine of credible yet minimal deterrence. According to informed sources, India's nuclear arsenal will eventually constitute between 124 and 150 weapons. Of these, at least three-quarters will be uranium-based and only a quarter will be plutonium-based. Furthermore, at least 80 percent of the stockpile will be strategic, large-pay-load warheads, whereas only 20 percent will be tactical warheads.

In an off-the-record conversation that we conducted with one of India's most senior decision makers, this dignitary asked us to describe a practical scenario in which India has been attacked with a nuclear weapon by either China or Pakistan and India retaliates with a nuclear strike of its own.[67] He probed this scenario further, asking whether—having delivered *one* weapon against an adversary that had wrought massive damage on the subcontinent—we could conceive of any situation that would compel India to deliver a *second* warhead to inflict further damage. His key message was that it is exceedingly doubtful that India would ever use *two* nuclear weapons in a conflict.

If so—if the assured capacity to deliver a single bomb against enemy territory is enough to create meaningful deterrent and retaliatory capacity—then India does not require a large arsenal at all. Although survivability and a second-strike capability demand a triad and reliable delivery systems, and though India believes that it needs to prepare for a two-front contingency, its leaders nevertheless have drawn hard conclusions from the massive arms buildup and deployment patterns of the Cold War and are determined not to repeat Soviet and American excesses.

These factors are essential to India's security calculations and to the refinement of its nuclear doctrine and force structure. In turn they are critical to a strategy premised on employing nuclear forces in defense of the nation and its vital interests. Minimal deterrence is where coping with the reality of a nuclear Asia coexists with New Delhi's political determination to work toward dismantling all the world's nuclear arsenals.

As discussed above, India is pursuing different strategies with respect to Pakistan and China. India's political decision makers evince absolutely no interest in leveraging India's nuclear weapons capability to wrest territory from Pakistan, to respond to a terrorist strike, or even to retaliate for state-sponsored acts of violence. They expect the Indian armed forces' conventional superiority to suffice for such contingencies, especially if the Cold Start Doctrine becomes a reliable war-fighting option. At the same time, they fret that Pakistan might escalate to the point of threatening or actually preparing to use nuclear weapons against India. As such, India must plan for all contingencies and deploy a credible, survivable nuclear force that can deter a Pakistani nuclear attack or deliver a retaliatory strike if the situation warrants.

Indian military commanders and officials share this line of thinking to an extent. They believe, however, that the Pakistani armed forces and intelligence establishment are intent on developing a credible first-strike force and on leveraging it for political ends. In this view, Islamabad is convinced that India will always blink first in the game of nuclear brinkmanship—a dangerous assumption if true. Consequently, as custodians of India's national defense, the military needs to deploy a robust rapid reaction capability and plan for a nuclear contingency in which the window for retaliation will slam shut after a few hours, not days or weeks. It is this differentiated reasoning and these conclusions that inform the refinement of India's nuclear doctrine and strategy.

As far as China is concerned, Indian leaders—both political and military—recognize that they are dealing with an adversary whose nuclear weapons capability is of a higher order of magnitude than India can match. They further believe that the adversary is devious, patient, and ruthless. But they also believe that China's rapid modernization of its overall military strength—including the nuclear component—is geared to making China the dominant power in Asia. Beijing's project in East Asia and the China seas will remain unfinished for quite some time. For the present, then, a direct Sino-Indian military confrontation ranks very low in Beijing's current strategic calculus.

India's China strategy flows from this logic. New Delhi has sought to engage Beijing by expanding trade ties and negotiating diverse economic and security arrangements while avoiding provoking a confrontation. Alongside this diplomatic outreach, India is building potent conventional and nuclear weapons capabilities that are mobile, secure, and survivable, in the expectation that the prospect of unacceptable damage will deter full-scale war.

Another dimension of Indian strategy stems from China's seemingly innocuous deepening of its economic and military ties with Pakistan, with India's other neighbors in South Asia, and with a broader buffer region. New Delhi has belatedly pursued a strategy of balancing growing Chinese influence through economic and military engagements of its own, often on terms highly beneficial to its partners. This strategy is beginning to establish a more fluid balance of power between New Delhi and Beijing, if not a dynamic equilibrium. It nonetheless remains to be seen how the two contenders will delineate their relative spheres of influence in the Asia-Pacific region. How they manage their differences along various fault lines promises to determine the longer-term outcome of their contest for power, influence, and prestige.

The International Order

If the military dimension of Indian nuclear strategy prevails on the regional level, where deterring threats is uppermost in policymakers' minds, the political ideals of nonproliferation and disarmament predominate in New Delhi's relations with the global community. New Delhi entertains a grand, multifaceted vision of what constitutes nuclear strategy. India long presented the global nuclear order with a persistent problem, because it challenged the ordering principles of the NPT for creating seemingly permanent categories of nuclear haves and have-nots. During the NPT's first four decades of existence, India at once represented the views of the Global South and developed capabilities that fitted better with the developed world. As a common if harsh observation puts it, India "acted like a trade union leader while seeking a seat at the business high table."

This situation has changed markedly since the successful conclusion of the United States–India civil nuclear cooperation agreement in 2007. The text of this agreement recognizes India as a "state with advanced nuclear capabilities and obligations," whereas the NSG exemption permits NSG member states—the forty-five countries with advanced nuclear capabilities—to engage India in nuclear commerce and other joint endeavors. In a nutshell, India is no longer seen as a target of sanctions but rather as a partner in global nonproliferation efforts. This represents a seismic shift in the international community's mindset, which is significant given how India prizes its prestige and the image it projects of playing a beneficent role in the international system. In practical terms, it matters because the legal framework now allows India to trade in dual-use items and to build high-technology strategic partnerships with major powers in the global system.

The WMD Act discussed earlier in the chapter meets the requirements of UN Security Council Resolution 1540, whereas the government's control lists and guidelines are aligned with those promulgated by the NSG and the Missile Technology Control Regime. India is now expected to pursue policies and enact enabling procedures that will converge with those of these two export-control programs, as well as those of the Australia Group (the arrangement that regulates the traffic in dual-use chemicals and some biological items and equipment) and the Wassenaar Arrangement (which regulates the flow of advanced conventional munitions and some missile-related aerospace items). These policy changes represent enablers for India to expand its high-technology trade on the global plane. In addition, New Delhi must continue its vigorous support for global antiterrorism efforts and measures to deny proliferators the use of cargo and transport conveyances.

Benchmarks for Indian Nuclear Success

India is a country on the march by any standard, including nuclear strategy. To gauge the evolution and prospects for success of Indian nuclear strategy, practitioners and scholars of South Asian affairs should monitor several benchmarks, including (1) public pronouncements and official statements about relations with China and Pakistan, counterterrorism, and other affairs that bear on nuclear deterrence and war fighting; (2) evidence of how strategic and doctrinal debates are unfolding on such matters as Cold Start, the viability of the nuclear triad, or a departure from minimal deterrence; (3) indicators of how well New Delhi is managing to solve the host of technical challenges associated with building a viable second-strike force; and (4) wild cards in the subcontinent's strategic environs that might skew the government's or the military's views on nuclear deterrence. In short, signs of technical progress will suggest how the material dimension of strategy is shaping up for New Delhi, whereas the words of key protagonists will show how India may employ its nuclear forces in times of peril.

It is striking how many of the nuclear strategic challenges facing New Delhi involve big organizations with distinct cultures and jealously guarded ways of transacting business. Political leaders' capacity to tame these clashing interests will help determine the future of the Indian nuclear strategy. Drawing up institutional arrangements that assure a modicum of rationality in the making of strategy, in force planning, and in efficiently fielding military hardware is only part of the challenge. Finding, installing, and empowering the right people to oversee these institutions—and to impose discipline on efforts involving multiple agencies—represent a leadership task of a high order.

Another benchmark for Indian progress, then, is how well the government fares in the domains of leadership and bureaucratic management. Outsiders can track movement in such specific areas as appointing a chief of the Defense Staff to orchestrate the joint endeavors of the Indian armed forces. Or parceling out command arrangements to appease various bodies—for example, allocating a leading role in the Strategic Forces Command to the Indian air force simply because the army and navy had been awarded other functions—represents a dubious practice, though not an unusual one among the world's armed forces. Max Weber is an unlikely ally in efforts to gauge the evolution of India's nuclear strategy. His writings are useful all the same.

Notes

1. Max Weber, *Economy and Society: An Outline of Interpretive Sociology*, edited by Guenther Roth and Claus Wittich and translated by Ephraim Fischoff and others, 3 vols. (New York: Bedminster Press, 1968), 223.
2. Ibid., 973.
3. Ibid., 223.
4. Ibid., 987.
5. Ibid., 988.
6. Ibid.

7. Ibid.

8. Ibid., 989.

9. Ibid., 961.

10. Ibid.

11. See, e.g., the analysis of India's policy on a nuclear option given by George Perkovich, *India's Nuclear Bomb: The Impact on Global Proliferation* (Berkeley: University of California Press, 1999).

12. Indian military exercises were traditionally conducted along the north–south axis. Leaders deemed this a nonthreatening gesture given Pakistan's proximate boundaries to the west of the exercise area. In 1987, however, General Sundarji deliberately chose a provocative east–west orientation for the exercise. It may have been this that prompted Khan to fire a stinging, preemptive volley of words across the border.

13. See, e.g., Adrian Levy and Catherine Scott-Clark, *Deception: Pakistan, the United States, and the Secret Trade in Nuclear Weapons* (New York: Walker, 2007).

14. Levy and Scott-Clark, *Deception*.

15. The entry-into-force clause identified India as one of forty-four countries that must accede to the CTBT for the treaty to come into force. And because unanimous approval is required at the Conference on Disarmament, India was forced to vote against it, which compelled the United States to later bring the same text to the UN General Assembly for signature.

16. National Security Advisory Board, *Indian Nuclear Doctrine* (New Delhi: Government of India, 1999).

17. G. Balachandran, "India's Nuclear Doctrine," Article 254, Institute of Peace and Conflict Studies, August 27, 1999, http://ipcs.org/article/nuclear/indias-nuclear-doctrine-254.html.

18. Government of India, "The Cabinet Committee on Security Reviews Operationalization of India's Nuclear Doctrine," New Delhi, January 4, 2002, available at www.acronym.org.uk/docs/0301/doc06.htm.

19. Ministry of External Affairs, Government of India, press release, January 4, 2003, http://meadev.nic.in/news/official/20030104/official.htm.

20. Ashok K. Mehta, "A Strategic Forces Command, Finally!" *Rediff.com*, February 10, 2003, www.rediff.com/news/2003/feb/10ashok.htm.

21. For an informed discussion about the reasons for reluctance on this issue, see General S. K. Sinha, "The Chief of Defense Staff," *Journal of Defense Studies*, August 2007, www.idsa.in/jds/1_1_2007_TheChiefOfDefenceStaff_SKSinha.

22. "Post of Chief of Defence Staff Is a Must: Naik," *Outlook* (India), March 30, 2010, http://news.outlookindia.com/item.aspx?678290.

23. "Chief of Defence Staff to Be Appointed after Political Consensus," *Thaindian News*, December 16, 2009, http://tinyurl.com/ydy3bfb.

24. For an alternate view, see Vinod Patney, "Jointness in Armed Forces and Institution of Post of Chief of Defence Staff Are Mutually Exclusive," *Journal of Defense Studies*, Summer 2008, http://tinyurl.com/y9ny3wz.

25. Arun Prakash, "India's Higher Defence Organization: Implications for National Security and Jointness," *Journal of Defense Studies*, August 2007, www.idsa.in/jds/1_1_2007_IndiasHigherDefenceOrganization_aprakash.

26. "Circular error probable" refers to the radius within which the missile will land at least 50 percent of the time if it misses a direct hit on its target. The CEP of Prithvi has

now been reduced to about 100 meters, a creditable figure for a nuclear-tipped short-range missile.

27. "Union Budget 2010: Govt Raises Defense Allocation to Rs 147,344 Cr," *Economic Times*, February 26, 2010, http://economictimes.indiatimes.com/articleshow/5619870.cms?prtpa ge = 1. The dollar figure is $32.74 billion.

28. The capital allocation to buy new equipment for the air force is $3.38 billion; for the navy, $1.54 billion; and for the army, $141 million. The Defense Research and Development Organization saw its acquisition budget hiked from $195 million to $1.17 billion, whereas the allocation for defense ordnance factories has been slashed by $407 million to $444 million. Germaine Lombardo, "An In-Depth Review on India Defence Budget 2010–11," *CEO World*, February 26, 2010, http://ceoworld.biz/ceo/2010/02/26/an-in-depth-review-on-indias-defence-budget-2010–11.

29. See Sandeep Unnithan, "The Secret Undersea Weapon," *India Today*, January 17, 2008, http://indiatoday.intoday.in/site/Story/3659/DEFENCE/The + secret + undersea + weapon.html; and "India Joins Elite Club with Nuclear Submarine Launch," *Rediff.com*, July 26, 2009, www.rediff.com/news/2009/jul/26pm-launches-nuke-submarine-arihant1.htm.

30. India has ship-to-ship, ship-to-land, land-to-land, and land-to-ship versions of BrahMos. See "Bravo BrahMos," *The Hindu* (Editorial), March 25, 2010, www.thehindu.com/2010/03/25/stories/2010032563641200.htm. See also "BrahMos Cruise Missile Test-Fired Successfully," *Times of India*, March 22, 2010, http://tinyurl.com/y68tvnt.

31. Anupam Srivastava, "India: Toward True Partnership," *Journal of International Security Affairs*, Fall 2006, 21–28.

32. "Navy to Launch Third Destroyer of 'Project 15 Alpha' on April 1 in Mumbai," *DNAIndia*, March 30, 2010, www.dnaindia.com/india/report_navy-to-launch-third-destroyer-of-project-15-alpha-on-april-1-in-mumbai_1365349.

33. "Walchandnagar Ind, French Co in JV for Submarine Parts," *Financial Express*, March 31, 2010, www.financialexpress.com/news/Walchandnagar-Ind-French-co-in-JV-for-submarine-parts/597814/.

34. "HCL Technologies Launches Center of Excellence with Boeing," press release, March 30, 2010, www.marketwatch.com/story/hcl-technologies-launches-center-of-excellence-with-boeing-2010–03–30?reflink = MW_news_stmp.

35. Pankaj Mishra, "Centre Plans to Restructure DRDO on Lines of Global Labs," *Economic Times*, March 12, 2009, http://economictimes.indiatimes.com/News/Economy/Policy/Centre-pl ans-to-restru cture-DRDO-on-lines-of-global-labs/articleshow/4253474.cms.

36. Press Information Bureau, Government of India, "Chiefs of Staff Committee Releases Joint Operational Doctrines," press release, February 9, 2010, www.pib.nic.in/release/release.asp?relid = 57725.

37. Mehta, "Strategic Forces Command." According to him, Arun Singh, who kick-started the establishment of the NCA in the 1980s, also steered the post-Kargil higher defense reforms, which included the SFC. He wrote an approach paper on this subject, and in September 2001 he began a twelve-month tour of the services and various departments of the government.

38. Walter C. Ladwig III, "The Challenge of Changing Indian Military Doctrine," www.india-seminar.com/2009/599/599_walter_c_ladwig_iii.htm.

39. Ibid.

40. Peter Gizewski, "Indian Nuclear Doctrine: A Critical Assessment of the Proposal for a Minimum Nuclear Deterrent," International Security Research and Outreach Program, Nonproliferation, Arms Control, and Disarmament Division, Department of Foreign Affairs and International Trade, Government of Canada, March 2000, www.in ternational.gc.ca/arms-armes/isrop-prisi/research-recherche/nuclear-nucleaire/gizewski 2000/section6.aspx.

41. Eric Arnett, "Facts and Fiction: Current Nuclear Weapon Capabilities in South Asia," www.sipri.se/projects/technology/Facts.html.

42. P. K. Subrahmanyam, "A Reasoned Policy in South Asia: Nuclear Deterrence in South Asia," *Harvard Asia-Pacific Review*, Winter 1998, www.hcs.harvard.edu/~hapr/winter98/subra.html.

43. For a detailed historical account, see Claude Arpi, "Can the India–China Border Issue Ever Be Solved?" *Rediff.com*, April 29 and 30, 2004, http://in.rediff.com/news/2004/apr/29claude.htm and www.rediff.com/news/2004/apr/30claude.htm.

44. Gizewski, "Indian Nuclear Doctrine."

45. Hans Kristensen, blog entry, May 15, 2008, www.fas.org/blog/ssp/2008/05/exten sive-nuclear-deployment-area-discovered-in-central-china.php.

46. Gizewski, "Indian Nuclear Doctrine."

47. In January 2002 General Khalid Kidwai, head of the Pakistani army's Strategic Plans Division, which oversees nuclear weapons development and deployment, listed the redlines in an interview to Paolo Cotta-Ramusino and Maurizio Martellini of the Landau Network, an Italian arms control organization; quoted by Kaushik Kapisthalam, "Pakistan Leaves Arms Calling Card," *Asia Times*, February 10, 2005, www.atimes.com/atimes/South_Asia/GB10Df06.html.

48. Vernie Liebl, "India and Pakistan: Competing Nuclear Strategies and Doctrines," *Comparative Strategy* 28, no. 2 (April 2009): 154–63.

49. "This may be due to the origin of all its missile technology being from China or North Korea. The missiles are liquid fueled and thus unstable platforms for storage of nuclear warheads." Liebl, "India and Pakistan."

50. Vipin Narang, "Posturing for Peace? Pakistan's Nuclear Postures and South Asian Stability," *International Security* 34, no. 3 (Winter 2009–10): 38–78, http://belfercenter .ksg.harvard.edu/files/Narang.pdf.

51. Narang, "Posturing for Peace?"

52. These include advance notification of missile tests and military exercises close to the border, annual exchange of nuclear sites, and hotlines at the level of the prime minister and director-general of military operations.

53. For detailed statistics on terrorist violence, see the South Asia Terrorism Portal, www.satport.org.

54. "Kasab Has Realized the Inevitability of His Fate," *Rediff.com*, April 9, 2010, http://news.rediff.com/interview/2010/apr/09/interview-with-26–11-prosecutor-ujjwal-nikam.htm.

55. Warren Richey, "David Headley Pleads Guilty in 2008 Mumbai Terrorist Attack," *Christian Science Monitor*, March 18, 2010, www.csmonitor.com/USA/Justice/2010/0318/David-Headley-pleads-guilty-in-2008-Mumbai-terrorist-attack.

56. Subhash Kapila, *India's New "Cold Start" Doctrine Strategically Reviewed*, South Asia Analysis Group Paper 991 (New Delhi: South Asia Analysis Group, 2004), www .southasiaanalysis.org/%5Cpapers10%5Cpaper991.html.

57. Ibid.

58. Maleeha Lodhi, "India's Provocative Military Doctrine," *News International* (Pakistan), January 5, 2010, *www.thenews.com.pk/print1.asp?id=216861*.

59. "Statement by Prime Minister Manmohan Singh at the Nuclear Security Summit, Washington DC," *The Hindu,* April 13, 2010, http://beta.thehindu.com/news/resources/article396372.ece.

60. Anupam Srivastava and Seema Gahlaut, "India and the NPT: Separating Substantive Facts from Normative Fiction," *Strategic Analysis* 34, no. 2 (March 2010): 287. The agreement granted all NSG members an exemption from their Comprehensive Safeguards requirements in order for them to engage India's safeguarded civilian complex. Following the exemption, India has negotiated expanded nuclear cooperation agreements with the United States, France, Russia, the United Kingdom, Canada, and Kazakhstan.

61. India was able to shut down its nuclear power reactor at Kalpakkam as the December 2004 tsunami waters reached the complex. It was able to restart operations within 48 hours. The complex withstood the adverse effects of corrosive ocean waters, prompting the IAEA to laud its design and ask India to organize a workshop to share details about reactor safety and procedures from its emergency response.

62. A. Vinod Kumar, "India and the CTBT: The Debate in New Delhi," *Bulletin of the Atomic Scientists,* November 2009, http://tinyurl.com/y2xj5nd. See also Srivastava and Gahlaut, "India and the NPT."

63. A detailed technical study demonstrates that while India has never accelerated weapons-grade fissile-material production since conducting the tests in 1998, Pakistan has done so. See Ashley J. Tellis, *Atoms for War? US–Indian Civilian Nuclear Cooperation and India's Nuclear Arsenal* (Washington, DC: Carnegie Endowment for International Peace, 2006), www.carnegieendowment.org/publications/index.cfm?fa=view&id=18443.

64. Srivastava and Gahlaut, "India and the NPT."

65. "Statement by Prime Minister Manmohan Singh." The center would consist of four schools dealing with advanced nuclear energy system studies, nuclear security, radiation safety, and the application of radioisotopes and radiation technology in the areas of health care, agriculture, and food.

66. The European Union and India are already partners in the construction of the international fusion tokamak International Thermonuclear Experimental Station. The agreement was signed at the EU–India Summit in New Delhi on November 6, 2009. India has strong, consolidated expertise on plasma and superconductors. It has been operating its own two tokamak machines for years. Euratom and India will establish a fast track for the exchange of both information on research issues and scientists in research projects. India already has ongoing collaborations with several European national research centers on fusion. Indian scientists will now join the major fusion experiments of Euratom. See "Europe and India Sign Cooperation Agreement—ITER Goes On," http://ec.europa.eu/research/index.cfm?pg=newsalert&lg=en&yea r=2009&na=na-061109.

67. These observations are based on off-the-record conversations by the authors with more than thirty key decision makers from the Indian national security, foreign policy, atomic energy, and missile apparatus over an extended period.

CHAPTER 9

THE FUTURE OF INDIA'S UNDERSEA NUCLEAR DETERRENT

Andrew C. Winner

THIS CHAPTER BUILDS upon the previous one by examining the maritime elements of Indian nuclear strategy and capability, both current and in prospect. It considers how India's current stationing of nuclear weapons on board surface ships and its planned stationing of nuclear weapons aboard submarines relates to its broader nuclear strategy and doctrine. The deployment of Indian nuclear weapons in submarines will clearly exert substantial influence on other nuclear powers in India's proximity, namely, China and Pakistan. This is particularly true if these rival navies also begin to deploy nuclear weapons in submarines cruising the Indian Ocean. In addition, all three states, and also potentially others, may modify their broader maritime strategies and doctrines, taking into account how conventional capabilities interact with nuclear-armed platforms at sea. Despite the long-awaited public launch of the Indian nuclear-powered submarine INS *Arihant* in July 2009, much of this chapter remains speculative, because this first platform was not yet operational as of this writing. Even after it is, it will take time for the true interactive effects to become clear.[1] Nevertheless, analyzing strategy, doctrine, and forces is worthwhile, even on a hypothetical basis, in light of the central role nuclear weapons can play in questions of war and peace.

This chapter examines the internal and external factors that have led India to pursue a nuclear-powered ballistic missile submarine (known as an "SSBN"), which stands for strategic submarine ballistic nuclear submarine) and that may influence its choices for retaining or deploying other maritime-based nuclear capabilities. It assesses what is known about Indian nuclear and naval strategies and doctrines and the insights that such documents provide into the possible activities of maritime nuclear platforms in peacetime, crisis, and war. Finally, the chapter examines interactions with Pakistan and China. Specifically, it looks at issues regarding the stabilizing or destabilizing nature of submarine-launched nuclear weapons and possible Pakistani and Chinese reactions to this new capability in strategy, procurement, doctrine, deployment, and operations. Although necessarily speculative, this last section draws upon past interactions among these protagonists as well as analysis of nuclear-armed submarine operations undertaken in the context of the US/Soviet nuclear rivalry during the Cold War.

Nuclear Origins and Doctrine

Although Indian national security analysts discussed potential Indian nuclear doctrine throughout the period when India was considering its nuclear options (there was an ambiguous period from 1974 until 1998; then, in 1998, it conducted nuclear tests), the Indian government apparently arrived at an official nuclear doctrine only sometime in 2003.[2] The only public evidence of this was a one-page press release discussing a Cabinet Committee on Security meeting that reviewed how to put the doctrine into effect.[3] The 2003 press release contained some elements similar to the much longer 1999 draft report from the National Security Advisory Board, which was set up to examine nuclear doctrine after the 1998 Indian nuclear tests. The 2003 press release also contained some new elements, one being a declaration that India had set up a formal Nuclear Command Authority with two subordinate councils, the Political Council and the Executive Council. The former, chaired by the prime minister, is the sole body that can authorize the use of nuclear weapons. The latter, chaired by the national security adviser, provides advice on nuclear weapons matters to the National Command Authority and appears to be the implementing body for decisions by the Political Council. In addition, the January 3, 2003, document announced the creation of a triservice Strategic Forces Command to administer all strategic forces. The press release, which is potentially relevant to sea-based nuclear capabilities, indicates that "nuclear retaliatory attacks can only be authorized by the civilian political leadership through the Nuclear Command Authority."

A third, and interesting, new element in the 2003 press release was an apparent alteration of India's declared no-first-use (NFU) policy. The traditional formulation of NFU means that a state will not use its nuclear weapons unless attacked by another state using nuclear weapons. The summary of the Cabinet Committee on Security meeting presented in the press release indicates that India's NFU doctrine is much narrower. It states that "in the event of a major attack against India, or Indian forces anywhere, by biological or chemical weapons, India will retain the option of retaliating with nuclear weapons." This is a difficult sentence to parse for precise meaning. At the very minimum, it appears to mean that India reserves the right to use nuclear weapons in retaliation for a chemical or biological attack and also a nuclear attack on Indian territory. It also appears to say that an Indian nuclear response could be triggered by such an attack on Indian forces regardless of where they are deployed—including, presumably, forces fighting on the territory of an adversary or naval units under way on the high seas. The statement could also indicate that India considers a nuclear attack against forces anywhere as the equivalent to a nuclear attack on Indian territory—an interesting variation that may be meant to guard against at least one Pakistani option for using nuclear weapons that has been discussed by analysts looking at Indo-Pakistani war scenarios. This would involve Pakistani use of a single or small number of nuclear weapons against Indian troops that had invaded Pakistani territory.

The longer but less authoritative document promulgated by the advisory board, which reported its findings in August 1999, contained some elements that are useful for thinking about the maritime aspects of Indian nuclear forces.[4] For one thing, India has embraced a doctrine of "credible minimum nuclear deterrence," but neither the draft doctrine nor any official government pronouncements since have defined what "minimum" means to New Delhi. Instead, spokesmen and official statements indicate it is a dynamic concept contingent on "the strategic environment, technological imperatives, and the needs of national security." Accordingly, the "actual size components, deployment and employment of nuclear forces will be decided in light of these factors." In other words, the size and makeup of India's nuclear arsenal—both numbers of weapons and numbers and types of delivery platforms—are neither fixed nor transparent.

India's draft nuclear doctrine statement vouchsafes that "India will not be the first to initiate a nuclear strike, but will respond with punitive retaliation should deterrence fail." The 2003 statement adds interesting language on the quality of that retaliation: "Nuclear retaliation to a first strike will be massive and designed to inflict unacceptable damage." This could say something about the range of forces, specifically delivery platforms, that India might use to carry out a retaliatory strike. The NFU stance roughly mirrors that of China but not of Pakistan, which has pointedly refrained from adopting an NFU stance. This asymmetry could affect strategic-level interactions between New Delhi, Islamabad, and Beijing in peacetime, crisis, or war.

In its very terse discussion of nuclear forces, the draft doctrine statement declares that Indian nuclear forces "will be based on a triad of aircraft, mobile land-based missiles, and sea-based assets." Although the doctrine specifies neither platforms nor types of weapons, then, it does explicitly stipulate that the Indian navy will have a hand in nuclear deterrence and warfighting. The 2003 announcement of the establishment of a triservice Strategic Forces Command also implied that the Indian navy will have a role in nuclear decision making within the military chain of command commensurate with its capabilities to contribute. The long-expected announcement of the launch of the INS *Arihant* finally confirmed that the Indian navy will have a nuclear weapon delivery mission beyond the very rudimentary surface ship program discussed below. Finally, the 1999 document declares that Indian nuclear forces and command-and-control arrangements will be designed and deployed to "ensure survival against a first strike and to endure repetitive attrition attempts with adequate retaliatory capabilities for a punishing strike which would be unacceptable to the aggressor."[5] As discussed below, the Indian navy and government clearly see this aspect of the doctrine as carrying direct implications for the maritime force structure.

The Indian Navy's Interest in a Nuclear Role

The Indian navy's 2004 Indian Maritime Doctrine includes an interesting if cursory discussion of trends in the nuclear force postures of the United States, Russia, France, and the United Kingdom. The document observes that the United States and

Russia are shifting much of their strategic nuclear deterrent to submarines, in keeping with arms control agreements concluded during and after the Cold War. It also notes that France and the United Kingdom are modernizing their submarine fleets. The Maritime Doctrine wraps up its brief discussion with a not-so-subtle appeal to Indian politicians and strategists, connecting undersea nuclear forces with great power status. Its framers proclaim that "it has become an unstated axiom of the post–Cold War era that an independent foreign policy posture is inexorably linked with this [submarine-based nuclear] deterrent capability."[6] Although, in 2004, work on India's first nuclear-powered, ballistic-missile-carrying submarine was already under way, it is clear from this short passage in its first public doctrine document that the Indian Navy felt it necessary to make a comparative case for an SSBN.

This passage constitutes an overt plea for a nuclear submarine force as a token of India's place among the world's great—that is, nuclear-armed—powers. Later in the Indian Maritime Doctrine, the authors make their case in even more succinct terms. "To achieve strategic deterrence," they say, "it is vital for a nation to possess nuclear submarines capable of launching missiles with nuclear warheads."[7] The Indian navy invokes the nuclear doctrine's requirement for a maritime force structure in its 2007 maritime strategy document, declaring that "the most 'credible' of all arsenals in a second strike is the nuclear-armed missile submarine."[8]

In the Indian Navy's newest iteration of its doctrine, statements about the navy's role in nuclear weapon delivery are less lofty and more in line with the relatively curt statements about India's nuclear doctrine, as outlined in the 2003 Indian government press release discussed above. In the 2009 Maritime Doctrine, the authors note that "by virtue of its stealth and attendant survivability of second-strike capability, a nuclear submarine is particularly suited for nuclear deterrence."[9] After that, the document clearly states the Indian navy's development plans and links them to the announced Indian nuclear doctrine: "The ways and means of deterrence by the [navy] would include developing a sea-based nuclear second-strike capability in keeping with the Indian Nuclear Doctrine that lays down an . . . NFU policy."[10]

Existing Capabilities

As of this writing, India fields no operational maritime leg for its nuclear triad. The Indian navy has tested a surface-ship-launched variant of its liquid-fueled Prithvi missile, called the Danush. Reports vary as to whether the Danush is a variant of the Prithvi I or the Prithvi II. The two missiles reportedly differ in range (150 vs. 250 kilometers) and payload (500 vs. 750 kilograms).[11] The Danush has been test-fired from the *Sukanya*-class offshore patrol craft, and at least one report indicates that it has been successfully launched from the INS *Rajput*, a destroyer. There are reports that the Indian Navy has ordered between 30 and 100 Danush missiles for its *Sukanya* patrol craft, but it remains unclear whether the Indian navy intends to deploy the missiles operationally, conducting regular deterrent patrols with nuclear warheads on board the ships. This is especially true in light of the now-public progress toward fielding a nuclear-powered missile submarine.[12]

As a practical matter, patrols by nuclear-missile-armed surface combatants would avail little except against Pakistan, one of India's two nuclear-armed rivals. Patrols against China are simply beyond the operational reach of the *Sukanya*-class vessels. On an even more practical level, it is doubtful whether surface-ship-based missiles constitute a serious nuclear deterrent at all, given the vulnerability of such vessels to anti-surface-warfare capabilities in the Pakistani and Chinese arsenals. Assuming the launch platform closed to two-thirds of the Danush's maximum range before firing—standard practice to bolster accuracy—the missile's short range would expose the *Sukanyas* to a variety of Pakistani countermeasures meted out by surface, subsurface, and air assets. Only if a lengthy conventional war preceded the deployment of the patrol craft, exacting a severe toll on Pakistani conventional capabilities, would a Danush force offer India a credible second-strike capability.

Ashley Tellis, a prominent American scholar of Indian nuclear development, offers a generous interpretation of the Danush. He maintains that the Danush missile possesses some strategic value vis-à-vis Pakistan, not as a nuclear delivery system but as part of a second-strike arsenal designed to deliver a punishing retaliatory blow after a Pakistani first use of nuclear weapons. Interestingly, Tellis's language— "punishing"—mirrors the "unacceptable and massive" language in the 2003 Indian government statement. This may suggest that any Indian second strike may involve a broad range of delivery platforms to ensure penetration of any enemy defenses and the delivery of a large enough number of warheads. This may have implications for the operational patterns of Indian nuclear submarines once they come on line. This will be discussed in more detail below. Tellis identifies a mix of bureaucratic and conventional military rationales for the Danush. First, he posits that the Indian navy wanted to get in early on the nuclear and ballistic missile game. Even a rudimentary system like the Danush made the navy a player vis-à-vis the army and air force. Second, the Indian navy wanted to continue pursuing modern, conventional land-attack capabilities, assuring its relevance in a variety of potential crisis and conflict situations involving India's historic antagonist.[13] Tellis posits that the mere existence of the Danush will complicate Pakistani defense planning efforts. Islamabad can never be sure whether the missile will be deployed and, if it is, whether it is tipped with conventional or nuclear warheads.

What Tellis neglects to mention is the destabilizing effect this sort of ambiguity— whether the missile constitutes a conventional or nuclear delivery system—could create under stressful circumstances. This effect applies not only to the Danush but also to land-based Prithvi missile systems. Conflating nuclear and conventional weapons could upset Pakistani strategic and operational calculations, particularly during the fog of war, which could have an unforeseeable impact on confrontations at sea or decisions about Pakistan's own nuclear use.

Future Capabilities

Only in December 2007, after decades of media reporting and analysts' speculation, did the Indian navy officially disclose its plans for a sea-based deterrent. Specifically, navy spokesmen indicated that the service intended to design and build its own nuclear-powered submarine, and in fact, revealed that the first of these boats was close to being launched. Admiral Sureesh Mehta, then the chief of navy staff, announced that India would begin testing a submarine dubbed the advanced technology vehicle in April 2009.[14] Admiral Mehta indicated that the Defense Research and Development Organization (DRDO) was overseeing the project, which would yield, in his words, a "technology demonstrator." This phrase carries unfortunate baggage, given India's decidedly uneven record on indigenous defense projects.[15] The Indian Department of Atomic Energy and Indian navy are involved in the effort alongside DRDO. Again, though, knowledgeable analysts such as retired submariner Rear Admiral Raja Menon portray government coordination and oversight of the project as less than stellar.[16] Other equally qualified experts, such as the retired chief of navy staff, Admiral Arun Prakash, are more positive, noting that the Indian navy, unlike its sister services, has learned how to get the best of DRDO projects by assigning navy officers directly to the research organization's staff.[17]

India's future maritime deterrent force took a more visible and significant step forward with the July 26, 2009, launch of the advanced technology vehicle—now christened the INS *Arihant*—at Visakhapatnam. This public "launch," which initially consisted of flooding the dry dock in which the submarine hull had been constructed, ended literally decades of rumors and speculation about what to that point had been a secret program. At this writing only a small amount of information has come out about the *Arihant*'s specifications and capabilities. The full range of its capabilities awaits sea trials and operational deployment.

What is known about this specific submarine and about the program to build additional nuclear-powered ballistic-missile-firing submarines is the following. The *Arihant* is a relatively small SSBN whose displacement is varyingly reported in the 5,000–6,000 ton range, a length of 106 meters, and a diameter of approximately 10 meters.[18] By way of comparison, the 1960s-era Soviet Charlie-class cruise missile submarine leased by India displaced 4,300 tons, and France's current Le Triomphant–class SSBNs displace twice as much, at 12,000 tons. The Indian submarine will be powered by an 80–85 megawatt, pressurized-water nuclear reactor fueled by highly enriched uranium. What exactly qualifies as "highly enriched" has not been made public, although the International Atomic Energy Agency defines it as exceeding 19.75 percent enrichment. Again, according to early reports, the engineering plant will have a ten-year life cycle before it needs to be refueled. Although it has been speculated that this reactor is based on or indeed represents a copy of the plant from the leased Charlie-class submarine, the chief of India's Atomic Energy Program, Anil Kakodkar, has stated that it is of purely Indian design and manufacture, built with Russian specialists acting in a consulting role.[19] In addition, one knowledgeable analyst reports that the sonar for the *Arihant* is Indian designed.

The submarine is reported to have twelve tubes for ballistic missiles. Most reports indicate that the first missile carried on board the *Arihant* will be the K-15 missile, also known as the Sagarika.[20] This single-warhead missile reportedly boasts a range of 700 to 750 kilometers.[21] At least one report, however, names the Shaurya missile as the primary missile for the *Arihant*. This missile, which has been reported as both a ballistic missile and as a hypersonic cruise missile capable of being fired from a canister on land or underwater, is also said to have a range of 750 kilometers.[22] A newer report indicates that the Shaurya is a land-based version of the Sagarika.[23] A longer-range, follow-on K-X missile that remains under development has also been mentioned as possible future armament for the *Arihant*. This missile, a variant of the Agni III, is slated to have a range of 3,000 to 3,500 kilometers and the ability to carry multiple warheads.[24] Its speed remains a question. The ground-based system, the Agni III, has yet to be fully inducted into the armed forces, meaning that it is not yet fully operational after commencing flight testing in 2006.[25] One leading Indian analyst has also noted that developing a missile with this longer range that could fit within the 10-meter-diameter hull of the *Arihant* poses a challenge for Indian scientists and engineers.[26] For comparison's sake, the 1960s-era US Polaris A2 missile, whose range was similar to that of the proposed K-X, was 31 feet long (approximately 9.5 meters).[27] The impact of these ranges on operating areas and interactions with potential nuclear adversaries is discussed below.

The Indian navy indicated that it expected the *Arihant* to be inducted into the service and operational in 2012. The chief of naval staff in 2010, Admiral Nirmal Verma, noted that the intervening two years would be used to address a range of challenges, such as "proving of new technology, getting the submarine fully operational, developing doctrines and procedures."[28] This last task—developing doctrines and procedures—indicates that the Indian navy is comfortable enough with what it is getting in the *Arihant* that the boat will not languish as a technology demonstrator. It will be a fully operational seagoing platform. Given that it is the first of its class, it will nevertheless provide both the developers and the operators with a great deal of information that will inform the construction of follow-on SSBNs. Construction has begun on a second Indian SSBN, and that submarine is expected to undertake sea trials in 2015.[29]

Exactly how many of those New Delhi will build and whether they will follow the *Arihant's* design directly or deviate from it based on the boat's at-sea performance remains somewhat unclear as of this writing. Admiral Verma has indicated, on the one hand, that India's submarine fleet should have five to six nuclear-powered ballistic missile submarines, but in the same interview he indicated that current plans call for only two additional SSBNs to "reinforce India's strategic deterrent force at sea."[30] He could have been expressing the Indian navy's desire as opposed to what was already in the design-and-building phase. One of the best book-length treatments of India's nuclear strategy, a work that deals at length with the sea-based leg, recommends a fleet of six SSBNs to equip New Delhi with a true second-strike capability.[31]

Details about the submarine and associated ballistic missile programs are sketchy in large part because the government has shrouded them both in official secrecy from their outset. This secrecy is understandable in part, both from the standpoint of general national security and because India has been the target of unilateral and multinational sanctions against its nuclear and military programs ever since its 1974 "peaceful nuclear explosion." If New Delhi had officially revealed that it was planning a sea-based nuclear deterrent at any point before September 2008, when the Nuclear Suppliers Group granted a waiver on transfers of nuclear technology to the Indian commercial power sector, its disclosure would have ended its chances for receiving such a waiver. Group members would have been more inclined to tighten sanctions than make an exception to the usual export control rules.

Some information suggests that India may be developing a submarine-launched cruise missile (SLCM) along a parallel track, perhaps with a view toward delivering tactical nuclear payloads. New Delhi has made no official announcements about an SLCM capability such as those that accompanied the launching of the *Arihant*, and there has been little public discussion such as that surrounding the K-15 and the Shaurya. It is very clear that India is pursuing a variety of cruise missile programs, both through indigenous development and through purchases from and joint development with Russia. It is less clear whether any of these missiles will ever carry nuclear warheads, although some press reports indicate as much.[32] That reports on such issues are often contradictory or ambiguous testifies to inexperience on the part of the Indian press and to the official penchant for secrecy in nuclear-related matters.

The cruise missile most frequently mentioned to fulfill a nuclear role is the BrahMos, a joint Russo-Indian project. The BrahMos is a supersonic cruise missile with antiship and land-attack capabilities. It is said to have a range of approximately 290 kilometers. Indian developers are discussing outfitting a variety of platforms with it. Thus far the Block I variant of the BrahMos has been installed in various Indian navy surface ships and accepted into various army units.[33] The BrahMos has reached a far more advanced stage of development than any purely indigenous Indian missile, which possibly lets it fill the gap between requirements and hardware until a system with greater range and payload can take its place. Again, press reports indicate that the Indian military is planning to field a longer-range cruise missile—on the order of 1,500 kilometers—capable of carrying a nuclear warhead.[34] It is an open question whether the government has approved or funded such a plan. It also remains unclear whether surface ships, submarines, or both would be fitted with the new system.

India has also purchased the Klub cruise missile from Russia. The Klub sports both an antiship and a land-attack capability. It can be launched from either torpedo tubes or a vertical launch system and has a range of approximately 220 kilometers.[35] Judging from the platforms and missiles already in the Indian inventory or that are about to be purchased or leased, the BrahMos or the Klub coupled with INS *Arihant* would constitute the most logical short-term candidate to serve as an initial third part of the Indian nuclear triad. Whether Indian weapons engineers have managed to miniaturize a nuclear warhead sufficiently to mount it on either the Klub or the BrahMos, however, remains to be seen. It is also unclear, largely because of the official secrecy cloaking nuclear force structure issues, whether India even wants SLCMs to be part of its long-term nuclear solution. The practical issues associated with using either the BrahMos or Klub as a nuclear weapon delivery vehicle are discussed below in the context of interactions between India, Pakistan, and China.

Interactive Effects

Now that India has publicly shown its commitment to a submarine-based nuclear delivery capability, what impact will this capability have on its regional rivals, Pakistan and China? How will Islamabad and Beijing react to this development, and what might be its ongoing impact in peacetime, crisis, and war? To the degree that the Indian government and indeed Indian analysts discuss the reasons for building such a capability, they generally cite the survivability of the platform relative to land-based delivery systems such as aircraft and missiles. It has long been an article of faith that it is more difficult to find and target a submarine intent on concealing its whereabouts than it is to strike at a plane or a land-based ballistic or cruise missile. This wisdom grew out of early experience with submarines during World War I and World War II and was reaffirmed in the early days of the Cold War, when the US and Soviet navies engaged in a back-and-forth struggle to hide their own and find the opponent's submarines.[36]

To be sure, combat experience has showed that road- and rail-based missiles are often very difficult to detect and target, even when one combatant enjoys air supremacy.[37] Although intelligence, surveillance, and reconnaissance techniques as well as precision strike capacity have improved immensely since Operation Desert Storm in 1991, mobile land targets continue to defy easy prosecution. Even so, the conviction that submarines are even more difficult to find and target persists—reinforcing the long-held belief that undersea craft are at once secure from enemy attack and a force for stability.

The concept that SLBMs impart stability to a contest between two rivals rests on a number of assumptions beyond the launch platform's relative security from detection. The two ideal stabilizing characteristics of any weapon system are its invulnerability to enemy attack and its being nonthreatening to an enemy's nuclear forces—presumably including the command-and-control structures governing those forces.[38] The latter characteristic relies both on that enemy's knowledge about the accuracy of such systems, particularly against hardened targets, and on whether the enemy estimates the number of these relatively invulnerable weapons (or warheads) as large enough to target a significant number of land-based nuclear forces or critical command-and-control nodes. This conception of stability relates to incentives to strike first, either generally or during a crisis. It was extensively debated as part of the broader set of controversies between the United States and Soviet Union over whether particular upgrades or additions to their oversized nuclear arsenals increased, decreased, or left unchanged the chances for global thermonuclear war.

Although some of the concepts from Cold War nuclear stability analysis offer a useful starting point for examining the likely impact of an Indian SSBN capability, both the surrounding context and the specifics of interactions among potential adversaries matter. Depending on how one views international security, important aspects of the context may include any history of enmity between the potential antagonists, the conventional military balance and operations, the domestic political situation in each country, and each side's modernization of its nuclear forces. Although these variables cannot all be examined in detail in this chapter, some of the major ones help illuminate the evolving strategic situation vis-à-vis Pakistan and China. Because India has only recently announced that it will seek an SLBM capability, and for the sake of brevity, the discussion below is limited to this dimension of Chinese–Pakistani–Indian interactions. I eschew examining how nuclear-armed cruise missiles might shape regional interactions, mainly because such weaponry, at least in the Indian arsenal, remains largely hypothetical for now.

The first question for India's next-door neighbor, Pakistan, is how to respond in peacetime to an openly acknowledged Indian nuclear delivery capability once it is operational. Islamabad responded rhetorically almost immediately after the launch of the *Arihant*, but the leadership must now decide whether, and how, to respond in terms of military acquisitions and adjustments to doctrine, planning, and operations.[39] In terms of military acquisitions, Pakistan has two basic choices. The first is to develop a parallel capability—a submarine platform capable of firing nuclear missiles. No information has come to light pointing to an indigenous Pakistani development effort akin to that which produced the *Arihant*. It is nearly unthinkable, furthermore, that any country with the capability to produce an SSBN would sell or otherwise transfer one to Pakistan. Although the Soviet Union and now Russia have leased nuclear-powered submarines to India, none of those were explicitly designed as nuclear weapons platforms. In all likelihood, presumed restrictions under the Nuclear Non-Proliferation Treaty plus concerns about past Pakistani proliferation activities would keep the United States, France, the United Kingdom, Russia, and even China from risking such a transfer.

Pakistan could, however, consider either purchasing or developing a submarine capable of carrying nuclear-armed SLCMs. Also conceivable is that submarines currently in the Pakistani fleet could be retrofitted to fire nuclear-tipped cruise missiles. Both the Pakistani navy's older submarines, the Agosta-70s, and newer submarines, the Agosta-90s, can already fire French-made Exocet antiship missiles. In addition, both classes of submarine can fire the United States–manufactured Harpoon antiship missile. Two questions arise. First, can either missile be converted from the antiship function for which it was designed to strike at land targets? And second, can Pakistani engineers master the intricacies of miniaturizing a nuclear warhead and mating it to a missile intended for different purposes?

At least one press report indicates that the US government thought that Pakistan was attempting to modify the Harpoon missile to strike land targets—a charge denied by Islamabad.[40] And to be sure, both the Exocet and the Harpoon have extremely limited ranges. It is doubtful either would be the weapon of choice for a mature Pakistani nuclear cruise missile program. A more promising candidate is the Babur cruise missile, whose variants boast ranges reported at 500 and 700 kilometers. Indeed, Pakistani military officials have told reporters that the Babur is capable of carrying a nuclear warhead.[41] Pakistan has announced plans to purchase new submarines from both France and China. The capacity to fire a longer-range land-attack cruise missile like the Babur may be part of Islamabad's requirements for its new boats.[42]

Pakistani acquisition of a submarine-based nuclear delivery system would not directly offset the Indian sea-based deterrent. In fact, one could argue that Pakistani development of such a capability would relate more directly to a desire for a more secure second-strike capability. Pakistan is likely concerned about a disarming Indian first strike that employs either nuclear weapons (in spite of New Delhi's official NFU doctrine) or the continually improving Indian conventional arsenal. But symbolism matters in the Indian–Pakistani relationship. Pakistani military and civilian officials insist that Pakistan will not allow itself to be rendered irrelevant on the international stage. Acquiring a submarine-based nuclear capability, therefore, represents one token of Islamabad's desire to be seen as a peer of New Delhi and as being able to match New Delhi in visible areas related to defense. Pakistan's campaign for a civil nuclear agreement with the United States resembling the deal struck between Washington and New Delhi may reflect similar prestige-driven logic.[43]

Once India begins operating INS *Arihant* and its successors, Pakistan will presumably start searching for ways to gather intelligence on the Indian undersea fleet's operational capabilities and seeking to acquire and exercise antisubmarine warfare (ASW) capabilities meant to counter this nuclear delivery platform in times of crisis or war. Indeed, the announcement that Pakistan hopes to purchase more and newer submarines from France and China marks the first step toward upgrading the navy's ASW capability. Intelligence gathering and ASW exercises would bring Pakistani forces—including submarines—into close proximity with Indian submarines. Close encounters intended to gather intelligence or test the skill and resolve of Indian submariners could give rise to "games of chicken" harking back to US–Soviet encounters during the Cold War.[44]

If a militarized crisis arises between India and Pakistan in the future, the presence of a nuclear-armed Indian submarine may prompt one or both adversaries to adopt and execute strategies that work against stability. As noted above, India's possession of a more secure second-strike platform may contribute to overall strategic stability in a static situation, but in a crisis, potential interactions between the submarine and Pakistani forces may actually escalate tensions. The propensity to escalate would depend on the specifics of the crisis and the operational-level strategy adopted by each side. For instance, if India chose to base its undersea nuclear forces on its east coast and sortie them to the northern Arabian Sea in times of trouble, Pakistan might consider any deployment provocative and take some preemptive conventional action against Indian submarines. The chances of a miscalculation or open conflict would rise if the Pakistani Navy were to harass or target Indian navy vessels with ASW forces.

Even if New Delhi chose to keep its submarine fleet close to its bases and away from Pakistan during a crisis, Islamabad might still attempt to track Indian naval movements. There is precedent for this. In the 1971 war Pakistan sent a submarine around the Indian subcontinent to lay mines outside the Indian eastern naval base at Visakhapatnam.[45] In that instance the Pakistani boat sank under disputed circumstances. (One narrative has it hitting its own mine, whereas another attributes responsibility to Indian naval action.) Whatever the case, this episode strongly suggests that Pakistan would be prepared to incur significant risks in wartime, dispatching its submarines on a long cruise that exposes them to enemy defenses. In thinking about crisis stability as it pertains to nuclear assets at sea, it is important to remember that military forces will likely interact closely with prospective foes, even if the crisis has not yet taken on military overtones and even if the two capitals are attempting to settle their differences through negotiations. Incidents are apt to occur at sea when passions run hot. They tend to escalate when rival forces find themselves in close quarters and communications with a higher authority prove tenuous.[46]

For the near term, the Indian submarine-launched nuclear capability will remain limited both in numbers and in its capacity to reach important targets in Pakistan. Assuming it carries a combat load of twelve single-warhead missiles, and that each possesses a range of approximately 700 to 750 kilometers, the INS *Arihant* features characteristics that qualify it as a stabilizing agent in a nuclear dyad. Again, these traits include relative invulnerability to attack and a limited ability to target an opponent's nuclear forces or the command-and-control elements overseeing those forces.[47] The *Arihant* enjoys the stealth of all undersea craft, whereas much of the Pakistani nuclear infrastructure lies out of the boat's range, to the north of the country. The seat of political and military power also lies out of missile range.[48]

However, the constraints on the *Arihant*'s ability to target Pakistani nuclear forces or command-and-control will remain in place only as long as the boat and its successors carry only single-warhead missiles with a limited range. The logic of Indo-Pakistani deterrence promises to change if New Delhi proceeds to develop and deploy the K-X missile, expanding the undersea fleet's coverage to the Pakistani political center and nuclear weapons sites. The other issue influencing the use of SSBNs for counterforce targeting involves the accuracy of the missiles they carry. For most of the Cold War, SLBMs were generally considered too inaccurate to successfully destroy hardened targets like missile silos. This changed in the late Cold War with the advent of the Trident D-5 missile on board US *Ohio*-class SSBNs. The accuracy of Indian SLBMs and therefore their potential for use as counterforce weapons remains to be seen as of this writing.

Submarines' relative invulnerability to attack also varies considerably, depending on the range of their missiles, the character of the operational plans governing submarine warfare, and the circumstances under which these plans are put into effect. Greater missile range obviously expands the arc within which an SSBN can reach its designated targets, and thus multiplies the sea areas in which it can hide. If the conventional Indian navy fleet is assigned to protect SSBNs in wartime, navy commanders might well opt to conduct substantial attacks on Pakistani ASW forces early on in a conflict. Although this would help safeguard Indian SSBNs, such action would also destroy a substantial portion of Pakistani military forces—prodding Islamabad toward the nuclear precipice.[49] In sum, while Indian SSBNs possess characteristics traditionally seen as stabilizing within a nuclear deterrent relationship, this may not hold true in the case of India's relations with Pakistan. How SSBNs will figure into peacetime, crisis, and wartime stability is a far more complex equation that depends significantly on Pakistani perceptions and actions.

How applicable are Cold War models for thinking about nuclear exchanges in the Indian Ocean? Intuitively, it appears that an SSBN force would let one side keep nuclear assets in reserve and possibly achieve escalation dominance over its opponent. But applying such models to the Indo-Pakistani context is not terribly fruitful, for at least the short to medium terms. Neither India nor Pakistan possesses large numbers of nuclear weapons. Accordingly, the relevance of the Cold War studies speculating about drawn-out nuclear exchanges would be limited in a South Asian scenario by the modest number of weapons available to the belligerents. In addition, the scant amount of publicly available information on Indian and Pakistani nuclear doctrines suggests that New Delhi and Islamabad think about using nuclear weapons as a last resort and as a one-time event, if it were to come to that. The 2003 press release described above modified India's NFU doctrine slightly. With regard to nuclear exchanges and escalation, however, it was explicit: "Nuclear retaliation to a first strike will be massive and designed to inflict unacceptable damage."[50] This wording seems to indicate that India sees nuclear use as a one-time, all-or-nothing endeavor. If so, there is little reason to hold back undersea nuclear capabilities. Indeed, depending on the percentage of India's nuclear forces that is eventually deployed in SSBNs, "massive" retaliation may demand the release of nuclear weapons at sea.

What about Sino-Indian deterrence? The interactive impact toward China of India's fielding an undersea deterrent will emerge over the longer term and therefore is even more speculative than that described above. There are several reasons why peacetime Chinese–Indian interactions relating to this new capability promise to unfold more slowly than Indian–Pakistani interactions. For one thing, Beijing probably considers the fledgling Indian capability unworthy of more than a rhetorical response for the moment. China has lived with the vastly more substantial submarine presence embodied by the US navy for many years. It will understandably regard the seagoing Indian deterrent as a lesser included case for peacetime strategy. This may not persist as the Indian deterrent advances. Beijing may undertake new operations in response as New Delhi incorporates new capabilities into its naval portfolio. Beijing may wish to gain more intelligence about Indian SSBNs' operating characteristics and practices and may step up surveillance of Indian navy patrol grounds in the Indian Ocean as a precaution. One incursion of a Chinese fishing trawler suspected of being a spy ship near the Andaman and Nicobar Islands may be an indication of such increased mapping and surveillance operations.[51]

Indian deployment patterns will also influence the Chinese operational calculus. For first-generation Indian SLBMs to reach targets in China, the *Arihant* or its sisters would need to steam at least into the South China Sea. Indian boats would need to cruise the Yellow Sea to target Beijing with missiles with a range of 700 to 750 kilometers. It is doubtful whether India has much appetite for peacetime deterrent patrols that far from Indian shores. If New Delhi chooses to undertake such patrols or to dispatch submarines or surface ships into the China seas to map the ocean floor or gather intelligence on Chinese surveillance and ASW capabilities, Beijing will probably respond in some fashion. Chinese vessels might harass the ships in question, much as it did US surveillance vessels in the vicinity of Hainan Island in 2009.[52] Such interactions would tend to fray relations between the two rising Asian powers. China might also opt to conduct patrols or surveillance operations of its own near Indian coasts or naval bases—exercising an option open to it even if India refrains from increasing its naval presence off the Chinese mainland.

As in the Pakistani case, sorting through the implications of Indian SSBNs during a Sino-Indian crisis is a bit more difficult than foreseeing the peacetime impact of an undersea Indian deterrent. One reason is that India and China have not had a serious militarized crisis since 1962. Second, the steaming distances involved and the fact that neither India nor China patrols regularly near the other's coasts mean that it might take some time for naval forces to get involved in any crisis—if they do at all. And, as noted above, an Indian submarine armed with shorter-range missiles would need to pass through one of the straits in Southeast Asia and position itself in the South China Sea or the Yellow Sea to threaten any large Chinese cities during a crisis. Whether India would forward-deploy a national asset like an SSBN to such exposed waters if a crisis were brewing is doubtful.

Part of the answer to this question depends on the ongoing Indian struggle to test and deploy land-based ballistic missiles able to reach key cities in China, including Beijing, and on whether New Delhi feels its land-based arsenal provides a sufficiently survivable deterrent. As of 2010 India had successfully tested and the Indian army had accepted delivery of the road- and rail-mobile Agni II missile. With a reported range in excess of 2,000 kilometers, the Agni II can range a number of large Chinese cities and military installations, but it cannot hit Beijing. New Delhi is currently testing the Agni III, with its 3,500-kilometer range. It successfully tested the 5,000-kilometer-range Agni V in April 2012.[53] The Agni III is progressing closer to induction into the Indian armed forces. Once in place, it will give New Delhi a more survivable capability that can target almost all of China, but the missile is suffering through a fitful set of trials. Even when New Delhi ultimately deploys a mobile, land-based arsenal able to cover the full range of potential targets in China, submarine-based nuclear capabilities will still offer a hedge against a Chinese technical or doctrinal breakthrough that would permit the People's Liberation Army to target land-mobile missiles or the command-and-control systems for the land-based leg of the Indian nuclear triad.

At the point in the future when the *Arihant*-class submarines are armed with the K-X missile, New Delhi would enjoy the option of ranging targets in Tibet and Sichuan and Hunan provinces from positions in the northern Bay of Bengal. Such deployments would complicate Beijing's calculations in a crisis and could provide the incentive for China to deploy ships or ASW-capable aircraft to the region, assuming nearby states such as Burma allowed Chinese units to operate out of bases on their soil. That Indian Ocean governments would grant such permission is far from a foregone conclusion. It is worth pointing out that the often-discussed but infrequently analyzed "string of pearls" strategy that many observers impute to China in the Indian Ocean is likely to encounter severe limits under stressful circumstances—assuming that such a string, or network of Chinese naval bases, comes into being at some point in the future.[54]

The string of pearls is not a well-documented Chinese strategy but rather an American conceptualization based on an American consulting firm's discussions with Indian navy officers.[55] The concept was developed as a way of thinking about how China might seek to acquire access or basing rights along the Indian Ocean littoral as a way to ensure the security of energy shipments from the Persian Gulf and Africa. Whether Beijing has indeed embarked on such a concerted strategy remains in doubt, as does the potential usefulness of such bases in a crisis or war embroiling China with India (or any other great power, for that matter). Suffice it to say that clashes like those discussed above—a crisis between India and China involving tracking or the combat use of nuclear-armed submarines—would severely test any access agreements negotiated by Beijing in peacetime in order to assure energy security. Both during and after the Cold War, the United States encountered numerous difficulties using bases and gaining overflight clearances, even from collective defense treaty allies. Beijing will face similar challenges if it seeks military access to or use of bases in a militarized crisis with India, the other claimant to great power in Asia. This is a choice few Indian Ocean governments would relish.

The addition of SSBNs to the Indian arsenal, then, only marginally changes the dynamics in a hypothetical wartime situation between India and China over the short to medium terms. Until New Delhi manages to arm its submarine-launched missiles with multiple, independently targetable reentry vehicles, the number of weapons coming from the sea in any Sino-Indian contingency will simply be too small to matter to wartime calculations. Flight-time differences between land-based and sea-based Indian missiles, furthermore, are not markedly different in terms of striking Chinese targets. This simplifies the dynamics between China and India to a degree. During the Cold War, both antagonists had to worry about decapitation attacks from the sea against command-and-control nodes. Geography and technology have spared Beijing and New Delhi this element of nuclear strategic rivalry for the time being.

Finally, it is worth briefly considering the part the future Indian SSBN force might play in a crisis or conflict were Beijing and Islamabad to make common cause against New Delhi. In one plausible future scenario, Pakistan and India might come to blows again. If India were getting the better of a conventional conflict with Pakistan, China might step in to threaten New Delhi, posing a two-front problem for the Indian forces. Given India's stated NFU doctrine, one would need to assume that the Chinese threat would be nuclear in this case. The question of how the *Arihant* would figure into the Indian strategy would depend on the range of the boat's current missile arsenal and on whether China believed it could credibly threaten New Delhi's land-based arsenal or hold other critical targets at risk. Dispatching the *Arihant* or another future SSBN through the Southeast Asian straits closer to China could send a useful signal, although it would also risk goading China into prosecuting an aggressive ASW campaign to find the Indian SSBN. As long as the range of Indian missiles remains modest, India may well opt to array its SSBN force to supply a retaliatory capability against Pakistan. If so, New Delhi would trust its mobile land-based arsenal as its primary deterrent against Chinese threats.

Other Issues and Considerations

How aggressively will New Delhi push ahead with its undersea deterrent? In economic terms the question arises of whether the Indian government will remain prepared to shoulder the burden of funding this very expensive and difficult technology.

The technological hurdles to constructing a reliable, nuclear-powered SLBM-armed submarine fleet remain formidable. India has spent more than three decades trying to bring its SSBN project to fruition. The project has only recently begun to bear fruit in the form of the INS *Arihant*. Indian navy officers have talked of putting to sea a fleet of between three and six submarines, but the pace at which such a force is assembled will depend not only on the costs of current research and development and shipbuilding but also on the expense of current operations. Straightforward operational and strategic logic may not dictate the configuration of the Indian submarine fleet.

Other obstacles may also crop up once the Indian navy places its SSBN fleet in operational service. Safety will be a priority, as it is for other navies. The need for a far more robust submarine rescue capability will bulk large once the Indian navy starts operating undersea craft with a far greater operational radius than the existing fleet.[56] Another challenge will be fielding trained officers and enlisted sailors in sufficient numbers to man a nuclear-powered submarine fleet. The Indian government's lease of a Russian *Akula*-class nuclear attack submarine is meant in part to help train Indian mariners to operate naval nuclear power plants, but such a program will encounter growing pains, judging from the experiences of other navies.

Government officials and lawmakers are not the only ones facing difficult trade-offs. If the Indian government does decide to proceed with submarine construction, is the Indian navy ready to fund it at the expense of other priorities such as conventional warships and aircraft? It is possible that New Delhi will fund the SSBN fleet through special budgetary allocations; but if not—if the Indian navy needed to construct a fleet out of existing resources, as seems probable—the naval command may decide that it can forgo nuclear submarines in favor of hardware that sees more day-to-day use. How the naval hierarchy's debate over trade-offs will unfold remains to be seen.

Another potential issue surrounds the requirement to miniaturize nuclear warheads for SLBMs or SLCMs. Whether Indian weapons engineers can create reliable missile payloads without nuclear testing is problematic. In fact, at least one nuclear scientist involved in India's 1998 nuclear tests maintains that the thermonuclear portion of the tests did not work as well as expected and that further testing may be required.[57] Renewed testing would raise political problems for India even if it resolved technical ones. If Indian nuclear scientists determine that more live testing is needed to perfect sea-based weapons, relations with the United States and other members of the Nuclear Suppliers Group will suffer. After all, these nations consented to civil nuclear cooperation with India on the premise that India would refrain from further tests. If the United States makes further progress toward President Barack Obama's declared goal of zeroing out nuclear arsenals worldwide, pressure may build on India to sign the Comprehensive Test Ban Treaty.

Finally, when India finally puts to sea a platform armed with nuclear weapons—something that will probably occur in the 2012 time frame—it will need to resolve significant issues involving command, control, and communications. Some of these challenges, including communicating with submerged submarines, involve known technologies and procedures. New Delhi should not find them insurmountable.

More interesting, and potentially thornier for India, are questions related to civilian control of nuclear weapons, and in particular to release authority for nuclear weapons. According to various reports, India has been working to develop a command-and-control system since 1998. It has also devoted significant work to integrating the Indian civil and military authorities and to managing the country's nuclear arsenal in general.[58] Sea-based nuclear weapons present unique challenges at the civil–military interface. A variety of possible solutions are conceivable—for instance, stationing civilians on board submarines under "dual-key" arrangements—but it will present a unique challenge for an Indian government that has traditionally kept very tight physical control of nuclear weapons and reserved decision making exclusively to civilians—both scientists and politicians. Again, these are not insurmountable challenges. But India must work through them in a way that satisfies Indian sensibilities.

Notes

1. Raja Menon, "Just One Shark in the Deep Blue Ocean," *Outlook India*, August 10, 2009, http://outlookindia.com/article.aspx?261048; Admiral Nirmal Verma, "Indian N-Sub to Be Operational in Two Years," *Domain-b.com*, February 8, 2010, http://domain-b.com/defence/sea/indian_navy/20100208_n_sub_operational.html.

2. For a comprehensive history of India's nuclear ambitions, discussions, and decisions since independence, see George Perkovich, *India's Nuclear Bomb: The Impact of Global Proliferation*, rev. ed. (Berkeley: University of California Press, 2002).

3. Ministry of External Affairs, "The Cabinet Committee on Security Reviews Operationalization of India's Nuclear Doctrine," press release, January 4, 2003, www.mea.gov.in/pressrelease/2003/01/04pr01.htm.

4. National Security Advisory Board, "Draft Report of National Security Advisory Board on Indian Nuclear Doctrine," August 17, 1999, http://meaindia.nic.in/disarmament/dm17aug99.htm.

5. Ibid.

6. Indian Navy, INBR 8, *Indian Maritime Doctrine* (Delhi: Indian Navy, Integrated Headquarters, Ministry of Defense, 2004), 49.

7. Ibid., 110.

8. Indian Navy, *Freedom to Use the Seas: India's Maritime Military Strategy* (Delhi: Indian Navy, Integrated Headquarters, 2007), 76.

9. Indian Navy, INBR 8, *2009 Indian Maritime Doctrine* (Delhi: Indian Navy, Integrated Headquarters, 2009), 27.

10. Ibid., 92–93.

11. *Jane's Naval Weapon Systems*, February 15, 2008.

12. *Jane's Missiles and Rockets*, December 1, 2004.

13. Ashley J. Tellis, *India's Emerging Nuclear Posture: Between Recessed Deterrent and Ready Arsenal* (Santa Monica, CA: RAND Corporation, 2001), 573–74.

14. Sandeep Unnithan, "The Secret Undersea Weapon," *India Today*, January 17, 2008, available at http://indiatoday.digitaltoday.in.

15. Timothy Hoyt of the US Naval War College has argued that the term "technology demonstrator" has applied to several Indian defense programs run by DRDO that produced items that were either unwanted by the Indian armed forces or that failed to meet military requirements. Many never made it into the active-duty inventory. Some were reengineered once significant military input was obtained, resulting in new, usable versions.

16. Raja Menon, *A Nuclear Strategy for India* (New Delhi: Sage, 2000), 226.

17. Arun Prakash, remarks at conference on "The Elephant at Sea: India's Maritime Strategy," Woodrow Wilson International Center for Scholars, Washington, DC, March 9, 2010, http://wilsoncenter.org/index.cfm?fuseaction = events.event_summary&event_id = 590861.

18. Raja Menon, "Launch of the Arihant: Relevance for India," National Maritime Foundation, August 5, 2009, www.maritimeindia.org/pdfs/Commentry05Aug09.pdf; Arun Prakash, "ATV: Out of the Closet at Last!" National Maritime Foundation, July 26, 2009, www.maritimeindia.org/pdfs/ATV.pdf.

19. Sandeep Unnithan, "Deep Impact," *India Today*, July 23, 2009; Anil Kakodkar, "INS Arihant Is an Indian Design: Anil Kakodkar," *The Hindu*, August 16, 2009, http://beta.thehindu.com/opinion/interview/article3502.ece.

20. Rahul Singh, "Arihant to Be Armed with Ballistic Missiles," *Hindustan Times*, February 17, 2010, www.hindustantimes.com/StoryPage/Print/509620.aspx.

21. Ibid.; Menon, "Launch of the Arihant: Relevance for India."

22. Ajai Shukla, "Shaurya Surfaces as India's Underwater Nuclear Missile," *Business Standard*, February 17, 2010.

23. Monika Chansoria, *India's Missile Program: Building Blocks for Effective Deterrence*, CLAWS Issue Brief 26 (New Delhi: Centre for Land Warfare Studies, 2011).

24. Radhakrishna Rao, "India Ups Ante on Coastal Security," *Central Chronicle*, August 10, 2009.

25. Pratap Chakravarty, "India Announces Long-Range Nuclear-Capable Missile Test," *ASDNews*, February 10, 2010.

26. Menon, "Just One Shark in the Deep Blue Ocean."

27. Federation of American Scientists, "Polaris A2," www.fas.org/nuke/guide/usa/slbm/a-2.htm.

28. Verma, "Indian N-Sub to Be Operational."

29. "Construction Commences on India's Second Nuclear Submarine," *Domain-B*, July 10, 2011, www.domain-b.com/defence/sea/indian_navy/20110711_nuclear_submarine.html.

30. Singh, "Arihant to Be Armed."

31. Menon, *Nuclear Strategy*, 226.

32. "BrahMos Cruise Missile Test-Fired Successfully," *Times of India*, March 22, 2010, http://timesofindia.indiatimes.com/india/BrahMos-cruise-missile-test-fired-successfully/articleshow/5709080.cms.

33. Ibid.

34. Ibid.

35. Mark Farrer, "Klub: Quantum Leap in Naval Strike," *Asia-Pacific Defense Reporter*, April 2005.

36. Owen R. Cote Jr., *The Third Battle: Innovation in the US Navy's Silent Cold War Struggle with Soviet Submarines*, Naval War College Newport Paper 16 (Newport: Naval War College Press, 2003).

37. Thomas A. Keaney and Eliot A. Cohen, "Gulf War Air Power Survey Summary Report," Federation of American Scientists, 1993, www.fas.org/sgp/library/gwpsum.doc.

38. Robert D. Glasser, "Enduring Misconceptions of Strategic Stability: The Role of Nuclear Missile-Carrying Submarines," *Journal of Peace Research* 29, no. 1 (February 1992): 24.

39. Shamin ur Rahman, "India Submarine to Trigger Arms Race: Pak Navy," *Dawn* (Karachi), July 27, 2009, www.dawn.com/wps/wcm/connect/dawn-content-library/dawn/news/pakistan/04-india-nuclear-submarine-to-trigger-arms-race-pak-navy-qs-07.

40. Eric Schmitt and David E. Sanger, "US Says Pakistan Made Changes to Missiles Sold for Defense," *New York Times*, August 30, 2009.

41. "Pakistan Test-Fires Nuclear Capable Missile," CNN.com, July 26, 2007, http://edition.cnn.com/2007/WORLD/asiapcf/07/26/pakistan.missile.test.reut/index.html.

42. "Navy to Buy Seven Submarines," *Dawn* (Karachi), March 25, 2010, www.dawn.com/wps/wcm/connect/dawn-content-library/dawn/news/pakistan/16-navy + to + buy + seven + submarines-hs-04.

43. "Pakistan Satisfied with US Nuclear Talks," *Dawn* (Karachi), March 25, 2010, www.dawn.com/wps/wcm/connect/dawn-content-library/dawn/news/pakis tan/16-qures hi + says + satisfied + with + us + talks + on + nukes-hs-03.

44. Desmond Ball, "Nuclear War at Sea," *International Security* 10, no. 3 (Winter 1985–86): 6.

45. Sardar F. S. Lodi, "An Agosta Submarine for Pakistan," Defensejournal.com, January 2000, www.defencejournal.com/2000/jan/agosta.htm.

46. One historical example involves Soviet submarine captains' not getting the word during the Cuban Missile Crisis that the US navy would only be using practice depth charges. For an up-to-date description of multiple close calls and missteps involving nuclear weapons and misperceptions, see Michael Dobbs, *One Minute to Midnight: Kennedy, Khrushchev and Castro on the Brink of Nuclear War* (New York: Alfred A. Knopf, 2008).

47. Glasser, "Enduring Misconceptions," 24.

48. For maps of Pakistan's nuclear infrastructure, see Center for Nonproliferation Studies, Selected "Pakistani Nuclear Facilities," http://cns.miis.edu/reports/pdfs/paki stan.pdf.

49. Feroz Hassan Khan, "Reducing the Risk of Nuclear War in South Asia," in *Pakistan's Nuclear Future: Reining in the Risk*, rev. ed. (Arlington, VA Nonproliferation Policy Education Center, 2008), www.strategicstudiesinstitute.army.mil/pubs/down load.cfm?q = 963.

50. Ministry of External Affairs, "Cabinet Committee on Security Reviews Operationalization."

51. Sudhi Ranjan Sen, "China Ship with 22 Labs Spied on India," *NDTV*, August 30, 2011, www.ndtv.com/article/india/china-ship-with-22-labs-spied-on-india-130174&cp.

52. Tom Shanker, "China Harassed US Ship, Pentagon Says," *New York Times*, March 10, 2009, www.nytimes.com/2009/03/10/world/americas/10iht-10military.2071 3498.html.

53. Rajat Pandit, "Pakistan's Nuke Arsenal Bigger Than India's," *Times of India*, June 3, 2010, http://timesofindia.indiatimes.com/India/Pakistans-nuke-arsenal-bigger-than-Indias/articleshow/6005178.cms.

54. For an informed Indian view of this concept, see Gurpreet S. Khurana, "China's 'String of Pearls' in the Indian Ocean and Its Security Implications," *Strategic Analysis* 32, no. 1 (January 2008): 1–39.

55. Booz Allen Hamilton, "Energy Futures in Asia," prepared for the Office of Net Assessment, US Department of Defense, 2005.

56. "Indian Navy: RFP for Submarine Rescue Vehicles Issued," *IndiaDefence*, April 16, 2008, www.india-defence.com/reports/3808.

57. Sanjoy Majumder, "India Nuclear Test 'Did not Work,'" BBC News, August 27, 2009, http://news.bbc.co.uk/2/hi/8225540.stm.

58. Harsh Pant, "India's Nuclear Doctrine and Command Structure," *Armed Forces and Society* 33, no. 2 (January 2007): 238–64.

CHAPTER 10

PAKISTAN'S NUCLEAR POSTURE

Thinking about the Unthinkable?

Timothy D. Hoyt

It HAS BEEN MORE THAN TEN YEARS NOW since Pakistan tested its first nuclear device—its first six nuclear devices, if one believes local reporting.[1] These nuclear weapons were the product of a twenty-five-year effort, which included collaboration with China, the creation of a covert international nuclear procurement network, and a misreading of US policy that led to a broad spectrum of economic and military sanctions.[2] During the past decade, Pakistan has weathered two changes of government, the assassination of a leading civilian politician, three crises that could have led to large-scale conventional war or regional nuclear exchanges, and the emergence of a transnational militant threat that not only has past links with Pakistani intelligence but also now threatens Islamabad itself. And when these factors are combined with Pakistan's truly abysmal nuclear proliferation record, which is rivaled only by China's, Pakistan's nuclear arsenal becomes a significant risk management problem for the international community, its neighbors, and its own government. When thinking about Pakistan, analysts need to seriously consider "the unthinkable."

This chapter briefly considers not only the costs and benefits of Pakistan's nuclear program but also the risks it raises at the domestic/internal, regional, and international levels of analysis. Pakistan's nuclear arsenal is examined in terms of intentions—the threats that drive nuclear acquisition, and existing nuclear doctrine—and capabilities. The bulk of the chapter looks at the risks posed by Pakistan's nuclear capability and the efforts that Pakistan and the international community have made to grapple with them. Finally, it looks at some possible futures derived not only from current trends but also from an examination of key policymaking institutions and of Pakistan's historical responses to opportunities, threats, and crises.

Intentions: Why Does Pakistan Have a Nuclear Arsenal?

Pakistan's nuclear arsenal is exclusively focused on India and is driven by a combination of security and normative concerns.[3] In Pakistan's case, however, the normative concerns have little to do with symbolism ("great powers have nukes"), and much more to do with issues of self-definition. Virtually since the creation of the state, Pakistani elites have defined themselves as being like India, but not India.[4] The most telling example of how this has affected nuclear decision making may be the actual decision to test a nuclear warhead in 1998. Despite an opportunity to drive a hard bargain and exact substantial gains from the United States and the international community, Pakistan was unable to resist proving its nuclear equivalence.

The security rationale for Pakistan's nuclear arsenal is clear and reasonably compelling.[5] Although India usually behaves as a status quo power, on rare occasions it has considered a more aggressive policy. At those times it placed the existence of Pakistan at significant risk.

India's far greater size has always created a military imbalance with Pakistan. At independence, India received 64 percent of the force structure and equipment of the old Imperial Indian Army and a much larger proportion of military industrial infrastructure (due to the location of the ordnance plants).[6] Although the Indian army carries out important internal security duties and must also guard against a conflict along the long Sino-Indian border, Pakistan assumes that the majority of Indian forces will be arrayed against it in any conflict. India's standing army since 1963 has been roughly twice the size of Pakistan's (before mobilization), and it has always maintained a significant quantitative edge in both equipment and major combat formations.[7]

When India wields this military advantage aggressively or opportunistically, Pakistan finds itself at significant risk—either of political coercion, or of actual conquest or dismemberment. The most significant example—and one burned into the perceptions of Pakistani elites even today—was the Indo-Pakistani War of 1971, which resulted in the creation of Bangladesh from what was once East Pakistan.

India had ample reason to consider intervention during the 1971 crisis. Pakistan's brutal suppression of East Pakistan's political aspirations created a wave of refugees that spilled into eastern India and caused great economic distress. However, the response of Indira Gandhi's administration to the crisis can only be described as opportunistic, if not actually Machiavellian. India decided to fight a war with Pakistan to take advantage of its ineptitude and internal disruption. During the next eight months, India signed a Treaty of Peace and Friendship with the Soviet Union, which gave assurances of a UN Security Council veto and a nuclear umbrella as well as extensive shipments of weapons, munitions, and spare parts. India provided sanctuary, training, and support for the Mukti Bahini—a Bengali national liberation movement formed from survivors of Pakistan's ethnic cleansing of East Pakistan's security and political institutions. By late October Indian forces were providing significant assistance and support to Mukti Bahini's operations inside East Pakistan. By late November Indian forces were actually infiltrating across the border and maintaining a presence in Pakistani territory. A mixture of careful Indian planning, masterful adaptation in combat, and Pakistani tactical and strategic ineptitude led to the rapid collapse of the Pakistani resistance after Pakistan attacked Indian military installations in early December. Ninety-three thousand Pakistanis surrendered to the Indian Army by mid-December 1971.[8]

Pakistani security planning has never recovered from this humiliation. The combination of reflexive fear and envy of India's greater power and stature, this clear historical example of Indian opportunism, and an acute awareness of ethnic tensions within the remainder of Pakistan generate an almost irrational sensitivity to the Indian threat. All of Pakistan's national security planning is based around a worst-case scenario that assumes India will repeat the 1971 war, but this time in the west.[9] Although worst-case planning is prudent and sometimes essential, using it as the basis for national security policy can spur actions that are provocative, destabilizing, and enormously counterproductive.

Capabilities: What Does the Arsenal Look Like, and What Can It Do?

Creating a nuclear arsenal in response to this threat perception is *not* irrational. Pakistan spent twenty-four years collecting the necessary infrastructure and knowledge from Chinese, Western European, and possibly North Korean sources. The government established competing entities—the Pakistan Atomic Energy Commission (PAEC) and Khan Research Laboratories (KRL)—to pursue different technological paths. PAEC pursued plutonium extraction technology, which had been severely hampered by Western technology transfer restrictions imposed after India's 1974 detonation of a "peaceful nuclear explosive" (which alarmed Pakistan and accelerated the nuclear weapons program). A. Q. Khan's KRL covertly worked the Western European commercial energy markets to create a uranium enrichment program. (Khan ran a gray market network, which enabled him to obtain weapons-related data and matériel abroad and further proliferation to other nuclear aspirants.) China obligingly provided a nuclear warhead design that employed highly enriched uranium and was optimized for missile delivery. In the 1990s PAEC acquired Chinese manufacturing technology for solid fuel missiles, while KRL lurched into the missile production business by acquiring the North Korean No Dong (known as Ghauri in the Pakistani service).[10]

Western analysts assume that Pakistan achieved the capability to assemble a working nuclear device in the early to middle 1980s, perhaps as early as 1983. There are reports of Chinese testing assistance involving either a "cold test" in the mid-1980s or, as more recent reports suggest, an actual detonation in China itself. By 1987 A. Q. Khan was willing to offer an interview to an Indian reporter in which he boldly claimed that Pakistan had the bomb—to the apparent dismay of General Zia ul-Haq, who was trying to downplay Pakistan's nuclear capability in the interest of minimizing friction with the United States.[11]

It is unsurprising, however, that the news was released at that time. The interview took place just after the height of the "Brasstacks" crisis, when Indian military exercises of unusual size, intended to test and demonstrate the operational decisiveness of newly restructured Indian army forces, were staged close to the Pakistani border.[12] These exercises took place under an unusual Indian political environment in which a troika of leaders appeared determined to test the limits and utility of military coercion. The "Sundarji Doctrine," promulgated by the Indian army chief of staff, called for rapid advances to penetrate deep into Pakistani territory. There is some indication that the Indian leadership sought to exploit a window of vulnerability and thus to preemptively or preventively attack Pakistan's nuclear capability before it could be institutionalized.[13] In addition, India simultaneously committed to an enormous military buildup on the Chinese border, which suggests again that India was intent on exercising its military power to redefine relationships with both of its nuclear-armed neighbors. This unusual suggestion of revisionist instincts is the exception rather than the rule in Indian foreign policy, but it only reinforces Pakistan's worst assumptions and justifies both nuclear acquisitions and sometimes bizarre policy responses.

The size and configuration of Pakistan's current nuclear arsenal are unknown but are susceptible to rough estimates.[14] Its potential stockpile of warheads certainly numbers in the dozens and may number in the low hundreds—fewer than the British arsenal but significantly greater than North Korea's.[15] These warheads include weapons specialized for airborne delivery by the Pakistani air force fleet of F-16 and Mirage III/V combat aircraft or by ballistic missile warheads. Pakistan possesses an arsenal of missiles with various ranges, capable of reaching most targets in India.[16] Referring to them by Cold War–inspired designations (e.g., medium- or intermediate-range ballistic missiles) makes little sense in Pakistan's case. Pakistan's missile force can cover most of the critical target set—across the Indian subcontinent.

The yield of Pakistani warheads remains a matter of some debate and confusion. The results of Pakistan's 1998 tests are disputed. Islamabad claimed to have tested six devices, five on May 28, 1998, and one on May 30, 1998.[17] Seismic evidence raises questions about the number of detonations and their yields, however, and according to some reports a second device may not have detonated on May 30.[18] Testing six warheads represents a powerful political symbol—at one stroke, Pakistan tested as many devices as India's combined total from 1974 and 1998—but it also would have constituted a substantial drain on Pakistan's available fissile material stockpile at the time. At a minimum Pakistan demonstrated the ability to detonate at least two devices of approximately Hiroshima-sized yield, somewhere in the range of 4 to 12 kilotons.[19]

In addition, A. Q. Khan transferred to Libya a nuclear weapon design that had apparently been obtained from China. There is no reason to believe this device is not in Pakistan's nuclear arsenal.[20] Finally, recent reports about the Khan network note that Switzerland recently had the International Atomic Energy Agency confirm its destruction of documents relating to a more advanced nuclear design. This design was found in the investigation of the Tinner family, Swiss members of the Khan network who were "turned" by Western intelligence. Press reports state that it might have been a second-generation weapon based either on an analysis of Pakistan's 1998 tests or on a separate design from China or other sources.[21]

Assessing Pakistan's capabilities is also a tricky business, because any assessment must take into account (1) the lack of transferability of key elements of Western thought derived from the Cold War to other nuclear arsenals and regional competitions; (2) the known relationship between Western nuclear analysis and the development of policies and doctrines in both Pakistan and India; and (3) the relative absence of discussion on the Pakistani side (at least in open sources).[22] The best starting point is the one document that clearly indicates some elements of Pakistani thinking: the interview given by General Khalid Ahmed Kidwai, the director of the Strategic Plans Division (responsible for Pakistani nuclear planning), in December 2001. This interview was released as part of a report by an Italian investigative team early in January 2002, at the height of another crisis between India and Pakistan (see below).[23]

According to General Kidwai, Pakistan has sketched four nuclear "redlines," conditions under which it will consider nuclear use of an undisclosed nature. These redlines are sufficiently precise to provide warning to both the Indians and the international community but are sufficiently vague to prevent precise calculation. They represent an admirable tool in some senses for reinforcing deterrence. The redlines reflect concerns about threats to the integrity of Pakistan's territory, to the integrity of its armed forces, to its economic well-being, and to efforts to take advantage of its ethnic diversity to divide the country or spark internal unrest. These redlines establish a space threshold, a military threshold, economic strangulation, and domestic destabilization as rationales for nuclear use.[24]

Threats to territorial integrity—the "space threshold"—constitute a natural concern for any government. In the event that India seizes significant but undisclosed portions of Pakistani territory, it is not surprising that Pakistan would consider nuclear use. In this instance vagueness probably reflects the diversity of Pakistani geography and demography. Large portions of Sindh Province are virtually vacant, so the threshold for retaliation might be much higher there than in Punjab, where major cities like Lahore and Rawalpindi lie close to the border.

A similar concern about the destruction of Pakistan's armed forces—the "military threshold"—is also entirely reasonable. General Kidwai specified significant destruction of either the army or the air force, again emphasizing rational calculation. The army is the dominant service in the Pakistani military, it is the dominant institution in Pakistan, and it considers itself the guardian of the nation. For the army leadership, significant destruction of the army would put the nation at risk, not only by making it more vulnerable to India's much larger ground forces (roughly twice the size of Pakistan's before reserves are mobilized) but also by depriving the nation of the one institution that would allow it to survive and recover. The air force not only defends the Pakistani population from air attack but also constitutes a crucial element in Pakistan's nuclear force. Significant attrition of the air force might put the Indians in a situation of "escalation dominance," so Pakistan may well have a low threshold in mind.

General Kidwai's construction of the redlines appears at first glance to give the Indians a "pass" if they destroy the Pakistani navy, the smallest and least institutionally important of Pakistan's armed forces. However, it appears that the navy may be covered by the third redline, or "economic strangling," which has been interpreted primarily in two ways. First, an extended blockade of the Pakistani coast would cut off sea lines of communication and Pakistani trade. Second, interference with the Indus River or termination of the Indus Waters Treaty is a threat that has been raised from time to time by more hawkish Indian analysts and politicians. The former interpretation suggests that attacks on the Pakistani navy, which protects those sea lanes, may also be bounded by a nuclear redline in some way.

Finally, threats to exploit Pakistan's ethnic minorities and divisions—"domestic destabilization"—reflect several concerns. The first is the reported Indian support for MQM, a Sindh separatist movement that raised significant concern for Pakistan in the 1990s and continues to exist in Karachi and other southern areas.[25] The second is Pakistan's border with Afghanistan and the Pashtun population that overlaps that border. Afghanistan still does not recognize the Durand Line, and Pashtun nationalism has often sought either to create an independent state or to unify the Pashtun population under Afghan rule, at Pakistan's expense.[26] Finally, a Baluch minority (overlapping both the Afghan and the Iranian borders) has often sought autonomy or independence through political action or insurgent activity.[27] Pakistan currently claims that Indian intelligence is stirring up problems with both the Baluch and Pashtun populations from its new consulates in Afghanistan. This claim is certainly exaggerated and is profoundly ironic and hypocritical given Pakistan's much greater use of this tactic against both India and Afghanistan.

The direct relationship between the redlines and Pakistan's fears of a repeat of its 1971 defeat warrants some comment. To some degree each of these redlines reflects Pakistan's experience in that conflict. The army and air force were overwhelmed in the East, whereas the Pakistani air force basically withdrew from fighting in the West, which would have created conditions of great vulnerability for Pakistan's ground forces if the war had continued in the west. Indian attacks on Pakistani shipping and denial of sea lanes (particularly in the east) made the liberation of Bangladesh a virtual fait accompli. Finally, Pakistan was cut in half by Indian military activity aimed at exploiting ethnic divisions, even if these were caused by Pakistani misgovernment and atrocities.

Thinking the Unthinkable No. 1: Nuclear Use in Conflict or Crisis

The question of how Pakistan might respond with nuclear weapons inspires conjecture rather than certainty. Again, Western analysis can be misleading here, particularly assumptions about "tactical nuclear weapons." In the NATO/Warsaw Pact confrontation, "tactical" was determined primarily by either yield (tactical weapons tended to have yields in the low kiloton range), by range (tactical delivery systems had ranges in the dozens or low hundreds of kilometers), or by delivery system (which included both artillery shells and static demolition devices).[28]

In South Asia, all warhead yields fall into the "tactical category." Although India claims to have tested a thermonuclear device (which remains a matter of dispute), the yield it claims is only 43 kilotons (which, again, is disputed).[29] Most weapons also have some kind of "strategic" utility. Due to the short ranges in theater, they can be targeted at command-and-control facilities, airfields, ground forces, or countervalue targets, which include cities, industrial complexes, and nuclear plants. In addition, the limited numbers of warheads available to each side make traditional considerations of counterforce strikes more problematic, particularly because both

India and Pakistan maintain their arsenals at very low alert levels under which any movement of materials or launchers constitutes a significant warning sign.

Furthermore, both India and Pakistan have demonstrated strong resistance to thinking or planning about actually using nuclear weapons. They have read and learned from Western literature but have been very slow to develop an analytical or institutional base for considering nuclear weapons as anything other than a kind of existential deterrent. Pakistan, for example, did not set up anything like a nuclear command-and-control network until after the 1998 tests, even though it had theoretically possessed nuclear weapons capability for as long as fifteen years.[30] Similarly, India's military was not involved in nuclear decision making for decades after independence.[31]

In considering nuclear Pakistan's options, therefore, it seems likely that these options will probably be rather simple. Nuclear weapons will be used either on the battlefield or against targets in India like cities or military installations. Precise calculations about how many weapons are required for certain kinds of options will be the exception rather than the rule. Concepts like redundancy (multiple weapons per target) or the number of nuclear strikes required to eliminate Indian field formations will be acquired through reading of outside sources rather than careful planning, gaming, or exercises. Until recently, with its small nuclear arsenal, Pakistan may well have considered a "use it or lose it" posture. As the arsenal expands, the possibility of warning shots or restrained initial use becomes more plausible.[32]

If a redline is crossed, Pakistan may use a nuclear device, and the longer the conflict persists, the greater the pressure for nuclear use. The nature of the breach will determine the response. For example, a "bolt out of the blue" strike that devastates the Pakistani air force would spark far greater alarm than a gradually escalating campaign. It seems unlikely that Pakistan would use large numbers of weapons in an initial response during most contingencies. A primary objective might be gaining international attention rather than inflicting destruction, on the assumption that international intervention might end the conflict short of nuclear catastrophe. From a military perspective the Pakistani armed forces might want to reserve substantial nuclear assets to deter India from some aggressive nuclear or conventional response. India has tried to hedge against this option by stating that an attack against Indian troops with nuclear weapons anywhere in the world will be interpreted as an attack against India proper.[33] It seems questionable, however, that India would actually launch a massive retaliatory strike against Pakistan if Pakistan detonated a nuclear device against Indian attackers on Pakistani soil. (The deserts of Rajasthan and Sindh would be an excellent place for battlefield nuclear use, due to low population density.)

This suggests that in the event of a South Asian war, a likely scenario in the event of Indian tactical successes on the conventional battlefield would be a Pakistani warning shot that might or might not target Indian forces, some modest Indian retaliation against Pakistani forces if necessary, and reliance by both sides on early diplomatic intervention by the international community to prevent further escalation.[34] If Pakistan's conventional forces are strong enough, short or limited wars can be maintained below the nuclear threshold. This belief has become enshrined in the thinking and doctrine of both the Indian and Pakistani armies. At least theoretically, in short, the existence of nuclear arsenals should contribute to predictability and therefore stability in the region. This constitutes a reasonable synopsis of the "nuclear optimist" argument on the consequences of proliferation.[35]

However, this may be an artificially stable scenario to begin with, which presupposes a highly controlled environment and an absence of friction. In fact, in the past, Indo-Pakistani crises have progressed in unusual and uncontrolled ways, with obvious assumptions being proven fundamentally flawed. For example, despite the presence of a hotline for direct communication in times of crisis, in 1990 the directors-general of military operations on each side declined to contact each other.[36] In the years 2001–2, terrorists belonging to groups affiliated with Pakistani intelligence attacked the Indian Parliament, leading to a ten-month confrontation, which suggested that (1) Pakistan no longer controlled its former proxies, (2) the regime no longer fully controlled its intelligence services, or (3) Pakistan had attempted to decapitate India's government.[37]

In the absence of perfect predictability, therefore, it is worth examining two other scenarios. The first is based on an Indian army doctrine called "Cold Start," which was instituted after the 2001–2 Operation Parakram crisis. The second is based on an alternative option that employs air instead of land power. Each represents a notional Indian military response to another terrorist event. And each also represents a reasonable scenario, given evidence that India considered and Pakistan may have expected a military response to the November 2008 terrorist attack on Mumbai.[38]

After the December 13, 2001, terrorist attack on India's Parliament, the Indian army undertook an unprecedented mobilization and forward deployment across the entire Indo-Pakistani border and the line of control in Kashmir. During the course of the mobilization, Indian commanders found that their short-term options for a military response were severely constrained. The bulk of the Indian army's combat power is deployed in three "strike corps," each of which is based around an armored division with substantial supporting elements. These units are positioned relatively far from the Indo-Pakistani border, and it took up to three weeks for them to assemble in their forward positions. The rest of the Indian army is organized in infantry and mountain corps ("holding corps") whose primary role is defensive and which are poorly equipped and postured for significant offensive operations.

As a result, the Indian army developed what it calls the Cold Start Doctrine to restructure the army for rapid, decisive operations within ninety-six hours of an incident or of political authorization for offensive or retaliatory action. The holding corps will be restructured and will receive new equipment that allows them to initiate near-immediate conventional assaults with the intent, according to some reports, of launching simultaneous penetrations of up to 100 kilometers into Pakistani territory on six to eight separate axes. If prosecuted effectively, Cold Start would not only threaten the territorial integrity of Pakistan but also threaten to collapse Pakistan's army by severing lines of communication and logistics while interfering with reserve mobilization patterns.[39]

The Indian army is years away from achieving its ambitious goals, which would require dramatic (and visible) increases in army capital expenditures and, more important, in officer training, forward infrastructure, and logistics capacity.[40] The fact that the Indian army has committed itself to studying the Cold Start Doctrine, however, means that Pakistan must take it seriously. It also raises the possibility that the Indian army may begin planning for deep penetration operations on short notice long before it acquires the necessary capabilities. If so, commanders will be able to offer this option to policymakers during a crisis even if the force structure is not in place.

How might Pakistan respond to what looks like a Cold Start attack, featuring multiple assaults on separate axes from one or more holding corps in response to a crisis?[41] Assuming even modest initial indications of success, Islamabad could easily interpret such a campaign as a violation of one or both of the first two redlines. Penetrations of tens of kilometers across the international border could threaten Lahore, Islamabad, or other metropolitan centers close to the border. Similar penetrations in the southern deserts could threaten communications with Karachi. Any of these might be viewed as crossing a territorial threshold, and if all occurred simultaneously, escalation might occur very rapidly. If simultaneous advances on multiple axes have the same operational effects as some analysts suggest (some compare Cold Start to the impact of the German advance into France in 1940), the integrity of the Pakistani army might be put at risk.[42] In this case, even if the Pakistani army did not lose significant numbers of troops, it might lose enough effectiveness to lead to escalation.[43] Cold Start—or Indian military actions that look like Cold Start—therefore constitutes a major incentive for Pakistan to consider moving up the escalation ladder.

A second form of Indian response might not involve ground forces at all in the initial stages but still could force Pakistan to leap up the escalation ladder. This would leverage Indian advantages in air power and precision strikes for punitive attacks on the Pakistani intelligence services and military leadership for supporting terrorist activities. Indian analysts rightly decry the option of bombing "terrorist camps," which are semipermanent and often colocated with Pakistani military facilities, as unproductive and trivial. In some circumstances, however, India might consider a more sophisticated attack on, for example, the headquarters of the Inter-Service Intelligence Directorate or on Pakistani command facilities to demonstrate that military leadership may no longer be able to avoid some form of meaningful retribution for the actions of its militant proxies.[44]

This scenario might be carried out by existing Indian air force assets. The air force boasts roughly twice the number of combat aircraft available to Pakistan, along with a growing spectrum of force multipliers ranging from precision-guided weapons to in-flight refueling and advanced airborne-early-warning aircraft.[45] Depending on the makeup of the strike package, the air force could try to sneak a small number of aircraft under Pakistani air defenses and warning for a limited strike, use standoff weapons against one or more targets near the border and line of control, or launch a larger mission aimed at multiple targets. The latter might require suppression of Pakistani air defenses and communications networks.

Any of these types of attacks, however, could be profoundly unsettling to Pakistan, which would generate a crisis atmosphere. Distances on the Indian subcontinent are very short, meaning that warning time is very limited. Pakistani defenders would have perhaps five minutes to react to missile launches, for example. First reports of Indian penetration of airspace or of actual attacks will lead Pakistan to scramble air defense assets, mobilize ground forces, and seriously consider the vulnerability of its nuclear and command-and-control facilities. Attacks may threaten nuclear command-and-control nodes, whether intentionally or inadvertently. Suppression of air defenses will threaten Pakistani air bases where delivery systems—aircraft and mobile missiles—are based, stored, or will be dispersed in crisis. Because Pakistan's weapons are reportedly stored in unassembled or quasi-assembled form, the Pakistani authorities may feel a need to move them immediately during the initial confusion of even a limited air strike. This would mark a significant step up the escalation ladder.[46] Alternatively, Pakistan may choose to move nuclear assets to higher levels of readiness in peacetime, which would remove a major obstacle to early nuclear use.

Thinking the Unthinkable No. 2: Managing Risk at Home

Unfortunately, history all too often demonstrates that even the most elegant theoretical assumptions can be challenged by the relentless pressures of human interaction and unpredictability. This final section looks at a series of elements that could challenge the stability of Pakistan's nuclear deterrent based on past experience, contemporary uncertainties, and future trends.

Deterrence and Stability

A stable nuclear environment demands some element of predictability and trust between nuclear antagonists. Such a relationship does not exist between India and Pakistan. As mentioned above, Pakistan is inherently distrustful of Indian intentions. This has not only prompted an almost paranoid focus on worst-case estimates but has also led Islamabad to adopt exceedingly dangerous policies intended to tie up Indian attention and resources. The use of militant forces to destabilize India, for instance, has become almost a permanent factor in the relationship.[47] In addition to sowing resentment and distrust on the Indian side—particularly after repeatedly promising to control infiltration into Kashmir, a promise that can be easily kept through policing Pakistan's five-mile exclusion zone near the Line of Control—this policy has created two extraordinarily dangerous regional crises.

On December 13, 2001, militants from two groups linked with Pakistan attempted to stage a suicide attack on the Indian Parliament. The last attacker was stopped only feet from the entrance. This incident gave rise to a ten-month standoff between India and Pakistan involving unprecedented levels of military mobilization. The crisis nearly escalated to conventional conflict in January 2002 and again in June 2002. More recently, the late November 2008 terrorist attack on Mumbai was launched by one of the two groups implicated in the 2001 crisis. In each case the Pakistani government initially denied any responsibility. In the case of the Mumbai assault it took months for Islamabad to actually admit that Pakistani citizens had taken part, even though Indian security forces took one attacker captive. An environment in which one side cannot control or account for the actions of its proxies creates an enormous risk of escalation. As long as Pakistan relies on the use of militant proxy forces as a key element of its foreign policy, this risk will remain high.

The Security of Nuclear Components

The physical security of nuclear components is absolutely critical for nuclear stability, particularly given Pakistan's appalling record of nuclear proliferation.[48] Since 2000 the Strategic Plans Division has gone to great lengths to provide for the physical security of the nuclear arsenal, for example, by training an establishment of more than eight thousand soldiers to provide for the security of nuclear installations.[49] According to press reports, Pakistani devices are stored in an unassembled or semi-assembled state and are not mated to delivery vehicles. This approach dramatically decreases the possibility of accidental detonation or launch.[50] Significant risks nonetheless persist.

Although the Strategic Plans Division has instituted a personnel reliability program, there is still considerable concern about the political allegiance of lower-level and midlevel officers in the Pakistani military.[51] Recruitment patterns for the officer corps have fundamentally changed. Both officers and enlisted personnel now come from much more conservative regions of the country, and the military as a whole is much more observant and conservative than it was in the past.[52] Zia ul-Haq's deliberate decision to increase Islamist influences within the officer corps has created a very different army in which Islam may compete with professionalism.[53] A 1995 coup attempt by a general and the participation of both army and Pakistani air force enlisted men and officers in assassination attempts against President Pervez Musharraf all suggest that personnel reliability should remain a concern.

Abundant reporting on the A. Q. Khan network clearly indicates that components have been removed from KRL and transshipped to foreign countries. This could not have occurred without some level of military complicity. Presumably this issue has been addressed in terms of both physical security and national policy, but the international community cannot reasonably accept Pakistani assurances on this issue without continued evidence of scrupulously correct adherence to nonproliferation norms and behavior. Greater transparency about Khan's transgressions is desirable but almost certainly will not be forthcoming. How secure Pakistani nuclear components are and how trustworthy Pakistani nuclear guardians are therefore remain topics of conjecture rather than certainty.

Even if physical security in normal peacetime circumstances is assured by recent reforms, in times of crisis Pakistan's nuclear materials will be at risk. At some point in a crisis, Pakistan may need to move its nuclear components, to fully assemble weapons, to mate them with delivery systems, or to reposition fully weaponized delivery systems to assure their safety and survivability. Reliance on road-mobile ballistic missiles for deterrence ensures that nuclear assets will be widely scattered and well away from safe storage areas at higher levels of alert.

It is unclear whether Pakistan installs safety devices like permissive action links (PALs) on its nuclear weapons once they are assembled. PALs provide enormous added confidence that weapons cannot be used without specific orders. This precaution significantly mitigates the risk of accidental detonation. Pakistan may be reluctant to accept this technology from the United States, however, and its transfer to a non–nuclear weapon state may be a violation of the Nuclear Non-Proliferation Treaty. Regardless, this shortcoming does create additional concerns about the safety and security of assembled Pakistani weapons.[54]

Any time these components are moved, the physical security risk expands enormously. Physically shifting components and delivery vehicles dramatically increases the opportunity for intelligence leaks. Components on the move are much more difficult to secure than components in bunkers and other locations, with limited access and established security protocols and operations procedures. It is during movement that materials (or, indeed, assembled devices) become most vulnerable to fall into the hands of any of the dozens of extremist groups that dot the Pakistani countryside and might find great value in possession of a nuclear device, either for use or for sale.[55]

Command and Control of Weapons during a Crisis

Some reliability and assurance over the command and control of weapons during a crisis is also a useful contribution to stability. Under Pervez Musharraf, Pakistan set up an institutional basis for this command and control. Committees chaired by the president and prime minister and that included both civilian and military representatives considered issues related to procurement, research and development, doctrine, and (if necessary) nuclear release.[56]

As Musharraf's administration evolved, however, the actual determination about who would make decisions became clouded. Musharraf permitted the election of a prime minister, resigned as chief of staff of the army, and eventually became a civilian president. More recently, since the election of a new civilian government headed by Prime Minister Yousuf Raza Gilani and President Asif Ali Zardari, the lines of authority have become even more ambiguous. Is the president or the prime minister in theoretical charge? Will the military permit civilians to make decisions of great magnitude, particularly given soldiers' past efforts to remove civilians from any role in the nuclear decision-making process? The head of the Strategic Plans Division throughout the Musharraf regime was General Kidwai, who is now retired. What role does Kidwai play in the new National Command Authority, if any? Are the command-and-control institutions considered permanent, or are they ad hoc?

This distinction becomes increasingly problematic as we see signs of civil/military friction in the new government. In 2008, the political leadership announced that it would put the military's Inter-Service Intelligence Directorate—a highly controversial organization with close links to Islamist militant groups—under the civilian-dominated Home Ministry.[57] But within twenty-four hours, the government had to rescind this decision under military pressure. Similarly, shortly after the Mumbai attack, the government announced that the new head of Inter-Service Intelligence would go to New Delhi and cooperate fully with the Indian government. But within twenty-four hours, this decision was also rescinded. Under military pressure, the government announced that it could not be seen as sending the Inter-Service Intelligence director "under Indian pressure."[58]

However, a third government decision appears to have passed through a potential military veto, and thus it may actually be an indicator of stability. Just before the Mumbai crisis, President Zardari announced that Pakistan would never attack India first with nuclear weapons.[59] This was a direct revocation of Pakistani nuclear doctrine, which is premised on leaving the option of first use open. Zardari did not retract his comment, which indicated that as president he may now wield the authority to change Pakistani nuclear doctrine. It may suggest, at a minimum, greater willingness on the military's part to allow civilians into debates about the nuclear arsenal. If so, this is a positive indicator. It nevertheless remains unclear whether in practice the military or the civilian leadership holds the ultimate say in critical decisions about doctrine and forces, or in fact how much influence civilian politicians have in any element of nuclear policy.

"Inside the Box": The Rise of Domestic Threats to Pakistan

Finally, the most significant risk for nuclear stability in the region lies in the rising internal threat to Pakistan that is emerging in the Federally Administered Tribal Areas (FATA) and the Khyber Pakhtunkhwa (formerly known as the North West Frontier Province).[60] Here, it appears that Pakistan's thirty-year romance with jihadi groups, and its reliance on them as an asset in and sometime substitute for foreign policy, may have engendered a very dangerous case of blowback.[61] Pakistan furnished tacit support and sanctuary for large numbers of Taliban and al-Qaeda survivors after Operation Enduring Freedom removed the former regime from power in Afghanistan.[62] The May 2, 2011, raid that killed Osama bin Laden in Abbottabad—the location of Pakistan's military academy—indicates how successfully key al-Qaeda figures were able to hide in Pakistan. And in the Pakistan border region and Afghanistan, Taliban forces have rebuilt themselves with substantial Pakistani help, official or unofficial.[63] They have restructured themselves in a series of loose alliances bound by mutual oaths of allegiance and are combating the United States–led international coalition and the Hamid Karzai government.

Many of these forces, however, are no longer strictly under the control of Pakistani intelligence. On at least two occasions—after the siege of the Lal Masjid (Red Mosque) in the summer of 2007, and after Pakistani Army attacks in the FATA in 2008—elements of the so-called Tehrik-i-Taliban Pakistan (TTP; Pakistan Taliban) and other nonaligned extremists have launched waves of terrorist attacks within

Pakistan. An Islamist militant group, Tehreek-e-Nafaz-e-Shariat-e-Mohammadi (TSNM), affiliated with TTP, seized control of the district of Swat. TSNM's action was effectively granted legitimacy through a series of military cease-fires. Large areas of FATA remain beyond government control, and Islamist violence has spread to other areas of the Khyber Pakhtunkhwa.[64] A series of Pakistani army offensives in Swat and Dir, along with ongoing operations in areas of the FATA over the past year, reasserted government control over some contested areas. The TTP and its allies nevertheless continue to prosecute terrorist attacks both in the northwest and in Punjab and have recently carried out a highly publicized attack on the Pakistani naval air station at Mehran, near Karachi.[65]

It is not clear whether this "militancy" (which some might call an insurgency) seriously threatens Islamabad's rule, but at a bare minimum it calls into question Islamabad's control of substantial portions of its Afghan border region and indeed of the provinces of Baluchistan and the Khyber Pakhtunkhwa. Combined with doubts about the professionalism and allegiance of the midlevel officer corps and perhaps the enlisted ranks, this militancy could threaten the central government. At the very least, it poses additional risks to the physical security of nuclear installations and components, particularly (as noted above) when they are moved about during a crisis.

The Dangers of Nuclear Mobilization

The areas where the Taliban and other militants enjoy their heaviest concentrations and influence are the very regions that provide Pakistan with the strategic depth to deploy mobile nuclear missiles while keeping them relatively safe from an Indian attack. Warheads mated to missiles in regions swarming with militants do not constitute an intrinsically stable deterrent. Indeed, they may well constitute a grave danger of nuclear leakage to militant forces.

The command-and-control problem Pakistan faces results not from a single glaring weakness but from a combination of factors. The country's foreign policy revolves around its troubled relationship with much larger India. To offset its size and material weakness, Pakistan has waged an aggressive, opportunistic campaign of support for separatists in India. This support includes arming and training sophisticated terrorists, who then operate under loose control from Pakistan's intelligence services. Their actions have provoked crises on three occasions that nearly touched off regional wars. The reliability and motives of the Pakistani intelligence services that play a critical role in national security thus remain suspect.

The militant groups themselves are suspected of participation in attacks on Pakistani institutions, and many have now been banned repeatedly. Some have links to al-Qaeda, which desires nuclear weapons. And the areas where Pakistan will hide and deploy its nuclear forces in the event of a crisis exhibit a strong presence of militant groups, which may work at cross-purposes with the national government—and certainly with the US national interest. Pakistan's nuclear doctrine and the range of potential threats to its nuclear forces once they are mobilized make every crisis a potential catastrophe. And Pakistan's irredentist and aggressive foreign policy makes regular crises with India almost a foregone conclusion.

Conclusion

Pakistan has made great strides in its nuclear institutions, planning, and doctrine since the 1998 nuclear tests. Primarily because most of these elements have remained firmly under the control of the military—the strongest institution in Pakistan—during an era of military dominance in the political sphere, Pakistan has made great strides toward assuring its neighbors and the international community that its nuclear arsenal is safe and secure. Yet the risks of instability or loss of control remain high—higher than in most nuclear states. This is because of Pakistan's unique combination of irresponsible activity in terms of both proliferation and regional policy, which lowers trust in its actions and even its competence, and its increasingly unstable domestic environment. Ironically, the military bears enormous responsibility for these destabilizing elements even as it claims credit for stabilizing peacetime nuclear control.

As a result, Pakistan remains one of the most dubious members of the nuclear community. Islamabad can upgrade its status only through a long period of impeccable behavior. Given the high degree of volatility and stress confronting Pakistan, both internally and regionally, the nation will remain an example of nuclear instability and a cause for concern both for its neighbors and for the international community. The result is that the international community will continue to have to engage Pakistan in an effort to influence its nuclear behavior, even as the community's leverage shrinks and Pakistan's nuclear arsenal continues to expand.

Notes

1. George Perkovich discusses Pakistan's claims of six nuclear tests—matching the combined total from India's tests in 1974 and 1998. See George Perkovich, *India's Nuclear Bomb: The Impact on Global Proliferation* (Berkeley: University of California Press, 1999), 433–35.

2. The Chinese connection has recently been highlighted by reports that China transferred 50 kilograms of highly enriched uranium to Pakistan in 1982. R. Jeffrey Smith and Joby Warrick, "A Nuclear Power's Act of Proliferation," *Washington Post*, November 13, 2009. A cautionary note on this report is sounded by David Albright, Paul Brannan, and Andrea Scheel Stricker, "Self-Serving Leaks from the A. Q. Khan Circle," Institute for Science and International Security, December 9, 2009, available at www.isis-online.org.

3. The idea that nuclear weapons are pursued for both normative and security reasons is explored by Scott D. Sagan, "Why Do States Build Nuclear Weapons? Three Models in Search of a Bomb," *International Security* 21, no. 3 (Winter 1996–97): 54–86. The evolution of Pakistan's nuclear capability and doctrine is traced by Zafar Iqbal Cheema, "Pakistan's Nuclear Use Doctrine and Command-and-Control," in *Planning*

the Unthinkable: How New Powers Will Use Nuclear, Biological, and Chemical Weapons, edited by Peter R. Lavoy, Scott D. Sagan, and James J. Wirtz (Ithaca, NY: Cornell University Press, 2000), 158–81; Hasan-Askari Rizvi, "Pakistan's Nuclear Testing," in *South Asia's Nuclear Security Dilemma: India, Pakistan, and China*, edited by Lowell Dittmer (Armonk, NY: M. E. Sharpe, 2005), 97–109; and Timothy D. Hoyt, "Strategic Myopia: Pakistan's Nuclear Doctrine and Crisis Stability in South Asia," in *South Asia's Nuclear Security Dilemma*, ed. Dittmer, 110–36.

4. For an overview of Pakistan's self-perception, see Stephen P. Cohen, *The Idea of Pakistan* (Washington, DC: Brookings Institution Press, 2004). On the emergence of Pakistan's national security policy, which drives its nuclear efforts, see Prevaiz Iqbal Cheema, *The Armed Forces of Pakistan* (New York: New York University Press, 2002); M. Asghar Khan, *We've Learnt Nothing from History* (Oxford: Oxford University Press, 2005); and Stephen P. Cohen, *The Pakistan Army* (Oxford: Oxford University Press, 1998).

5. Feroz Hassan Khan and Peter R. Lavoy, "Pakistan: The Dilemma of Nuclear Deterrence," in *The Long Shadow: Nuclear Weapons and Security in 21st Century Asia*, edited by Muthiah Alagappa (Stanford, CA: Stanford University Press, 2008), 215–40.

6. Lorne J. Kavic, *India's Quest for Security: Defense Policies, 1947–1965* (Berkeley: University of California Press, 1967), 82, 126–27; Cohen, *Pakistan Army*, 4–8.

7. Rodney Jones did a good study of the military imbalance in the subcontinent; see Rodney W. Jones, *Conventional Military Imbalance and Strategic Stability in South Asia*, Research Paper 1, South Asian Strategic Stability Unit, March 2005, www.policyarchitects.org/pdf/Conventional_imbalance_RJones.pdf.

8. Studies of the 1971 conflict include those by Robert Jackson, *South Asian Crisis: India, Pakistan, Bangladesh* (London: Chatto & Windus and International Institute for Strategic Studies, 1975); D. K. Palit, *The Lightning Campaign: Indo-Pakistani War 1971* (New Delhi: Thomson Press–India), 1972); and Richard Sisson and Leo E. Rose, *War and Secession: Pakistan, India, and the Creation of Bangladesh* (Berkeley: University of California Press, 1990).

9. Pakistan's "nuclear redlines," discussed below, can be interpreted as specifically aimed at denying a repeat of India's 1971 efforts.

10. The evolution of Pakistan's nuclear infrastructure is discussed by Adrian Levy and Catherine Scott-Clark, *Deception: Pakistan, the United States, and the Secret Trade in Nuclear Weapons* (New York: Walker, 2007); Gordon Corera, *Shopping for Bombs* (Oxford: Oxford University Press, 2006); William Langewiesche, *The Atomic Bazaar: The Rise of the Nuclear Poor* (New York: Farrar, Straus & Giroux, 2007); Douglas Frantz and Catherine Collins, *The Nuclear Jihadist* (New York: Twelve Press, 2007); and Bhumitra Chakma, *Pakistan's Nuclear Weapons* (London: Routledge, 2009).

11. This bizarre incident is describe in detail by Devin T. Hagerty, *The Consequences of Nuclear Proliferation: Lessons from South Asia* (Cambridge, MA: MIT Press, 1998), 102–5.

12. Sumit Ganguly and Devin T. Hagerty, *Fearful Symmetry: India-Pakistan Crises in the Shadow of Nuclear Weapons* (Oxford: Oxford University Press, 2005), 68–81.

13. Kanti Bajpai, *Brasstacks and Beyond: Perception and Management of Crisis in South Asia* (Urbana-Champaign: Program in Arms Control, Disarmament, and International Security, University of Illinois, 1995).

14. See, e.g., Chakma, *Pakistan's Nuclear Weapons*, 58–80; and Peter R. Lavoy, "Islamabad's Nuclear Posture: Its Premises and Implementation," in *Pakistan's Nuclear Future: Worries beyond War*, edited by Henry D. Sokolski (Carlisle, PA: Strategic Studies Institute, US Army War College, 2008), 129–65.

15. Chakma, *Pakistan's Nuclear Weapons*, 59, cites estimates ranging from 30 to 130 weapons; Lavoy, "Islamabad's Nuclear Posture," 141, provides a range of 70–115. More recently, see Karen DeYoung, "Pakistan Doubles Its Nuclear Arsenal," *Washington Post*, January 31, 2011, www.washingtonpost.com/wp-dyn/content/article/2011/01/30/AR 2011013004682.html.

16. Lavoy, "Islamabad's Nuclear Posture," 142.

17. Carey Sublette, "Pakistan's Nuclear Weapons Program: 1998—The Year of Testing," Nuclear Weapons Archive, http://nuclearweaponarchive.org/Pakistan/PakTests .html.

18. "Pakistan Nuclear Weapons," Federation of American Scientists, www.fas .org/nuke/guide/pakistan/nuke/.

19. Sublette, "Pakistan's Nuclear Weapons Program."

20. Mohan Malik, "Nuclear Proliferation and A. Q. Khan's China Connection," *Epoch Times*, May 23, 2004, www.theepochtimes.com/news/4–5-23/21583.html.

21. Peter Crail, "Swiss Destroy Key A. Q. Khan Evidence," *Arms Control Today*, July–August 2008, www.armscontrol.org/act/2008_07–08/Swiss; Peter Grier, "Did Rogue Network Leak Nuclear Bomb Design?" *Christian Science Monitor*, June 18, 2008, www.csmonitor.com/USA/Foreign-Policy/2008/0618/p02s01-usfp.html.

22. See, e.g., S. Paul Kapur, "India and Pakistan's Unstable Peace: Why Nuclear South Asia Is Not Like Cold War Europe," *International Security* 30, no. 2 (Fall 2005): 127–52.

23. Quoted by Centro di Cultura Scientifica Alessandro Volta, *Nuclear Safety, Nuclear Stability and Nuclear Strategy in Pakistan: A Concise Report of a Visit by Landau Network—Centro Volta* (Como: Centro di Cultura Scientifica Alessandro Volta, 2002), www.centrovolta.it/landau/content/binary/pakistan%20Januray%202002.pdf.

24. Ibid., section 5.

25. C. Christine Fair, *Urban Battle Fields of South Asia* (Santa Monica, CA: RAND Corporation, 2004), 113–17.

26. Daniel Markey, *Securing Pakistan's Tribal Belt*, Council Special Report 36 (New York: Council on Foreign Relations, 2008).

27. Frederic Grare, *Pakistan: The Resurgence of Baloch Nationalism* (Washington, DC: Carnegie Endowment for International Peace, 2006).

28. Timothy D. Hoyt, "The Buddha Frowns? Tactical Nuclear Weapons in South Asia," in *Tactical Nuclear Weapons: Emergent Threats in an Evolving Security Environment*, edited by Brian Alexander and Alistair Millar (Washington, DC: Brassey's, 2003), 95–109.

29. For a synopsis of key points in the debate, see Shiv Sastry, "Sizzle or Fizzle: The Indian Nuclear Test Soap Opera," *Security Research Review* 4, no. 1 (October 2009), www.adl.gatech.edu/research/brmsrr/2009/SRRP04010901.pdf.

30. Lavoy states that "a thoroughly considered and planned nuclear deterrence strategy took shape only after the country conducted its first nuclear explosive tests in May 1998"; Lavoy, "Pakistan's Nuclear Posture," 129–30. See also Cheema, "Pakistan's Nuclear Use Doctrine," 159.

31. Perkovich, *India's Nuclear Bomb*.

32. I am indebted to Chris Cleary for pointing this out. A 2009 assessment of Pakistan's nuclear arsenal puts the potential number of warheads in the range of 70 to 90. See International Panel of Fissile Materials, *Global Fissile Material Report 2009: A Path to Nuclear Disarmament* (Princeton, NJ: International Panel of Fissile Materials, 2009), www.fissilematerials.org/ipfm/site_down/gfmr09.pdf. See also Neil Joeck, "The Indo-Pakistani Nuclear Confrontation: Lessons from the Past, Contingencies in the Future," in *Pakistan's Nuclear Future: Reining in the Risk*, edited by Henry Sokolski (Carlisle, PA: Strategic Studies Institute, US Army War College, 2009), 19–61.

33. "India Nuclear Update, 2003," *Risk Report 9*, no. 5 (September–October 2003), www.wisconsinproject.org/countries/india/nuke2003.htm; Ali Ahmed, *Reviewing India's Nuclear Doctrine*, IDSA Policy Brief (New Delhi: Institute for Defence Studies and Analyses, 2009), www.idsa.in/policybrief/reviewingindiasnucleardoctrine_aahmed_240409.

34. This possibility is discussed by Vipin Narang, "Posturing for Peace? Pakistan's Nuclear Postures and South Asian Stability," *International Security* 34, no. 3 (Winter 2009–10): 59–60.

35. The case that nuclear weapons will create peace in South Asia and elsewhere is made most forcefully in a book by Kenneth Waltz; in the same volume, Scott Sagan counters that nuclear war is more likely. See Scott D. Sagan and Kenneth N. Waltz, *The Spread of Nuclear Weapons: A Debate Renewed*, 2nd ed. (New York: W. W. Norton, 2002).

36. Michael Krepon and Mishi Faruqee, eds., *Conflict Prevention and Confidence-Building Measures in South Asia: The 1990 Crisis*, Occasional Paper 17 (Washington, DC: Henry L. Stimson Center, 1994), vi.

37. For more on the 2001–2 crisis, see Polly Nayak and Michael Krepon, "US Crisis Management in South Asia's Twin Peaks Crisis" (Washington, DC: Henry L. Stimson Center, 2006); and Sumit Ganguly and Michael R. Kraig, "The 2001–2002 Indo-Pakistani Crisis: Exposing the Limits of Coercive Diplomacy," *Security Studies* 14, no. 2 (April–June 2005): 290–324.

38. Rajesh Basrur, Timothy Hoyt, Rifaat Hussain, and Suyojini Mandal, *The Mumbai Terrorist Attacks: Strategic Fallout*, RSIS Monograph 17 (Singapore: S. Rajaratnam School of International Studies, 2009). See also Angel Rabasa, Robert D. Blackwill, Peter Chalk, Kim Cragin, C. Christine Fair, Brian A. Jackson, Brian Michael Jenkins, Seth G. Jones, Nathaniel Shestak, and Ashley J. Tellis, *The Lessons of Mumbai* (Santa Monica, CA: RAND Corporation, 2009), www.rand.org/pubs/occasional_papers/2009/RAND_OP249.pdf.

39. The most comprehensive discussion of Cold Start is given by Walter C. Ladwig III, "A Cold Start for Hot Wars? The Indian Army's New Limited War Doctrine," *International Security* 32, no. 3 (January 2008): 158–90. Other sources include A. Vinod Kumar, "A Cold Start: India's Response to Pakistan-Aided Low-Intensity Conflict," *Strategic Analysis* 33, no. 3 (2009); Gurmeet Kanwal, *Indian Army Vision 2020* (New Delhi: HarperCollins, 2008); and Subhash Kapila, *India's New "Cold Start" War Doctrine Strategically Reviewed*, South Asia Analysis Group Paper 991 (Delhi: South Asia Analysis Group, 2004), www.southasiaanalysis.org/%5Cpapers10%5Cpaper991.html.

40. This argument was explored in detail by Timothy D. Hoyt, "Cold Start in Context: Wrong Doctrine, Wrong Time," paper presented at conference on "Cold Start: India's New Strategic Doctrine and Its Implications," Naval Postgraduate School, Monterey, CA, May 29–30, 2008.

41. Pakistani assessments of the threat of Cold Start tend to be rather optimistic. See Brigadier General (retired) Shaukat Qadir, "OP-ED: India's "Cold Start" Strategy," *Daily Times*, May 8, 2004, www.dailytimes.com.pk/default.asp?page = story_8-5-2004_ pg3_3; and Shaukat Qadir, "OP-ED: Cold Start—The Nuclear Side," *Daily Times*, May 16, 2004, www.dailytimes.com.pk/default.asp?page = story_16-5-2004_pg3_4.

42. Walter C. Ladwig III, "An Overview and Assessment of the Indian Army's Cold Start Strategy," paper presented at conference on "Cold Start: India's New Strategic Doctrine and Its Implications," Naval Postgraduate School, Monterey, CA, May 29–30, 2008, http://users.ox.ac.uk/~mert1769/Ladwig,%20Cold%20Start%20NPS%20Paper .pdf.

43. An excellent study of factors contributing to military collapse or catastrophe is provided by Eliot A. Cohen and John Gooch, *Military Misfortunes: The Anatomy of Failure in War* (New York: Free Press, 1990).

44. An example might be US air strikes on Iraqi intelligence headquarters in 1993 after an assassination plot against former president George H. W. Bush.

45. A Pakistani perspective with some questionable numbers can be found in Air Marshal (retired) Ayaz Khan, Pakistani air force, "Military Balance in South Asia," *South Asia Investor Review*, http://southasiainvestor.blogspot.com/2009/01/military-balance-in-south-asia.html.

46. Narang, "Posturing for Peace?" 66–70.

47. Praveen Swami, *India, Pakistan and the Secret Jihad: The Covert War in Kashmir, 1947–2004* (New York: Routledge, 2007); Hassan Abbas, *Pakistan's Drift into Extremism: Allah, the Army, and America's War on Terror* (Armonk, NY: M. E. Sharpe, 2005).

48. Since 2000, there have been significant reforms. See International Institute for Strategic Studies, *Nuclear Black Markets: Pakistan, A. Q. Khan and the Rise of Proliferation Networks* (London: International Institute for Strategic Studies, 2007), 107–18.

49. Feroz Hassan Khan, "Nuclear Security in Pakistan: Separating Myth from Reality," *Arms Control Today*, July–August 2009, www.armscontrol.org/act/2009_07–08/ khan.

50. See, e.g., "Pakistan's Nuclear Bases Attacked by Al-Qaeda," *Daily Telegraph*, August 11, 2009, www.telegraph.co.uk/news/worldnews/asia/pakistan/6011668/Paki stans-nuclear-bases-targeted-by-al-Qaeda.html.

51. There is also an increasing volume of analysis on the role of Pakistan's Inter-Service Intelligence Directorate and its ultimate allegiance to either army or civilian leadership. See Frederic Grare, *Reforming the Intelligence Agencies in Pakistan's Transitional Democracy* (Washington, DC: Carnegie Endowment for International Peace, 2009); Robert B. Oaklet and Franz-Stefan Gady, *Radicalization by Choice: ISI and the Pakistani Army*, Strategic Forum 247 (Washington, DC: Institute for National Strategic Studies, 2009); and Mark J. Roberts, "Pakistan's Inter-Services Intelligence Directorate: A State within a State?" *Joint Force Quarterly* 48 (1st Quarter 2008): 104–10.

52. Shuja Nawaz, *Crossed Swords* (Oxford: Oxford University Press, 2008), 570–77. See also Brian Cloughley, *War, Coups & Terror* (New York: Skyhorse, 2008).

53. Husain Haqqani discusses the changing relationship between the army and Islam. Husain Haqqani, *Pakistan: Between Mosque and Military* (Washington, DC: Carnegie Endowment for International Peace, 2005).

54. An argument that Pakistan has assembled an indigenous variant of a PAL system is made by Shaun Gregory, "The Terrorist Threat to Pakistan's Nuclear Weapons," *CTC*

Sentinel, July 2007, 1–4, www.ctc.usma.edu/sentinel/CTCSentinel-Vol2Iss7.pdf. Narang argues that it is unlikely that Pakistan has robust PALs; Narang, "Posturing for Peace?" 68–69.

55. A brief summary of Pakistan's militant threats is given by C. Christine Fair and Seth G. Jones, "Pakistan's War Within," *Survival* 51, no. 6 (December 2009–January 2010): 161–88.

56. Zafar Iqbal Cheema, *The Domestic Governance of Nuclear Weapons: The Case of Pakistan,* Case Study Report (Geneva: Geneva Centre for the Democratic Control of Armed Forces, 2008).

57. "Interior Ministry Gets ISI, IB Control," *The Nation* (Karachi), July 27, 2008, www.nation.com.pk/pakistan-news-newspaper-daily-english-online/Politics/27-Jul-2008 /Interior-Ministry-gets-ISI-IB-control.

58. "Pakistan Warns West: We Cannot Fight Al-Qaida If Crisis Escalated," *Guardian* (London), December 1, 2008, www.guardian.co.uk/world/2008/dec/01/terrorism-paki stan-india-conflict.

59. "Pakistan Ready for No First Use of Nukes," *The News* (Karachi), November 23, 2008, www.thenews.com.pk/top_story_detail.asp?Id = 18538.

60. Markey, *Securing Pakistan's Tribal Belt.*

61. Sameer Lalwani, "Pakistani Capabilities for a Counterinsurgency Campaign: A Net Assessment" (Washington, DC: New America Foundation, 2009).

62. Ahmed Rashid, *Descent into Chaos* (New York: Viking, 2008).

63. Antonio Giustozzi and Seth Jones both provide significant data on Pakistan's role in providing sanctuary and support for Taliban factions in Afghanistan and Pakistan. See Antonio Giustozzi, *Koran, Kalashnikov, and Laptop: The Neo-Taliban Insurgency in Afghanistan* (New York: Columbia University Press, 2008); and Seth G. Jones, *Counterinsurgency in Afghanistan* (Santa Monica, CA: RAND Corporation, 2008).

64. International Crisis Group, *Pakistan: The Militant Jihadi Challenge,* Asia Report 164 (Brussels: International Crisis Group, 2009).

65. "Inside Help Suspected in PNS Mehran Base Attack," *The News* (Karachi), May 27, 2011, www.thenews.com.pk/TodaysPrintDetail.aspx?ID = 6290&Cat = 13.

CHAPTER 11

REGIME TYPE, NUCLEAR REVERSALS, AND NUCLEAR STRATEGY

The Ambiguous Case of Iran

Scott A. Jones and James R. Holmes

THE NATURE OF A REGIME may exert less influence on nuclear strategy and force structure than it might appear. Tehran pursued a policy of nuclear ambiguity starting during the rule of Shah Reza Pahlavi, which yielded to today's Islamic regime following the Revolution in 1979.[1] The Iranian nuclear program, then, has endured over the span of four decades and across two very dissimilar regimes. That both the shah's regime and the Islamic regime saw fit to push ahead with a nuclear program that could have military applications is telling. It suggests that there may exist a logic of nuclear proliferation that is independent of regime type. In other words, the link appears tenuous between the type of regime that rules a country, the decision to go nuclear, and the kind of strategy the regime puts in place to govern the use of nuclear weapons.

If so, strategies aiming at forcible regime change are of doubtful utility in reversing proliferation. This could be instructive as one peers into the second nuclear age. How different regimes approach questions related to strategy and force structure once they have breached the nuclear threshold remains an open question. Thucydides furnishes a useful starting point for this, as for so many questions about politics, war, and strategy. The chronicler of the Peloponnesian War declares that "three of the strongest motives" animating states' actions are "fear, honor, and interest." States that disregard these motives, says Thucydides, flout "the law that the weaker should be subject to the stronger."[2] The historian makes little allowance for the nature of the regime as a variable in the fear–honor–interest calculus he imputes to states. Freewheeling democratic Athens complied with this logic of statecraft. So did oligarchic Sparta.

Consider these motives in turn. Thucydides' third driver, interest, is reasonably tangible and quantifiable. By applying raw intellect, representatives of different societies and cultures will probably come up with the same list of interests and options for a given state situated in given geopolitical surroundings. In the nuclear strategy sphere, likewise, an enduring logic appears to govern the actions of disparate states.

In the second nuclear age, this logic seemingly nudges new entrants into the nuclear club toward minimal deterrence. This helps explain the apparent continuity in Iranian nuclear strategy since the days of the shah.

Thucydides' other two drivers for states' actions, honor and fear, color perceptions of national interests and of the best courses of action to attain those interests. Iranians across the political spectrum take pride in past grandeur, for instance, and they see nuclear weapons as a token of greatness. The Islamic regime adds religious motives to the pursuit of national greatness. Not only must Iran recover its past glory; it must stake its claim to leadership within the Muslim world. There would clearly be some differences in emphasis between a religious and a more secular regime, but the desire for some form of nuclear arsenal would remain essentially constant. Here again, continuity would prevail across types of regime.

In Thucydidean terms, fear promises to act as the arbiter of future Iranian nuclear strategy. How Tehran sizes up the external threat environment when governed by different regimes could result in different nuclear postures. A secular regime would presumably incline to routine power politics and might not entertain exaggerated views of regional and global powers intents and capabilities. A minimal nuclear posture would buffer against likely rivals. Such a regime would likely content itself with a few nuclear weapons kept at fairly low readiness levels.

By contrast, a clerical regime like the current one, which defines itself in opposition to the secular West, would be prone to see hostile designs lurking everywhere. All-consuming fear of outside menaces could goad Tehran—much like the South African regime under apartheid or the Pakistani regime today—toward a mania for security of the arsenal. For instance, the leadership could incorporate measures into its nuclear strategy intended to make a nuclear reversal impossible. Fielding a sizable arsenal rather than just a few score weapons would be one option. Concealment and dispersal among hardened sites would constitute an obvious step. Imposing tight central control of release authority would be another option. Cultivating ambiguity about Iranian redlines for using nuclear weapons would be yet another.

Nuclear weapons, then, serve dual purposes. They burnish Iranian prestige, and they provide top cover under which the regime can pursue its goals through instruments of statecraft such as diplomacy, economics, and conventional military force. Yet despite the constants in Iranian politics, Iranian strategy and behavior could look quite different from regime to regime—even under doctrines formally classified as minimal deterrence. Pariah states are not irrational, but subjective factors like fear and honor condition their rational actions.

Glimpsing how Iran's Islamic regime or some successor would handle such questions is a matter of considerable significance for outside powers like the United States that hope to craft a wise policy and strategy toward Iran. Accordingly, we first examine why regime type is not all-important in nuclear decision making. Analyzing previous nuclear reversals in Africa and Latin America illuminates this question. Having established this, we then move on to explore the likely contours of Iranian nuclear strategy, doctrine, and force structure, in hopes of discerning how Tehran will conduct business under the Islamic regime or some more secular successor.

Regime Change and Nuclear Reversals

The question of nuclear reversal is really a question about whether to persist with a given force structure that a state's armed forces have procured—that is, a particular implement of strategy—or to disarm. It is important to note that only South Africa has dismantled a working nuclear arsenal, albeit a small one. As we recount below, Argentina and Brazil abandoned nuclear programs for Thucydidean reasons of their own, but there is reason to believe that Iran will depart from this pattern. Although the premises of this volume are that proliferation has occurred and that it is time to think about proliferators' strategies, it is at least worth entertaining the possibility of an Iranian nuclear reversal. This should shed light on the future Iranian posture under different forms of political rule.

Although most nuclear proliferation studies consist of either technical itemizations or analyses of motives and mechanisms for acquisition, few studies have examined nuclear reversals.[3] Within that limited subset, the role of regime change has remained case-specific. Given the compelling role played by regime change in historical nuclear reversal cases, the further study of regime change as a critical "reversal" variable merits further consideration. Examining the Iranian nuclear proliferation case in the context of regime range has both practical and theoretical merit. In the case of the former, regime change figured prominently in the Bush administration's nuclear nonproliferation policy for both Iraq and Iran. Whether such strategies work constitutes a question of major significance for policymakers. In the case of the latter, the causal role of regime change and regime type merits further study in order to augment current theories of nuclear acquisition and renunciation.

The Iranian case shows that regime change is a necessary but insufficient causal variable in a state's decision to renounce nuclear weapons after embarking on a nuclear program. Regime type is important, but not all-important, in decisions of such moment. The case raises theoretical questions about our understanding of why states—and certain types of states in particular—give up their nuclear aspirations, or at least engage in nuclear hedging. With regard to actual versus potential proliferation, the Iranian case also prompts wider questions about exactly what it means "to go nuclear." In this chapter, accordingly, we also canvass issues pertaining to the relationship between regime type and nuclear proclivities.

In this section we present exploratory research into some of the above-mentioned questions using Iran as a case study of regime change and type and the relation, if any, to nuclear persistence or restraint. We begin by reviewing theoretical treatments of the standard canon of nuclear restraint cases—Argentina, Brazil, and South Africa. The subsequent section examines the persistence of the nuclear issue across regimes in Iran. We then delve into prospective Iranian nuclear strategy, doctrine, and force structure and dispositions, bearing in mind how speculative such an endeavor remains.

In explaining rationales and outcomes, the literature on nuclear reversals and restraint deploys a standard battery of external and internal variables: objective and subjective security analyses, security assurances, economic incentives, parochial considerations (e.g., prestige or honor), and regime change.[4] Recent studies have begun to examine the regime change variable in more depth by examining not only the phenomenon of regime change itself but also that of regime type.[5] Nevertheless, though no single variable can explain nuclear reversal, a more in-depth analysis of regime change in nuclear reversal cases may offer more insight into how the sundry variables interrelate, determine the casual role played by regime type, and help discern the concomitant policy implications.[6] As noted above, the Iranian case is of particular interest given its current topicality, the recent application of regime change strategy in Iraq, and the ambiguous role played by past and—as we will argue—future regime changes in Iran.[7]

To examine "regime change" as a nonproliferation variable, it is necessary to formulate a working definition of this term. Surprisingly, both theoretical and policy treatments tend to use the term vaguely or even contradict one another as to its meaning. In examining the perceived failure of democracy and democratization in the Middle East, for example, Holger Albrecht and Oliver Schlumberger define regime change by what it is not: "Regime change is not equal to transition: The latter means a systemic change of the type of polity, while the former refers to *any* sort of change, thus also to change *within* a given type of political regime while the systemic attributes of the polity remain in place" (emphasis in the original).[8] Robert Litwak uses the term to describe the political changes in Iraq in 2003, where Saddam Hussein's government was completely overthrown and supplanted.[9] In the context of US government policy toward Iran, Congress passed the Iran Freedom and Support Act of 2005, which appropriated $10 million and directed the president to use these resources to fund groups that oppose the Iranian government.[10] For the purposes of this chapter we define regime change as a fundamental shift in a country's form and practice of governance.

Before exploring the illustrative cases in which regime change has been a decisive factor in reversing a state's course toward nuclear weapons, it is important to review the past and current contexts surrounding proliferation and to define "nuclear reversal." Ariel Levite offers perhaps the most widely accepted definition of this concept: "Nuclear reversal refers to the phenomenon in which states embark on a path leading to nuclear weapons acquisition but subsequently reverse course, though not necessarily abandoning altogether their nuclear ambitions. At the core of this definition is the distinction between states that have launched (indigenously or with external assistance) nuclear weapons program and then abandoned it and those that never had such a program in the first place."[11]

On the basis of this definition, Levite plots nuclear proliferation along a continuum from nuclear abstinence to acquisition. Unlike Levite we view the South African case not as a nuclear reversal but as indistinct, and thus classifiable both as a reversal and as a divestiture case.[12]

Consider the cases of nuclear reversal as a category of proliferation status. In each case in which regime change occurred, the decision to abandon nuclear weapons was directly related to—and dependent upon—the change of governing arrangements. In other words, if regime change had not taken place, it is highly unlikely that a nuclear reversal would have resulted.[13] The other interesting aspect of the regime change factor is that each of these cases involved a transformation from an authoritarian/military regime to a democratic government. Hence the nature of the regime may be a critical component in understanding the correlation between regime change and nuclear reversal. We leave that question until later in the chapter. Here we examine the regime change nuclear reversal cases—Argentina, Brazil, and South Africa.

Argentina and Brazil

The nuclear reversal cases in Argentina and Brazil are interlinked.[14] In addition to the roles played by the United States and other external parties, regime change facilitated an actual and perceptual shift in the security relationship between these two states.[15] Argentina's move to civilian, democratic rule in 1983 acted as the catalyst for a significant alteration in Argentine nuclear and security policy. The country's nuclear program was placed under civilian control, and the new government enacted legislation to legally prohibit the development of nuclear weapons.[16] Argentina unilaterally ratified the Nuclear Non-Proliferation Treaty (NPT) in 1995. (Brazil did not ratify the NPT until 1998.)

Military rule ended in Brazil in 1985, and in 1988 the Brazilian Congress approved a new constitution mandating that all nuclear activities be conducted solely for peaceful purposes.[17] Even so, the new liberal government did not consolidate the nation's nuclear reversal until the middle to late 1990s. For example, the only change President José Sarney made to the nuclear program came in 1986, when he ordered work at the Cachimbo installation to cease.[18] Subsequently, Brazil renounced nuclear weapons and, with Argentina, established mutual verification and inspection procedures in 1990 under the bilateral Declaration on the Common Nuclear Policy of Brazil and Argentina. A Common Accounting and Control System agreement signed in 1991 was followed the same year by the "Exclusively Peaceful Use of Nuclear Energy" agreement, which created the Agency for Accounting and Control of Nuclear Materials (Agência Brasileiro-Argentina de Contabilidade e Controle de Materiais Nucleares).[19] In 1994 Brazil ratified the Treaty of Tlatelolco. And it ratified the NPT on July 13, 1998, ratifying the Comprehensive Test Ban Treaty the same day.[20] Brazil joined the Nuclear Suppliers Group as a full member on April 23, 1996, at the Buenos Aires Plenary Meeting.

South Africa

South Africa's nuclear weapons program began in the early 1970s under the apartheid regime, particularly under the P. W. Botha administration.[21] Pretoria's decision to produce nuclear weapons was predicated on national security considerations, such as South Africa's sense of encirclement and the deteriorating regional security environment in the region. Concerns about the communist threat emanating from neighboring Angola were especially acute.[22] During the 1970s South Africa acquired a complete nuclear fuel cycle and built a limited nuclear deterrent comprising at least six nuclear weapons.[23] With the dismantlement of the apartheid regime,

the F. W. de Klerk government disassembled the entire weapons program, complet-
ing the process in June 1991.[24] In July 1991 South Africa acceded to the NPT as
a non–nuclear weapon state, and it implemented the International Atomic Energy
Agency's Comprehensive Safeguards Agreement in November 1991. In 1993 President de Klerk publicly disclosed that a nuclear arsenal had once existed.[25] South
Africa joined the Nuclear Suppliers Group in 1995.

Initial Conclusions

What initial conclusions can we draw from these three cases? Before answering
this question, it is important to point out that the South African case deserves some
qualification, insofar as the nuclear reversal was not coterminous with regime
change. Strictly speaking, and in contrast to the Argentinean and Brazilian cases, the
South African nuclear reversal took place before the actual change in government.[26]
Nevertheless, until the election of F. W. de Klerk, the defining characteristic of South
African politics was the apartheid system. From 1990 to 1991 the de Klerk administration completely dismantled the apartheid system, lifting the ban on rival political
parties like the African National Congress, the United Democratic Front, the Pan
Africanist Congress, and the Communist Party of South Africa.[27]

In all successful reversals involving regime change, the resultant political form
was democratic.[28] Specifically, each state made the transition from a military/author-
itarian regime to a more democratic form of national governance. This finding com-
ports with Etel Solingen's distinction between "internationalizing" and "backlash"
constituencies.[29] Regime change is insufficient in and of itself to bring about a
nuclear reversal. Nevertheless, it would appear that the *type* of regime is also a
qualifying factor in determining a nuclear reversal. A focus on regime type may
explain in part why the nuclear program survived regime change in Iran.

Iran: Regime Change without Reversal?

By most accounts Iran appears to be on the path to nuclear weapons. Tehran's serial
obfuscation, dissimulation, and deliberate ambiguity suggest motives beyond the
development of nuclear energy—the stated goal of its nuclear program.[30] Yet the
quest to harness the atom began not with the current regime, the Islamic Republic
of Iran, but with its predecessor. Under Shah Mohammed Reza Pahlavi, Iran began
its nuclear pursuit in 1957, under a "proposed agreement for cooperation [between
the United States and Iran] in research in the peaceful uses of atomic energy" under
the auspices of President Dwight D. Eisenhower's Atoms for Peace program.[31] In
1960, after the agreement was made public, the shah established the Tehran Nuclear
Research Center and negotiated with the United States to supply a 5-megawatt reactor.[32] US nuclear assistance continued throughout the 1960s.[33] In 1968 Iran became
one of the first signatories to the NPT.

The process of transferring nuclear technology continued throughout the 1970s.[34] Canada, France, and Germany joined the United States in providing assistance to the Iranian nuclear program. Interestingly, Iran and South Africa signed a nuclear agreement under which six hundred tons of yellowcake uranium were sent from South Africa to Iran for further processing.[35] In March 1974 the shah established the Atomic Energy Organization of Iran. Throughout the nuclear development process, the publicly avowed goal of the Iranian program was peaceful, aimed at generating energy and furthering scientific research. Nevertheless, the United States suspected that Tehran was interested in weapons development.[36] Despite the shah's insistence that Iran's nuclear program was exclusively peaceful, his regime's interest in reprocessing plutonium and its insistence on a "full right" to do so fanned concerns in Western capitals.[37]

The end of the Pahlavi regime did not mark an end to Iran's nuclear aspirations. Despite Ayatollah Ruhollah Khomeini's antinuclear rhetoric, nuclear research-and-development efforts continued. With Chinese assistance, for instance, Iran established a nuclear research facility at Isfahan in 1984 and sought nuclear partnerships throughout the 1980s.[38] In other words, there was no clear break between these two very different regimes with regard to nuclear issues. Of course, a great deal of ambiguity surrounds the apparent Iranian weapons program. Were the shah or elements of his regime pursuing a nuclear weapons capability?[39] When exactly did the post-1979 Islamic regime decide to pursue a weapons option? How did regime change affect nuclear policy, if at all?

The Iranian regime change is of particular interest when compared with other nuclear reversal cases in which regime change was a prominent if not decisive factor in the decision to roll back or dismantle a weapons program. In the absence of complete information—an intrinsic shortfall for research of this type—we can assume that the shah's intentions were not completely benign. They were ambiguous, at the very least.[40] The effort to develop the capacity to generate nuclear energy consequently imparted momentum to Iranian infrastructure and personnel. This nuclear momentum was not halted by the subsequent regime.[41] Indeed, nuclear politics became common currency within the revolutionary regime, particularly after the lacerating effects of the Iran-Iraq War.[42] Nevertheless, we still lack a clear understanding of the issues at play between regimes. Deeper study of the dynamic between regime change and nuclear reversal—or, more to the point, between regime change and the decision to forgo nuclear reversal—should better inform theory and practice.

Does Regime Type Matter?

In the cases examined earlier in the chapter—Argentina, Brazil, and South Africa—the connection between regime change and nuclear reversal was highly robust. Moreover, regime type seems to be a qualifying feature of regime change, particularly when compared with the Iranian case. Regime change in each case was marked by a move from an authoritarian/military administration to a more democratic political system. (The same held true to a lesser extent in nuclear reversals in South Korea and Taiwan.) This correlation squares with Solingen's work on liberalizing versus nationalist coalitions, although Solingen is not as concerned with regime type per se.[43]

Robert Litwak acknowledges the important causative role played by regime type, particularly in the cases reviewed above. Nevertheless, he concludes that "the historical record indicates that regime intention, not regime type, is the critical proliferation indicator. The crux issue is whether regime *change*—whether forcibly imposed from without, as in Iraq, or precipitated by indigenous force from within—will produce a change in regime *intention*" (emphasis in the original).[44]

Litwak connects regime intention with a country's "strategic personality."[45] To the extent that the shah's regime entertained ambitions toward nuclear weapons, the concept of strategic personality, or "strategic culture," may explain why Tehran's nuclear quest endured after a fundamental change in governance. The concept may also suggest that, in the case of Iran, even regime change to a more generically democratic form of government may not bring about a nuclear reversal. In Thucydidean parlance, fear of the menaces in a tough neighborhood remains more or less constant for leaders of very different political traditions. This imposes a modicum of constancy on the methods and tools used to protect the nation.

The first scholarly treatment of Iranian regime change as a nonproliferation variable appeared in a 2001 study by the Iran scholar Geoffrey Kemp, who developed a matrix mapping each form of Iranian regime to a corresponding policy approach to nuclear weapons. He concluded that a "moderate" regime was no more likely to eschew nuclear weapons than a "radical" variant.[46] In a similar vein a 2005 National Defense University study of Iranian nuclear options determined that regime type was largely irrelevant to Tehran's pursuit of nuclear weapons.[47] A more recent survey of Iranian popular opinion about a range of issues connected with the country's nuclear developments renders the current understanding of regime change as a nonproliferation tool even more problematic. According to Christine Fair and Stephen Shellman,

> Contrary to common belief and Tehran's own rhetoric, Iranian impressions of Israel do not drive support for the country's nuclear efforts. On the other hand, negative beliefs about the United States do appear to predict this support. While these results do not refute—and indeed generally comport with—the conventional wisdom about the nation's program, they do suggest that there is less distance between the sentiment of the public and that of the regime than may be popularly believed. Indeed in some measure the premise of American "regime change" funds presumes a degree of difference in preferences that is not supported by these data.[48]

These data suggest that even if Iran were to undergo a transition to a more popular form of governance, the Iranian nuclear program would not follow, say, the Argentinean or Brazilian model. In February 2003 congressional testimony, remarkably, former Central Intelligence Agency director George Tenet interjected a cautionary note regarding the theory and practice of regime change as a nonproliferation tool: "Although a crisis for the regime might come about were reformers to abandon the government or hardliners to initiate a broad suppression on leading advocates of change, the resulting disorder would do little to alleviate US concern over Iran's international behavior. No Iranian government, regardless of its ideological leanings, is likely to willingly abandon WMD [weapons of mass destruction] programs that are seen as guaranteeing Iran's security."[49] Tenet's policy conclusion confirms Levite's inference that academic studies of nuclear reversal—and, more broadly, nuclear nonproliferation—have been unable to establish a direct link between the *nature* of a regime and its orientation toward nuclear matters.[50] Nevertheless, the case studies do suggest a causal link between nuclear reversals and the type of regime change, as does a recent study of the South African case.[51]

If the type of regime change represents a critical variable in nuclear reversals (or restraint), then understanding its underlying mechanisms is essential to our overall understand of proliferation. In other words, will a democratic regime change in Tehran increase the probability of a nuclear reversal? If so, what causal mechanisms will make it so? Addressing these and related questions demands a combined international relations and comparative politics approach to the proliferation puzzle.[52] Solingen's 2007 work on nuclear logics can be viewed as an effort to apply such an approach while outlining the means by which nuclear logic is realized or frustrated. As noted above, Solingen is less concerned with regime type, but her typologies of liberalizing/internationalizing coalitions as nuclear weapons opponents would suggest a more generically "democratic" form of governance. The historical nuclear reversal/regime change cases empirically appear to validate this connection.

Prospective Nuclear Doctrine and Deployment

Although regime type may not necessarily determine a government's proclivities toward nuclear development or rollback, it may afford insights into nuclear doctrine and deployment. Recall that neither Argentina nor Brazil breached the nuclear barrier before relinquishing its weapons aspirations, whereas South Africa's apartheid regime dismantled only a small arsenal, and only under very unusual circumstances. Once a sizable arsenal exists, abandoning it would be a difficult decision for any leadership—religious, secular authoritarian, or secular democratic—to make. Seldom do nation-states buckle under to fear or forswear instruments of war that let them ameliorate fear. Seldom do they forswear claims to honor or prestige or give up important interests. In short, Tehran will probably press ahead with its bomb-making efforts, as the literature on nuclear reversals implies.

As noted at the outset, however, one Thucydidean driver for policy and strategy—fear—could elicit different emphases in nuclear strategy from regime to regime, assuming that strategic logic will prod *any* rulers in Tehran to field a minimal deterrent of some kind. Nuclear weapons are essentially tools of statecraft, with a direct bearing on foreign and national security policy and strategy. Most treatments of the Iranian nuclear weapons issue have focused almost entirely on the status of weapons development and on the likelihood and the best means—whether through diplomacy, military action, or regime change—to dissuade Tehran from taking this route.

In this section we take nuclear weapons as a given and examine the possible nuclear doctrine of the current regime and likely near-term forms of government.

The present form of Iranian government is predicated on a Khomeini-inspired form of Shia Islamic jurisprudence, the *velayat-i faqih* (the rule of the jurist), which was promulgated as a revolutionary ideology that promotes international political reform.[53] From the establishment of the Islamic Republic in 1979, revolutionary fervor and focus has shifted, particularly following the tempering effects of a brutal nine-year war with Iraq. Nevertheless, the essence of the revolutionary ideology and the regime's raison d'être remains intact. Namely, the Islamic Republic emerged in response to perceived apostasy, political corruption, and foreign usurpation. Alleged US predations remain foremost in the revolutionary canon.[54]

Although the various motives behind possible nuclear weapons development before and after the Iranian Revolution were assessed in the preceding sections, it is instructive to revisit conceivable drivers as they relate to the current government, the immediate security threats the leadership perceives, and therefore Tehran's likely approach to nuclear deployment. It is important to note that nuclear ambiguity helps Iran achieve important strategic effects, namely, deterrence by uncertainty.[55] In terms of core motivations, that is, Iranian nuclear weapons would deter adversaries, bolster national prestige, and project power in an uncertain regional environment—as they have for a number of other nuclear states.[56] Iran's perceived encirclement by US military forces, Israel's undeclared nuclear arsenal, and regional security concerns such as the Arab-Sunni Gulf states pose potential security challenges. In the cases of Israel and the United States in particular, Tehran is similarly concerned with maintaining the viability of the current regime.[57] No regime lightly forgoes instruments that promise to help it survive such challenges.

The current regime, under the second term of President Mahmoud Ahmadinejad, is frequently characterized as revanchist, morbidly conservative, and a decided departure from the relatively moderate Khatami administration.[58] Nuclear negotiations under the Ahmadinejad administration have been intractable, characterized by obstruction and a shrill rhetoric of defiance. With respect to the nuclear question, analysts have emphasized the ideological composition of Ahmadinejad's choices for the "power" ministries, meaning the bodies that wield the state monopoly of force. All his appointees hail from the Islamic Revolutionary Guard Corps (IRGC), as he does himself. To a man, they were deeply involved in the military aspects of the 1979 Revolution and the subsequent war with Iraq.[59] The formative impact of the Iran-Iraq War on this generation cannot be overstated. Even a comparative moderate like former president Ali Akbar Hashemi-Rafsanjani once proclaimed, "With regards to chemical, bacteriological and radiological weapons, it was made clear during the war that these weapons are very decisive. We should fully equip ourselves in both offensive and defensive use of these weapons."[60]

In practice, despite the increased prominence of the security and intelligence ministries under the Ahmadinejad administration, Iranian nuclear doctrine may not conform to Tehran's belligerent rhetoric. A menacing official doctrine may only isolate Iran further and, potentially, invite military intervention. Again, regime survival is the mullahs' paramount concern. Nuclear opacity helps delay the resolution of the nuclear standoff and complicates allied plans to muster an international consensus, let alone intervene in Iran by force.[61] In short, obfuscating about nuclear weapons ambitions represents a straightforward way to gain time while deferring concrete action on the international community's part.

In terms of force structure, strategy, and doctrine, Iran's options are very limited. How would different types of regimes do things differently in this sphere, assuming that the Islamic regime undergoes some kind of significant evolution, falls, or is overthrown? History suggests that continuity may prevail within the military establishment, regardless of who rules Iran. It is important to note that the clerical regime installed during the 1979 Revolution vested security and military power in separate, Islamicized versions of the already-existing military command structure. Likewise, absolute authority, including security decision making, nominally rests with the Islamic Republic's supreme leader, Ayatollah Ali Khamenei. The regular army, or Artesh, was stripped of practical power and of order-of-battle planning after the revolution.

To protect the Revolution and the clerical establishment, Khomenei and his advisers created a parallel military structure, the IRGC. Most analysts concur that the IRGC will play the dominant part in any nuclear weapons development, including that of missile delivery systems. Furthermore, IRGC troops would operate nuclear-armed Iranian missile forces if they are deployed.[62] Whether a post-Islamic regime would maintain such a guardian force to guarantee its rule—and entrust the nuclear arsenal to this force rather than the regular military—remains a matter of speculation, but one with significant strategic importance. A new government might well restore control of all forces to the regular armed services as a means of asserting its control over military affairs. Tighter civil control of the military, which would presumably characterize a more liberal form of governance in Tehran, ought to assure that political calculations govern doctrine and strategy more closely. This would represent a welcome development from the Western standpoint. Accordingly, it is worth monitoring for signs that the civilian political leadership is modifying the system of civil–military relations and, if so, how.

In the near term, Iran could field only a small arsenal of perhaps ten to fifteen warheads. The 1981 Israeli air raid on the Iraqi nuclear installation at Osirak constituted a seminal learning event for Iranians. The chief lessons taken by aspiring nuclear states: to avoid preemptive action, dig in and disperse. In keeping with the lessons of Osirak, any Iranian nuclear arsenal will most likely be heavily fortified, concealed, and scattered about rugged Iranian territory to prevent any single strike from eliminating the entire force and to preserve a second-strike capability.[63]

To avoid preemptive air or missile strikes from the sea, the IRGC would likely position launchers in the rough terrain of northwestern Iran, far from the Persian Gulf. Underground facilities could be constructed to make use of mountainous topography. Shortfalls in US military capacity to strike at bunkers and other underground sites have been amply documented, vindicating such options. Mobile launchers represent another attractive option. The US military's fruitless 1991 "Scud hunt" in the western Iraqi desert illustrated the potential of mobile launchers. The Chinese military seemingly has great confidence in the survivability of its road-mobile missile force, whereas the US military itself has employed rail-mobile intercontinental ballistic missiles. Tehran could well reach similar conclusions about the value of land-based missiles, especially given its difficult maritime geography. Launch sites could conceivably be placed near the frontiers with important countries like Russia or Turkey, moreover, which would complicate any Western decision to strike at them. In effect Tehran could dare the West to attack these sites and risk the ensuing political fallout from friendly or neutral powers. Some combination of dug-in and mobile launchers probably represents the optimal mix for a modest Iranian nuclear force.

These scenarios remain largely speculative for now, given that warhead delivery represents a serious technical challenge. Although Tehran has stepped up its ballistic missile development efforts, the underlying technology has not fundamentally advanced beyond basic Scud technology.[64] Cruise missile development is likewise limited. Indeed, the current generation of cruise missiles is geared almost exclusively toward antiship missions, in keeping with Tehran's desire to keep US navy warships as far from Iranian coasts as possible.[65] Warhead miniaturization poses yet another technical obstacle to a credible, working nuclear deterrent.

Sea-launched options appear more viable, although Iran's aging fleet of Russian-built Kilo-class submarines is reportedly incapable of launching ballistic or cruise missiles.[66] Kilos are not equipped with vertical launch capability, and the navy possesses no land-attack cruise missile that can be launched from torpedo tubes. By no means is this shortcoming insurmountable from a technical standpoint. More modern Kilo-class boats can launch antiship cruise missiles, meaning that they could conduct land-attack missions, provided suitable payloads and guidance systems are developed for the navy's submarine-launched missiles.[67]

The Iranian navies, both the regular force and the IRGC, though fairly capable in basic surface-fleet resources, have displayed too little competence to inspire confidence in their ability to manage and use fully functioning nuclear warheads.[68] The IRGC possesses a large number of fast-attack craft. Recently, there have been a number of international interdictions involving speedboats bound for Iran. Some analysts suggest that fast-attack craft could serve as delivery platforms for nuclear munitions.[69] Although this possibility cannot be ruled out entirely, such craft are so small and so vulnerable to surface and air attacks that such an option would represent a temporary expedient at best—much as it is for the Indian navy, which has reportedly experimented with nuclear-capable missiles on board its own small combatants.

The maritime environment would be inhospitable for a seagoing nuclear force in any event. The Persian Gulf is shallow, which complicates antisubmarine warfare but also makes it hard for the launch platform to hide for long. Iranian Kilos have reportedly mastered techniques for resting on the bottom of the Gulf and exploiting temperature and salinity gradients to elude antisubmarine warfare surface ships and aircraft. Though highly effective, such tactics can only be for the short term. If Tehran opted for an undersea deterrent, the navy would likely need to dispatch its submarines to the Indian Ocean for concealment. This would raise issues of its own, because Iranian submarines would be compelled either to transit the Strait of Hormuz on the surface, exposing them to detection, or to make the transit underwater, with the perils that would entail. Patrolling the Arabian Sea or the Indian Ocean, moreover, might well complicate relations both with neighboring Pakistan and with India, which views maritime South Asia as its own preserve. These are questions that Tehran must ponder if the leadership decides to field an undersea nuclear force. In all likelihood the technical, tactical, and diplomatic hurdles render a submarine-based deterrent a long-term prospect for Iran.

Of more immediate concern is the prospect of asymmetrical deployment—in other words, the use of some proxy group as an indirect delivery platform for unconventional weaponry. Iranian financial, political, and military support for the Islamist militant groups Hezbollah and Hamas adds another dimension to speculation about deployment options.[70] Most analysts consider arming nonstate groups with nuclear weaponry highly improbable given the likely retaliation it would provoke.[71] Releasing nuclear explosives to a militant group would also remove them—and the decision to use them—from direct Iranian operational control. This would be a move out of desperation, however strong the affinities between the Islamic Republic regime and the radicals. Tehran might well be held accountable for a nuclear terrorist strike, even if it withheld specific permission to execute the strike. Despite the shortcomings of forensics—that is, of efforts to determine the origin of a nuclear device—such difficulties may not shield Tehran from an overwhelming Israeli or US response. At the very least, the prospect of seeing its covert activities exposed would give the leadership pause.

Asymmetrical deployment nonetheless constitutes perhaps the most vexing question pertaining to regime change and Iranian nuclear weapons. Even though a more democratic government would probably not curtail efforts to field a nuclear arsenal, it probably would forgo certain destabilizing strategic options like turning unconventional arms over to Islamist militants. As noted above, close supervision of questions relating to nuclear weapons is a hallmark of popular government. If a more liberal regime balked at entrusting nuclear weapons to an ideological body like the IRGC, still less would it entrust them to a mercurial group like Hamas or Hezbollah. Iran watchers should remain watchful for evidence of distrust toward these groups—distrust that could prompt Tehran to keep its distance. Equipping them with rockets or conventional explosives is one thing; furnishing them with the ultimate weapon is another. Although regime change may not keep Iran from entering the circle of nuclear weapon states, in short, the advent of more liberal governance could alter Iranian behavior in important, and probably healthy, ways.

Tehran's nuclear doctrine and deployment options, it appears, will remain extremely limited for the foreseeable future. A limited missile capability, an aging air force, a submarine force ill configured for nuclear missions, and technical limitations on warhead design and development all constrain Iranian options with regard to force structure, strategy, and doctrine. Though possible, delivery by proxy is highly improbable and will become more so if the Islamic regime gives way to something more liberal. Iran remains steadfast in its nuclear development efforts, however oriented, but nuclear ambiguity will characterize both its doctrine and any demonstrations of technical capability, such as underground testing.

Conclusion

Iran launched a domestically produced communications satellite using a two-stage rocket on February 2, 2009, in tandem with thirtieth-anniversary celebrations of the founding of the Islamic Revolution. The underlying rocket technology is identical to the Shahab family of ballistic missiles—missiles many experts believe are being developed to carry nuclear payloads.[72] Nuclear ambiguity is currently one of the foremost international security issues pertaining to Iran. As such, in addition to diplomacy and sanctions, regime change has been bruited about as a corrective to nuclear intransigence. The underlying but dubious logic of regime change suggests that a more democratic regime in Tehran would decline to exercise the nuclear option. From an empirical standpoint, internal regime change that results in more democratic forms of governance correlates with nuclear reversals.[73] Even so, the proposition that democratic states forgo nuclear weapons altogether is patently absurd—witness the five officially declared nuclear weapon states, most of which are under democratic rule. Instead the question is about the dynamics of regime change, the type of regime that results from regime change, and the corresponding impact on a nation's nuclear status.

The Iranian case is of interest to this line of inquiry because of its past regime change, its nuclear ambiguity, and its evolving domestic political situation. Current economic and demographic trends in Iran portend significant political changes to the clerical system of governance. On the basis of this initial review of cases, future political change in a more democratic direction should increase the probability of a nuclear reversal, provided that the military has not yet fielded a working arsenal. But the type of regime provides no guarantee in itself. It must be understood in relation to other variables, such as regional security dynamics and the Iranian national strategic personality. At a minimum, a more controlled study of the effects of regime change on regime types, and of regime type on strategic behavior, is necessary to yield firmer, more theoretically informed conclusions that can help solve the methodological and conceptual problems plaguing the literature on proliferation and strategy.[74]

Beyond regime type is the problem of latent nuclear weapons capability or, as Ariel Levite puts it, "nuclear hedging," which refers to a strategy of amassing the makings of a nuclear arsenal without actually staging a nuclear breakout. Even if Tehran abjures a nuclear weapons program, in other words, it will remain doubtful that it has forsworn nuclear weapons altogether. A hedging strategy would give the leadership the option of going nuclear in short order without incurring the consequences of openly fielding a nuclear arsenal—and thereby abandoning the policy of nuclear ambiguity that has paid off handsomely. The imprecision in what constitutes proliferation—an imprecision deliberately being exploited by Tehran—will continue to complicate policy and strategy toward Iran. Iranian strategists will doubtless take a similar, indirect approach toward nuclear strategy if Tehran proceeds to field a nuclear force. Regime type clearly matters in nuclear affairs. But as Thucydides counsels, it does not override the fundamental motives driving states' actions.

Notes

1. International Atomic Energy Agency, *Implementation of the NPT Safeguards Agreement and Relevant Provisions of Security Council Resolutions 1737 (2006), 1747 (2007), 1803 (2008), and 1835 (2008) in the Islamic Republic of Iran*, Report by the Director-General GOV/2009/74 (Vienna: International Atomic Energy Agency, 2009), 2.

2. Robert B. Strassler, ed., *The Landmark Thucydides* (New York: Touchstone, 1996), 43.

3. Ariel Levite, "Never Say Never Again: Nuclear Reversal Revisited," *International Security* 27, no. 3 (Winter 2002–3): 59–88.

4. Illustrative treatments of nuclear reversals and regime change include Rebecca Hersman and Robert Peters, "Nuclear U-Turns: Learning from South Korean and Taiwanese Rollback," *Nonproliferation Review* 13, no. 3 (November 2006): 539–53; and Levite, "Never Say Never Again," 59–88. More generally, selected theoretical treatments of nuclear decision making include T. V. Paul, *Power versus Prudence: Why Nations Forgo Nuclear Weapons* (Montreal: McGill–Queen's University Press, 2000). See also Mitchell Reiss, *Bridled Ambitions: Why States Constrain Their Nuclear Capability* (Washington, DC: Woodrow Wilson Center Press, 1995); Scott D. Sagan, "Why Do States Build Nuclear Weapons? Three Models in Search of a Bomb," *International Security* 21, no. 3 (Winter 1996–97): 54–86; Mitchell Reiss, *Without the Bomb: The Politics of Nuclear Nonproliferation* (New York: Columbia University Press, 1988); Barry R. Schneider and William L. Dowdy, eds., *Pulling Back from the Nuclear Brink: Reducing and Countering Nuclear Threats* (London: Frank Cass, 1998); Etel Solingen, "The Political Economy of Nuclear Restraint," *International Security* 19, no. 2 (Fall 1994): 126–69; Leonard S. Spector, "Repentant Nuclear Proliferants," *Foreign Policy* 88 (Fall 1992): 3–20; and William C. Potter, *The Politics of Nuclear Renunciation: The Cases of Belarus, Kazakhstan, and Ukraine*, Occasional Paper 22 (Washington, DC: Henry L. Stimson Center, 1995).

5. As Hughes observes, "Other scholars have noted the role of domestic organizational and other variables in influencing states' decisions to develop (or reverse) their nuclear weapons programs, although the causal weight assigned to systemic versus domestic explanations typically varies." In the case of Pakistan, Samina Ahmed argues that although the perceived security threat from India was a necessary condition in Pakistan's drive to develop and test a nuclear device, the marginalization of the political leadership and the dominance of the military in Pakistan's security policy architecture played a decisive role in nuclear decision making across time. David Karl notes that in the case of India, the military leadership was reticent about developing a nuclear-weapons program because of fears it would enable civilian leaders to meddle in military decision-making. The French decision to develop an independent nuclear deterrent, similarly, is arguably driven by national prestige as well as systemic variables. Finally, Ariel Levite writes that domestic factors have been important causes of "nuclear reversal," that is, when a state chooses to abandon a nascent nuclear-weapons program. Llewelyn Hughes, "Why Japan Will Not Go Nuclear (Yet): International and Domestic Constraints on the Nuclearization of Japan," *International Security* 31, no. 4 (Spring 2007): 67–96. See also Stephen Burgess, "South Africa's Nuclear Weapons Policies," *Nonproliferation Review* 13, no. 3 (November 2006): 519–26.

6. Robert Litwak, "Non-Proliferation and the Dilemmas of Regime Change," *Survival* 45, no. 4 (Winter 2003–4): 7–32. In Litwak's study of regime change and nuclear

proliferation, he concludes that "the historical record indicates that regime intention, not regime type, is the critical proliferation indicator. The crux issue is whether regime *change*—whether forcibly imposed from without, as in Iraq, or precipitated by indigenous force from within—will produce a change in regime *intention*" (author's emphases). Regime intention is a useful heuristic in understanding behavior over time. However, this insight does not negate the need to explore the causal impact of regime type on nuclear decisions, particularly in light of the historical record. See also Paul, *Power versus Prudence*.

7. The Bush administration enumerated regime change amongst policy options for reversing nuclear gains in Iran. See, e.g., Litwak, "Non-Proliferation." See also Seymour Hersh, "The Iran Plans," *New Yorker*, April 16, 2006, www.newyorker.com/archive/2006/04/17/060417fa_fact?currentPage=all.

8. Holger Albrecht and Oliver Schlumberger, " 'Waiting for Godot': Regime Change without Democratization in the Middle East," *International Political Science Review* 25, no. 4 (2004): 371–92.

9. Robert Litwak, *Regime Change: US Strategy through the Prism of 9/11* (Washington and Baltimore: Woodrow Wilson Center Press and Johns Hopkins University Press, 2007).

10. In the press, this section was dubbed the "regime change provision." See, e.g., Kelley Vlahos, "Capitol Hill Mulls 'Regime Change' in Iran," Fox News, February 4, 2005, www.foxnews.com/story/0,2933,146342,00.html.

11. Levite, "Never Say Never Again," 61.

12. International Atomic Energy Agency, *Implementation of the NPT Safeguards Agreement in the Arab Republic of Egypt*, Report by the Director-General (Vienna: International Atomic Energy Agency, 2005).

13. Of course, there were other mitigating factors in the cases of Argentina, Brazil, and South Africa, e.g., reduced external security threats, none of which are simultaneously necessary and sufficient. See, e.g., Benjamin Frankel, "The Brooding Shadow: Systemic Incentives and Nuclear Weapons Proliferation," and Richard K. Betts, "Paranoids, Pygmies, Pariahs, and Nonproliferation Revisited," both in *The Proliferation Puzzle: Why Nuclear Weapons Spread (and What Results)*, edited by Zachary S. Davis and Benjamin Frankel (Portland: Frank Cass, 1993), 37–38, 100–124.

14. At the November 1985 Foz de Iguazú presidential meeting between Argentina and Brazil, a "Joint Declaration on Nuclear Policy" was issued that stressed the exclusively peaceful purposes of the nuclear programs of both countries and their intent to cooperate very closely in this area. See Julio Carasales, "The Argentine–Brazilian Nuclear Rapprochement," *Nonproliferation Review* 2, no. 3 (Spring–Summer 1995): 39–49. See also Jose Goldemberg, "Looking Back: Lessons from the Denuclearization of Brazil and Argentina," *Arms Control Today*, April 2006, www.armscontrol.org/act/2006_04/lookingback.

15. An interesting case study is provided by Etel Solingen, "Middle East Denuclearization? Lessons from Latin America's Southern Cone," *Review of International Studies* 27 (2001): 375–94.

16. Joseph Cirincione, Jon B. Wolfsthal, and Miriam Rajkumar, *Deadly Arsenals: Tracking Weapons of Mass Destruction* (Washington, DC: Carnegie Endowment for International Peace, 2005), 383–92.

17. In August 2005 former Brazilian president José Sarney confirmed that the Brazilian military had endeavored to develop nuclear weapons to counter political and military competition from Argentina. See Sharon Squassoni and David Fite, "Brazil's Nuclear History," *Arms Control Today*, October 2005, www.armscontrol.org/act/2005_10/Oct-Brazil#BrazilHistory.

18. Cachimbo was designated as the test site for nuclear explosives. See Michael Barletta, *The Military Nuclear Program in Brazil*, CISAC Working Paper (Stanford, CA: Center for International Security and Cooperation, Stanford University) http://cisac .stanford.edu/docs/barletta.pdf. See also Squassoni and Fite, "Brazil's Nuclear History."

19. In December 1991 Brazil and Argentina concurrently signed agreements with the International Atomic Energy Agency authorizing full-scope safeguards at nuclear installations in both countries. Inspections by the International Atomic Energy Agency began in 1994. See the ABAAC website, www.abaac.com.br. See also Joseph Cirincione, Jon Wolfsthal, Miriam Rajkumar, "Brazil," in *Deadly Arsenals: Nuclear, Biological, and Chemical Threats*, 2nd rev. ed., edited by Joseph Cirincione, Jon B. Wolfsthal, and Miriam Rajkumar (Washington, DC: Carnegie Endowment for International Peace, 2006), 393–407.

20. Brazil initially opposed the Nuclear Non-Proliferation Treaty for decades, arguing that it discriminates against non–nuclear weapon states and infringed on national sovereignty. See Barletta, *Military Nuclear Program*, 15.

21. Arguably, the official initiation for a nuclear weapons program took place under Prime Minister Johannes Vorster. See, e.g., Hannes Steyn, Richardt van der Walt, and Jan van Loggerenberg, *Armament and Disarmament: South Africa's Nuclear Weapons Experience* (Pretoria: Network Publishers, 2003). US nuclear assistance was also a critical variable. US support included the construction of a research reactor in Pelindaba, the supply of highly enriched uranium, and training for nuclear technicians.

22. Peter Liberman, "The Rise and Fall of the South African Bomb," *International Security* 26, no. 4 (Fall 2001): 58.

23. See Verne Harris, Sello Hatang, and Peter Liberman, "Unveiling South Africa's Nuclear Past," *Journal of Southern African Studies* 30, no. 3 (September 2004): 457–76.

24. According to Waldo Stumpf, head of the Atomic Energy Commission during this period, "de Klerk informed the South African Parliament that South Africa had embarked on the development of a limited nuclear deterrent in the years covering the 1970s and 1980s. He also confirmed that the weapons program had been fully dismantled before South Africa's accession to the NPT and signature of a Comprehensive Safeguards Agreement with the [International Atomic Energy Agency], a mere 7 weeks later, on 16 September 1991. He also granted permission, for full access by [the agency] to facilities and records of facilities, which in the past had been used for the development of the nuclear deterrent capability." See Waldo Stumpf, "Birth and Death of the South African Nuclear Weapons Program," presentation given at the conference "Fifty Years after Hiroshima," organized by Unione Scienziati per il Disarmo, Castiglioncello, Italy, September 28–October 2, 1995, available at Federation of American Scientists website, www.fas .org/nuke/guide/rsa/nuke/stumpf.htm.

25. Interestingly, as noted by Liberman, "neither sanctions nor norms appear to have had much impact on P. W. Botha's nuclear policy, although they did lead Minerals and Energy Minister Steyn to recommend joining the NPT to P. W. Botha around 1987. An avalanche of new Western anti-apartheid sanctions in 1985 and 1986, combined with a

debt crisis in South Africa, might have put the NPT on the agenda. De Klerk speculates that Botha's 1987 NPT remarks might have reflected an interest in exploring whether the nuclear program could be used as a bargaining chip to relieve economic sanctions." Liberman, "Rise and Fall," 79.

26. The [problematic] definition of regime change will be discussed in the concluding section.

27. Robert M. Price, *The Apartheid State in Crisis: Political Transformation in South Africa, 1975–1990* (New York: Oxford University Press, 1991).

28. In the case of Argentina and Brazil, e.g., Robert Litwak notes: "In Brazil and Argentina, the transition to democracy and civilian rule was instrumental in terminating covert nuclear weapon programmes under military control and in bringing about the nations' 1994 accession to the 1967 Treaty of Tlatelolco, which had created a nuclear weapons-free zone in Latin America." See Litwak, "Non-Proliferation," 10. The cases of South Korea and Taiwan offer similar insights, although the connection between nuclear reversal and democracy is more chronologically attenuated. For more on the two cases see Rebecca Hersman and Robert Peters, "Nuclear U-Turns: Learning from South Korean and Taiwanese Rollback," *Nonproliferation Review* 13, no. 3 (November 2006): 539–53. The authors suggest that the transition to more democratic forms of government may have influenced Seoul and Taipei to roll back their nuclear weapons plans. However, they caution that increased transparency, e.g., is an insufficient guarantor of continued nuclear restraint.

29. Solingen's theory differentiates between outward-looking regimes that derive domestic legitimacy from ensuring economic growth through global integration and inward-oriented ones that employ import-substituting models favoring extreme nationalism and economic autonomy. It does not, however, address regime change per se but focuses on coalitions within a standing government structure. In the case of Argentina and Brazil's nuclear reversals, Solingen notes: "The Argentine leadership understood the requirements of an internationalizing strategy—on both sides—increasing its confidence in Brazil's future accession to the NPT, *once domestic political conditions in that country allowed this*" (emphasis added). See Solingen, "Middle East Denuclearization?" 393. See also Etel Solingen, "The Political Economy of Nuclear Restraint," *International Security* 19, no. 2 (Fall 1994): 126–69; and Etel Solingen, *Nuclear Logics: Alternative Paths in East Asia and the Middle East* (Princeton, NJ: Princeton University Press, 2007).

30. See, e.g., Paul Kerr, *Iran's Nuclear Program: Status*, Report for Congress RL34544 (Washington, DC: Congressional Research Service, 2008), and International Atomic Energy Agency, "Report on Iran Nuclear Safeguards Sent to IAEA Board," November 9, 2011, www.iaea.org/newscenter/news/2011/bog091111.html.

31. See Paul Kerr, *Iran's Nuclear Program*, and Greg Bruno, "Iran: Nuclear Overview," December 2009, both at Nuclear Threat Initiative website, www.nti.org/e_research/profiles/Iran/Nuclear/index.html. See also Peter Grier, "It Was Uncle Sam Who First Gave Iran Nuclear Equipment," *Christian Science Monitor*, October 2, 2009, www.csmonitor.com/USA/Foreign-Policy/2009/1002/p04s01-usfp.html.

32. Andrew Koch and Jeanette Wolf, "Iran's Nuclear Procurement Program: How Close to the Bomb?" *Nonproliferation Review* 5, no. 1 (Fall 1997): 123–34.

33. Foe example, the United States was willing to supply Iran with reprocessing technology according to 1975 and 1976 National Security Council documents. Tehran also had a 1976 contract for a pilot uranium enrichment facility using lasers; see International

Atomic Energy Agency, *Iran*, Report by the Director-General GOV/2007/58 (Vienna: International Atomic Energy Agency, 2007). Also see Kerr, *Iran's Nuclear Program: Status*, 2.

34. Many of the formerly classified US government documents detailing Iranian nuclear developments can be found at the Nuclear Vault, www.gwu.edu/~nsarchiv/nukevault/ebb268/index.htm. See also Gawdat Bahgat, "Nuclear Proliferation: The Islamic Republic of Iran," *Iranian Studies* 39, no. 3 (September 2006): 307–27, www.informaworld.com/smpp/title~db = all~content = t713427941~tab = issueslist~branches = 39-v39.

35. Much of this feedstock supplied Iran's current pool of uranium hexafluoride (UF_6) gas and resulting stock of enriched uranium. David Albright, Jacqueline Shire, and Paul Brannan, "Is Iran Running Out of Yellowcake?" Institute for Science and International Security, February 11, 2009, www.nti.org/e_research/profiles/Iran/Nuclear/index.html.

36. "Special National Intelligence Estimate: Prospects for Further Proliferation of Nuclear Weapons," August 23, 1974, available at National Security Archive website, www.gwu.edu/~nsarchiv/NSAEBB/NSAEBB240/snie.pdf. In 1974 the shah declared that Iran would have nuclear weapons "without a doubt and sooner than one would think." The statement is denied by Iran's embassy in France, and the shah later backed off the statement, reaffirming that "not only Iran, but also other nations in the region should refrain from planning to gain atomic arsenals." This citation comes from John K. Cooley, "More Fingers on Nuclear Trigger?" *Christian Science Monitor*, June 25, 1974, quoted by Anne Hessing Cahn, "Determinants of the Nuclear Option: The Case of Iran," in *Nuclear Proliferation in the Near-Nuclear Countries*, edited by Onkar Marwah and Ann Shulz (Cambridge, MA: Ballinger, 1975).

37. Foe example, Akbar Etemad, the chairman of Iran's Atomic Energy Organization, argued that Iran should have the "full right to decide whether to reprocess or otherwise dispose or treat the materials provided under the agreement." William Burr, "The History of Iran's Nuclear Program," *Bulletin of the Atomic Scientists*, January 19, 2009.

38. *Nuclear Engineering International*, December 1984, 13; Akbar Etemad, "Iran," in *European Non-Proliferation Policy*, edited by Harald Muller (Oxford: Oxford University Press, 1987), 9; "Proliferation: Pulling a Bomb Apart," *Economist*, March 14, 1992, 46.

39. At some point in the 1970s, the United States obtained intelligence data indicating that the shah had set up a clandestine nuclear weapons development program. Also, according to Akbar Etemad, director of the Atomic Energy Organization of Iran until October 1978, researchers at the Tehran Nuclear Research Center are involved in laboratory experiments that could have applications for reprocessing spent fuel. See Leonard Spector, *Going Nuclear: The Spread of Nuclear Weapons 1986–1987* (Cambridge, MA: Ballinger, 1987), 50–55.

40. As noted by Ariel Levite, "empirical data on proliferation in general and nuclear reversal in particular often are incomplete or otherwise unreliable because of a combination of extraordinary secrecy, intentional cover-up, and deliberate misinformation. Yet the literature manifests little appreciation of the gravity of these data problems." See Levite, "Never Say Never Again," 64.

41. In some respects the Islamic revolutionary ideology espoused by Khomeini and others could logically accommodate the possession of nuclear weapons as a means of continuing the radical Shi'a ideology of *moqavamat*, or "resistance." See David E. Thaler,

Alireza Nader, Shahram Chabin, Jerrold D. Green, Charlotte Lynch, and Frederic Weh-
rey, *Mullahs, Guards, and Bonyads: An Exploration of Iranian Leadership Dynamics*,
RAND National Defense Research Institute Report (Santa Monica, CA: RAND Corporation, 2010), 13.

42. See, e.g., Shahram Chubin and Robert S. Litwak, "Debating Iran's Nuclear Aspirations," *Washington Quarterly* 26 (Fall 2003): 99–114.

43. Solingen, *Nuclear Logics*, 17.

44. Litwak, "Non-Proliferation," 11. Litwak goes on to suggest that while intentions
matter, the particular aspects of democratic forms of government (e.g., transparency and
accountability) are valid as nonproliferation determinants. He observes that "the positive
outcomes in South Africa and Ukraine, as well as in Brazil and Argentina, offered the
promise of a new post–Cold War model: nonproliferation through democratization,
security assurances and integration into the globalized economy of the liberal international order."

45. The concept is taken from Caroline Ziemke's fascinating study of Iraq and Iran in
terms of national identify typologies. Ziemke defines strategic personality as "the underlying motivations for any state's strategic conduct [that] can be found by focusing on its
Ultimate Concerns—the set of material, moral, or ideological factors that have emerged
over the course of the state's history as the keys to its long-term survival, cohesion, and
sense of national well-being." See Caroline Ziemke, *Strategic Personality and the Effectiveness of Nuclear Deterrence: Deterring Iraq and Iran* (Washington, DC: Institute for
Defense Analysis, US Defense Threat Reduction Agency, 2001), www.dtra.mil/docu
ments/asco/publications/IranIraq.pdf.

46. Kemp and his colleagues concluded that "it is clear that even if the moderate forces
in Tehran led by President Khatami were to eventually succeed in achieving control over
all key instruments of power, including the armed forces, the police, the judiciary, and
the intelligence agencies, it is unlikely their attitudes to Iraq or Israel would be any different than their more conservative brethren. In fact, most reformers show a remarkable
congruence with the conservatives in their assertion of Iranian nationalism. This is
reflected in the fact that some of the staunchest critics of Iran's participation in international arms control regimes have moderate reformist perspectives on domestic politics."
Farideh Farhi, "To Have or Not to Have? Iran's Domestic Debate on Nuclear Options,"
in *Iran's Nuclear Weapons Options: Issues and Analyses*, edited by Geoffrey Kemp
(Washington, DC: Nixon Center, 2001), 35–53, www.nixoncenter.org/publications/
monographs/Iran%27s%20Nuclear%20Weapons%20Options%20-%20Issues%20and
%20Analysis2.pdf.

47. The authors concluded that "support for the acquisition of advanced nuclear technology crosses ideological and factional lines. Few believe that a more reformist-minded
government would deny its right to take any measure it deemed necessary for national
security. More broadly, press commentaries suggest Iranians increasingly resent foreign
efforts to shape their policies on nuclear energy or deny them what is seen as a natural
and national right." Judith Yaphe and Charles Lutes, eds., *Reassessing the Implications
of Nuclear-Armed Iran* (Washington, DC: Institute for National Strategic Studies,
National Defense University, 2005), 11.

48. Christine Fair and Stephen Shellman, "Determinants of Popular Support for Iran's
Nuclear Program: Insights from a Nationally Representative Survey," *Contemporary
Security Policy* 29, no. 3 (December 2008): 538–58, at 553. An earlier analysis of public

polling data was done by Michael Herzog, "Iranian Public Opinion on the Nuclear Program: A Potential Asset for the International Community," *Policy Focus* 56 (Washington, DC: Washington Institute for Near East Policy, 2006).

49. Statement by Director of Central Intelligence George J. Tenet before the Senate Select Committee on Intelligence on the "Worldwide Threat in 2003: Evolving Dangers in a Complex World," www.au.af.mil/au/awc/awcgate/cia/worldwidethreatbriefing2003 .htm.

50. Levite continues: "Thus, even in those rare cases where the United States might be able to encourage a regime change, this would *not* guarantee, by itself, nuclear reversal or restraint. The issue of regime change is more intriguing and the effect more complex." Levite, "Never Say Never Again," 83.

51. For example, in his study of the South African nuclear reversal, Stephen Burgess suggests that "democratic reforms may prove to be a successful long-term factor in reversing the development of nuclear weapons." See Burgess, "South Africa's Nuclear Weapons Policies," 519. It is important to note, however, that the causal link between regime type and nuclear reversal is still underspecified. For example, in a recent quantitative study examining the variables of nuclear weapons development and peaceful nuclear cooperation, Matt Fuhrmann notes: "Many policymakers assume that proliferation is a problem caused by 'rogue' or undemocratic states. Although some autocratic states such as North Korea have proliferated in recent years, on average democracy is less salient in explaining the spread of nuclear weapons than the conventional wisdom suggests." See Matthew Fuhrmann, "Spreading Temptation: Proliferation and Peaceful Nuclear Cooperation Agreements," *International Security* 34, no. 1 (Summer 2009): 36.

52. Potter and Mukhatzhanova highlight this important distinction in the nonproliferation literature, that it generally operates from either an international relations or a comparative politics perspective. See William Potter and Gaukhar Mukhatzhanova, "Divining Nuclear Intentions: A Review Essay," *International Security* 33, no. 1 (Summer 2008): 139–69.

53. The basic principle of the Islamic Republic's political system is the *velayat-i faqih* (the government of the jurist) system, as developed by Ayatollah Khomeini and reinforced in 1988 by adding a new dimension, the absolute governance of the jurist (*velayat-e motlaqah-e faqih*), according to which the supreme leader (*vali-e faqih*) is the titular and actual head of the political system, despite the existence of the office of the president. Under Article 110 of the 1979 Constitution, the supreme leader retains the constitutional right to declare war and call for general troop mobilization. He is also the supreme commander of both the IRGC and the Artesh. See Eva Patricia Rakel, "The Political Elite in the Islamic Republic of Iran: From Khomeini to Ahmadinejad," *Comparative Studies of South Asia, Africa and the Middle East* 29, no. 1 (2009): 105–25.

54. See Daniel Byman, Shahram Chubin, Anoushiravan Ehteshami, and Jerrold D. Green, *Iran's Security Policy in the Post-Revolutionary Era* (Santa Monica, CA: RAND Corporation, 2009), 87–92, www.rand.org/pubs/monograph_reports/MR1320/index .html.

55. Regarding nuclear ambiguity as a deterrence strategy, Robert Litwak notes: "Perceptions that Washington's objective is regime change create incentives for nuclear hedging and the strategic use of weapons-program ambiguity." See Robert S. Litwak, "Living with Ambiguity: Nuclear Deals with Iran and North Korea," *Survival* 50, no. 1 (2008): 91–118.

56. Iran scholar Ray Takeyh suggests that Iran's nuclear motivations are highly typical of other nuclear weapon states. See Ray Takeyh and Colin Dueck, "Iran's Nuclear Challenge," *Political Science Quarterly* 122, no. 2 (2007): 189–205.

57. Iran borders two states that have suffered coercive regime change at the hands of the United States. Likewise, the Bush administration explicitly pursued a policy of promoting (albeit indirectly) regime change as a means by which to facilitate nuclear transparency and control. See Patrick Clawson and Michael Eisenstadt, eds., *Deterring the Ayatollahs: Complications in Applying Cold War Strategy to Iran*, Policy Focus 72 (Washington, DC: Washington Institute for Near East Policy, 2007). See also Trita Parsi, *The Treacherous Alliance: The Secret Dealings of Israel, Iran, and the United States* (New Haven, CT: Yale University Press, 2007).

58. As noted by Elliot Hen-Tov, "the defining feature of Ahmadinejad's administration is the intertwining of formal government decision-making with the revolutionary military-security complex, in contrast to the conventional armed forces, which lack influence in the Islamic republic. . . . One should view Iran's quest for nuclear weapons through the prism of elite factionalism and regime development. The successful acquisition of nuclear weapons would accelerate a militarization of Iran's regime." Elliot Hen-Tov, "Understanding Iran's New Authoritarianism," *Washington Quarterly* 30, no. 1 (winter 2007): 163–79, at 166, 169.

59. According to Takeyh, "Iran's nuclear calculations have been further hardened by the rise of war veterans such as President Mahmoud Ahmadinejad to positions of power. Although the Iran-Iraq war ended nearly twenty years ago, for many within the Islamic Republic, it was a defining experience that altered their strategic assumptions." Takeyh and Dueck, "Iran's Nuclear Challenge," 196.

60. Cited by Wyn Bowen and Joanna Kidd, "The Iranian Nuclear Challenge," *International Affairs* 5, no. 1 (March 2004): 257–76.

61. Litwak, "Living with Ambiguity," 91–118. Anthony Cordesman and Khalid Al-Rodhan observe that "Iran can gain as much from concealing and obfuscating its weaponization activities as from hiding or obfuscating the nature of its nuclear program. As long as Iran does not actually test a full nuclear explosion, it can develop and test potential weapons and warhead designs in a wide range of ways." Anthony H. Cordesman and Khalid R. Al-Rodhan, *Iranian Nuclear Weapons? The Uncertain Nature of Iran's Nuclear Programs* (Washington, DC: Center for Strategic and International Studies, 2006), 19, available at www.csis.org/burke.

62. According to Anthony Cordesman: "The IRGC operates most of Iran's surface-to-surface missiles and is believed to have custody over potentially deployed nuclear weapons, most or all other chemical, biological, radiological, and nuclear (CBRN) weapons, and to operate Iran's nuclear-armed missile forces if they are deployed. The links between the IRGC and Iran's nuclear program are so close that its leaders were singled out under the UN Security Council Resolutions passed on December 23, 2006, and March 24, 2007, and had their assets frozen." Anthony H. Cordesman, *Iran's Revolutionary Guards, the Al Quds Force, and Other Intelligence and Paramilitary Forces* (Washington, DC: Center for Strategic and International Studies, 2007), available at www.csis.org/burke.

63. The open talk of a military option has also increased the likelihood that Iran would disperse and heavily fortify any nuclear holdings. See Austin Long and Whitney

Raas, "Osirak Redux? Assessing Israeli Capabilities to Destroy Iranian Nuclear Facilities," *International Security* 31, no. 4 (2007): 7–33.

64. A comprehensive technical overview of Iran's ballistic missile programs is given by Theodore Postol, "Technical Addendum to the Joint Threat Assessment on the Iran's Nuclear and Missile Potential: A Technical Assessment of Iran's Ballistic Missile Program," East-West Institute, 2009, http://docs.ewi.info/JTA_TA_Program.pdf.

65. Scott Jones, "Ra'ad Cruise Missile Boosts Iran's Military Capability," *Jane's Intelligence Review*, April 1, 2004.

66. Iran's submarine force currently consists of three Russian Kilo-class diesel-electric submarines. See "Iranian Navy," GlobalSecurity.org, www.globalsecurity.org/military/world/iran/navy.htm.

67. "Kilo Class—Project 636," Federation of American Scientists website, www.fas.org/man/dod-101/sys/ship/row/rus/877.htm.

68. According to Cordesman and the International Institute for Strategic Studies, the Iranian Navy is composed of three submarines, three frigates, two corvettes, ten missile patrol craft, five mine-warfare ships, fifty-two coastal and inshore patrol craft, and ten amphibious ships. See Anthony H. Cordesman and Khalid R. Al-Rodhan, *The Gulf Military Forces in an Era of Asymmetric War: Iran* (Washington, DC: Center for Strategic and International Studies, 2006), available at www.csis.org/burke.

69. Jo Becker, "Web of Shell Companies Veils Trade by Iran's Ships," *New York Times*, June 7, 2010, www.nytimes.com/2010/06/08/world/middleeast/08sanctions.html?pagewanted=all.

70. See, e.g., Robert L. Pfaltzgraff, "An Iran with Nuclear Weapons," *Foreign Policy Challenges for the New Administration: Iran and the Middle East*, Fares Center for Eastern Mediterranean Studies, Tufts University, March 6, 2009; William Harris, "Iran, Hezbollah, and the Bomb: The Futility of Containment," *Weekly Standard*, May 7, 2010, www.weeklystandard.com/blogs/iran-hezbollah-and-bomb; and Masoud Kazemzadeh, "Ahmadinejad's Foreign Policy," *Comparative Studies of South Asia, Africa and the Middle East* 27, no. 2 (2007): 423–49.

71. See Mark Fitzpatrick, "Assessing Iran's Nuclear Program," *Survival* 48, no. 3 (Autumn 2006): 5–26.

72. See, e.g., Anthony H. Cordesman and Martin Kleiber, *Iran's Military Forces and Warfighting Capabilities: The Threat in the Northern Gulf* (Washington, DC: Center for Strategic and International Studies, 2007).

73. Externally imposed regime change can, at the very least, result in unintended policy outcomes. For example, in their study of the evolution of greater Libyan cooperation with the West, Jentleson and Whytock note that "pursuing regime change can be counterproductive to achieving policy change. There are some situations in which regime change rhetoric can have utility. But if there still are doubts about the costs and risks that can be incurred in actually making regime change a policy objective, Iraq should be dispelling them. Alternatively, the Libya case shows what can be achieved when regime change is taken off the table. The repeated reassurances the United States and Britain gave Libya of policy change not regime change were absolutely crucial. Rogue states need to know both that the coercer is firm about not accepting too little and also trustworthy about not pushing for too much. This runs counter to the view that keeping regime change as an option enhances leverage and coercive pressure." Bruce W. Jentleson and Christopher

A. Whytock, "Who 'Won' Libya? The Force-Diplomacy Debate and Its Implications for Theory and Policy," *International Security* 30, no. 3 (Winter 2005–6): 47–86.

74. Potter and Mukhatzhanova suggest that "one of the major problems in distilling useful, future-oriented information from the enormous body of literature on nuclear proliferation that has been produced during the past half century is the extent to which it is largely speculative and contradictory in its insights. Contributing to this Rashomon effect is a lack of agreement about what constitutes nuclear proliferation, the appropriate level of analysis for study, the importance to be attached to a multitude of plausible proliferation determinants, and how best to penetrate the veil of secrecy surrounding nuclear decisions." Potter and Mukhatzhanova, "Divining Nuclear Intentions," 152.

CHAPTER 12

CONCLUSION

Thinking about Strategy in the Second Nuclear Age

Toshi Yoshihara and James R. Holmes

As **WAS NOTED AT THE OUTSET**, the premise of this book is that proliferation is now a fact and nuclear rollback is a remote prospect at best. Western analysts and officials must accept these uncomfortable realities. Notwithstanding some thinkers' acknowledgment that the nuclear landscape has changed, little policy energy has gone into appraising how new nuclear players' postures have matured. Strategic assessment remains limited and sporadic. The apparent lag in a coherent response to the nuclear challenge is attributable in part to intellectual inertia. Because nonproliferation remains the worthy ideal it has always been, analysts in the West typically focus on why nuclear proliferation takes place, how to quell it, and how it will affect the West if it indeed occurs.

The famous theoretical debate between Scott Sagan and Kenneth Waltz over whether proliferation is a good, bad, or indifferent thing comes to mind.[1] The Sagan–Waltz exchange enriched our understanding of the perils and supposed benefits of proliferation, and it remains useful on its own terms. Nonetheless, it is time to move on. Stemming new proliferation certainly remains worthwhile, but nuclear breakouts have already taken place in every case examined in this volume. For the foreseeable future, there is little chance that these countries will disarm and thus let the nuclear geometry revert to something simpler, more predictable, and more manageable. The rare alignment between domestic and international conditions that prompted disarmament in South Africa is unlikely to happen again. The need to accept the reality of a postproliferation world represents our key conceptual leap.

The second nuclear age is as much about the human factor as about missile flight profiles, the size of inventories, warhead yields, and other numerical indices of nuclear capability. By zeroing in on strategy—again, defined for our purposes as the political and military use or nonuse of disruptive nuclear technology—this study breaks with the familiar mode of net assessment, with its emphasis on quantifiable factors like hardware and manpower. Measuring what we can measure is an understandable tendency, but it obscures data that defy quantification but are nevertheless useful, such as insights into nuclear aspirants' motives and ways of strategic thought. In this book we have aspired to take a substantial analytical step beyond the crowded field of work focusing on the motives and structural forces that lead to proliferation. Our narrow-gauge view has examined the much-neglected area of *how* states manage their nuclear weaponry in the immediate aftermath of a breakout and, in some cases, for many years afterward. The following overall findings emerge from our analyses in the preceding chapters.

New Entrants Will Consolidate Strategies, Doctrines, and Forces

Our first finding is that relatively recent entrants into the circle of nuclear weapon states—including India, Pakistan, and North Korea—will consolidate and refine their arsenals with the goal of maximizing their efficacy for this postbreakout era. They have little reason to discard weaponry constructed at such expense, effort, and hazard. Consequently, international efforts to persuade them to disarm have made little headway. On the contrary, all three states have moved on to the next phase of proliferation, and thus they are devising nuclear doctrines while bolstering confidence in the credibility and security of their nuclear arsenals. As the authors of the pertinent chapters above have shown, India is constructing its first undersea deterrent, Pakistan has assumed a stance predicated on nuclear ambiguity, and North Korea has—evidently—expanded its modest arsenal while exploring creative basing options for its missile force. In the case of Iran, a key component of its strategy is to make a breakout impervious to domestic and international pressures to roll back. In short, we should expect these nuclear players to optimize their strategies and doctrines to suit their local circumstances. They will not prove as pliant as diplomats and disarmament proponents hope.

What incentives or punishments the members of the international community could levy to dissuade these new nuclear weapon states from such measures is unclear. We believe the West must anticipate that these new entrants will undertake further efforts to consolidate their nuclear postures and thus convert their forces into working implements of statecraft. For their part, established powers like the United States and its allies must appraise the strategies, doctrines, and force structures taking shape among both nuclear newcomers and old hands. By gazing through a glass darkly, they can design responses that reinforce deterrence amid vastly more complex strategic circumstances.

The Numbers Are Smaller

The quantitative dimension of nuclear strategy stands out as another stark contrast to the Cold War. Admittedly, force size is a relative concept that must be compared with other factors, including adversaries' force structures and a country's own financial and economic wherewithal to develop nuclear weapons. Nevertheless, the states examined in this volume generally command too few resources to build very large forces numbering in the thousands, along with sprawling nuclear infrastructures resembling those of the Cold War. They may suffer from limited access to fissile materials. Insecure regimes may balk at expending finite capital to develop complex command-and-control systems that delegate decision-making authority to lower echelons—that is, to officers whose political reliability could prove suspect. Geographic realities such as the size and proximity of adversaries' targets may demand more modest nuclear forces.

On a related point, the capability and credibility of nuclear states' arsenals—the twin pillars of deterrence—may be modest compared with Cold War standards. The low-yield warheads and short- to medium-range missiles that the superpowers regarded as tactical or perhaps theater strike weapons could qualify as strategic weaponry for the new players. Even a limited nuclear war, that is, could spell national disaster or destruction for small, weak states. As a result, nuclear newcomers' notions of sufficiency may differ radically from those of the Cold War. Considerations of reputation and moral stature could apply a brake on arms buildups, particularly in democracies like India.

These constraints suggest that most players will adopt existential or minimum-deterrence postures for many years to come. Minimalist approaches come in many varieties and go by different names, including "recessed" or "virtual" postures. States may take a low nuclear profile, for example, and thus keep their arsenals at very low readiness during peacetime. They could opt to deploy their warheads and delivery systems at different geographic sites. Such an arrangement would leave open the option of taking a launch-on-warning posture only in times of crisis to signal resolve. Newcomers could perceive weapons not mated to their delivery platforms as viable. Some states may regard the existence of crude nuclear devices that can be assembled quickly as a sufficient deterrent.

Even a nuclear old-timer like China allowed its nuclear forces to remain small, more or less static in size, and technologically stagnant for decades until recently. Some analysts believe that Beijing's "minimum means of reprisal" will remain the defining feature of Chinese nuclear strategy for the foreseeable future.[2] India has also declared that it is content with a minimalist posture, despite its economic potential to construct a substantially larger force. These words are convincing. More than a decade has passed since India's 1998 nuclear tests, but there is still no evidence that New Delhi has embarked on a crash program to amass a large arsenal.

But a low ceiling on force totals may generate its own sets of instabilities. Smaller nuclear powers, recent breakout states, and threshold nuclear players are typically quite vulnerable to great power preemption or threats of preemption. Knowing this, the great powers may be tempted to eliminate emerging programs before they become viable or irreversible. The United States, for instance, seriously considered striking at North Korea's nuclear infrastructure at the height of the 1994 nuclear crisis.[3] Policymakers backed away from forcible disarmament only when the frightful costs of a second Korean war sank in.

Long-standing enmities may color perceptions under certain circumstances, which drives great powers to cling to the military option. When this happens, new nuclear entrants find themselves stuck in a "valley of vulnerability" from which they cannot escape for many years. Maoist China, for instance, did not escape the danger of a preemptive US or Soviet attack for nearly a decade following its 1964 breakout.

In recent years analysts have speculated openly about the risks and benefits of possible US and/or Israeli action to forestall Iranian nuclear ambitions.[4] Even those resigned to Iran's eventual acquisition of nuclear weapons hold open the option of a preemptive attack if Iran undertakes provocative actions such as placing its nuclear forces on alert.[5] As in the case of China in the 1960s, Washington may consider Tehran an object of preemption for many years after its breakout. In other words, a stable deterrent relationship is neither a given nor an immediate prospect when a new player joins the nuclear club.

Do Not Overstate the Importance of Quantitative Measures

The social, psychological, and logistical dimensions of nuclear strategy are as important as technology and operations, for reasons spelled out by Michael Howard and Peter Paret in their commentary on Carl von Clausewitz's *On War*. Clausewitz warns against letting numbers and abstract theories "cheerfully go on elaborating absolute conclusions and prescriptions"; thus, he insists that precepts remote from human affairs "would be no use at all in the real world."[6] In this vein, our chief goal was to glimpse the thinking of the protagonists, helping US and allied practitioners of statecraft adapt their own policies and strategies to a bewilderingly intricate geometry. Discerning the basic assumptions held by new players toward the utility of nuclear weapons may tell us much about how their strategies may converge with—or diverge from—the baseline established during the first nuclear age.

We acknowledge the methodological reality that it is hard to discern how recent proliferators truly think about nuclear strategy. But what is worse, from our standpoint—as pointed out above—is that most of the states appraised in this volume deliberately obscure their intentions and capabilities. If, as Clausewitz opines, war is "a trial of moral and physical forces through the medium of the latter," nuclear newcomers disclose neither aspect of their national strength willingly.[7] Newcomers' doctrines and operational practices will likely remain shadowy for many years to come. Material weakness and deep-seated insecurity will reinforce newcomers' determination to cloak their nuclear programs in mystery. Many such states seemingly regard ambiguity as a source of credibility for their nuclear deterrents. Obfuscating suits their interests, as they construe them.

A case in point: Interviews with Iraqi leaders following the fall of Baghdad in 2003 suggested that Saddam Hussein deliberately prevaricated about whether the Iraqi military possessed weapons of mass destruction. This was part of a political strategy dubbed "deterrence by doubt." In short, Saddam sought to keep outsiders guessing about Iraq's nuclear capabilities. He believed that Iraq's adversaries, particularly Iran, would refuse to take the gamble that Baghdad *might* use weapons of mass destruction against them.[8] His deception proved all too successful, misleading the United States–led coalition into forcible regime change. The perceived virtues of secrecy—and the unintended consequences of such ambiguity—amplify the urgency of understanding how potential antagonists may approach deterrence, and of foreseeing whether they would try war-winning nuclear strategies. To borrow a term common in wargaming, we hope this volume advances our thinking about the "red team's," or adversaries', side of the deterrent relationship.

Nuclear Geometry Is Multifaceted

There are other complicating features of the second nuclear age beyond piercing the veil of secrecy that shrouds nuclear programs. The entry of new players has multiplied the number and types of deterrent interactions that take place in the international system, which has yielded a newly complex geometry of deterrence. This volume shines light on deterrence between great powers and regional powers (the United States and China), between new nuclear powers (India and Pakistan), and between nuclear and nonnuclear powers (China and Japan, North Korea, and Japan).[9] To compound the intricacies, deterrent axes between two states often intersect to form trilateral and even quadrilateral deterrent configurations. The United States' extending deterrence to Japan to counter Chinese nuclear coercion is one example. Or China might feel compelled to intervene against India on behalf of its client state, Pakistan, during some South Asian crisis or conflict. Third-party intervention in a nuclear crisis or conflict will likely prove a delicate affair. The stakes involved, furthermore, may be of dubious value to outside powers. Signs of indecision could keep them from credibly signaling resolve or deescalating tensions. Opponents might be emboldened, and allies and partners might be disheartened.

In contrast to the Cold War, the threat perceptions that drive these multilayered deterrent interactions are often ambiguous. Muthiah Alagappa detects an intriguing "quiet competition" in Asia, where bilateral relationships "are all subject to multiple and competing dynamics, including interdependence, cooperation, conflict, and confrontation."[10] Both strategic ambivalence and unprecedented economic integration, says Alagappa, typify Sino-Japanese and United States–China ties. Crosscutting interests and contradictory impulses could muddy the policymaking process and thus impair efforts to devise coherent, consistent strategies toward nuclear challengers, old and new alike. The political resolve to mobilize a decisive response to emerging nuclear threats may evanesce when enmity and amity compete for policy attention within a single relationship. That is, frank discussions about strategy, operations, and plans are next to impossible for protectors of the status quo when it is politically incorrect to identify a specific adversary. One need only recall the outcry that engulfed the 2001 US Nuclear Posture Review when its framers explicitly listed China as a potential nuclear target.

Smaller, weaker nuclear newcomers may prefer such implicit rivalries, which give them maneuvering space. Such a power can court—or manipulate—audiences among its potential adversaries, encouraging engagement or at least avoiding overt confrontation. In so doing it can steer antagonists away from a zero-sum, all-or-nothing approach to proliferation. Successful diplomacy of this kind leaves a nuclear aspirant freer to develop its nuclear arsenal without triggering an overreaction that sets a countervailing buildup in motion. Cordial or indifferent relations with prospective opponents, then, spare the newcomer a prohibitively costly, destabilizing arms race. Chinese analysts often invoke the Soviet collapse as a cautionary tale about the grave risks of undertaking an unwinnable strategic competition against the United States. The corollary to this Cold War lesson is that disadvantaged states must deny Washington and its allies any cause for undertaking such an unremitting struggle. Obfuscating the nature of the threat, then, benefits those intent on securing their nuclear positions and gains.

People, Not Hardware, Engage in Conflict

Clearly, then, the intellectual dimension of nuclear strategy constitutes another intriguing theme of this study. Learning is a critical pillar not only of nuclear strategy but also of strategy making in general. Even advanced powers must devote substantial time and energy to managing nuclear weapons and thus apply all their intellectual, technological, institutional, and doctrinal resources. Many of the contributors to this volume find that states exhibit diverse patterns of learning that reflect their own unique strategic circumstances. The long shadow cast by Mao Zedong, for instance, inhibited Beijing from venturing a fundamental reassessment of nuclear strategy for nearly two decades after the Great Helmsman's death. Open discussions about rethinking deterrence remain a rare phenomenon in the People's Republic of China to this day.

For their part the South Asian nuclear powers have approached doctrinal development and command-and-control issues at a pace that many Western observers find glacial. As a consequence, institutional control over nuclear weaponry appears to lag behind the demonstrated technical capacity to build and use it. Both New Delhi and Islamabad have repeatedly reassured the international community that they possess the know-how and the skill to ensure the safety and security of their mass destruction arsenals. Yet doubts persist, particularly with regard to Pakistan. It is unclear whether Western observers find Indian and Pakistani explanations unpersuasive because of their own biases or unreasonable expectations.

The case studies also suggest that existing and potential newcomers track debates over nuclear deterrence and strategy in the United States. Indeed, some strategic communities overseas exhibit an impressive mastery of Western deterrence theory. Yet ideas do not map from one nation-state or civilization to another on a strict one-to-one basis. That is, for foreign strategists, neither their awareness nor deep study of American debates means that they share or even accept basic Western assumptions about deterrence. Some players, then, may draw different lessons from the Cold War or find these lessons inapplicable to their particular strategic circumstances. They will doubtless factor their distinctive interests, histories, traditions, and geographic surroundings into the strategy-making process.

For some of these strategists East/West competition offers an intellectual point of departure rather than a paradigm to emulate. Chinese, Indian, and Pakistani thinkers commonly deprecate the relevance of US theoretical developments in nuclear affairs. For years Chinese strategists discounted the war-fighting potential of nuclear weapons, although such attitudes may be changing. Benign neglect seems to characterize Japanese thinking about nuclear matters. Tokyo is seemingly content to let its superpower patron perform the intellectual heavy lifting on extended deterrence. Different learning processes heighten the potential for states to enter nuclear confrontations with expectations that could produce spiraling escalation when unfulfilled. Surprises lurk.

Interactions Are Profoundly Complex

Given the findings noted above, political and strategic leaders lose sight of the human factor at their peril. But understanding the national strategy of an individual state is not enough. Forecasting how these strategies may interact and change during times of extreme stress is as crucial as conducting deep study of a single country and society. The impact of nuclear interactions—a mass destruction variant of what Clausewitz aptly termed a "collision" of "living forces"—on the regional and international orders promises to be at once profound and extraordinarily complex.[11] Many new players possess nuclear infrastructures and doctrines for employing nuclear forces that are peculiar to their local circumstances. For their part, the established players covered in this study are developing hardware and doctrines that are so at variance with past approaches that they may as well be starting anew.

This is a familiar phenomenon. The United States underwent growing pains of its own during the 1950s, as strategists struggled with the intricacies and ambiguities of the first nuclear age. Some of today's nuclear newcomers could be suffering from similar theoretical underdevelopment. If so, these states may be unprepared to cope with the full range of nuclear-related contingencies—which could come about suddenly and unexpectedly and thus compress policymakers' time to think and decide to near zero. And the unfounded overconfidence of these states' leaders in their material and intellectual preparedness could goad them into unwisely disparaging adversaries' resolve or capacity to react. Barring a trauma on par with the Cuban Missile Crisis that concentrates the mind, such sentiments may go unchallenged. Consequent errors in judgment, compounded by mutual misperceptions, could exacerbate the instabilities inherent in crisis or conflict. Insights into the disparate well-crafted, flawed, and indifferent national strategies deployed by various players could help Western leaders glimpse the interactions that will be likely when these players collide, either with one another or with nuclear old-timers.

Power Disparities Compound Uncertainty

The nuclear newcomers will likely remain insecure for years to come while they strive to consolidate their methods of deterrence and come to terms with this fluid strategic environment. In the meantime they must accept a degree of risk unthinkable among established nuclear weapon states as they live with their temporary inability to ride out a first strike. Yet the compelling logic of deterrence and the persistence of small nuclear forces do not necessarily portend a stable or predictable future, even once conditions settle into a new equilibrium. The contributors to this volume demonstrate convincingly that plausible scenarios for instability and escalation abound in the second nuclear age. These dangers arise from mutual misperceptions and stark power differentials between weak and strong powers.

In times of tension or crisis, relatively weak states could adopt highly destabilizing nuclear postures for entirely rational purposes. China, North Korea, or Pakistan could see value in increasing the readiness of their forces as a political mechanism and thus telegraph their resolve to a stronger adversary. They may deploy or fuel missiles or place their forces on alert in ways designed to indicate that they are preparing to launch. Chinese doctrinal writings even suggest firing demonstration shots with live nuclear warheads onto China's own soil as a warning to others. They may engage in such provocative behavior in the counterintuitive belief that escalation may compel an enemy to deescalate. According to this line of reasoning, displaying recklessness could frighten enemies into backing down.

Given the potential asymmetries in value that each party attaches to the political stakes, the weaker side may calculate that such risky tactics stand a good chance of success. The logic underwriting this strategy of the weak powers illustrates the "rationality of irrationality." Those powers on the receiving end of such signals, however, may assess the situation quite differently. The United States and India, to name two, may perceive what their antagonists intend as limited shows of force as preludes to first or all-out strikes. Such misperceptions may prompt decision makers in Washington or New Delhi to choose preemption or escalation. If so, they would take precisely the steps that the signaling was meant to deter.

The stronger side may also feed escalation in a vicious cycle. Technological advances have already begun to blur the line dividing strategic nuclear capabilities from conventional weapons. The advent of the reconnaissance/precision-strike complex, aided by quantum leaps in information technology, has made deep, surgical attacks against enemy targets a real prospect. As highly offensively oriented concepts like the United States' "prompt global strike" capability reach maturity, conventional warfare could generate operational effects similar to nuclear warfare while promising to reduce politically hazardous collateral damage. This may tempt statesmen to order preemptive strikes. But at the same time, this technical virtuosity might prompt the weaker side to cease distinguishing conventional attacks from nuclear ones. As such, even limited conventional retaliation by the strong powers could look like a precursor to a disarming first strike, triggering classic use-it-or-lose-it fears for the weak powers.

The collision between the rationality of irrationality and the reconnaissance/precision-strike complex could quickly unravel efforts at controlling escalation. Consider, for instance, a crisis on the Korean Peninsula. If North Korea demonstrated resolve by displaying preparations for a nuclear launch, it might back the United States into a preemptive strike. How the Kim Jong-un regime might react to an early warning of US preemption is anybody's guess. A theme that emerges from this study, accordingly, is that stratagems, intimidation tactics, and superior technology may prove counterproductive or even self-defeating in crises involving nuclear weapons. No one has a silver bullet in the chamber.

Prospective interactions between the strong and the weak nuclear powers highlight another theme of this volume. The importance of great powers outside the other powers' region, particularly the United States, is evident across all the case studies. For instance, in a Taiwan Strait conflagration, China would logically hope that the integrity of its growing retaliatory forces would keep the United States out of the conflict or at least delay its entry. Nuclear weapons, then, could constrain US power and options. In contrast, Pakistan sees the presence of nuclear weapons on the subcontinent and the potential for a nuclear exchange as incentives to draw in Washington during a confrontation between Islamabad and New Delhi. Pakistani leaders believe that US intervention would constrain India, especially if things were going badly for Pakistan. For traditional US allies like Japan and South Korea, national survival hangs on the credibility of the American nuclear umbrella. Washington's security commitment, furthermore, not only defrays the costs for its East Asian allies of building independent nuclear deterrents but also empowers Tokyo and Seoul to exert regional influence that they might otherwise lack.

However, the United States might confound these diverse expectations. For example, as noted above, Chinese efforts to convey resolve could in fact accelerate the momentum toward US intervention on behalf of Taiwan. If Washington views Islamabad as the provocateur in a future crisis, it may instead side with New Delhi, an outcome made all the more likely by the emerging US–Indian entente. Washington's prolonged strategic overextension in other parts of the world might reinforce long-standing allied skepticism about US staying power. Missteps or visible reluctance to respond decisively in an Asian crisis could persuade segments of the Japanese and South Korean strategic communities that America's extended deterrence is no longer credible. These examples suggest that states—even those enjoying close ties with Washington—are inclined to misread US intentions and steadfastness.

The propensity for ugly surprises, therefore, is yet another plausible trend. US policymakers habitually impute unpredictability to others, but Washington may prove just as likely to spring strategic surprises—on friends and foes alike.

Power Disparities Spell Pathological Behavior

Deterrent interactions between small and large nuclear powers generate their own pathologies that could likewise work against stability. Some analysts question whether American conventional military and nuclear superiority would deter smaller, nuclear-armed regional powers from reckless, destabilizing behavior. Fundamental asymmetries in the stakes involved may render moot US threats of proportionate retaliation or even annihilation. Antagonists simply might not believe that Washington attaches enough importance to its goals to launch cataclysmic strikes, with all the human suffering such attacks entail.

Alternatively, the prospects for certain military defeat and regime change may radically alter the strategic calculus of a weaker nuclear state, making last-ditch nuclear options thinkable. In a conflict with the United States, an adversary's leadership may conclude that the regime's very survival is in grave danger. Under such dire circumstances, it may believe that it has no choice but to employ nuclear weapons to preclude a regime-toppling outcome. For instance, the potential for a use-it-or-lose-it dilemma could give pause to US policymakers contemplating their military options in a conflict on the Korean Peninsula. As two RAND Corporation analysts observe, "Pyongyang can credibly threaten to use nuclear weapons against a range of assets valued by its adversaries because decision makers in Washington and Seoul know that Kim and company may perceive that they will be no worse off than they already are should the United States retaliate in kind." As a result, they argue, *"the weaker side has, in a sense, achieved escalation dominance"*[12] (emphasis in the original).

At the same time, however, others contend that the US military still possesses usable options against an intractable nuclear challenger like North Korea. The conventional wisdom holds that Pyongyang's ability to inflict unacceptable damage on Seoul would be enough to force Washington to back down in a crisis or conflict. Pyongyang's massive conventional forces, particularly its long-range artillery aimed at Seoul, provide an insurance policy against US military escalation or preemption.

Yet some US analysts apparently believe that the US reconnaissance/precision-strike complex can "smother" Pyongyang's artillery positions and thus limit the damage done to Seoul.[13] Accurate and lethal suppression fires, goes this line of reasoning, would severely weaken Pyongyang's capacity to retaliate and thus liberate Washington to strike against nuclear-related targets. North Korea's counterdeterrent, then, may not guarantee US restraint or inaction. In other words, Pyongyang cannot confidently discount the possibility that Washington will succumb to the temptation to strike first, especially under severe duress.

These scenarios suggest that deterrence failures could arise both from the inherent vulnerabilities of a weaker nuclear power and from the material superiority of a stronger contender. The bleak reality is that both the weak and the strong have incentives to escalate or contemplate nuclear strikes in certain stressful situations.

Parity Is No Guarantee

Beyond such asymmetrical dynamics, the second nuclear age is propelled by competition between regional states possessing roughly similar nuclear capabilities, measured by both quantity and quality. As noted above, most newcomers are likely to assume recessed nuclear postures, which keep their forces at low readiness during peacetime. This is arguably one of the central features that distinguishes the second nuclear age from the first. During the Cold War, deterrence among Paris, London, and Beijing—the so-called second-tier nuclear powers—was tangential if not irrelevant to the larger global competition.[14] Rather than concentrate on one another, each of these capitals devoted its attention primarily to deterring its superpower adversary or adversaries.

In the case of China, Beijing sought to deter both the United States and the Soviet Union. Today, by contrast, nuclear-armed powers within geographic subregions have locked their sights on one another. The rivalry between India and Pakistan— punctuated by hair-raising crises, low-intensity conflicts, and close calls with major war—attracts the most attention at present. An unfamiliar but no less dangerous competition involves China and India. Beijing has deployed long-range, nuclear-capable missiles on the Tibetan Plateau to shore up deterrence along its southern flank, while New Delhi is pursuing similar systems to hold major Chinese targets at risk. Some form of future dyadic relationship between Iran and Israel is conceivable, assuming that the international community acquiesces in Tehran's nuclear breakout.

Conventional military imbalances, some admittedly more severe than others, typify these nuclear dyads. The prospect that the Indian armed forces will overrun Pakistani defenses and dismember the state deeply vexes military planners in Islamabad. China's crushing victory during its punitive 1962 war against India, followed by Beijing's impressive military modernization of the past two decades, exerts constant pressure on New Delhi to catch up. Israel's qualitative military superiority over Iran remains unquestioned, but this may tempt the weaker party to use its nuclear arsenal as a backstop for conventional inferiority.

The pressure to rely on nuclear weapons as a stopgap is perhaps most acute in South Asia. Pakistan has never renounced its first-use option. Islamabad's thresholds for first nuclear use remain disturbingly vague and low, which suggests that a wide range of Indian military actions could trigger retaliation.[15] As nuclear redlines multiply, so do scenarios featuring nuclear escalation. To make matters worse, India has adopted the "Cold Start" doctrine for limited war. Cold Start envisions rapidly seizing the initiative against the Pakistani armed forces, on Pakistani territory, in order to control and dominate escalation.[16] New Delhi and Islamabad are thus engaged in a two-level game of nuclear and conventional interactions that could fan instability during a crisis. Size matters in nuclear deterrence, but it is clearly no guarantee of success.

Interactions among Newcomers Are Problematic

Substantial controversy surrounds the study of potential interactions among the new nuclear powers. Here, too, scholarly disagreements center primarily on the integrity and fragility of deterrence in South Asia. The theoretical sparring between Paul Kapur and Sumit Ganguly is an excellent example.[17] Kapur contends that Pakistan's possession of nuclear weapons emboldened it to take provocative actions aimed at redefining the status quo.[18] He argues that Pakistan initiated the 1999 Kargil crisis because its leaders convinced themselves that the Indian leadership, fearing nuclear escalation, would self-limit the military measures it deployed to punish or defeat Pakistani forces. Kapur asserts that Indian policymakers' decision to refrain from applying more coercive military pressure—even when they had the wherewithal to do so—validated Pakistan's calculation. Nuclear weapons thus provided a strategic cover for lower-level military efforts, compelling New Delhi to do Islamabad's bidding.

Disputing claims that the stability/instability paradox was at work in South Asia, Ganguly avers that nuclear deterrence remained robust during the post-nuclear-breakout crises of 1999 and 2001–2.[19] He points out that the origins of these crises far predated the nuclear tests. Thus the Pakistani risk calculus was independent of the new nuclear arsenal. Indian restraint stemmed more from New Delhi's confidence that it could manage the crisis without further escalation than from fears of Islamabad's nuclear weapons. That two reputable scholars like Kapur and Ganguly interpret the same set of events so differently suggests that policymakers should keep an open mind when attempting to forecast potential interactions among states with minimal-deterrent postures.

Fundamental Strategic Logic Reigns

Despite the uncertainties and worries elucidated here, an overriding lesson from the preceding chapters is that a "fundamental strategic logic" underpins nuclear strategy, validating our premise that strategy as defined in this study follows universal principles.[20] Both large and small states have all sought to align their respective strategies and force structures with national objectives. They engage in what Michael Handel considers "an essentially rational activity involving the careful and continuous correlations of ends and means." Handel likens investigations of strategic theory to discovering natural laws that apply from region to region, civilization to civilization, and state to state.[21] Thus far, nuclear newcomers have refrained from designing, building, or fielding arsenals disproportionate to their perceived needs. Thus pariah states ruled by unpredictable regimes, like North Korea or Iran, have nonetheless pursued nuclear weapons in a manner moored to rational aims. Even apartheid-era South Africa, whose leadership feverishly exaggerated the malign intent of its external enemies, both near and far, kept its ambitions modest.

The pursuit of deterrence—via the political use or nonuse of nuclear weapons—is thus alive and well. New and potential nuclear players have all played up deterrence against external aggression as a central rationale for their nuclear gambits. Although we concede that some states clearly hope to use nuclear weapons as a cover for altering the status quo, the role of deterrence is no less relevant. Most analysts worry far more about a failure of deterrence than about states' attempts to conduct war-winning nuclear attacks. The case studies examined in this book further show that countries confronting mortal dangers respond rationally by pursuing the ultimate weapon to deter attack. A corollary relevant to the nonproliferation debate is that states do not go nuclear because the international community has acquiesced in previous breakouts. Rather, they react to stimuli unique to their own internal and external environments. Proliferation will occur, but it will not spread uncontrollably in random directions.

Even as proliferation becomes a permanent reality for the breakouts examined in this study, substantial evidence indicates that force buildups will remain relatively limited, including among old-timers like China. Though speculation about Beijing's "race to parity" amid US–Russian arms control efforts has persisted during the past decade, the rate of China's buildup and the scale of the US–Russian builddown remain insufficient to let Beijing reach equality any time soon. India, the other rising power, also seemingly rejects the notion that size alone determines the credibility of its deterrent. New Delhi clearly prefers to keep its nuclear forces to a minimum. Threshold nuclear powers, such as Japan and South Korea, are neither eager nor prepared to break out, despite deteriorating strategic environments. North Korea, Pakistan, and even energy-rich Iran lack the economies of scale necessary to engineer rapid or very large increases in their weapons inventories. In short, a spiraling, escalating arms race resembling that of the Cold War is not in the making. Rather, competitive buildups will unfold in slow motion. Quantitative indicators designed to gauge the state of rivalries during the current second nuclear age will provide a picture that is incomplete at best and misleading at worst.

The reason that there is no easy correlation between economic size and the scale of the nuclear infrastructure is simple: All governments must weigh their nuclear options against their other pressing priorities. Thus they are likely to be far more sensitive to the costs of a nuclear program than were the Cold War superpowers. With the possible exception of North Korea, most nuclear newcomers are finely attuned to national development, which they rightly see as the key to sustaining their long-term well-being. For China, economic growth is a nearly inviolable imperative. Beijing thus keeps a vigilant eye on the potential for strategic modernization to crowd out efforts to manage broader socioeconomic programs. Competing constituencies in India's open democracy clamor incessantly for scarce resources, which keeps advocates of a larger nuclear force in check. Both Iran and Pakistan appear quite responsive to the external climate, including their access to the international economic system. In short, all the newcomers acknowledge that their nuclear weapons constitute only one narrow dimension of their national power and international standing.

Because of these constraints on force structure, weaker nuclear powers are under constant pressure to increase the survivability of their modest arsenals, particularly against the threat of preemption. The contributors to this volume agree that nuclear weapon states consider an undersea deterrent the gold standard for invulnerability. China may be nearing an assured retaliatory strike capability with its second-generation strategic submarines, whereas India has demonstrated a keen interest in exercising a nuclear option beneath the waves and has achieved substantial progress. It may behoove Japan to concentrate its resources on an undersea deterrent and thus to rely on land-based and air-launched nuclear forces as interim measures. Yet all these measures represent enormously expensive and technically challenging undertakings, which are open only to a few well-resourced powers.

As a consequence, smaller states need to think inventively about protecting their forces. But each option carries its own risks. Geographic depth offers unreliable sanctuary against long-range strike systems. Hardened facilities and hidden sites no longer guarantee safety from deep-penetrating precision munitions. Mobility on land and the associated delegation of launch authority pose command-and-control issues and also security and safety problems. If a fundamental strategic logic indeed governs such matters across national, cultural, and social boundaries, common ways of thinking should lend a certain predictability to the newcomers' actions.

Yet the Unthinkable Is Thinkable

A final if implicit theme of this study is that the use of nuclear weapons remains a distinct possibility in the coming years. It has become an article of faith for some that the nuclear taboo increasingly carries the weight of a global norm, and thus nuclear use is simply beyond the pale. Even nuclear newcomers will view their arsenals as unusable in virtually any imaginable circumstance. Yet as the chapters of this volume demonstrate, this normative prohibition is quite fragile. Under certain stressful conditions, nuclear use—either inadvertent or deliberate—is entirely conceivable and could even be construed as rational. Accordingly, policymakers must not wish away the odious prospect of a nuclear exchange. The complex task of managing the risks inherent in interactive nuclear crises and confrontations represents the challenge of our time. As Washington and its allies face this challenge, a firmer grasp of the logic underlying nuclear strategy will help them untangle the intricacies of the second nuclear age.

Notes

1. Scott D. Sagan and Kenneth N. Waltz, *The Spread of Nuclear Weapons: A Debate Renewed*, 2nd ed. (New York: W. W. Norton, 2002).

2. Jeffrey G. Lewis, *The Minimum Means of Reprisal: China's Search for Security in the Nuclear Age* (Cambridge, MA: MIT Press, 2007).

3. Joel S. Wit, Daniel B. Poneman, and Robert L. Gallucci, *Going Critical: The First North Korean Nuclear Crisis* (Washington, DC: Brookings Institution Press, 2004), 175–82.

4. Whitney Raas and Austin Long, "Osirak Redux? Assessing Israeli Capabilities to Destroy Iranian Nuclear Facilities," *International Security* 31, no. 4 (Spring 2007): 7–33.

5. James M. Lindsay and Ray Takeyh, "After Iran Gets the Bomb," *Foreign Affairs* 89, no. 2 (April–May 2010): 33–49.

6. Carl von Clausewitz, *On War*, edited and translated by Michael Howard and Peter Paret (Princeton, NJ: Princeton University Press, 1976), 86.

7. Ibid., 127.

8. Michael R. Gordon and Bernard E. Trainor, *Cobra II: The Inside Story of the Invasion and Occupation of Iraq* (New York: Pantheon, 2006), 65.

9. For the five ideal types of deterrent relationships, see T. V. Paul, "Complex Deterrence: An Introduction," in *Complex Deterrence: Strategy in the Global Age*, edited by T. V. Paul, Patrick M. Morgan, and James J. Wirtz (Chicago: University of Chicago Press, 2009), 9.

10. Muthiah Alagappa, "Introduction: Investigating Nuclear Weapons in a New Era," in *The Long Shadow: Nuclear Weapons and Security in 21st Century Asia*, edited by Muthiah Alagappa (Stanford, CA: Stanford University Press, 2008), 12.

11. Clausewitz, *On War*, 75, 77.

12. David Ochmanek and Lowell H. Schwartz, *The Challenge of Nuclear-Armed Regional Adversaries* (Santa Monica, CA: RAND Corporation, 2008), 42.

13. Austin Long, *Deterrence from the Cold War to Long War: Lessons from Six Decades of RAND Research* (Santa Monica, CA: RAND Corporation, 2008), 77–80.

14. For a comparative analysis, see Avery Goldstein, *Deterrence and Security in the 21st Century: China, Britain, France, and the Enduring Legacy of the Nuclear Revolution* (Stanford, CA: Stanford University Press, 2000).

15. Feroz Hassan Khan, "Reducing the Risk of Nuclear War in South Asia," in *Pakistan's Nuclear Future: Reining in the Risk*, edited by Henry Sokolski (Carlisle, PA: Strategic Studies Institute, US Army War College, 2009), 79.

16. Walter C. Ladwig III, "A Cold Start for Hot Wars? The Indian Army's New Limited War Doctrine," *International Security* 32, no. 3 (Winter 2007–8): 163–67.

17. For a dialogue among a group of scholars about this controversy, see Sumit Ganguly and S. Paul Kapur, eds., *Nuclear Proliferation in South Asia: Crisis Behavior and the Bomb* (London: Routledge, 2008).

18. S. Paul Kapur, "Ten Years of Instability in a Nuclear South Asia," *International Security* 33, no. 2 (Fall 2008): 71–94.

19. Sumit Ganguly, "Nuclear Stability in South Asia," *International Security* 33, no. 2 (Fall 2008): 45–70.

20. Michael I. Handel, *Masters of War: Classical Strategic Thought*, 3rd ed. (London: Frank Cass, 2001).

21. Ibid., 1, 79.

CONTRIBUTORS

Stephen F. Burgess is a professor in the Department of International Security Studies of the US Air War College. His books include *South Africa's Weapons of Mass Destruction* (with Helen Purkitt); and *The United Nations under Boutros Boutros-Ghali, 1992–97*. He has published numerous articles and book chapters on African and South Asian security issues.

Michael S. Chase is associate research professor in the Warfare Analysis and Research Department of the US Naval War College, where he previously taught in the Strategy and Policy Department. He earned a PhD in international affairs from the Paul H. Nitze School of Advanced International Studies at Johns Hopkins University. In addition, he studied at the Johns Hopkins University–Nanjing University Center for Chinese and American Studies in Nanjing. Before joining the faculty of the Naval War College, he was a research analyst with Defense Group Inc. and the RAND Corporation.

Andrew S. Erickson is associate professor in the Strategic Research Department of the US Naval War College and a founding member of the China Maritime Studies Institute. He is an associate in research at Harvard University's Fairbank Center for Chinese Studies. He received a PhD and an MA in international relations and comparative politics from Princeton University and a BA in history and political science from Amherst College. His research has appeared in such journals as *Asian Security*, the *Journal of Strategic Studies*, *Orbis*, *The American Interest*, and *Joint Force Quarterly*. He is coeditor of and a contributor to the Naval Institute Press book series Studies in Chinese Maritime Development.

Seema Gahlaut is assistant director for training and outreach at the University of Georgia's Center for International Trade and Security and an adjunct professor in the university's School of Public and International Affairs. She contributed to *Combating Weapons of Mass Destruction* and *To Supply or to Deny*, and she coedited *Engaging India*. She received her PhD from the University of Georgia.

James R. Holmes is associate professor of strategy at the US Naval War College. He previously served on the faculty of the University of Georgia's School of Public and International Affairs, as a senior political-military analyst at Energy Security Associates Inc., as a research associate at the Institute for Foreign Policy Analysis, and as a US navy surface warfare officer. He is a Phi Beta Kappa graduate of Vanderbilt University and earned graduate degrees from the Fletcher School at Tufts University, Providence College, and Salve Regina University. He was the recipient of the Naval War College Foundation Award in 1994, signifying the top graduate in his Naval War College class. His most recent book (with Toshi Yoshihara) is *Red Star over the Pacific: China's Rise and the Challenge to US Maritime Strategy.*

Timothy D. Hoyt is professor of strategy and policy and the holder of the John Nicholas Brown Chair of Counterterrorism at the US Naval War College. He received his PhD in international relations and strategic studies from Johns Hopkins University's School of Advanced International Studies in 1997. In addition to teaching at the Naval War College, he has taught at Georgetown University, worked for the US Army and the Congressional Research Service, and served as a lecturer or consultant at other US military schools and government agencies. He is the author most recently of *Military Industries and Regional Power,* along with more than forty book chapters and articles.

Scott A. Jones is executive director of the University of Georgia's Center for International Trade and Security. He is the author of *The Evolution of the Ukrainian Export Control System: State Building and International Cooperation.* He is also a contributor to *Arms on the Market: Reducing the Risk of Proliferation in the Former Soviet Union* and a coeditor of and contributor to *Crossroads and Conflict: Security and Foreign Policy in the Caucasus and Central Asia.*

Helen E. Purkitt is professor of political science at the US Naval Academy. Her publications include *Africa's Environmental and Human Security in the 21st Century* (editor); *South Africa's Weapons of Mass Destruction* (with Steve Burgess); *World Politics: Annual Edition (2001–11)* (editor); and dozens of articles in scholarly journals. Her current research interests include covert nuclear, biological, chemical, and radiological research and development in the developing world; the nexus of transnational crime and terror in Africa; and the impact of climate change on ecotourism and development in southern Africa.

Terence Roehrig is professor of national security affairs and the director of the Asia-Pacific Studies Group at the US Naval War College. He has written extensively on Korean and East Asian politics and security and is the author of *From Deterrence to Engagement: The US Defense Commitment to South Korea* and the forthcoming book *Japan, South Korea, and the US Nuclear Umbrella: Extended Deterrence and Nuclear Weapons in the Post–Cold War.* He received his PhD from the University of Wisconsin–Madison and is a past president of the Association of Korean Political Studies.

Joshua Rovner is associate professor of strategy and policy at the US Naval War College. He is also an adjunct professor in the School of International and Public

Affairs at Columbia University and the book review editor for the *Journal of Strategic Studies*. He is the author, most recently, of *Fixing the Facts: National Security and the Politics of Intelligence*.

James L. Schoff is senior adviser for East Asia policy in the Office of the Secretary of Defense, where he focuses on US alliance relations with Japan and South Korea, as well as regional security cooperation initiatives and extended deterrence issues. He is on a two-year assignment at the Defense Department on loan from the Institute for Foreign Policy Analysis, where he has been director of Asia-Pacific studies. His publications include *Nuclear Matters in North Korea: Building a Multilateral Response for Future Stability in Northeast Asia* (coauthor). He received a BA from Duke University and an MA in international relations from the Paul H. Nitze School of Advanced International Studies at Johns Hopkins University.

Anupam Srivastava is director of Asia projects at the University of Georgia's Center for International Trade and Security and an adjunct professor at the university's School of Public and International Affairs. He directs multiyear projects at the center that provide training and research on nuclear nonproliferation and technology security to licensing and enforcement officials across the governmental and corporate circles in China, India, and several other countries in the Asia-Pacific region. He coedited *Engaging India*, has published a variety of journal articles and opinion pieces, and is a frequent commentator for such outlets as the BBC.

Andrew C. Winner is professor of strategic studies in the Strategic Research Department and director of the Indian Ocean Studies Group at the Naval War College. His areas of focus are South Asia, nuclear nonproliferation, maritime strategy, the Middle East, and US national security. He received a PhD from the University of Maryland, College Park, an MA from the Paul H. Nitze School of Advanced International Studies at Johns Hopkins University, and an AB from Hamilton College.

Christopher T. Yeaw is chief scientist at Air Force Global Strike Command, where he advises the commander on all technical and deterrence science matters, represents the Command to external research organizations, and guides the development of suitable technology for inclusion in the world's foremost nuclear forces. He received a PhD in nuclear engineering and engineering physics from the University of Wisconsin, where he was a Department of Energy fellow. He has served as a fusion fellow for the Department of Energy, a lead engineer for the US navy in ballistic missile defense, an officer at the Defense Intelligence Agency, principal adviser on nuclear and strategic issues to the assistant secretary of state for verification and compliance, and associate professor at the US Naval War College.

Toshi Yoshihara holds the John A. van Beuren Chair of Asia-Pacific Studies and is an affiliate member of the China Maritime Studies Institute at the US Naval War College. Previously, he was visiting professor in the Strategy Department at the Air War College. He has also served as an analyst at the Institute for Foreign Policy

Analysis at RAND Corporation and at the American Enterprise Institute. He received a PhD from the Fletcher School at Tufts University, an MA from the Paul H. Nitze School of Advanced International Studies at Johns Hopkins University, and a BS from the School of Foreign Service at Georgetown University. He is the coauthor of *Red Star over the Pacific: China's Rise and the Challenge to US Maritime Strategy*; *Indian Naval Strategy in the Twenty-First Century*; and *Chinese Naval Strategy in the Twenty-First Century: The Turn to Mahan*. He is the coeditor of *Asia Looks Seaward: Power and Maritime Strategy*.

INDEX